A SUPPLEMENT TO THE PLAYS OF WILLIAM SHAKSPEARE:

COMPRISING

THE SEVEN DRAMAS

WHICH HAVE BEEN ASCRIBED TO HIS PEN, BUT WHICH ARE NOT INCLUDED WITH HIS WRITINGS IN MODERN EDITIONS, NAMELY:

THE TWO NOBLE KINSMEN,
THE LONDON PRODIGAL,
THOMAS LORD CROMWELL,
SIR JOHN OLDCASTLE,
THE PURITAN, OR THE WIDOW OF WATLING STREET,
THE YORKSHIRE TRAGEDY,
THE TRAGEDY OF LOCRINE.

EDITED,

With Notes, and an Introduction to each Play,

BY WILLIAM GILMORE SIMMS, ESQ.

AUBURN AND ROCHESTER:
ALDEN AND BEARDSLEY.
NEW YORK:
J. C. DERBY, 119 NASSAU STREET.
1855.

TO THE

REV. ALEXANDER DYCE,

OF ENGLAND:

The acute and laborious worker in the old, but still ample and green, fields of British Dramatic Literature, this humble labor, a FIRST American edition of the imputed Plays of SHAKSPEARE, is

Very Respectfully Inscribed,

BY THE EDITOR.

WOODLANDS, SOUTH CAROLINA,
January 20, 1848.

GENERAL INTRODUCTION.

In undertaking to supply the American reader with an edition of the plays which have been ascribed to Shakspeare, but which are not usually included among his writings, the publishers do not, by any means, propose to decide upon their authenticity. They prefer to leave this question, as they find it, to future criticism and the sagacity of the reader. It is enough for them that the question of authorship is still under discussion, and may long remain so — that some of the best critics of the age that is passing incline to the belief that several, if not all, of these imputed productions, however inferior to the generally-received performances of Shakspeare, are nevertheless from his pen — and, that the weight of external testimony clearly corresponds with this opinion. For this matter, the reader will see the separate prefaces to the several plays, as they occur in this edition, where an endeavor has been made to bring together, for the purpose of facilitating the popular judgment, all the known facts in the history of their production and publication in past periods. The object of the present publishers is to afford to the general reader an opportunity, if not of deciding for himself upon the genuineness of these plays, at least of becoming familiar with their merits. Such a purpose, indeed, appears to belong particularly to the duties of a publisher, who, though his aim be gain, is yet required to regulate his selfish desires by a due and equal regard to the claims of the public, and the writer whose works he brings before them. He stands in a relation of double responsibility; and it seems scarcely proper that the publisher of Shakspeare's writings, or of any writings, should presume to settle a difficulty so important to his author, by excluding, on the merest conjectures of criticism, a large body of literature which has been confidently ascribed to his pen, either by his contemporaries or by those nearest to him in point of time; — and this, simply because of their inferiority, whether obvious or only supposed, to the average merits of his received performances. They do not see that they enjoy the right, in the case of any author, of rejecting testimony, however inadequate as proof, at the simple instance of shrewd but conjectural criticism; and are persuaded, in the case of so great a master, that, while the incorporation, with his recognised productions, of the plays which are doubtful, can by no means disparage or impair his acknowledged excellences, their exclusion, while any doubt exists, is an absolute wrong and injustice to the reader, who should at least be permitted to enter into a similar inquiry with his critic, and to decide for himself upon what is intrinsic in the discussion. At all events, he should be permitted to believe that he possesses all of the writings of his favorite, though this conviction be coupled with the misgiving that he possesses something more. That he should arrive at the ordinary opinion — the justice of which the present publishers do not propose to gainsay — that these doubtful plays are, in point of merit, far below those which usually complete the body of Shakspeare's writings, will not, in any respect, lessen the propriety — assuming it as possible that the former are really his — of bringing the two classes together. They may, or may not, form a part of the same great family — changelings, perhaps — sons of premature birth — of inferior stature and proportion — "scarce half made up," "and sent into the world before their time;" but this inferiority, or even deformity, should constitute no sufficient objection to the scheme of uniting them in the same household. There shall be a decrepit, a mute, or an idiot, in a noble family, while the true heir shall be of erect and symmetrical figure, with all attributes perfect and superior; but the practice would be pronounced Scythian and barbarous, which should destroy summarily, or banish to a desert cave to perish, the imperfect or inferior progeny, because of its unhappy disparity with him upon whom the hopes of the family are placed. The case finds its exact parallel in these instances of premature birth and imperfect organization in the literary world; and there is an equal cruelty and impolicy in our consigning to oblivion the more homely or feeble production, because it so strikingly contrasts with that which we have learned to study and to love. This very contrast has its uses, since the defects of the one more strikingly impress us with the beauties of the other; and we frame our own standards of excellence quite as frequently from the contemplation of the humble and the faulty, as of the perfect and the high.

In the recognition of this opinion, the literary student has a leading interest, since he is naturally curious to see in what manner his predecessor has worked — from what small beginnings, against what obstructions, and with what inferior tools. It is important, indeed, that he should see where, and how frequently, the great master has faltered, or has fallen, in his experiments. The very inequalities of the exemplar commend him somewhat more to our sympathies, as they tend to bring him within the laws of a humanity which is notoriously imperfect. We are pleased to see how much was toil and trouble — how much was care and anxiety — how much was industry and perseverance — how much was in mortal powers, in the secret of his successes; — to discover that it was not all Genius — all inspiration — all the fruit of a special gift of Heaven, to a chosen individual, which no follower may hope to share. We are pleased to see how, feebly, step by step, he has continued to struggle, onward and upward, until, from awkwardness, he arrives at grace; from weakness, he has grown to strength; from a crude infancy, he has risen into absolute majesty and manhood. Those inequalities which declare the transition periods in the progress of the mind, and show the natural but laborious advance of the thinking faculties, from sentiment to idea, and from idea to design and structure, are particularly grateful to the student, who, delighting in the excellences of a favorite author, acquires a personal and familiar interest in him, when thus permitted to follow him into his workshop — to trace his gradual progresses — the slow marches of his intellect through its several stages of acquisition and utterance, infancy preparing the way for childhood, childhood for youth, and youth for manhood, as naturally as in the physical world; and the curiosity which requires to behold the singular processes of each individual self-training, the results of which have been eminence and fame, is the fruit of a just ambition, enlivened by instincts, which make it equally profitable and pleasant to survey the *modus operandi* of the great genius, not yet fairly conceiving the peculiar mission which follows from his endowment, yet preparing, step by step, for the consummation of its objects. It is, indeed, by the faults and errors, rather than by the more symmetrical achievements of the masters, that we improve. The perfect models, seen by themselves, and totally uncoupled with those qualifying exuberances and failings, which are the necessary shadows to their successes, are rather more likely to discourage us by their manifest superiority, than invite by their examples. The difficulty of the model might impair our hope to excel or equal it, were we not permitted to know how frequently its author has failed, and how many abortive efforts have fallen from his hands, before he attained the degree of success in which he felt that his art could go no farther. We are encouraged when the laborious artist takes us into his studio, and reveals to us the painful difficulties which he has been compelled to overcome — the rudeness of his own first conceptions and designs — the feeble prurience of his childish fancies — the unsymmetrical crudenesses of his thought, and the huge, ungainly fragments that lie about his workshop, which prove the pains, the labors, and frequent miscarriages, which preceded the perfect birth. This study of the artist in his cell, or of the author in his garret — the familiarity thus acquired with his tools, and a proper idea of the toils, the obstacles, and the trials, which his patience, courage, study, and genius, have finally overcome, is, indeed, the true field of research for all those who would follow in his footsteps; — discouraging the vain and feeble, humbling the presumptuous, and fully unfolding, to the resolute and endowed worker, the true nature of that destiny for which he was chosen. It is mere *dilettantism* alone, which shrinks from such a development — preferring only the knowledge of the perfect results of labor, without being troubled with its processes. The mind of the true worker is best seen in these very processes. The genuine student — and to such alone is it permitted to behold and to appreciate the highest objects and excellences of art — prefers this survey, in connexion with the final results attained, simply as it unveils the peculiar processes of an individual mind: giving birth to an original thought, a new truth, shaped by imagination into a form which the world finally receives as a model and a law.

It was the misfortune of Shakspeare, perhaps, that his early critics and commentators — to say nothing of their more modern and recent successors — have not been willing to acknowledge these considerations. Regarding their idol, most properly, as, perhaps, the most various wonder that mortal genius ever displayed, they were not willing that he should be found mortal in any respect. They entertained the vulgar notion that, in order to enhance his merits, they were to depreciate his advantages — overlooking the notorious truth, that all successful art, no matter what has been its social fosterings or privileges, must still depend upon self-education — a training of the inner nature, adapted particularly to the individual characteristics of the man, and to be conceived and carried on wholly by one's self. The achievements of Shakspeare, according to these philosophers, were to derive their value from the fact that his genius was totally unassisted by the usual school acquisitions, and his successes were to flow to him in spite of a condition of social life more than commonly unfriendly and adverse. He was to be wretchedly poor and destitute of training, and it was for accident alone, or a call of Providence rather, to prompt his mind to that direction, by which it was to effect its wondrous performances. Banished from his native hamlet, as a profligate and deer-stealer, he was to wander off to London as a link-boy, and the merest appanage of a theatre; and, all of a sudden, he was to confound the world with the wonders of a genius to which his domestic fortunes had shown themselves hostile to the last. Most of this history is untrue, and much of it is absurd. The life of Shakspeare is gradually to be rewritten The earnest activity of such workers as Dyce, Collier, Knight, and the gentlemen connected with the Shakspeare Society, in England, will continue to make discoveries, such as they have already made, which will most probably lead us to such an approximation of the true, in Shakspeare's career, as, at least, to relieve his biography of the gross exaggerations and errors which have disfigured it. We shall probably learn, as in part we do already, that his family was one of good repute and condition, though somewhat reduced in fortune, and not so much stinted but that his education was quite as good as could be afforded in that part of England during his boyhood — that he was not only somewhat informed in Greek and Latin, as Jonson, indeed, tells us,— though the wilful biographers of Shakspeare have perversely construed his line —

"And though thou hadst small Latin and less Greek,"—

into the possession of neither — but that he was probably, in some degree also, acquainted with the French and Italian, and visited the continent, at some early period of his life — making a personal acquaintance at Venice with the Rialto, and receiving his prompting for that most perfect of all love stories, Romeo and Juliet, at the very tomb of the Capulets in Verona. It is also highly probable that, on leaving the grammar-school of Stratford, he passed into the office of an attorney, and picked up that familiarity with legal phrases, which his writings betray to a greater extent than those of all his contemporary dramatists together. Here, it is probable — we will suppose at fifteen or sixteen — that his mind received its first dramatic direction. Several of his townsmen seem to have been players — several of those who afterward appeared in his pieces — the famous Burbage among them; and Stratford had its theatre when John Shakspeare, the father of William, was bailiff of the town. It might be that the office of the father procured for the son some peculiar theatrical privileges. Here, then, at this period, relieving the daily toils of an attorney's office by an occasional nocturnal frolic with the players, at the expense of Sir Thomas Lucy's park at Charlecote, he most probably commenced his first feeble career as a dramatic author. To suppose that he wrote any of the plays usually ascribed to him, at this early period, or, indeed, at any period of his life before his twenty-fifth year, unless Titus Andronicus and Pericles,* is almost an absurdity. These all betray, in addition to the manifest possession of the highest genius, the equal maturity of experience and reflection, — the fruits of contemplation — a knowledge only derivable from long and active association among men — an art made confident by frequent successes — a taste polished and refined by repeated and long exercise — an imagination invigorated by habitual training — a fancy curbed in its excesses by attrition with rival wits, and a constant familiarity with books from the best hands, not to dwell upon the singular knowledge of dramatic situation and stage effect, which his more mature pieces exhibit — a knowledge which could only arise, as in the case of Sheridan Knowles, from a long practice in theatricals. These possessions are not gifts, but acquisitions. They are the work of time and practice. They are not to be found in youth, even in the case of the highest genius, since they contemplate human standards which fluctuate — arts which depend upon a social condition, and a knowledge which is not derived from the natural or external world, but the capricious world of man, and the appreciation of his finite characteristics and conditions.

If, then, the great masterpieces of Shakspeare, such as his Othello, Macbeth, and Hamlet, were not likely to have been the work of his boyhood — not likely to have been produced before his twenty-fifth year at least — in what manner did he employ his genius during the ten years which preceded this period? To suppose that he remained idle, pursuing a mere

* Shakspeare went to London in his twenty-third year, and Titus Andronicus appeared soon after, and became instantly popular. Indeed, it was one of the best pieces that had yet appeared on the English stage, however much we may despise it now; and the very horrors and stateliness for which we condemn it, were the peculiar and distinguishing features of the English drama at that period, and commended it more especially to the taste of its unlettered audience. In Shakspeare's subsequent improvement, it is his merit, as it was that of Chaucer, to have lifted his people with him.

vegetable life in Stratford, from his fifteenth to his twenty-third year, when he went to London, would be a strangely unreasonable supposition. It is, ordinarily, about the fifteenth year that the poetic germ, in persons thus endowed, usually begins to exhibit itself with zeal and activity. To suppose that he did nothing until his twenty-fourth year, when Titus Andronicus first appeared, and that his *first* attempt should place him above all his predecessors, from whom he must have learned the very first rudiments of his art, is quite improbable. Rejecting Titus Andronicus wholly, is it not equally unreasonable to imagine that he leaped to perfection at a single bound, armed in all the panoply, not merely of genius, but of thought, study, and experience, like Minerva, full clad and grown, from the thigh of Jupiter? How much more reasonable to assume that his youth was employed in those crude performances which have been ascribed to him by his contemporaries and their immediate successors; — that it was with his Locrines and Titus Andronicuses that he first began his career in tragedy, and that some of the feeble comedies in this collection were the first fruits of his boyish embraces with the comic muse. There is nothing improbable or unreasonable in the conjecture, even if you show, not only that these crude productions are immeasurably inferior to his great works, but that they are totally unlike them in all the peculiar characteristics by which the master makes himself known. In these, a mere beginner, for the first time practising in an unfamiliar art, he naturally wrote in the fashion of the times. The horrors of Locrine and Titus Andronicus — the unbroken stateliness of the lines, the swelling pomp of the diction, the free use of the heathen mythology, and the extravagant rant of all the characters — were the common characteristics of all dramatic writing at this period; but it is no less remarkable than true, that, though in these respects partaking of all the vices common to the dramatic authors of the time, the author of Titus Andronicus was still their superior: and this very production was as far superior, in its real merits and proofs of genius, to most of its contemporaries, as Shakspeare's better dramas are superior to it.

We have said that the deficiency of these works, in the usual characteristics of Shakspeare — though we are far from admitting this deficiency in all respects — is by no means to be regarded as an argument against their legitimacy. The opinion is not entertained without serious deliberation. The truth is, that a young author seldom writes from himself at first. He is more apt to write like anybody but himself. He subdues and suppresses himself. He does not feel himself. He is compelled to look out of himself for models and authorities, before he can properly unfold himself, and he naturally turns his regards upon the writers who are most popular — whose books are most cried up by his neighbors, and whose stature most imposingly rises upon his young and timid imagination. This very unfolding of self is the great business of life — never wholly effected, even with the utmost diligence, until the author has reached the mellow period of middle life, and seldom entirely then. We have numerous illustrative examples of this history in modern times, with which the reader is familiar. Who, for example, ever looked to the feeble ballads of Walter Scott, poor imitations of Monk Lewis, for the splendid creations of Marmion and Ivanhoe? Who, in the boyish ditties and college exercises of Lord Byron, so cruelly but justly cut up by Brougham, in the Edinburgh Review, would have looked for signs of that genius which afterward brought forth Manfred, Childe Harold, and Cain? Or who, in Cloudesley, the work of Godwin's senility, would recognise the daring and vigorous writer of Caleb Williams and St. Leon? The inequalities between the imputed and the acknowledged writings of Shakspeare are hardly greater than these contrasted performances of writers in our own period, and the dawnings are equally unlike the characteristics of the day which followed. The beginnings of a young writer are necessarily feeble, and, mostly, grossly imitative. His first aim is not idea or structure. It is the power of voice only — such as his peculiar art requires — the command of language in oratorical array. This very necessity makes him imitative of various authors; — and he never becomes in any degree original, until he has acquired such a flexibility of speech as to enable him to clothe his thoughts, as they arise, with utterance.

Gradually, his original vein unfolds itself. You have, amid masses of common-place, an occasional germ which betrays freshness. You see a certain peculiarity of thought and manner, and possibly glimpses of design and conception, which are only buried where they occur, but which the author will be apt, finally, to extricate from the places where they were first planted, as in a nursery, and set out elsewhere in a connexion which shall enable them to flourish appropriately, and to their most legitimate effect.

In these plays, whether by Shakspeare or not, will be found several instances of the germ, which has afterward been developed nobly in his subsequent performances. Here and there a line or thought, and here the glimpses of a scene or scheme, which the timid and unpractised hand of the boy-beginner had not courage or patience to pursue to its complete successes in the first premature endeavors of his muse. Let us pursue this point a little farther, by a reference to the supposed order in which his plays are thought to have been produced. This conjectural arrangement, by the way, is exceedingly illusory. It resolves itself, apart from the evidence of the author himself, into mere guesswork, since, even the first publishing of a piece affords us no certain assurance that there are not others in his possession that do not precede it in point of time. Nor are the intrinsic qualities of the piece any better guides, since the experience of all literature shows the frequent fact of the failure following the successful effort, quite as commonly as it precedes it. But, taking these estimates for what they are worth, let us see how the case appears. We have before us the several conjectures of Chalmers, Malone, and Drake. Titus Andronicus was produced upon the stage when Shakspeare was twenty-three years of age. The Comedy of Errors, according to Chalmers and Drake, appeared first in 1591; and Malone says 1592. This would make Shakspeare, who was born in 1564, twenty-seven or twenty-eight years of age. Now, we are free to declare the opinion, that, of the two pieces, Titus Andronicus is immeasurably the best, and exhibits an immense superiority over the Comedy of Errors, in all the essential proofs of poetry and character. Hamlet is supposed to have been produced (Chalmers and Drake) in 1597; Malone, more probably we think, makes it 1600, or nine years after the production of the Comedy of Errors, and twelve years after that of Titus Andronicus. Now, if we compare the relative gain of Shakspeare's genius, in this stretch, whether of nine or twelve years, as illustrated by the superiority of his Hamlet over the Comedy of Errors, what may we assume it to have been during the interval from his twenty-seventh year, when the Comedy was produced, and the period of his life at Stratford, from fifteen to twenty-three, when it is scarcely rational to suppose that he lay completely idle? He who examines carefully the plays in this collection, will find no such wonderful inequality between them, and the Titus Andronicus, Comedy of Errors, and Pericles — pieces which any attempt to wrest from Shakspeare is eminently absurd — as exists between these latter pieces and the great works which make him the wondrous master that he is. In the three plays just mentioned, his now-admitted works, there is greater polish, symmetry, dexterity, and worldly knowledge; but the germs of poetry are not more frequent, nor more decided, nor the proofs of originality and invention more certain or satisfactory. The acknowledged plays of Shakspeare, thirty in number, including Pericles and Titus Andronicus, occupy, in the period of their production, a space of time ranging from 1588 to 1614 — a period of twenty-seven years. This, if he began at twenty-four, the period when Titus Andronicus was produced, and ceased to produce in 1613, when he left the theatre, and retired from London to Stratford, would show an average production of one play to every eight months. How many, then, should he have written during the long period of probation, when, if we receive not the writings of this volume, he did absolutely nothing. Supposing him, however, to have been equally industrious and prolific, as Ben Jonson and others of his contemporaries tell us that he was, is it not highly probable that he carried with him a considerable stock to London. He went thither in 1587. Two things may be assumed for him in this connexion, namely, that he would seek publication as soon as possible, and that he would bring out his best production first. Titus Andronicus, accordingly, appeared in 1588–'9

Pericles, according to Drake, in 1590; and, as we have seen, the Comedy of Errors appeared the year after. These were, no doubt, the best pieces in our young poet's collection — Titus Andronicus being really the best of these. Their success may have stifled his inferior productions in the birth, or have prompted him to put them forth indifferently or anonymously, under the obvious necessity of not risking the renown which he had already won, by works, the crudities of which his now-rapidly growing experience enabled him to see. His Love's Labor's Lost, another of these inferior productions, but less offensive by its crudities, and more decidedly a work of art, was suffered to appear in 1591 (according to Drake), 1592 (Malone), 1594 (Chalmers). The conjecture of Drake is the most reasonable, though we must repeat that nothing can be more unsatisfactory or doubtful than these speculations. We need not continue them. Taking them for what they are worth — and they embody no improbabilities — and we have reason to assume, that he whose progress in dramatic art had been so moderate between the period when he produced these latter pieces, and the first, might naturally enough have written the works in the following collection at a still earlier date. We insist that the characteristics of the pieces above mentioned are not much more decidedly like those of the great — the full-grown — Shakspeare, than the performances which have been imputed and denied. But, our opinion is, that the prolific youth took with him to London the germs of all these early plays — the Comedy of Errors, as well as Pericles, and Titus Andronicus, the Love's Labor's Lost, and the Two Gentlemen of Verona — that he there altered and amended them, as his increasing experience with the stage and people counselled, and that the inequalities of thought and language, to be found in all these pieces, and which so constantly compel the critics to cry aloud that they see two different hands at work, are due entirely to these graffings, made by the more practised hand, upon the imperfect growth of its more feeble and inexperienced planting. Doubtless, if time had been allowed him — were not his muse too prolific and too fond of the provocation of new scenes and subjects, which diverted him from works, the topics of which could no longer excite his imagination — we should have seen these pieces furbished up in the same manner, and have been compelled, by the obvious impress of the master, shown here and there by a decisive thought and fancy, and such lines as betray a grace which genius knows how to snatch from nature without the assistance of art, to admit the still-abortive production as from the unquestionable hand of Shakspeare. These pieces were thus suffered to find their way to the stage and the public, without the paternal care which they could no more reward; or, it is possible that they preceded even Titus Andronicus in performance, and that they were brought out by his friends, the players, at Stratford, or were carried up, by the same hands, to London, even before he adventured to the great city himself, and were finally left to their fate, in consequence of that condition of things in the theatrical world, a proper knowledge of which would tend to account for that otherwise singular indifference which the dramatic authors of that time have shown toward their productions. A few words on this head, in explanation, may not be unadvisable.

There was really no such indifference of the author, to the fate of his writings, as our frequent wonder and lamentations have unjustly made to appear. The old dramatists were as jealous of their fame, their name, and the fortunes of their pieces, as the most sensitive writers now. By constant squabbles and controversies, which not unfrequently grew from words to blows, they proved themselves to be true members of the *genus irritabile ratum.* A world of pamphlets, essays, critiques, prefaces, and epigrams, remain to us, illustrating this belligerent disposition, from the pens of a host of angry combatants; and when their pieces were denounced and driven from the stage, they rushed to the press, and made their final appeal — their temper quite as apparent as their logic — to the judgments of a higher class, or to the more deliberate, the sober second thought, of the very critics by whom the pieces had been censured. *The plays, accordingly, which we have received from the hands of the authors themselves, are those, chiefly, which failed upon the stage. These, consequently, are likely to have come to us in the most perfect condition. That such should be the case, is not a subject of surprise to those who remember that the legitimate mode of dramatic publication is from the stage, and not from the press. A successful play was a property of the theatre,* for which it was usually written, not unfrequently under contract with the manager; and it derived its value almost entirely from the fact that it was *kept from the press.* It was thus preserved as a novelty, and always bore an air of freshness when it was produced. The great cause of the decline of modern theatricals, is to be found in the fact that the press has made the people familiar with the pieces played; and those who attend the theatre, accordingly, go only to discriminate between the styles of actors — thus substituting one art for another — to witness the pageantry, hear the music, and see the company. In withholding the play from the press, the manager equally withheld it from the author. The latter had sold entirely the right of property in his production, and no longer held any control over its destination. The work of his hands was thus entirely released from his jurisdiction. It could be lopped or lengthened at the pleasure of the manager, played or suppressed, altered in title, and subjected to alterations and interpolations, to suit particular exigencies and occasions; and these alterations were as frequently confided to the hands of strangers as to those of the original author. In this way, it is not unreasonably supposed, that Shakspeare himself has given his peculiar impress to the works of inferior artists, and that his own great productions have been impaired by the unskilled efforts of common workmen, to adapt his pieces to the common standard, or the particular occasion. The great body of English dramatic literature never found its way to the press at all, until in the ascendency of the puritans, when the theatres being overthrown and abolished, the property ceased to have a value in the original and legitimate form of publication, and was sold to, or seized upon by, the early publishers, to whose carelessness and ignorance we owe the wretched mangling to which the finest strains of tragic song have been subjected, and from which the original and perfect versions have, to this day, but imperfectly recovered. To any one who has ever seen a first edition of Shakspeare's Hamlet, it is scarcely necessary to say, that the piece is not to be recognised at all, compared with the restored production, faulty as that still is, which we now possess. The breaking up of the theatres led to the dispersion equally of players and plays. The latter, scattered abroad in various hands, were lost and destroyed in immense numbers. Where they survived the tender mercies of such appreciating critics as the Cook of Warburton, they still suffered from a treatment which nothing but the native hardihood of their constitutions enabled them to withstand. Neither the sway of the Stuarts, nor that of Cromwell, was favorable to the higher forms of art and poetry. The divine genius of Milton succumbed under the one, and was compelled to work as a politician only for the other; while the bald comedy of an inferior school, to which a vastly inferior talent was the minister, failed utterly to compensate the nation for the manhood, the soul, the vigorous, sinewy, and deeply-energetic blood and courage, of the earlier and the nobler muse. That Dryden must be recognised as a redeeming worker in the more modern period, will not impair the justice of its general condemnation. When the plays of the old dramatists found their way to the press at first, they enjoyed none of the advantages of editorship. The players themselves, unless in the case of their own writings, which they seldom edited, were indifferent as to what became of pieces which no longer yielded them a livelihood. The proprietors gave or sold them to the press, without feeling or affection; and the publishers, if not so indifferent as the players, were less capable of correct readings of the manuscript. Titlepages were lost, blurred, or obliterated; titles themselves were changed, to suit the whim of the publisher, or meet the fashions of the times. The plays were hurried through the press, with all their imperfections on their heads. The original draughts of the author — the copies of the player, covered with his private marks or opinions — were published just as the printer found them, defaced with extraneous matter, which was perversely incorporated with the text. Verse was printed as if it were prose, and prose as verse. Stage directions were mingled with the matter, lengthening the line, and baffling the sense; and even the *cues* of actors, and their sometimes whimsical and mischievous comments, were studiously set forth to the reader, in the body of the play, to the equal disparagement of the sense and symmetry of the piece. It is only of late days that the press has been repairing its own mischief, in the case of the early dramatists; whose fortunes have been thus peculiar, from the peculiar characteristics of their profession, and not from any such wholesale indifference to the awards of fame as has been so thoughtlessly ascribed to them. English and German criticism, with an ingenuity and industry which can scarcely be too highly commended, has done wonders in retrieving many noble writings from oblivion, by correcting the mistakes, and amending the decisions, of a preceding age; restoring the purity of the text of favorite authors — particularly Shakspeare — so as to afford us a tolerably fair substitute for writings which no substitute, not of an author's own choosing, can possibly hope to render altogether satisfactory.

The undoubted plays of Shakspeare, published in his lifetime, were Othello, Troilus and Cressida, King Lear, Hamlet, Merry Wives of Windsor, Much Ado about Nothing, Midsummer Night's Dream, Merchant of Venice, the first and second parts of Henry IV., Henry V., parts II. and III. of Henry VI., Love's Labor's Lost, Romeo and Juliet, and Richard II. and III. To these are to be added Pericles and Titus Andronicus. The editions thus published were all imperfect, apparently from copies surreptitiously obtained; and some, as in the case of Hamlet, from reporters at the theatre, relying chiefly on the ear for the text, during the rapid and passionate enunciation of the performers. Both proprietor and author were equally interested in arresting such a practice; but it was one for which the crude and imperfect legislation of that day — scarcely much bettered, in respect of copyright, in our own — could suggest no remedy.

The pieces in the collection which follows — the Two Noble Kinsmen excepted — were also printed, either with his name or his initials, in the lifetime of Shakspeare. An edition of his works, put forth after his death, by Heminge and Condell, his friends, associate proprietors with him of the Globe theatre, contained (making the same exception) the same body of plays: and the dedications and prefaces to this edition are supposed, with reason, to have been from the pen of Ben Jonson, his intimate friend, and most profound and discriminating admirer. They and he ought to have known whether these plays could properly, or should, be imputed to his pen. They include them without comment, and, seemingly, without doubt or misgiving.

The plays which have been imputed to Shakspeare, but which the critics have concluded to regard as doubtful, may be divided into two classes. The one consists of those plays only which have been (wholly or in part) ascribed to his pen, and included, at an early period, among his works; the other, of those which a vague tradition, no longer to be followed, has assigned him, or which have been assumed to be his, in consequence of certain supposed resemblances to his writings, in thought and manner, which have been discovered in them by ingenious criticism. The present publication is confined wholly to the former class. It comprises seven dramas. The first of these — the Two Noble Kinsmen — is supposed to be from the joint hands of Shakspeare and Fletcher. The first act, indeed, has been confidently ascribed to the pen of the former, not merely by the critics, on the strength of its peculiar merits, but by a tradition of the playhouse. On this point, our opinion, which is offered with great deference, will be found in the immediate introduction to the play in question. The six other plays are in the order of the old folio of Heminge and Condell: the London Prodigal; the History of Thomas Lord Cromwell; Sir John Oldcastle — Lord Cobham; The Puritan, or the Widow of Watling Street; a Yorkshire Tragedy; and the Tragedy of Locrine.

The history of these six plays, so far as it is now known to us, will be found in the separate introductions, as they occur at the opening of each, and will not require farther notice. Indeed, most of these introductions have been rendered copious, somewhat at the expense of the "general introduction," suggesting views and arguments which might have been examined here. They will not, accordingly, require our farther consideration.

Of the second class of imputed plays, which do not appear in this volume, the list is quite as large as the former. It comprises "Arden of Feversham"—a piece of considerable merit; "the Reign of King Edward III."—a work so like Shakspeare's, in the respects of versification and manner, that it is difficult to hit upon any writer who could so happily have imitated him; "George a-Greene, the Pinner of Wakefield"—which is now supposed to have been written by Robert Greene, but upon the most slender of all sorts of evidence; "Fair Emma"—which Mr. Knight assigns to a period subsequent to the death of Shakspeare; "Mucedorus," of which we know nothing, and can express no opinion,—Tieck and Horn, the German critics, pronounce it a youthful production of Shakspeare; Mr. Knight gives us a brief analysis of the story, describes it as a lively play, with some few passages of merit, but, otherwise, speaks of it slightingly;—"The Birth of Merlin"—which, in its first known edition, that of 1662, was announced as the joint production of Shakspeare and Rowley; and "The Merry Devil of Edmonton"—a performance which, as Mr. Knight justly remarks, is that of a true poet, whoever he may be.

These seven plays, constituting the whole number of those, the ascription of which to William Shakspeare rests chiefly upon opinion, may be made, hereafter, to constitute the materials for an additional volume to that which is now offered to the public. In compiling and preparing such a collection for the press, the object will be, as in the present instance, not to assert, or even to assume, that the writings in question are those of Shakspeare, or so to argue as in anywise to give a direction to the question which denies their legitimacy, but simply to enable the reader to be sure that he loses nothing, even of what is puerile and immature, in the writings of so great a master. It is thought better and safer to impute to him, erroneously, those productions to which no other author presents an equally reasonable claim, than to leave the reader in doubt whether some of the performances of his favorite have not been withheld from his possession.

INTRODUCTION

TO

THE TWO NOBLE KINSMEN.

THIS play was first printed in 1634, with the following title: "The Two Noble Kinsmen: presented at the Black Friers by the King's majesty's servants, with great applause: written by the memorable worthies of their time, Mr. John Fletcher and Mr. William Shakspeare, gent., and printed at London by Thos. Cotes, for John Waterstone, and are to be solde at the signe of the Crowne in Paul's churchyard—1634." In the first folio edition of the works of Beaumont and Fletcher, in 1647, the Two Noble Kinsmen did not appear. It is reprinted in the second folio edition, with some slight alterations from the quarto.

The story is taken from the "Knight's Tale," in the Canterbury Tales of Chaucer. It is certainly a very fine performance; marked by considerable inequalities of execution, but lifted by frequent passages of great nobleness, delicacy and power. In some portions, the plot is managed with skill and spirit; the slightest suggestions of Chaucer's muse being seized upon and brought out with the happiest and most dramatic effect. In other parts, we have to regret that the dramatist has slurred over some of the points made by the old poet, which might have been illustrated with rare scenic ability. The opening scene, considering the action only, is quite worthy of Shakspeare's hand, even if it did not employ it. It presents a dramatic spectacle of great and tragic interest. Other scenes correspond with this in merit: we may instance that in which the brothers assist each other in putting on their armor before the duel, and that in which they appear severally before their favorite deities with their invocations and offerings. These scenes must have shown very impressively upon the stage. They unite high tragic dignity with a progressive dramatic interest, which, while it raised the expectations of the audience, filled their hearts with solemnity and emotion.

The story is one of considerable difficulties, being better suited, in some of the most interesting portions, for narrative and epic, than for dramatic purposes. Some of the most important events are conveyed to the spectator by narration, rather than in action. It is enough to indicate the combat between the rivals and their friends, and the final catastrophe which determines the fate of the triumphant party. Another of the obstacles to the complete dramatic success of this tragedy, is that want of personal prominence and individual superiority in either of the chief characters, on which so much of the success of a play depends. The rival youths, Palamon and Arcite, are distinguished rather by the descriptive passages of the author, than by their own performances, or, in these, only in the minor and less impressive portions of the piece. There is no such inequality of character, between the princes, as will permit the audience to choose between them. The spectator knows not which to make his favorite, and dare not yield his sympathies to one of the parties, lest he should do wrong to the claims of the other. They are both equally pure, brave, and virtuous—equally accomplished in arms, and alike graceful and winning in deportment. To decide between them, the author himself finds impossible, and can only extricate himself from his embarrassment by throwing the catastrophe upon the gods—an accident determining the success of one of the princes, after the prize has actually been awarded to his opponent.

The question of the authorship of this play is one much more difficult to decide than its merits. An old tradition of the play-house reports that the first act was written by Shakspeare, and the rest by Fletcher. The tradition, with the titlepage of the quarto of 1634, are therefore the only direct external evidence in favor of the notion that Shakspeare had a hand in its production. The evidence is almost equally doubtful, indeed, of Fletcher's participation in it. The first editors of the collected edition of Beaumont and Fletcher's works omit the Two Noble Kinsmen, with seventeen other plays, because it had been printed before in separate form. It is included in the second edition of 1679, in order, as they allege, that the writings of these authors may be "perfect and complete." That they were not prepared to make it so, with proper circumspection, may be inferred from the fact that they included in this collection one, at least, of the known performances of another writer. The truth is, the external testimony is very nearly a blank in regard to the claims of both dramatists. It may be Shakspeare's, or it may be Fletcher's. The claim of the latter, from intrinsic evidence, seems to me the better founded. On the same evidence, could we rely upon it solely — were it not, indeed, the most uncertain and most illusory of all modes of determining authorship — we should say that Shakspeare never wrote a syllable of the piece before us, though much of it is directly imitated from Shakspeare. Yet we must express ourselves with becoming deference. Mr. Pope supposes that the hand of Shakspeare may be discerned in some of the scenes. Dr. Warburton believes that he "wrote the first act, but in his worst manner." Mr. Coleridge says boldly, though, as he was wont to say many things, adventurously: "I can scarcely retain a doubt as to the first act's having been written by Shakspeare." Charles Lamb speaks of some of the scenes as giving "strong countenance to the tradition that Shakspeare had a hand in this play. . . . . They have a luxuriance in them which strongly resembles Shakspeare's manner, in those parts of his plays where, the progress of the scene being subordinate, the poet was at leisure for description." The German critics, who claim to know more about Shakspeare than the English, and who certainly have shown a just sympathy with his genius, by their fine and instinctive appreciation of it, concur in this opinion; but their speculations, as well as those which we have quoted, are wholly conjectural, and based upon assumptions, few of which will bear the test of a close examination.

As we have seen, we have not a tittle of external evidence available at the present moment, which can furnish any sufficient clues to the mystery. A glance at the internal proofs satisfies us that the Two Noble Kinsmen — a noble play, worthy of Fletcher, Chapman, or Ben Jonson — is yet not Shakspeare's. It does not show, to us at least, any satisfactory marks of his footstep. *Ex pede Herculem.* The versification is not his. In spite of what Mr. Lamb has said on this subject, it lacks his flow and vivacity. The great marks of Shakspeare are his equal profundity and lucidity. He rises always with a wing from his subject, however low that may be, as we see birds skim along the surface of the ground, just above and without touching it. His most difficult thoughts, ordinarily, are those which flow most musically; and the more comprehensive the range of his passions and ideas, they seem to choose for themselves an utterance of special clearness in due degree with the natural obstacles of the conception. Now, let the reader examine the metaphysical verse of the Two Noble Kinsmen, and he will see what embarrassments occur to the utterance of the writer in proportion to the subtlety of the sentiment. The nearest approach which he makes to Shakspeare's acknowledged writings, is to portions of such plays as Troilus and Cressida, of which the piece before us seems partly an imitation. Nor are these difficulties of utterance, when profound thoughts are to be expressed, calling for a new phraseology, to be accounted for by supposing that this was a production of our great dramatist in his youth. The Two Noble Kinsmen is not the work of an apprentice. It shows the familiarity of a master with his tools — one who would have done greatly better, had he trusted to himself wholly, avoiding anything like imitation His versification, if not that of Shakspeare, has force, readiness, compactness and animation. It is distinct and manly, if wanting something in freedom; and the sentiment is declared with confidence and promptness, as the voice of one who has been long accustomed to speak. Were there less promptness, less skill and spirit, we might better be prepared to admit Shakspeare's agency in the piece at a time when he had not yet learned the extent and strength of his own resources. It is too confident a performance for the inexperienced writer, and too wanting in the higher freedoms of music and imagination, for Shakspeare, in the day of his mature manhood. It is very certain that Shakspeare never conceived the clumsy copy of his Ophelia which appears in this performance. Is it probable that he would have participated in the composition of a play in which his associate should presume upon such a gross caricature?

THE TWO NOBLE KINSMEN.

PERSONS REPRESENTED.

THESEUS, *Duke of* Athens.
PALAMON, } The Two Noble Kinsmen, *in love with*
ARCITE, } Emilia.
PERITHOUS, *an* Athenian *general.*
VALERIUS, *a* Theban *nobleman.*
Six valiant knights.
Herald.
Gaoler.
Wooer to the Gaoler's Daughter.
Brothers, } *to the* Gaoler.
Friends, }
GERROLD, *a schoolmaster.*

HIPPOLYTA, *bride to* Theseus.
EMILIA, *her sister.*
Three Queens.
Gaoler's Daughter, in love with Palamon.
Servant to Emilia.

A Taborer, Countrymen, Soldiers, Nymphs, &c.

SCENE,—ATHENS; *and in part of the First Act,* THEBES.

ACT I.

SCENE I.

Enter HYMEN, *with a torch burning; a* Boy, *in a white robe, before, singing, and strewing flowers; after* HYMEN, *a* Nymph, *encompassed in her tresses, bearing a wheaten garland; then* THESEUS, *between two other* Nymphs, *with wheaten chaplets on their heads; then* HIPPOLYTA, *the bride, led by* PERITHOUS, *and another holding a garland over her head, her tresses likewise hanging; after her,* EMILIA, *holding up her train.*[1]

SONG.

Roses, their sharp spines being gone,
Not royal in their smells alone,
But in their hue;
Maiden-pinks, of odor faint,
Daisies smell-less, yet most quaint,
And sweet thyme true.

Primrose, first-born child of Ver,
Merry, spring-time's harbinger,
With her bells[2] dim;
Oxlips in their cradles growing,
Marigolds on death-beds blowing,
Larks'-heels trim.

All, dear Nature's children sweet,
Lie 'fore bride and bridegroom's feet,
Blessing their sense! [*Strew flowers.*
Not an angel of the air,[3]
Bird melodious, or bird fair,
Be[4] absent hence.

The crow, the slanderous cuckoo, nor
The boding raven, nor chough hoar,[5]
Nor chatt'ring pie,
May on our bridehouse perch or sing,
Or with them any discord bring,
But from it fly!

Enter three Queens, *in black, with veils stained, with imperial crowns. The first* Queen *falls down at the foot of* THESEUS; *the second falls down at the foot of* HIPPOLYTA; *the third before* Emilia.

1 *Queen.* For pity's sake, and true gentility,
Hear and respect me!
2 *Queen.* For your mother's sake,
And as you wish your womb may thrive with fair [ones,
Hear and respect me!
3 *Queen.* Now for the love of him whom Jove hath marked
The honor of your bed, and for the sake
Of clear virginity, be advocate
For us, and our distresses! This good deed
Shall raze you out o' the book of trespasses
All you are set down there.
Thes. Sad lady, rise!
Hip. Stand up!
Emi. No knees to me!
What woman I may stead that is distressed,
Does bind me to her.
Thes. What's your request? Deliver you for all.
1 *Queen.* We are three queens, whose sovereigns fell before
The wrath of cruel Creon; who endured
The beaks of ravens, talons of the kites,
And pecks of crows, in the foul fields of Thebes.
He will not suffer us to burn their bones,
To urn their ashes, nor to take th' offence
Of mortal loathsomeness from the blessed eye
Of holy Phœbus, but infects the winds

[1] This is the original stage-direction; with the exception that Hippolyta, by a manifest error in the old copies, is led by Theseus.
[2] Query: *Harebells?*
[3] *Angel* is used for bird. Dekker calls the Roman *eagle* "the Roman *angel*."—*Gifford's Massinger*, vol. i., p. 36.
[4] *Be.* The early copies, *is.*
[5] *Clough he* is the reading of the old editions.

With stench of our slain lords. Oh, pity, duke!
Thou purger of the earth, draw thy feared sword,
That does good turns to the world; give us the bones
Of our dead kings, that we may chapel them!
And, of thy boundless goodness, take some note,
That, for our crownèd heads, we have no roof
Save this, which is the lion's and the bear's,
And vault to everything!

Thes. Pray you kneel not!
I was transported with your speech, and suffered
Your knees to wrong themselves. I have heard the fortunes
Of your dead lords, which gives me such lamenting
As wakes my vengeance and revenge for them.
King Capaneus was your lord: the day
That he should marry you, at such a season
As now it is with me, I met your groom
By Mars's altar; you were that time fair,
Not Juno's mantle fairer than your tresses,
Nor in more bounty spread;[1] your wheaten wreath
Was then nor thrashed, nor blasted. Fortune at you
Dimpled her cheek with smiles. Her'cles, our kinsman,
(Then weaker than your eyes) laid by his club;
He tumbled down upon his Nemean hide,
And swore his sinews thawed. Oh, grief and time,
Fearful consumers, ye will all devour!

1 *Queen.* Oh, I hope some god,
Some god hath put his mercy in your manhood,
Whereto he'll infuse power, and press you forth
Our undertaker!

Thes. Oh, no knees; none, widow!
Unto the helmeted Bellona use them,
And pray for me, your soldier.—Troubled I am.
[*Turns away.*

2 *Queen.* Honored Hippolyta,
Most dreaded Amazonian, that hast slain
The scythe-tusked boar;—that, with thy arm as strong
As it is white, wast near to make the male
To thy sex captive; but that this thy lord
(Born to uphold creation in that honor
First nature styled[2] it in) shrunk thee into
The bound thou wast o'erflowing; at once subduing
Thy force and thy affection;—soldieress,
That equally canst poise sternness with pity,
Who now, I know, hast much more power on him
Than ever he had on thee; who own'st his strength,
And his love too, who is a servant[3] for
The tenor of thy speech; dear glass of ladies,
Bid him, that we, whom flaming war doth scorch,
Under the shadow of his sword may cool us!
Require him he advance it o'er our heads;
Speak't in a woman's key, like such a woman
As any of us three; weep ere you fail;
Lend us a knee;
But touch the ground for us no longer time
Than a dove's motion, when the head's plucked off!
Tell him, if he in the blood-sized[4] field lay swoll'n,
Showing the sun his teeth, grinning at the moon,
What you would do!

Hip. Poor lady, say no more!
I had as lief trace this good action with you
As that whereto I'm going, and never yet
Went I so willing way.[5] My lord is taken,
Heart deep with your distress. Let him consider;
I'll speak anon.

3 *Queen.* Oh, my petition was
[*Kneels to* EMILIA.
Set down in ice, which by hot grief uncandied
Melts into drops; so sorrow wanting form
Is pressed with deeper matter.

Emi. Pray stand up;
Your grief is written in your cheek.

3 *Queen.* Oh, woe!
You cannot read it there; here, through my tears,
Like wrinkled pebbles in a glassy stream,
You may behold them! Lady, lady, alack,
He that will all the treasure know o' the earth,
Must know the centre too. He that will fish
For my least minnow, let him lead his line
To catch one at my heart. Oh, pardon me!
Extremity, that sharpens sundry wits,
Makes me a fool.

Emi. Pray you, say nothing; pray you!
Who cannot feel nor see the rain, being in't,
Knows neither wet nor dry. If that you were
The ground-piece of some painter, I would buy you
To instruct me 'gainst a capital grief indeed;
Such heart-pierced demonstration!—but, alas,
Being a natural sister of our sex,
Your sorrow beats so ardently upon me,
That it shall make a counter-reflect 'gainst
My brother's heart, and warm it to some pity
Though it were made of stone; pray have good comfort!

Thes. Forward to the temple! leave not out a jot
Of the sacred ceremony.

1 *Queen.* Oh, this celebration
Will longer last, and be more costly, than
Your suppliants' war! Remember that your fame
Knolls in the ear o' the world. What you do quickly
Is not done rashly; your first thought is more
Than others' labored meditance; your premeditating
More than their actions: but, (oh Jove!) your actions,
Soon as they move, as ospreys do the fish,[6]
Subdue before they touch. Think, dear duke, think
What beds our slain kings have?

2 *Queen.* What griefs our beds,
That our dear lords have none!

3 *Queen.* None fit for the dead.
Those that with cords, knives', drams,[6] precipitance,[7]
Weary of this world's light, have to themselves
Been death's most horrid agents;—human grace
Affords them dust and shadow.

1 *Queen.* But our lords
Lie blistering 'fore the visitating[9] sun,
And were good kings, when living.

Thes. It is true: and I will give you comfort,
To give your dead lords graves. The which to do,
Must make some work with Creon.

1 *Queen.* And that work now presents itself to the doing:

1 "Nor in more bounty spread *her*," is the old reading. The omission equally helps the sense and the measure.

2 I should prefer to read "*stoled* it in," that is, dressed or habited in,—meaning the masculine dignity with which man was endowed, as superior, at the creation, and with which, though an Amazon, the queen of Theseus must not conflict.

3 Servant, attendant, one who even now waits to hear what you have to say.

4 Blood stained. *Size or sizing*, is a glutinous ground employed by painters.

5 Query: *willingly?* 6 Osprey, or ospring, the sea-eagle.

7 Dram, in the sense of drug; suicide, by poison.

8 This is usually printed—
"Those that with cords, knives, drams, precipitance."
We receive "cords," &c., as genitive cases to "precipitance."

9 Query: *vegetating?*

Now 't will take form. The heats are gone to-morrow;
Then bootless toil must recompense itself
With its own sweat. Now, he's secure,
Nor dreams we stand before your puissance,
Rinsing your holy begging in our eyes,
To make petition clear.

2 Queen. Now you may take him,
Drunk with his victory.[1]

3 Queen. And his army full
Of bread and sloth.[1]

Thes. Artesius, that best know'st
How to draw out, fit to this enterprise
The prim'st for this proceeding, and the number
To carry such a business; forth and levy
Our worthiest instruments, whilst we despatch
This grand act of our life, this daring deed
Of fate in wedlock!

1 Queen. Dowagers, take hands!
Let us be widows to our woes! Delay
Commends us to a famishing hope.

All. Farewell!

2 Queen. We come unseasonably; but when could grief
Cull forth, as unpanged judgment can, fitt'st time
For best solicitation?

Thes. Why, good ladies,
This is a service whereto I am going,
Greater than any war;[2] it more imports me
Than all the actions that I have foregone,
Or futurely can cope.

1 Queen. The more proclaiming
Our suit shall be neglected, when her arms,
Able to lock Jove from a synod, shall
By warranting moonlight corslet thee. Oh, when
Her twinning[3] cherries shall their sweetness fall[4]
Upon thy tasteful lips, what wilt thou think
Of rotten kings, or blubberéd[5] queens? what care
For what thou feel'st not,—what thou feel'st being able
To make Mars spurn his drum? Oh, if thou couch
But one night with her, every hour in't will
Take hostage of thee for a hundred, and
Thou shalt remember nothing more than what
That banquet bids thee to.

Hip. Though much I like[6]
You should be so transported, as much sorry
I should be such a suitor; yet I think
Did I not, by the abstaining of my joy,
Which breeds a deeper longing, cure their surfeit,
That craves a present medicine, I should pluck
All ladies' scandal on me: therefore, sir,
As I shall here make trial of my prayers,
Either presuming them to have some force,
Or seeing[7] for aye their vigor dumb, prorogue
This business we are going about, and hang
Your shield afore your heart, about that neck
Which is my fee, and which I freely lend
To do these poor queens service!

All Queens. Oh, help now!
Our cause cries for your knee. [*To* EMILIA.

Emi. If you grant not
My sister her petition, in that force,
With that celerity and nature, which
She makes it in, from henceforth I'll not dare
To ask you anything, nor be so hardy
Ever to take a husband.

Thes. Pray stand up!
I am entreating of myself to do
That which you kneel to have me. Perithous,
Lead on the bride! Get you and pray the gods
For success and return; omit not anything
In the pretended celebration. Queens,
Follow your soldier, as before. Hence you,
And at the banks of Aulis meet us with
The forces you can raise, where we shall find
The moiety of a number, for a business
More bigger looked!—Since that our theme is haste,
I stamp this kiss upon thy currant lip.
Sweet, keep it as my token! Set you forward;
For I will see you gone.

[*Exeunt toward the Temple.*

Farewell, my beauteous sister! Perithous,
Keep the feast full; bate not an hour on 't!

Per. Sir,
I'll follow you at heels; the feast's solemnity
Shall want[8] till your return.

Thes. Cousin, I charge you
Budge not from Athens; we shall be returning
Ere you can end this feast, of which I pray you,
Make no abatement. Once more, farewell all.

1 Queen. Thus dost thou still make good the tongue o' the world.

2 Queen. And earn'st a deity equal with Mars.

3 Queen. If not above him; for,
Thou, being but mortal, mak'st affections bend
To godlike honors; they themselves, some say,
Groan under such a mastery.

Thes. As we are men,
Thus should we do; being sensually subdued,
We lose our humane title. Good cheer, ladies!

[*Flourish.*

Now turn we toward your comforts. [*Exeunt.*

SCENE II.

Enter PALAMON *and* ARCITE.

Arc. Dear Palamon, dearer in love than blood,
And our prime cousin, yet unhardened in
The crimes of nature; let us leave the city,
Thebes, and the temptings in't, before we further
Sully our gloss of youth!
And here to keep in abstinence were[9] shame
As in incontinence: for not to swim
In the aid of the current, were almost to sink;
At least to frustrate striving; and to follow
The common stream, 'twould bring us to an eddy
Where we should turn or drown; if labored[10] through,
Our gain but life and weakness.

[1] See the speech in Hamlet, where Hamlet, forbearing to slay the king at his prayers, proposes to take him "when he is drunk," &c., as his father had been taken "when full of bread," &c.

[2] *War.* The early copies, *was.*

[3] Other copies read twining. Twinned, is the proper word.

[4] *Fall*—an active verb.

[5] Weeping.

[6] In former editions, "Though much *unlike*," &c. She addresses Theseus, and means to say, though it pleases her, his passion, and though it makes her sorry to have such a painful visit to him, yet she is compelled to join with the suitors, even to the delay of her own happiness. As it formerly read, the sense was wanting.

[7] "*Sentencing* for aye," is the language of former copies.

[8] Query: *wait?*

[9] "*We* shame," in former copies.

[10] "*Labor* through," is the old reading.

Pal. Your advice
Is cried up with examples. What strange ruins,
Since first we went to school, may we perceive
Walking in Thebes! Scars, and bare weeds,
The gain o' the martialist, who did propound
To his bold ends, honor and golden ingots,
Which, though he won, he had not; and now flurted[1]
By peace, for whom he fought,—who then shall offer
To Mars's so-scorned altar? I do bleed
When such I meet, and wish great Juno would
Resume her ancient fit of jealousy,
To get the soldier work; that peace might purge
For her repletion, and retain anew
Her charitable heart, now hard, and harsher
Than strife or war could be.

Arc. Are you not out?
Meet you no ruin but the soldier in
The cranks and turns of Thebes? You did begin
As if you met decays of many kinds:
Perceive you none that do arouse your pity,
But th' unconsidered soldier?

Pal. Yes; I pity
Decays where'er I find them; but such most,
That, sweating in an honorable toil,
Are paid with ice to cool 'em.

Arc. 'Tis not this
I did begin to speak of; this is virtue
Of no respect in Thebes. I spake of Thebes,
How dangerous, if we will keep our honors,
It is for our residing; where every evil
Hath a good color; where every seeming good's
A certain evil; where not to be even jump[2]
As they are here, were to be strangers, and
Such things to be mere monsters.

Pal. It is in our power,—
Unless we fear that apes can tutor us—to
Be masters of our manners. What need I
Affect another's gait, which is not catching
Where there is faith? or to be fond upon
Another's way of speech, when, by mine own,
I may be reasonably conceived,—saved too,
Speaking it truly? Why am I bound,
By any generous bond, to follow him
Follows his tailor—haply so long, until
The followed make pursuit! Or, let me know,
Why mine own barber is unblessed with him;
My poor chin too, for 'tis not scissored just
To such a favorite's glass? What canon's there
That does command my rapier from my hip,
To dangle 't in my hand; or to go tiptoe
Before the street be foul? Either I am
The fore-horse in the team, or I am none
That draw i' the sequent trace! These poor slight sores
Need not a plantain; that which rips my bosom
Almost to the heart's—

Arc. Our uncle Creon.

Pal. He!—
A most unbounded tyrant, whose successes
Make Heaven unfeared, and villany assured,
Beyond its power there's nothing;—almost puts[3]
Faith in a fever,[4] and deifies alone
Voluble chance—who only attributes
The faculties of other instruments
To his own nerves and act commands men's service,
And what they win in't, boot and glory too—
That fears not to do harm—good dares not—let
The blood of mine thats sib[5] to him be sucked
From me with leeches: let them break and fall
Off me with that corruption!

Arc. Clear-spirited cousin,
Let's leave his court, that we may nothing share
Of his loud infamy! for [still] our milk
Will relish of the pasture, and we must
Be vile or disobedient; not his kinsmen
In blood, unless in quality.

Pal. Nothing truer!
I think the echoes of his shames have deafed
The ears of heav'nly justice: widows' cries
Descend again into their throats, and have not
Due audience of the gods.—Valerius!

Enter VALERIUS.

Val. The king calls for you; yet be leaden-footed
Till his great rage be off him! Phœbus, when
He broke his whipstock, and exclaimed against
The horses of the sun, but whispered to
The loudness of his fury.

Pal. Small winds shake him
But what's the matter?

Val. Theseus (who where he threats appals) hath [sent
Deadly defiance to him, and pronounces
Ruin to Thebes; who is at hand to seal
The promise of his wrath.

Arc. Let him approach.
But that we fear the gods in him, he brings not
A jot of terror to us. Yet what man
Thirds his own worth (the case is each of ours)
When that his action's dregged with mind assured
'Tis bad he goes about?

Pal. Leave that unreasoned!
Our services stand now for Thebes, not Creon.
Yet, to be neutral to him, were dishonor,
Rebellious to oppose; therefore, we must,
With him, stand to the mercy of our fate,
Who hath bounded our last minute.

Arc. So we must.
Is't said this war's afoot? or it shall be,
On fail of some condition?

Val. 'Tis in motion;
The intelligence of state came in the instant
With the defier.

Pal. Let's to the king! [6]Were he
A quarter carrier of that honor which
His enemy comes in, the blood we venture

1 *Flurt*—to snap the fingers derisively. We may read *flouted.*

2 *Jump*—just—exactly.

3 This passage is ordinarily printed:—

"A most unbounded tyrant, whose *successes*
Make Heaven unfeared, and villany assured,
Beyond its power; there's nothing almost puts," &c.

Seward suggested the punctuation which we have adopted, in the third line; but by leaving the plural nominative *successes* he left the remainder of the sentence unintelligible—at least to modern readers, who require strict grammatical construction.*

* Thus Mr. Knight. I prefer to restore *successes*, as essential to the rhythm, and, by the omission of the letter *s* from *makes*, in the next line, to repair the grammatical hurts which are complained of. I have also changed the punctuation; though the last three lines, which I have left untouched, are still very obscure, and are susceptible of improvement.

4 Theobald reads it "faith in a fear," and I think with great propriety,—to the manifest improvement of the verse, and to the equally evident elevation of the sense.

5 *Sib*—kin.

6 Previous editions read, "Who were he," thus rendering the line unmusical, without helping the sense.

Should be as for our health; which were not spent;
Rather laid out for purchase. But alas,
Our hands advanced before our hearts, what[1] will
The fall o' the stroke do damage?

Arc. Let th' event,
That never-erring arbitrator, tell us
When we know all ourselves; and let us follow
The becking[2] of our chance! [*Exeunt.*

SCENE III.

Enter PERITHOUS, HIPPOLYTA, *and* EMILIA.

Per. No further!

Hip. Sir, farewell! Repeat my wishes
To our great lord, of whose success I dare not
Make any timorous question; yet I wish him
Excess and overflow of power, an't might be,
To dure[3] ill-dealing fortune. Speed to him!
Store never hurts good governors.

Per. Though I know
His ocean needs not my poor drops, yet they
Must yield their tribute there. My precious maid,
Those best affections that the Heavens infuse
In their best-tempered pieces, keep enthroned
In your dear heart!

Emi. Thanks, sir! Remember me
To our all-royal brother! for whose speed
The great Bellona I'll solicit: and
Since, in our terrene state petitions are not
Without gifts understood, I'll offer to her
What I shall be advised she likes. Our hearts
Are in his army, in his tent!

Hip. In 's bosom!
We have been soldiers, and we can not weep
When our friends don their helms, or put to sea,
Or tell of babes broached on the lance, or women
That have sod their infants in (and after eat them)
The brine they wept at killing 'em; then if
You stay to see of us such spinsters, we
Should hold you here for ever.

Per. Peace be to you,
As I pursue this war! which shall be then
Beyond further requiring. [*Exit.*

Emi. How his longing
Follows his friend! Since his depart, his sports,
Though craving seriousness and skill, past slightly
His careless execution, where nor gain
Made him regard, or loss consider; but
Playing[4] one[5] business in his hand, another
Directing in his head, his mind nurse equal
To these so diff'ring twins! Have you observed him
Since our great lord departed?

Hip. With much labor,
And I did love him for't. They two have cabined
In many as dangerous, as poor a corner;
Peril and want contending; they have skiffed
Torrents, whose roaring tyranny and power
I' th' least of these was dreadful; and they have
Fought out together, where death's self was lodged;
Yet fate hath brought them off. Their knot of love
Tied, weaved, entangled, with so true, so long,
And with a finger of so deep a cunning,
May be outworn, never undone. I think
Theseus can not be umpire to himself,
Cleaving his conscience into twain, and doing
Each side like justice, which he loves best.

Emi. Doubtless,
There is a best, and Reason has no manners
To say it is not you. I was acquainted
Once with a time, when I enjoyed a playfellow;
You were at wars when she the grave enriched,
Who made too proud the bed;—took leave o' th' moon
(Which then looked pale at parting) when our count
Was each eleven.

Hip. 'Twas Flavina.

Emi. Yes.
You talk of Perithous and Theseus' love:
Theirs has more ground, is more maturely seasoned,
More buckled with strong judgment, and their needs
The one of th' other may be said to water
Their intertangled roots of love; but I
And she (I sighed and spoke of) were things innocent;
Loved, for we did, and, like the elements
That know not what, nor why, yet do affect
Rare issues by their operance,—our souls
Did so to one another. What she liked,
Was then of me approved; what not, condemned;
No more arraignment. The flower that I would pluck
And put between my breasts (oh, then but beginning
To swell about the blossom) she would long
Till she had such another, and commit it
To the like innocent cradle, where phœnix-like
They died in perfume. On my head no toy
But was her pattern; her affections[6] (pretty,
Though happily her careless wear) I followed
For my most serious decking. Had mine ear
Stolen some new air, or at adventure hummed one
From musical coinage, why, it was a note
Whereon her spirits would sojourn (rather dwell on)
And sing it in her slumbers; this rehearsal,
Which every innocent wots well, comes in,
Like old importment's bastard, has this end,
That the true love 'tween maid and maid may be
More than in sex dividual.

Hip. You're out of breath;
And this high speeded pace is but to say,
That you shall never, like the maid Flavina,
Love any that's called man.

Emi. I am sure I shall not.

Hip. Now, alack, weak sister,
I must no more believe thee in this point
(Though in't I know thou dost believe thyself)
Than I will trust a sickly appetite,
That loaths even as it longs. But sure, my sister,
If I were ripe for your persuasion, you
Have said enough to shake me from the arm
Of the all-noble Theseus; for whose fortunes
I will now in and kneel, with great assurance,
That we, more than his Perithous, possess
The high throne in his heart.

Emi. I am not
Against your faith; yet I continue mine. [*Exeunt.*

1 *How* will.
2 Qu.: *Beckon?* or beckoning?
3 *Dure.* So the original, for *endure.* Some read *cure*; others, *dare.*
4 Should not *plying* be the word instead of playing?
5 *One* is suggested by M. Mason. The original has *ore.*

6 *Affections*—what she affected—liked.*
* Affections in the sense of affectations,—but pretty ones, and so gracefully and happily worn as to prompt my serious imitation.

SCENE IV.

A battle struck within ; then a retreat ; flourish. Then enter Theseus, *victor ; the three* Queens *meet him, and fall on their faces before him.*

1 *Queen.* To thee no star be dark!
2 *Queen.* Both Heaven and earth
'Friend thee for ever!
3 *Queen.* All the good that may
Be wished upon thy head, I cry "amen" to't!
Thes. Th' impartial gods, who, from the mounted heavens,
View us, their mortal herd, behold who err,
And in their time chastise. Go and find out
The bones of your dead lords, and honor them
With triple ceremony! Rather than a gap
Should be in their dear rites, we would supply't.
But those we will depute which shall invest
You in your dignities, and even[1] each thing
Our haste does leave imperfect: so adieu,
And Heaven's good eyes look on you! — What are those ?[2] [*Exeunt* Queens.
Herald. Men of great quality, as may be judged
By their appointment; some of Thebes have told us
They are sisters' children, nephews to the king.
Thes. By the helm of Mars, I saw them in the war,
Like to a pair of lions, smeared with prey,
Make lanes in troops aghast. I fixed my note
Constantly on them; for they were a mark
Worth a god's view! What prisoner was't that told [me,
When I inquired their names?
Herald. With leave, they're called
Arcite and Palamon.
Thes. 'Tis right; those, those.
They are not dead?
Herald. Nor in a state of life. Had they been taken
When their last hurts were given, 'tis possible
They might have been recovered; yet they breathe,
And have the name of men.
Thes. Then like men use 'em!
The very lees of such, millions of rates
Exceed the wine of others. All our surgeons
Convent[3] in their behoof; our richest balms,
Rather than niggard, waste! Their lives concern us
Much more than Thebes is worth. Rather than have them
Freed of this plight, and in their morning state,
Sound and at liberty, I would them dead;
But, forty thousand fold, we had rather have them
Prisoners to us than death. Bear 'em [in] speedily
From our kind air (to them unkind), and minister
What man to man may do! — for our sake more!
Since I have known frights, fury, friends' behests,
Love's provocations, zeal, a mistress' task,
Desire of liberty, a fever, madness,
Hath set a mark which Nature could not reach to
Without some imposition — sickness in will
Or wrestling strength in reason for our love
And great Apollo's mercy — all our best
Their best skill tender! — Lead into the city:
Where, having bound things scattered, we will post
To Athens 'fore our army. [*Exeunt.*

1 *Even*—make even.
2 Here we are to suppose the bodies of the wounded Arcite and Palamon to be borne along.
3 Convent for convene, assemble.

SCENE V.

Enter the Queens *with the hearses of their* Kings, *in a funeral solemnity, &c.*

Urns and odors bring away,
Vapors, sighs, darken the day!
Our dole more deadly looks than dying!
Balms, and gums, and heavy cheers,
Sacred vials filled with tears,
And clamors through the wild air flying:
Come, all sad and solemn shows,
That are quick-eyed Pleasure's foes!
We convent naught else but woes.
We convent, &c.

3 *Queen.* This funeral path brings to your household's grave:[4]
Joy seize on you again! Peace sleep with him!
2 *Queen.* And this to yours!
1 *Queen.* Yours this way! Heavens lend
A thousand differing ways to one sure end!
3 *Queen.* This world's a city, full of straying streets;
And death's the market-place, where each one meets.
Exeunt severally.

ACT II.

SCENE I.

Enter Gaoler *and* Wooer.

Gaoler. I may depart[5] with little while I live,
Something I may cast to you, not much: Alas!
The prison I keep, although it be for great ones,
They seldom come. Before one salmon, you
Shall take a number of minnows. I'm given out
To be better lined than 't can appear to me
Report is a true speaker. I would I were,
Really, that I am delivered to be.
Marry [but] what I have — be't what it will —
I will assure upon my daughter at
The day o' my death.
Wooer. Sir, I demand no more
Than your own offer; and I will estate
Your daughter in what I've promised.
Gaoler. Well!
We'll talk more of this when the solemnity
Is past: but have you a full promise of her?
When that shall be seen, I tender my consent.
Wooer. I have, sir; — here she comes.

Enter Daughter.

Gaoler. Your friend and I
Have chanced to name you here on the old business;
But no more of that now! Soon as the court-hurry
Is over, we will make an end of it.
I' the meantime look to the two prisoners,
Tenderly;—I can tell you they are princes.
Daughter. These strewings for their chamber. It is pity
They are in prison, and [yet] 'twere pity that
They should be out. I do think they've patience

4 *Household's grave.* So the quarto. The ordinary reading is *household graves.* Each king had *one* grave.*
* So Mr. Knight;—and yet the "household graves" were those of the family. The plural seems to me the more antique and the more legitimate reading. It affords that freedom from the *literal* which poetry most prefers.
5 Depart with—*part with.*

To make adversity ashamed. The prison,
Itself, is proud of them; and they have all
The world in their chamber.
Gaoler. They are famed to be
A pair of absolute men.
Daughter. By my troth I think
[That] Fame but stammers them. They stand a-grees[1]
Above the reach of report.
Gaoler. I have heard them
Reported, in the battle, to have been
The only doers.
Daughter. Ay,[2] most likely,
For they are noble sufferers. I marvel how
They would have looked, had they been victors, that
With such a constant nobleness[3] enforce
A freedom out of bondage, making [of] misery
Their mirth, and [of] affliction [but] a toy
To jest at.
Gaoler. Do they so?
Daughter. It seems to me,
They've no more sense of their captivity,
Than I of ruling Athens. They eat well,
Look merrily, discourse of many things,
But nothing of their own straits[4] and disaster;
Yet, sometimes, a divided sigh, martyred,
As 'twere in the deliverance, will break
From one of them; when t' other, presently,
Gives it so sweet[5] rebuke, that I could wish
Myself a sigh to be so chid, or at least,
A sigher to be comforted.
Wooer. I ne'er saw 'em.
Gaoler. The duke himself comes private[6] in the night,
And so did they; [but] what the reason of it,
I know not.—Look [you] yonder [where] they are!
That's Arcite [that] looks out.

Enter Palamon *and* Arcite *above.*

Daughter. No, sir, that's Palamon:
Arcite's the lower of the twain. You may
Perceive a part of him.
Gaoler. Go to,—leave[6] pointing!
They'd not make us their object. Out of[7] sight.
Daughter. It is a holiday to look on them!
Lord, Lord! the difference of men.[8] [*Exeunt.*

SCENE II.

Enter Palamon *and* Arcite, *in prison.*[9]

Pal. How do you, noble cousin?
Arc. How do you, sir!
Pal. Why, strong enough to laugh at misery,
And bear the chance of war yet. We are prisoners
I fear for ever, cousin.
Arc. I believe it;
And to that destiny have patiently
Laid up my hour to come.
Pal. Oh, cousin Arcite,
Where is Thebes now? where is our noble country?
Where are our friends and kindred? Never more
Must we behold those comforts; never [more] see
The hardy youths strive for the games of honor,
Hung with the painted favors of their ladies,
Like tall ships under sail; then start amongst 'em,
And, as an east wind, leave 'em all behind us
Like lazy clouds, whilst Palamon and Arcite,
Even in the wagging of a wanton leg,
Out-strip the people's praises, win the garlands,
Ere they have time to wish 'em ours. Oh, never
Shall we two exercise, like twins of honor,
Our arms again, and feel our fiery horses,
Like proud seas under us! Our good swords now,
(Better the red-eyed god of war ne'er wore)
Ravished our sides, like age, must run to rust,
And deck the temples of those gods that hate us.
These hands shall never draw them out like lightning,
To blast whole armies more!
Arc. No, Palamon,
These hopes are prisoners with us: here we are,
And here the graces of our youths must wither,
Like a too timely spring. Here age must find us,
And, which is heaviest, Palamon unmarried.
The sweet embraces of a loving wife,
Laden with kisses, armed with thousand Cupids,
Shall never clasp our necks! no issue know us;
No figures of ourselves shall we e'er see,
To glad our age, and like young eagles teach them
Boldly to gaze against bright arms, and say,
Remember what your fathers were, and conquer!
The fair-eyed maids shall weep our banishment,
And, in their songs, curse ever-blinded Fortune,
Till she for shame see what a wrong she has done
To youth and nature. This is all our world;
We shall know nothing here, but one another;
Hear nothing but the clock that tells our woes;
The vine shall grow, but we shall never see it;
Summer shall come, and with her all delights,
But dead-cold winter must inhabit here!
Pal. 'Tis too true, Arcite! To our Theban hounds,
That shook the agéd forest with their echoes,
No more now must we halloo; no more shake
Our pointed javelins, whilst the angry swine
Flies like a Parthian quiver from our rages,
Struck with our well-steeled darts! All valiant uses
(The food and nourishment of noble minds)
In us two, here shall perish; we shall die,
(Which is the curse of honor!) lazily,[10]
Children of grief and ignorance.
Arc. Yet, cousin,
Even from the bottom of these miseries,
From all that fortune can inflict upon us,
I see two comforts rising, two mere[11] blessings,

1 *Grees*—Seward reads "grief" and Mr. Knight follows him. *Grees*, or *grese*, means steps or stairs, and may mean degrees. Either of these makes sense of the passage, which *grief* does not.

2 Previous editions read "nay." The sense of the speech requires the alteration.

3 Previous copies read, "*nobility.*"

4 Former copies read, "*restraints.*"

5 "So sweet *a* rebuke," elsewhere.

6 "Privately," in Knight and Seward's edition.

7 Leave *your* pointing.
8 Out of *their* sight.
} These omissions, which do not affect the sense, are demanded by the verse. The whole scene which Mr. Knight prints as prose is in the usual dramatic blank verse, and is so printed by Mr. Seward. I have thrown in, here and there, a particle or preposition, where the measure seemed to require it.

9 The position of Palamon and Arcite in the prison, with the power of observing what passes in the garden when Emilia enters, implies a double action which requires the employment of the secondary stage. See Othello, Act v.

10 Mr. Knight, following the old copy, has "*lastly*"—a word without significance in this connexion. I follow the reading of Mr. Seward. Sloth, laziness, and not death, is here meant by "the curse of honor."

11 *Mere*—absolute.—So Mr. Knight. "Mere" is certainly used by the old writers in the sense of absolute; but I half incline to think that the proper word is *new*, which might well be converted into "mere" by the printer. *More* would answer better than *mere*.

If the gods please to hold here ; — a brave patience,
And the enjoying of our griefs together.
Whilst Palamon is with me, let me perish
If I think this our prison.

Pal. Certainly,
'Tis a main goodness, cousin, that our fortunes
Were twinned together : 'tis most true, two souls
Put in two noble bodies, let them suffer
The gall of hazard, so they grow together,
Will never sink ; they must not say they could ;[1]
A willing man dies sleeping, and all's done.

Arc Shall we make worthy uses of this place,
That all men hate so much ?

Pal. How, gentle cousin?

Arc. Let's think this prison holy sanctuary,
To keep us from corruption of worse men !
We are young, and yet desire the ways of honor,
That liberty and common conversation,
The poison of pure spirits, might, like women,
Woo us to wander from. What worthy blessing
Can be, but our imaginations
May make it ours ? And here being thus together,
We are an endless mine to one another ;
We are one another's wife, ever begetting
New births of love ; we are father, friends, acquaintance ;
We are, in one another, families ;
I am your heir, and you are mine ; this place
Is our inheritance ; no hard oppressor
Dare take this from us ; here, with a little patience,
We shall live long, and loving ; no surfeits seek us ;
The hand of war hurt none here, nor the seas
Swallow their youth. Were we at liberty,
A wife might part us lawfully, or business ;
Quarrels consume us ; envy of ill men
Crave[2] our acquaintance. I might sicken, cousin,
Where you should never know it, and so perish
Without your noble hand to close mine eyes,
Or prayers to the gods : a thousand chances,
Were we from hence, would sever us.

Pal. You have made me
(I thank you, Cousin Arcite !) almost wanton
With my captivity : what a misery
It is to live abroad, and everywhere !
'Tis like a beast, methinks ! I find the court here,
I'm sure, a more content ; and all those pleasures,
That woo the wills of men to vanity,
I see through now ; and am sufficient [bold]
To tell the world, 'tis but a gaudy shadow,
That old Time, as he passes by, takes with him.
What had we been, old in the court of Creon,
Where sin is justice, lust and ignorance
The virtues of the great ones ! Cousin Arcite,
Had not the loving gods found this place for us,
We had died as they do, ill old men unwept,
And had their epitaphs, the people's curses !
Shall I say more ?

Arc. I would hear you still.

Pal. You shall.
Is there record of any two that loved
Better than we do, Arcite ?

Arc. Sure there can not.

Pal. I do not think it possible our friendship
Should ever leave us.

Arc. Till our deaths it can not ;

Enter EMILIA *and her* Servant, *in the garden below.*

And after death our spirits shall be led
To those that love eternally. Speak on, sir !

Emi. This garden has a world of pleasures in't.
What flower is this ?

Serv. 'Tis called Narcissus, madam.

Emi. That was a fair boy, certain, but a fool
To love himself ; were there not maids enough ?

Arc. (*above*). Pray, forward ![3]

Pal. Yes.

Emi. Or were they all hard-hearted ?

Serv. They could not be to one so fair.

Emi. Thou wouldst not ?

Serv. I think I should not, madam.

Emi. That's a good wench !
But take heed to your kindness though !

Serv. Why, madam ?

Emi. Men are mad things.

Arc. (*above*). Will you go forward, cousin?[4]

Emi. Canst not thou work such flowers in silk, wench ?

Serv. Yes.

Emi. I'll have a gown full of them, and of these ;
This is a pretty color : will't not do
Rarely upon a skirt, wench ?

Serv. Dainty, madam.

Arc. Cousin ! How do you, sir ? Why, Palamon !

Pal. Never 'till now was I in prison, Arcite.

Arc. Why, what's the matter, man ?

Pal. Behold, and wonder !
By Heaven, she is a goddess !

Arc. (*sees Emilia*). Ha !

Pal. Do reverence !
She is a goddess, Arcite !

Emi. Of all flowers,
Methinks a rose is best.

Serv. Why, gentle madam !

Emi. It is the very emblem of a maid :
For when the west wind courts her gently,
How modestly she blows, and paints the sun
With her chaste blushes ! When the north comes near her,
Rude and impatient, then, like chastity,
She locks her beauties in her bud again,
And leaves him to base briars.

Serv. Yet, good madam,
Sometimes her modesty will blow so far
She falls for it : a maid,
If she have any honor, would be loath
To take example by her.

Emi. Thou art wanton.

Arc. She's wondrous fair !

Pal. She's all the beauty extant

Emi. The sun grows high ; let's walk in ! Keep these flowers ;
We'll see how near art can come near[5] their colors.
I'm wondrous merry-hearted ; I could laugh now.

1 This line is usually divided thus—"they must not ; say they could"—but the meaning is, they must not admit to themselves that they can sink, lest they do so, since to despair is to die sleeping, willingly.

2 *Crave* is the word of the early copies. M. Mason proposes to read *cleave*—that is, separate—the *acquaintance* of the two friends. We receive the passage as—the envy which characterizes ill men may crave that we also should become acquainted with that passion.

3 That is—"speak on"—respecting a former entreaty.

4 Palamon has been silent in watching Emilia.

5 We might read "compare" in this place, instead of come near. "How near art can come near," is such an awkwardness as might well justify the substitute.

Serv. I could lie down, I'm sure.
Emi. And take one with you?
Serv. That's as we bargain, madam.
Emi. Well agree[1] then. [*Exit with* Serv.
Pal. What think you of this beauty?
Arc. 'Tis a rare one.
Pal. Is't but a rare one?
Arc. Yes, a matchless beauty.
Pal. Might not a man well lose himself, and love her?
Arc. I can not tell what you have done; I have!—
Beshrew mine eyes for it! Now I feel my shackles.
Pal. You love her, then?
Arc. Who would not?
Pal. And desire her?
Arc. Before my liberty.
Pal. I saw her first.
Arc. That's nothing.
Pal. But it shall be.
Arc. I saw her too.
Pal. Yes; but you must not love her.
Arc. I will not, as you do; to worship her,
As she is heavenly, and a blessed goddess:
I love her as a woman, to enjoy her;
So both may love.
Pal. You shall not love at all.
Arc. Not love at all? who shall deny me?
Pal. I that first saw her; I that took possession
First, with mine eye, of all those beauties in her
Revealed [un]to mankind! If thou lovest her,
Or entertainest a hope to blast my wishes,
Thou art a traitor, Arcite, and a fellow
False as thy title to her. Friendship, blood,
And all the ties between us, I disclaim,
If thou once think upon her!
Arc. Yes, I love her;
And if the lives of all my name lay on it,
I must do so. I love her with my soul!
If that will lose you, farewell, Palamon!
I say again, I love; loving her, maintain
I am as worthy and as free a lover,
And have as just a title to her beauty,
As any Palamon, or any living,
That is a man's son.
Pal. Have I called thee friend?
Arc. Yes, and have found me so. Why are you moved thus?
Let me deal coldly[2] with you! am not I
Part of your blood, part of your soul? you've told me
That I was Palamon, and you Arcite.
Pal. Yes.
Arc. Am I not liable to those affections,
Those joys, griefs, angers, fears, my friend shall suffer?
Pal. You may be.
Arc. Why then would you deal so cunningly,
So strangely, so unlike a noble kinsman,
To love alone? Speak truly; do you think me
Unworthy of her sight?
Pal. No; but unjust
If thou pursue that sight.
Arc. Because another
First sees the enemy, shall I stand still,
And let mine honor down, and never charge?
Pal. Yes, if he be but one.

1 Or, "we'll agree"—that is, to take as we bargain.
2 Coolly, calmly, as a reasoning being; or it may be, *boldly*.

Arc. But say that one
Had rather combat me?
Pal. Let that one say so,
And use thy freedom! else, if thou pursuest her,
Be as that cursèd man that hates his country,
A branded villain!
Arc. You are mad.
Pal. I must be,
Till thou art worthy. Arcite, it concerns me;
And, in this madness, if I hazard thee
And take thy life, I deal but truly.
Arc. Fie, sir!
You play the child extremely. I will love her,
I must, I ought to do so, and I dare;
And all this, justly.
Pal. Oh, that now, that now,
Thy false self, and thy friend, had but this fortune,
To be one hour at liberty, and grasp
Our good swords in our hands! I'd quickly teach thee
What 't were to filch affection from another!
Thou'rt baser in it than a cutpurse! But put
Thy head but once out of this window more,
And, as I have a soul, I'll nail thy life to't!
Arc. Thou darest not, fool; thou canst not; thou art feeble!
Put my head out? I'll throw my body out,
And leap the garden, when I see her next,

Enter GAOLER.

And pitch[3] between her arms, to anger thee.
Pal. No more; the keeper's coming: I shall live
To knock thy brains out with my shackles.
Arc. Do.
Gaoler. By your leave, gentlemen.
Pal. Now, honest keeper?
Gaoler. Lord Arcite, you must presently to the duke:
The cause I know not yet.
Arc. I am ready, keeper.
Gaoler. Prince Palamon, I must awhile bereave you
Of your fair cousin's company.
[*Exit with* ARCITE.
Pal. And me too,
Even when you please, of life!—Why is he sent for?
It may be, he shall marry her: he's goodly;
And like enough the duke hath taken notice
Both of his blood and body. But his falsehood!
Why should a friend be treacherous? If that
Get him a wife so noble and so fair,
Let honest men ne'er love again. Once more
I would but see this fair one Blessed garden,
And fruit, and flowers more blessed, that still blossom
As her bright eyes shine on ye! 'Would I were,
For all the fortune of my life hereafter,
Yon little tree, yon blooming apricot!
How I would spread, and fling my wanton arms
In at her window! I would bring her fruit!
Fit for the gods to feed on. Youth and pleasure,
Still, as she tasted, should be doubled on her;
And, if she be not heavenly, I would make her
So near the gods in nature, they should fear her;
And then I'm sure she'd love me.

Enter GAOLER.

How now, keeper!
Where's Arcite?
Gaoler. Banished. Prince Perithous

3 Qu.: *Perch?*

Obtained his liberty; but never more,
Upon his oath and life, must he set foot
Upon this kingdom.
Pal. He's a blessèd man!
He shall see Thebes again, and call to arms
The bold young men, that, when he bids them charge,
Fall on like fire. Arcite shall have a fortune,[1]
If he dare make himself a worthy lover,
Yet in the field to strike a battle for her;
And if he lose her then, he's a cold coward:
How bravely may he bear himself to win her,
If he be noble Arcite, thousand ways!
Were I at liberty, I would do things
Of such a virtuous greatness, that this lady,
This blushing virgin, should take manhood to her,
And seek to ravish me.
Gaoler. My lord, for you
I have this charge too.
Pal. To discharge my life?
Gaoler. No; but from this place to remove your lordship;
The windows are too open.
Pal. Devils take them,
That are so envious to me! Prithee kill me!
Gaoler. And hang for't afterward!
Pal. By this good light,
Had I a sword, I'd kill thee.
Gaoler. Why, my lord?
Pal. Thou bringest such pelting scurvy news continually,
Thou art not worthy life! I will not go.
Gaoler. Indeed you must, my lord.
Pal. May I see the garden?
Gaoler. No.
Pal. Then I'm resolved I will not go.
Gaoler. I must
Constrain you then! and, for you're dangerous,
I'll clap more irons on you.
Pal. Do, good keeper,
And I will shake 'em so, you shall not sleep;
I'll make you a new morris! Must I go?
Gaoler. There is no remedy.
Pal. Farewell, kind window!
May rude wind never hurt thee! Oh, my lady,
If ever thou hast felt what sorrow was,
Dream how I suffer! Come, now bury me. [*Exeunt.*

SCENE III.

Enter Arcite.

Arc. Banished the kingdom! 'Tis a benefit,
A mercy I must thank them for; but banished
The free enjoying of that face I die for,
Oh, 'twas a studied punishment, a death
Beyond imagination! Such a vengeance,
That, were I old and wicked, all my sins
Could never pluck upon me. Palamon,
Thou hast the start now; thou shalt stay and see
Her bright eyes break each morning 'gainst thy window,
And let in life unto thee; thou shalt feed
Upon the sweetness of a noble beauty,
That nature ne'er exceeded, nor ne'er shall.
Good gods, what happiness has Palamon!
Twenty to one he'll come to speak to her;
And, if she be as gentle as she's fair,
I know she's his. He has a tongue will tame
Tempests, and make the wild rocks wanton.
Come what can come, the worst is [only] death
I will not leave this kingdom:
I know my own is but a heap of ruins,
And no redress there! If I go, he has her.
I am resolved: another shape shall make me,
Or end my fortunes; either way, I'm happy:
I'll see her, and be near her, or no more.

Enter four Country People; *one with a garland before them.*

1 *Coun.* My masters, I'll be there, that's certain.
2 *Coun.* And I'll be there.
3 *Coun.* And I.
4 *Coun.* Why then, have with ye, boys! 'tis but a chiding;
Let the plough play to-day! I'll tickle't out
Of the jades' tails to-morrow!
1 *Coun.* I am sure
To have my wife as jealous as a turkey:
But that's all one; I'll go through, let her mumble.
3 *Coun.* Do we all hold against the maying?[2]
4 *Coun.* Hold! what should ail us?
3 *Coun.* Arcas will be there.
2 *Coun.* And Sennois,
And Rycas; and three better lads ne'er danced
Under green tree. Ye know what wenches. Ha!
But will the dainty *domine*, the schoolmaster,
Keep touch, do you think? for he does all, ye know.
3 *Coun.* He'll eat a hornbook, ere he fail: Go to!
The matter is too far driven between
Him and the tanner's daughter, to let slip now;
And she must see the duke, and she must dance too.
4 *Coun.* Shall we be lusty?
2 *Coun.* All the boys in Athens,
Blow wind i'the breech on us! . . .
(*Sings*)—And here I'll be
And there I'll be,—
For our town . . . .
And here again,
And there again.
Ha, boys! Heigh for the weavers.
1 *Coun.* This must be done i' the woods.
4 *Coun.* Oh, pardon me!
2 *Coun.* By any means; our thing of learning says so;
Where he himself will edify the duke
Most parlously in our behalfs: he's excellent
I' the woods. Bring him to the plains,
His learning makes no cry.
3 *Coun.* We'll see the sports;
Then every man to his tackle; and,
Companions, let's rehearse by any means,
Before the ladies see us; and do't sweetly,
And God knows what may come on't!
4 *Coun.* Content:
The sports once ended, we'll perform. Away, boys;
And hold!
Arc. By your leaves, honest friends! I pray you,
Whither go you?
4 *Coun.* Whither? why, what a question's that!

1 *Fortune*—a chance.

2 When we open Beaumont and Fletcher's works, we encounter grossnesses entirely of a different nature from those which occur in Shakspeare. They are the result of impure thoughts, not the accidental reflection of loose manners. They are meant to be corrupting. We have four lines here conceived in this spirit, and we omit them without hesitation. No one has thought that these comic scenes were written by Shakspeare.

Arc. Yes, 'tis a question,
To me, that know not.
3 *Coun.* To the games, my friend.
2 *Coun.* Where were you bred, you know it not?
Arc. Not far, sir.
Are there such games to-day?
1 *Coun.* Yes, marry are there;
And such as you ne'er saw: the duke himself
Will be in person there.
Arc. What pastimes are they?
2 *Coun.* Wrestling and running. 'Tis a pretty fellow.
3 *Coun.* Thou wilt not go along?
Arc. Not, yet, sir.
4 *Coun.* Well, sir,
Take your own time. Come, boys!
1 *Coun.* My mind misgives me,
This fellow hath a vengeance trick o' the hip;
Mark, how his body's made for't!
2 *Coun.* I'll be hanged though
If he dare venture; hang him; he, plum-porridge!
He wrestle? He roast eggs. Come, let's be gone, lads! [*Exeunt* Countrymen.
Arc. This is an offered opportunity
I durst not wish for. Well I could have wrestled;
The best men called it excellent;—and run,—
Swifter the wind upon a field of corn
(Curling the wealthy ears) ne'er flew![1] I'll venture,
And in some poor disguise be there: who knows
Whether my brows may not be girt with garlands,
And happiness prefer me to a place
Where I may ever dwell in sight of her? [*Exit.*

SCENE IV.

Enter Gaoler's DAUGHTER.

Daugh. Why should I love this gentleman. 'Tis odds
He never will affect me. I am base;
My father the mean keeper of his prison,
And he a prince: to marry him is hopeless,
To be his whore is witless. Out upon 't!
What pushes are we wenches driven to,
When fifteen once has found us! First, I saw him;
I, seeing, thought he was a goodly man.
He has as much to please a woman in him,
(If he please to bestow it so) as ever
These eyes yet looked on: next, I pitied him;
And so would any young wench, o'my conscience,
That ever dreamed, or vowed her maidenhead
To a young handsome man: then, I loved him,
Extremely loved him, infinitely loved him!
And yet he had a cousin, fair as he too;
But in my heart was Palamon, and there,
Lord what a coil he keeps! [Only[2]] to hear him
Sing in an evening, what a heaven it is!
And yet his songs are sad ones. Fairer spoken
Was never gentleman: when I come in,
To bring him water in a morning, first
He bows his noble body, then salutes me:
"Fair gentle maid, good morrow! may thy goodness
Get thee a happy husband!"—Once he kissed me;
I loved my lips the better ten days after:
'Would he would do so every day! He grieves much,
And me as much to see his misery:
What should I do to make him know I love him?
For I would fain enjoy him: say I ventured
To set him free? what says the law then?
Thus much for law, or kindred! I will do it,
And this night or to-morrow. He shall love me!
[*Exit.*

SCENE V.—*A short flourish of cornets, and shouts within.*

Enter THESEUS, HIPPOLYTA, PERITHOUS, EMILIA, *and* ARCITE, *with a garland, &c.*

Thes. You have done worthily. I have not seen,
Since Hercules, a man of tougher sinews:
Whate'er you are, you run the best and wrestle,
That these times can allow.
Arc. I am proud to please you.
Thes. What country bred you?
Arc. This; but far off, prince.
Thes. Are you a gentleman?
Arc. My father said so;
And to those gentle uses gave me life.
Thes. Are you his heir?
Arc. His youngest, sir.
Thes. Your father
Sure is a happy sire then. What prove you?
Arc. A little of all noble qualities:
I could have kept a hawk, and well have halloo'd
To a deep cry of dogs. I dare not praise
My feat in horsemanship, yet they that knew me
Would say it was my best piece; last, and greatest,
I would be thought a soldier.
Thes. You are perfect.
Per. Upon my soul, a proper man!
Emi. He is so.
Per. How do you like him, lady?
Hip. I admire him:
I have not seen so young a man so noble
(If he say true) of his sort.
Emi. Believe [me[3]]
His mother was a wondrous handsome woman!
His face, methinks, goes that way.
Hip. But his body,
And fiery mind, illustrate a brave father.
Per. Mark how his virtue, like a hidden sun,
Breaks through his baser garments.
Hip. He's well got, sure
Thes. What made you seek this place, sir?
Arc. Noble Theseus,
To purchase name, and do my ablest service
To such a well-found wonder as thy worth;
For only in thy court, of all the world,
Dwells fair-eyed Honor.
Per. All his words are worthy.
Thes. Sir, we are much indebted to your travel,

1 The ordinary reading is:—
"And run,
Swifter *the* wind upon a field of corn
(Curling the wealthy ears) *ne'er* flew."
The original has *than*, which has been altered to *the*. By changing *ne'er* to *e'er* we obtain a better construction.*
* And with Mr. Knight's permission, I have ventured to restore the reading of *the* for *than*, with a new punctuation, preferring, though with great deference, the present construction to his own.

2 "Only," is here an interpolation, to render the line complete and musical. In Seward's edition, he interpolates "to sit," thus—"To sit and hear," &c.

3 Former copies simply say, "believe." I add the word, "me," as equally necessary to the rhythm and the idiom. "His face goes that way," means, he looks like his mother—he has a feminine aspect.

Nor shall you lose your wish. Perithous,
Dispose of this fair gentleman.

Per. Thanks, Theseus! —
Whate'er you are, you're mine, and I shall give you
To a most noble service; — to this lady —
This bright young virgin: pray observe her goodness:
You've honored her fair birthday with your virtues,
And, as your due, you're hers; kiss her fair hand, sir.

Arc. Sir, you're a noble giver. — Dearest beauty,
Thus let me seal my vowed faith! When your servant
(Your most unworthy creature) but offends you,
Command him die, he shall.

Emi. That were too cruel.
If you deserve well, sir, I shall soon see't:
You're mine, and somewhat better than your rank
I'll use you.

Per. I'll see you furnished: and because you say
You are a horseman, I must needs entreat you
This afternoon to ride; but 't is a rough one.

Arc. I like him better, prince; I shall not then
Freeze in my saddle.

Thes. Sweet, you must be ready;
And you, Emilia; and you, friend; and all;
To-morrow, by the sun, to do observance
To flowery May, in Dian's wood. Wait well, sir,
Upon your mistress! Emily, I hope
He shall not go afoot.

Emi. That were a shame, sir,
While I have horses. Take your choice; and what
You want at any time, let me but know it:
If you serve faithfully, I dare assure you
You'll find a loving mistress.

Arc. If I do not,
Let me find that[1] my father ever hated,
Disgrace and blows!

Thes. Go, lead the way; you've won it;
It shall be so: you shall receive all dues
Fit for the honor you have won; 'twere wrong else.
Sister, beshrew my heart, you have a servant,
That if I were a woman, would be master;
But you are wise. [*Flourish.*

Emi. I hope too wise for that, sir. [*Exeunt.*

SCENE VI.

Enter Gaoler's DAUGHTER.

Daugh. Let all the dukes and all the devils roar,
He is at liberty! I've ventured for him;
And out I've brought him to a little wood
A mile hence. I have sent him, where a cedar,
Higher than all the rest, spreads like a plane
Fast by a brook; and there he shall keep close,
Till I provide him files and food; for yet
His iron bracelets are not off. Oh, Love,
What a stout-hearted child thou art! My father
Durst better have endured cold iron than done it.
I love him beyond love, and beyond reason,
Or wit or safety! I have made him know it.
I care not; I am desperate. If the law
Find me, and then condemn me for't, some wenches,
Some honest-hearted maids, will sing my dirge,
And tell to memory my death was noble,
Dying almost a martyr. That way he takes,
I purpose, is my way too: sure, he can not
Be so unmanly as to leave me here!
If he do, maids will not so easily
Trust men again. And yet he has not thanked me
For what I've done; no, not so much as kissed me;
And that, methinks, is not so well; nor scarcely
Could I persuade him to become a freeman,
He made such scruples of the wrong he did
To me and to my father. Yet, I hope,
When he considers more, this love of mine
Will take more root within him: let him do
What he will with me, so he but use me kindly!
For use me so he shall, or I'll proclaim him,
And to his face, no man. I'll presently
Provide him necessaries, and pack my clothes up,
And where there is a path of ground I'll venture,
So he be with me! By him, like a shadow,
I'll ever dwell. Within this hour the hubbub
Will be all o'er the prison. I am then
Kissing the man they look for. Farewell, father!
Get many more such prisoners, and such daughters,
And shortly you may keep yourself. Now to him!
[*Exit.*

ACT III.

SCENE I.—*Cornets in sundry places. Noise and hallooing, as people a-maying.*

Enter ARCITE.

Arc. The duke has lost Hippolyta; each took
A several land. This is a solemn rite
They owe bloomed May, and the Athenians pay it
To the heart of ceremony. Oh, queen!
Emilia, fresher than [the] May, [and] sweeter
Than her gold buttons on the boughs, or all
Th' enamelled knacks o' the mead or garden! yea,
We challenge, too, the bank of any nymph,
That makes the stream seem flowers; thou, oh jewel
Of the wood, of the world, hast likewise blessed a place
With thy 'sole presence. In thy rumination
That I, poor man, might eftsoons come between,
And chop[1] on some cold thought! — Thrice blessed chance,
To drop on such a mistress,— expectation
Most guiltless of 't! Tell me, oh, lady Fortune,
(Next after Emily my sovereign), how far
I may be proud. She takes strong note of me,
Hath made me near her, and this beauteous morn
(The prim'st of all the year) presents me with
A brace of horses; two such steeds might well
Be by a pair of kings backed, in a field
That their crowns' titles tried. Alas, alas,
Poor cousin Palamon, poor prisoner! thou
So little dream'st upon my fortune, that
Thou think'st thyself the happier thing, to be
So near Emilia. Me, thou deem'st at Thebes,
And therein wretched, although free: but if

[1] There is something quite obscure in this passage. I should prefer to substitute "*forget*," for "find that." To forget that his father's lessons always taught a hatred of disgrace and blows, would be necessary to one whose conduct is supposed to deserve them.—KNIGHT.

[1] *Chop*, on a sudden, to meet by chance. Still the passage is obscure. Why a cold thought, unless it is meant that as she ruminates coldly and indifferently, her heart is still accessible to a new passion?

Thou knew'st my mistress breathed on me, and that
I eared her language, lived in her eye, oh, coz,
What passion would enclose thee!

Enter PALAMON *as out of a bush, with his shackles; bends his fist at* ARCITE.

Pal. Traitor kinsman!
Thou shouldst perceive my passion, if these signs
Of prisonment were off me, and this hand
But owner of a sword. By all oaths in one,
I, and the justice of my love, would make thee
A confessed traitor! Oh, thou most perfidious
That ever gently looked! The void'st of honor
That e'er bore gentle token! Falsest cousin
That ever blood made kin! Call'st thou her thine?
I'll prove it in my shackles, with these hands
Void of appointment,[1] that thou liest, and art
A very thief in love, a chaffy lord,
Not[2] worth the name of villain! Had I a sword,
And these house-clogs away—

Arc. Dear cousin Palamon—

Pal. Cozener Arcite, give me language such
As thou hast showed me feat!

Arc. Not finding, in
The circuit of my breast, any gross stuff
To form me like your blazon, holds me to
This gentleness of answer. 'Tis your passion
That thus mistakes; the which, to you being enemy,
Can not to me be kind. Honor and honesty
I cherish, and depend on, howsoe'er
You skip them in me; and, with them, fair coz,
I'll maintain my proceedings. Pray be pleased
To show in generous terms your griefs, since that
Your question's with your equal, who professes
To clear his own way, with the mind and sword
Of a true gentleman.

Pal. That thou durst, Arcite!

Arc. My coz, my coz, you have been well advertised
How much I dare. You've seen me use my sword
Against th' advice of fear. Sure, of another
You would not hear me doubted, but your silence
Should break out, though i' the sanctuary.

Pal. Sir,
I've seen you move in such a place, which well
Might justify your manhood; you were called
A good knight and a bold: but the whole week's not [fair,
If any day it rain! Their valiant temper
Men lose, when they incline to treachery;
And then they fight like compelled bears,—would fly
Were they not tied.

Arc. Kinsman, you might as well
Speak this, and act it in your glass, as to
His ear, which now disdains you!

Pal. Come up to me!
Quit me of these cold gyves, give me a sword
(Though it be rusty), and the charity
Of one meal lend me; come before me then,
A good sword in thy hand, and do but say
That Emily is thine, I will forgive
The trespass thou hast done me, yea, my life,
If then thou carry't; and, brave souls in shades,
That have died many, which will seek of me
Some news from earth, they shall get none but this,
That thou art brave and noble.

1 Without preparation of armor or weapons.
2 Other editions read "nor."

Arc. Be content;
Again betake you to your hawthorn-house!
With counsel of the night, I will be here
With wholesome viands; these impediments
Will I file off; you shall have garments, and
Perfumes to kill the smell o' the prison; after,
When you shall stretch yourself, and say but, 'Arcite,
I am in plight!' there shall be at your choice
Both sword and armor.

Pal. Oh, you heavens, dare any
So noble, bear a guilty business? None
But only Arcite; therefore none but Arcite,
In this kind, is so bold.

Arc. Sweet Palamon—

Pal. I do embrace you, and your offer: for
Your offer do't; ay, only, sir: your person,
Without hypocrisy, I may not wish
More than my sword's edge on't.
[*Wind horns of cornets.*

Arc. You hear the horns:
Enter your musit,[3] lest this match between us
Be crossed ere met. Give me your hand: farewell?
I'll bring you every needful thing: I pray you
Take comfort, and be strong!

Pal. Pray hold your promise
And do the deed with a bent brow! most certain
You love me not: be rough with me, and pour
This oil out of your language: by this air,
I could for each word give a cuff! my stomach
Not reconciled by reason.

Arc. Plainly spoken!
Yet pardon me hard language: when I spur
My horse, I chide him not; content and anger
[*Wind horns.*
In me have but one face. Hark, sir! they call
The scattered to the banquet: you must guess
I have an office there.

Pal. Sir, your attendance
Can not please Heaven; and I know your office
Unjustly is achieved.

Arc. I've a good title,
I am persuaded: this question, sick between us,
By bleeding must be cured. I am a suitor,
That, to your sword, you will bequeath this plea,
And talk of it no more.

Pal. But this one word:
You are going now to gaze upon my mistress;
For, note you, mine she is—

Arc. Nay, then—

Pal. Nay, pray you!—
You talk of feeding me to breed me strength:
You are going now to look upon a sun
That strengthens what it looks on; there you have
A vantage o'er me; but enjoy it till
I may enforce my remedy. Farewell! [*Exeunt*

SCENE II.

Enter Gaoler's DAUGHTER.

Daugh. He has mistook the brake[4] I meant; is gone
After his fancy. 'Tis now well-nigh morning;

3 The original has, "enter your *music.*" Seward reads "*muse quick,*" explaining *muse* to be "the muse of a hare." Weber adopts *muse,* but omits *quick.* We substitute *musit,* which has the same meaning.
4 The original has *beake.* M. Mason suggested *brake.**
* Mr. Seward has it *beck.* "Brook" is probably the proper word. She has previously said:—
"I have sent him," &c.,
"Fast by a brook."

No matter! Would it were perpetual night,
And darkness lord o' the world! — Hark! 'tis a wolf:
In me hath grief slain fear, and, but for one thing,
I care for nothing; and that's Palamon.
I reck not if the wolves would jaw me, so
He had this file. What if I hallooed for him?
I can not halloo: if I whooped, what then?
If he not answered, I should call a wolf,
And do him but that service. I have heard [be
Strange howls this live-long night; why may't not
They have made prey of him? He has no weapons;
He cannot run; the jingling of his gyves
Might call fell things to listen, who have in them
A sense to know a man unarmed, and can
Smell where resistance is. I'll set it down
He's torn to pieces; they howled many together,
And then they fed on him: so much for that!
Be bold to ring the bell; how stand I then?
All's chared[1] when he is gone. No, no, I lie;
My father's to be hanged for his escape;
Myself to beg, if I prized life so much
As to deny my act; but that I would not,
Should I try death by dozens! — I am moped:
Food took I none these two days; only sipped
Some water. Two nights have not closed mine eyes,
Save when my lids scowered off their brine; alas,
Dissolve, my life! Let not my sense unsettle,
Lest I should drown, or stab, or hang myself!
Oh, state of nature, fail together in me, [now?
Since thy best props are warped! — So! which way
The best way is the next way to a grave:
Each errant step beside is torment. Lo!
The moon is down, the crickets chirp, the screech-owl
Calls in the dawn! All offices are done,
Save what I fail in: but the point is this,
An end, and that is all! [*Exit.*

SCENE III.

Enter ARCITE, *with meat, wine, and files.*

Arc. I should be near the place. Ho, Cousin Palamon!

Enter PALAMON.

Pal. Arcite?
Arc. The same: I've brought you food and files.
Come forth, and fear not; here's no Theseus.
Pal. Nor none so honest, Arcite.
Arc. That's no matter;
We'll argue that hereafter. Come, take courage;
You shall not die thus beastly; here, sir, drink!
I know you're faint; then I'll talk further with you.
Pal. Arcite, thou might'st now poison me.
Arc. I might;
But I must fear you first. Sit down; and, good now,
No more of these vain parleys! Let us not,
Having our ancient reputation with us,
Make talk for fools and cowards. To your health!
Pal. Do—
Arc. Pray sit down then; and let me entreat you,
By all the honesty and honor in you,
No mention of this woman! 'Twill disturb us;
We shall have time enough.
Pal. Well, sir, I'll pledge you.
Arc. Drink a good hearty draught! it breeds good blood, man.
Do not you feel it thaw you?
Pal. Stay; I'll tell you
After a draught or two more.
Arc. Spare it not;
The duke has more. Eat now.
Pal. Yes.
Arc. I am glad
You have so good a stomach.
Pal. I am gladder
I have so good meal to't.
Arc. Is't not mad lodging
Here, in the wild wood, cousin;
Pal. Yes, for them
That have wild consciences.
Arc. How tastes your victuals?
Your hunger needs no sauce, I see.
Pal. Not much:
But if it did, yours is too tart, sweet cousin.
What is this?
Arc. Venison.
Pal. 'Tis a lusty meat.
Give me more wine; here, Arcite, to the wenches
We have known in our days? The lord-steward's
Do you remember her? [daughter;
Arc. After you, coz.
Pal. She loved a black-haired man.
Arc. She did so: well, sir?
Pal. And I have heard some call him Arcite; and—
Arc. Out with it, faith!
Pal. She met him in an arbor:
What did she there, coz? Play o' the virginals?
Arc. Something she did, sir.
Pal. Made her groan a month for't;
Or two, or three, or ten.
Arc. The marshal's sister
Had her share too, as I remember, cousin,
Else there be tales abroad: you'll pledge her?
Pal. Yes.
Arc. A pretty brown wench 'tis! There was a time
When young men went a-hunting, and a wood,
And a broad beech; and thereby hangs a tale.—
Heigh-ho! [*Sighs.*
Pal. For Emily, upon my life! Fool,
Away with this strained mirth! I say again,
That sigh was breathed for Emily: base cousin,
Darest thou break first?
Arc. You're wide. [honest!
Pal. By Heaven and earth, there's nothing in thee
Arc. Then I'll leave you:
You are a beast now.
Pal. As thou mak'st me, traitor.
Arc. There's all things needful; files, and shirts and perfumes:
I'll come again some two hours hence, and bring
That that shall quiet all.
Pal. A sword and armor?
Arc. Fear me not, you are now too foul: farewell!
Get off your trinkets; you shall want naught.
Pal. Sirrah—
Arc. I'll hear no more! [*Exit.*
Pal. If he keep touch, he dies for't! [*Exit.*

1 *All's chared.* Weber says that this means "my task is done,"—*chare* being used in the sense of a task. *Chare* is a turn—a job of work. We doubt the explanation.*

* Why not "all's cleared?" The sentence which follows seems to imply some such signification: "No, no," she says, "I lie; my father's to be hanged," &c.

SCENE IV.

Enter Gaoler's DAUGHTER, *mad.*

Daugh. I'm very cold, and all the stars are out too,
The little stars, and all that look like aglets:
The sun has seen my folly. Palamon!
Alas, no; he's in heaven!—Where am I now?—
Yonder's the sea, and there's a ship; how't tumbles!
And there's a rock lies watching under water;
Now, now, it beats upon it! now, now, now!
There's a leak sprung, a sound one; how they cry!
Upon her before the wind,[1] you'll lose all else!
Up with a course or two, and tack about, boys!
Good night, good night; you're gone!—I'm very
hungry:
Would I could find a fine frog! he would tell me
News from all parts o' the world; then would I make
A carrack of a cockle-shell, and sail
By east and northeast to the king of pigmies,
For he tells fortunes rarely. Now my father,
Twenty to one, is trussed up in a trice
To-morrow morning; I'll say never a word.

SONG.

For I'll cut my green coat a foot above my knee;
And I'll clip my yellow locks an inch below mine e'e
Hey, nonny, nonny, nonny.
He's buy me a white cut, forth for to ride,
And I'll go and seek him, through the world that is so wide.
Hey, nonny, nonny, nonny.

Oh, for a prick now, like a nightingale,
To put my breast against![2] I shall sleep like a top
else. [*Exit.*

SCENE V.

Enter GERROLD, *four* Countrymen, (*and the* Bavian[3]), *two or three* Wenches, *with a* Taborer.

Ger. Fie, fie!
What tediosity and disensanity
Is here among ye! Have my rudiments
Been labored so long with ye, milked unto[4] ye,
And, by a figure, even the very plum-broth
And marrow of my understanding laid upon ye,
And do ye still cry "where," and "how," and "where-
fore?"
Ye most coarse frieze capacities, ye jape[5] judgments,
Have I said "thus let be," and "there let be,"
And "then let be," and no man understand me?
Proh Deum, medius fidius; ye are all dunces!
For why? here stand I; here the duke comes; there
are you,
Close in the thicket; the duke appears, I meet him,
And unto him I utter learned things,
And many figures; he hears, and nods, and hums,
And then cries "rare!" and I go forward; at length
I fling my cap up; mark there! then do you,
As once did Meleager and the boar,
Break comely out before him, like true lovers,
Cast yourselves in a body decently,
And sweetly, by a figure, trace, and turn, boys!

1 Coun. And sweetly we will do it, Master Gerrold,

2 Coun. Draw up the company. Where's the taborer?

3 Coun. Why, Timothy!

Tab. Here, my mad boys; have at ye!

Ger. But, I say, where's the women?

4 Coun. Here's Friz and Maudlin

2 Coun. And little Luce, with the white legs, and bouncing Barbary.

1 Coun. And freckled Nell, that never failed her master.

Ger. Where be your ribands, maids? Swim with your bodies,
And carry it sweetly, and deliverly;[6]
And now and then a favor, and a frisk!

Nell. Let us alone, sir.

Ger. Where's the rest o' the music?

3 Coun. Dispersed as you commanded.

Ger. Couple then,[7]
And see what's wanting. Where's the Bavian?
My friend, carry your tail without offence
Or scandal to the ladies; and be sure
You tumble with audacity, and manhood!
And when you bark, do it with judgment.

Bav. Yes, sir.

Ger. *Quo usque tandem?* Here's a woman wanting.

4 Coun. We may go whistle; all the fat's i' the fire!

Ger. We have,
As learned authors utter, washed a tile;
We have been *fatuus*, and labored vainly.

2 Coun. This is that scornful piece, that scurvy hilding,
That gave her promise she would faithfully
Be here, the sempster's daughter, Cicely!
The next gloves that I give her shall be dog's skin!
Nay, an she fail me once—You can tell, Arcas,
She swore, by wine and bread, she would not break.

Ger. An eel and woman,
A learned poet says, unless by the tail
And with thy teeth thou hold, will either[8] fail.
In manners;—this was false position.

1 Coun. A fire ill[9] take her! does she flinch now?

3 Coun. What
Shall we determine, sir?

Ger. Nothing;
Our business is become a nullity.
Yea, and a woful, and a piteous nullity! [it,

4 Coun. Now, when the credit of our town lay on

---

1 So the original. There have been several attempts to render this proper nautical language. Weber reads, "*spoom* her before the wind."*

* "*Put* her before the wind," is just as likely to be the reading. Mr. Sympson recommends, "Up with her 'fore the wind;" and Mr. Theobald, "Spoon her before," &c. The choice is with the reader.

2 The nightingale is fabled to sing most sweetly when thus suffering from the thorn.

3 Fletcher uses this term for a character in the morris-dance.*

* The Bavian, according to Nares, is a baboon or monkey, but not a regular character in the old morris-dance. His office here is to bark, to tumble, play antics of all sorts, and exhibit an enormous length of tail, with a due regard to decency.

4 Quere: "Milked *into* ye"?

5 *Jape.* The original has *jave.* Seward reads *sleave.* As no one can explain *jave,*—and *sleave,* the sleave of silk, is almost meaningless,—we substitute *jape,*—belonging to a buffoon, a *japer.**

* The original is "jabe." This may be only a misprint for "*have.*"—"Ye have judgments," spoken ironically.

6 We might read, "deliver ye"—i. e., speak what you have to say.

7 Or, "them."

8 "Ever" would seem to be the word.

9 Mr. Seward reads "feril," or "ferule" take her—a not inappropriate notion of punishment on the part of a pedagogue.

Now to be frampal! Now to wet the nettle;[1]
Go thy ways: I'll remember thee, I'll fit thee!

Enter Gaoler's DAUGHTER.

Daugh. The George alow came from the south,
From the coast of Barbaree-a.
And there he met with brave gallants of war,
By one, by two, by three-a.

Well hailed, well hailed, you jolly gallants!
And whither now are you bound-a?
Oh, let me have your company
Till I[2] come to the Sound-a!

There was three fools, fell out about an howlet:
The one said 'twas an owl,
The other he said nay,
The third he said it was a hawk,
And her bells were cut away.

3 *Coun.* There is a dainty mad woman, master,
Comes i' the nick; as mad as a March hare!
If we can get her dance, we're made again:
I warrant her, she'll do the rarest gambols!
1 *Coun.* A mad woman? We are made, boys!
Ger. And are you mad, good woman?
Daugh. I would be sorry else;
Give me your hand.
Ger. Why?
Daugh. I can tell your fortune:
You are a fool. Tell ten: I've pozed him. Buz!
Friend, you must eat no white bread; if you do,
Your teeth will bleed extremely. Shall we dance, ho?
I know you; you're a tinker: sirrah tinker,
Stop no more holes, but what you should![3]
Ger. *Dii boni!* A tinker, damsel?
Daugh. Or a conjurer:
Raise me a devil now, and let him play
Quipassa, o' the bells and bones!
Ger. Go, take her,
And fluently persuade her to a peace.
Atque opus, exegi, quod nec Jovis ira, nec ignis—
Strike up, and lead her in!
2 *Coun.* Come, lass, let's trip it!
Daugh. I'll lead. [*Wind horns.*
3 *Coun.* Do, do.
Ger. Persuasively, and cunningly; away, boys!
[*Exeunt all but* GERROLD.
I hear the horns: give me some meditation,
And mark your cue. Pallas inspire me!

Enter THESEUS, PERITHOUS, HIPPOLYTA, EMILIA, ARCITE, *and* Train.

Thes. This way the stag took.
Ger. Stay, and edify!

1 I have altered a single word in this sentence, where to avoid a vulgarism, Mr. Knight omits it altogether.
2 *I* is omitted in the original. Weber reads *we*.
3 It is not incumbent on an editor to make sense of the speeches of a mad woman, the author himself being seldom inclined to do so;—still there is a necessity for a certain economy even in nonsense, and a degree of method must needs be found in most cases of dramatic madness. I am inclined to think that the stuff here spoken by the daughter should be distributed in parts among some of her companions; and would read the passage thus:—
Daugh. I can tell your fortune:—
You are a fool.
Ger. Tell ten. [Tell't then.]
Daugh. I've pozed him.
Ger. Buz.
Daugh. Friend, you must eat no white bread;
If you do; &c.

Thes. What have we here?
Per. Some country-sport, upon my life, sir.
Thes. Well, sir, go forward: we will edify.
Ladies, sit down! we'll stay it.
Ger. Thou doughty duke, all hail! all hail, sweet ladies!
Thes. This is a cold beginning.
Ger. If you but favor, our country pastime made is
We are a few of those collected here,
That ruder tongues distinguish villager;
And to say verity, and not to fable,
We are a merry rout, or else a rabble,
Or company, or by a figure, chorus,
That 'fore thy dignity will dance a morris.
And I that am the rectifier of all,
By title Pedagogus, that let fall
The birch upon the breeches of the small ones,
And humble with a ferula the tall ones,
Do here present this machine, or this frame:
And, dainty duke, whose doughty dismal fame
From Dis to Dedalus, from post to pillar,
Is blown abroad: help me, thy poor well-willer,
And with thy twinkling eyes, look right and straight
Upon this mighty *morr*;—of mickle weight,
Is—now comes in, which, being glued together,
Makes *morris*, and the cause that we came hither.
The body of our sport, of no small study,
I first appear, though rude, and raw, and muddy,
To speak before thy noble grace, this tenor:
At whose great feet I offer up my penner.[4]
The next, the lord of May, and lady bright,
The chambermaid, and servingman by night,
That seek out silent hanging: then, mine host,
And his fat spouse, that welcome to their[5] cost
The galled traveller, and with a beck'ning
Inform the tapster to inflame the reck'ning:
Then the beast-eating clown, and next the fool,
The Bavian, with long tail, and eke long tool;
Cum multis aliis, that make a dance:—
Say "ay," and all shall presently advance.
Thes. Ay, ay, by any means, dear domine!
Per. Produce.
Ger. *Intrate filii!* Come forth, and foot it.

Enter Countrymen, *&c.* *They dance.*

Ladies, if we have been merry,
And have pleased ye with a derry,
And a derry, and a down,
Say the schoolmaster's no clown.
Duke, if we have pleased thee too,
And have done as good boys should do,
Give us but a tree or twain
For a Maypole, and again,
Ere another year run out,
We'll make thee laugh, and all this rout.

Thes. Take twenty, domine.—How does my sweetheart?
Hip. Never so pleased, sir.
Emi. 'Twas an excellent dance;
And, for a prefase, I never heard a better.
Thes. Schoolmaster, I thank you. One see them all rewarded.

4 *Penner*—case for holding pens.
5 I should prefer to read:—
"Welcome to *his* cost,
The galled traveller," &c.

Per. And here's something to paint your pole withal.
Thes. Now to our sports again!
Ger. May the stag thou huntest stand long,
And thy dogs be swift and strong!
May they kill him without letts,
And the ladies eat's dowsets!
Come, we're all made! [*Wind horns.*
Dii Deæque omnes!
Ye have danced rarely, wenches. [*Exeunt.*

SCENE VI.

Enter PALAMON *from the bush.*

Pal. About this hour my cousin gave his faith
To visit me again, and with him bring
Two swords, and two good armors; if he fail,
He's neither man, nor soldier. When he left me,
I did not think a week could have restored
My lost strength to me; I was grown so low
And crest-fallen with my wants. I thank thee, Arcite,
Thou'rt yet a fair foe; and I feel myself,
With this refreshing, able once again
To out-dure[1] danger. To delay it longer
Would make the world think, when it comes to hearing,
That I lay fatting, like a swine, to fight,
And not a soldier: therefore, this blessed morning
Shall be the last; and that sword he refuses,
If it but hold, I kill him with: 'tis justice:
So, Love and Fortune for me! Oh, good morrow!

Enter ARCITE, *with armors and swords.*

Arc. Good morrow, noble kinsman!
Pal. I have put you
To too much pains, sir.
Arc. That too much, fair cousin,
Is but a debt to honor, and my duty.
Pal. 'Would you were so in all, sir! I could wish you
As kind a kinsman, as you force me find
A beneficial foe; that my embraces
Might thank you, not my blows.
Arc. I shall think either,
Well done, a noble recompense.
Pal. Then I shall quit you.
Arc. Defy me in these fair terms, and you show
More than a mistress to me: no more anger,
As you love anything that's honorable!
We are not bred to talk, man; when we're armed,
And both upon our guards, then let our fury,
Like meeting of two tides, fly strongly from us!
And then to whom the birthright of this beauty
Truly pertains (without upbraidings, scorns,
Despisings of our persons, and such poutings,
Fitter for girls and schoolboys) will be seen,
And quickly, yours or mine. Will't please you arm, sir?
Or, if you feel yourself not fitting yet,
And furnished[2] with your old strength, I'll stay, cousin,
And every day discourse you into health,
As I am spared. Your person I am friends with,
And I could wish I had not said I loved her,
Though I had died; but, loving such a lady,
And justifying my love, I must not fly from't.
Pal. Arcite, thou art so brave an enemy,
That no man but thy cousin's fit to kill thee:
I'm well, and lusty; choose your arms!

1 Here I should certainly prefer to read, "*outdare*."
2 Should we not rather read, "unfurnished" for "and furnished"?

Arc. Choose you, sir
Pal. Wilt thou exceed in all, or dost thou do it
To make me spare thee?
Arc. If you think so, cousin,
You are deceived; for, as I am a soldier,
I'll not spare you!
Pal. That's well said!
Arc. You will find
Pal. Then, as I am an honest man, and love
With all the justice of affection,
I'll pay thee soundly! This I'll take.
Arc. That's mine then
I'll arm you first.
Pal. Do. Pray tell me, cousin,
Where gott'st thou this good armor?
Arc. 'Tis the duke's
And, to say true, I stole it. Do I pinch you?
Pal. No.
Arc. Is't not too heavy?
Pal. I've worn a lighter,
But I shall make it serve.
Arc. I'll buckle't close.
Pal. By any[3] means.
Arc. You care not for a grand-guard?[4]
Pal. No, no; we'll use no horses. I perceive
You would fain be at that fight.
Arc. I'm indifferent.
Pal. Faith, so am I. Good cousin, thrust the buckle
Through, far enough!
Arc. I warrant you.
Pal. My casque now!
Arc. Will you fight bare-armed?
Pal. We shall be the nimbler.
Arc. But use your gauntlets though: those are o' the least;
Prithee take mine, good cousin!
Pal. Thank you, Arcite!
How do I look? am I fallen much away?
Arc. Faith, very little; Love has used you kindly.
Pal. I'll warrant thee I'll strike home.
Arc. Do, and spare not!
I'll give you cause, sweet cousin.
Pal. Now to you, sir!
Methinks this armor's very like that, Arcite,
Thou wor'st that day the three kings fell, but lighter.
Arc. That was a very good one; and that day,
I well remember, you outdid me, cousin;
I never saw such valor when you charged
Upon the left wing of the enemy;
I spurred hard to come up, and, under me,
I had a right good horse.
Pal. You had, indeed;
A bright-bay, I remember.
Arc. Yes. But all
Was vainly labored in me; you outwent me,
Nor could my wishes reach you: yet a little
I did by imitation.
Pal. More by virtue;
You're modest, cousin.
Arc. When I saw you charge first
Methought I heard a dreadful clap of thunder
Break from the troop.
Pal. But still, before that, flew
The lightning of your valor. Stay a little!
Is not this piece too strait?

3 "Any," for "all."
4 *Grand-guard*—armor for equestrians.

Arc. No, no; 'tis well.
Pal. I would have nothing hurt thee but my sword;
A bruise would be dishonor.
Arc. Now I'm perfect.
Pal. Stand off, then!
Arc. Take my sword! I hold it better.[1]
Pal. I thank you, no; [you] keep't; your life lies on't:
Here's one, if it but hold; I ask no more
For all my hopes. My cause and honor guard me!
[*They bow several ways; then advance and stand.*
Arc. And me, my love! Is there aught else to say?
Pal. This only, and no more: thou art mine aunt's son,
And that blood we desire to shed is mutual;
In me, thine, and in thee mine: my sword
Is in my hand, and if thou killest me
The gods and I forgive thee! If there be
A place prepared for those that sleep in honor,
I wish his weary soul that falls may win it!
Fight bravely, cousin; give me thy noble hand!
Arc. Here, Palamon! This hand shall never more
Come near thee with such friendship.
Pal. I commend thee.
Arc. If I fall, curse me, and say I was a coward;
For none but such dare die in these just trials.
Once more, farewell, my cousin!
Pal. Farewell, Arcite! [*Fight.*
[*Horns within; they stand.*
Arc. Lo, cousin, lo! our folly has undone us!
Pal. Why?
Arc. This is the duke, a-hunting, as I told you;
If we be found, we're wretched! Oh, retire,
For honor's sake and safety; presently
Into your bush again, sir! We shall find
Too many hours to die in. Gentle cousin,
If you be seen you perish instantly,
For breaking prison; and I, if you reveal me,
For my contempt: then all the world will scorn us,
And say we had a noble difference,
But base disposers of it.
Pal. No, no, cousin;
I will no more be hidden, nor put off
This great adventure to a second trial!
I know your cunning, and I know your cause.
He that faints now, shame take him! Put thyself
Upon thy present guard —
Arc. You are not mad?
Pal. Or I will make th' advantage of this hour
Mine own; and what to come shall threaten me,
I fear less than my fortune. Know, weak cousin,
I love Emilia! and in that I'll bury
Thee, and all crosses else!
Arc. Then come what can come;[2]
Thou shalt know, Palamon, I dare as well
Die, as discourse, or sleep: only this fears me,
The law will have the honor of our ends.
Have at thy life!
Pal. Look to thine own well, Arcite!
[*Fight again. Horns.*

Enter THESEUS, HIPPOLYTA, EMILIA, PERITHOUS, *and* Train.

Thes. What ignorant and mad malicious traitors
Are you, that, 'gainst the tenor of my laws,
Are making battle, thus, like knights appointed,
Without my leave, and officers of arms?
By Castor, both shall die!
Pal. Hold thy word, Theseus.
We're certainly both traitors, both despisers
Of thee, and of thy goodness: I am Palamon,
That can not love thee; — he that broke thy prison;
Think well what that deserves! — and this is Arcite;
A bolder traitor never trod thy ground,
A falser ne'er seemed friend: this is the man
Was begged[3] and banished; this is he contemns thee
And what thou darést do; and, in disguise,[4]
Against thy[5] known edict, follows thy sister,
That fortunate bright star, the fair Emilia,
(Whose servant, if there be a right in seeing,
And first bequeathing of the soul to, justly
I am;) and, which is more, dares think her his!
This treachery, like a most trusty lover,
I called him now to answer. If thou be'est,
As thou art spoken, great and virtuous,
The true decider of all injuries,
Say, "Fight again!" and thou shalt see me, Theseus,
Do such a justice, thou thyself wilt envy.
Then take my life! I'll woo thee to't.
Per. Oh, Heaven,
What more than man is this!
Thes. I've sworn.
Arc. We seek not
Thy breath of mercy, Theseus! 'Tis to me
A thing as soon to die, as thee to say it,
And no more moved. Where this man calls me traitor,
Let me say thus much: if love[6] be treason,
In service of so excellent a beauty,
As I love most, and in that faith will perish;
As I have brought my life here to confirm it;
As I have served her truest, worthiest;
As I dare kill this cousin, that denies it;
So let me be most traitor, and you please me.
For scorning thy edict, duke, ask that lady
Why she is fair, and why her eyes command me
Stay here to love her; and if she say "traitor,"
I am a villain fit to lie unburied.
Pal. Thou shalt have pity of us both, oh, Theseus,
If unto neither thou show mercy; stop,
As thou art just, thy noble ear against us;
As thou art valiant, for thy cousin's soul,
Whose twelve strong labors crown his memory,
Let's die together at one instant, duke!
Only a little let him fall before me,
That I may tell my soul he shall not have her.
Thes. I grant your wish; for, to say true, your cousin
Has ten times more offended; — for I gave him
More mercy than you found, sir; your offences
Being no more than his. None here speak for them.
For, ere the sun set, both shall sleep for ever.
Hip. Alas, the pity! now or never, sister;
Speak, not to be denied: that face of yours
Will bear the curses else of after-ages,
For these lost cousins!

1 That is, "I consider it the best."
2 I would omit the "come" at the close of this line, as injurious to the verse, and not necessary to the sense.
3 He was admitted to mercy at the instance of Prince Perithous.
4 Previous copies read "in *this* disguise."
5 In former editions, "*this* known edict."
6 According to former copies, "if *in* love."

Emi. In my face, dear sister,
I find no anger to them, nor no ruin;
The misadventure of their own eyes kills them:
Yet, that I will be woman, and have pity,
My knees shall grow to the ground but I'll get mercy.
Help me, dear sister! in a deed so virtuous,
The powers of all women will be with us.
Most royal brother—
Hip. Sir, by our tie of marriage—
Emi. By your own spotless honor—
Hip. By that faith,
That fair hand, and that honest heart you gave me—
Emi. By that you would have pity in another,
By your own virtues infinite—
Hip. By valor—
By all the chaste nights I have ever pleased you—
Thes. These are strange conjurings!
Per. Nay, then I'll in too:
By all our friendship, sir; by all our dangers;
By all you love most, wars,—and this sweet lady—
Emi. By that you would have trembled to deny,
A blushing maid—
Hip. By your own eyes; by strength,
In which you swore I went beyond all women,
Almost all men,—and yet I yielded, Theseus—
Per. To crown all this, by your most noble soul,
Which can not want due mercy! I beg first.
Hip. Next hear my prayers!
Emi. Last, let me entreat, sir!
Per. For mercy!
Hip. Mercy!
Emi. Mercy on these princes!
Thes. You make my faith reel: say I felt
Compassion to them both, how would you place it?
Emi. Upon their lives; but with their banishments.
Thes. You're a right woman, sister; you have pity,
But want the understanding where to use it.
If you desire their lives, invent a way
Safer than banishment: can these two live,
And have the agony of love about them,
And not kill one another? Every day
They'll fight about you; hourly bring your honor
In public question with their swords: be wise then,
And here forget them! it concerns your credit,
And my oath equally: I have said, they die!
Better they fall by the law than one another.
Bow not my honor.
Emi. Oh, my noble brother,
That oath was rashly made, and in your anger;
Your reason will not hold it: if such vows
Stand for express will, all the world must perish.
Beside, I have another oath 'gainst yours,
Of more authority; I'm sure more love;
Not made in passion neither, but good heed.
Thes. What is it, sister?
Per. Urge it home, brave lady!
Emi. That you would ne'er deny me anything
Fit for my modest suit, and your free granting:
I tie you to your word now; if you fail in't,
Think how you maim your honor;
(For now I'm set a-begging, sir, I'm deaf
To all but your compassion!) how their lives
Might breed the ruin of my name's opinion![1]
Shall anything that loves me perish for me?
That were a cruel wisdom! do men prune
The straight young boughs that blush with thousand blossoms,
Because they may be rotten? Oh, duke Theseus,
The goodly mothers that have groaned for these,
And all the longing maids that ever loved,
If your vow stand, shall curse me and my beauty,
And, in their funeral songs for these two cousins,
Despise my cruelty, and cry woe-worth me,
Till I am nothing but the scorn of women:
For Heaven's sake save their lives, and banish them!
Thes. On what conditions?
Emi. Swear them never more
To make me their contention, or to know me,
To tread upon thy dukedom, and to be,
Wherever they shall travel, ever strangers
To one another.
Pal. I'll be cut to pieces
Before I take this oath! Forget I love her?
Oh, all ye gods, despise me then! Thy banishment
I not mislike, so we may fairly carry
Our swords, and cause along; else, never trifle
But take our lives, duke! I must love, and will;
And for that love, must and dare kill this cousin,
On any piece the earth has!
Thes. Will you, Arcite,
Take these conditions?
Pal. He's a villain then!
Per. These are men!
Arc. No, never, duke; 'tis worse to me than begging,
To take my life so basely. Though I think
I never shall enjoy her, yet I'll preserve
The honor of affection, and, dying[2] for her,
Make death a devil!
Thes. What may be done? for now I feel compassion.
Per. Let it not fall again, sir!
Thes. Say, Emilia,
If one of them were dead, as one must, are you
Content to take the other to your husband?
They can not both enjoy you. They are princes
As goodly as your own eyes, and as noble
As ever Fame yet spoke of. Look upon them,
And if you can love, end this difference!
I give consent! are you content, too, princes?
Both. With all our souls.
Thes. He that she refuses
Must die then.
Both. Any death thou canst invent, duke.
Pal. If I fall from that mouth, I fall with favor,
And lovers yet unborn shall bless my ashes.
Arc. If she refuse me, yet my grave will wed me,
And soldiers sing my epitaph.
Thes. Make choice then!
Emi. I can not, sir; they're both too excellent:
For me, a hair shall never fall of these men.
Hip. What will become of them?
Thes. Thus I ordain it:
And, by mine honor, once again it stands,
Or both shall die!—You shall both to your country:
And each, within this month, accompanied
With three fair knights, appear again in this place,
In which I'll plant a pyramid: and whether,[3]
Before us that are here, can force his cousin

[1] We adopt a suggestion of M. Mason. The original has, "name, opinion." *Opinion* is used in the sense of reputation.

[2] All other editions read, "and die for her"—the grammar and sense, seem equally to require the alteration.

[3] "When either," which might be abridged, and written thus—"Whe'ther."

By fair and knightly strength to touch the pillar,
He shall enjoy her; the other lose his head,
And all his friends: nor shall he grudge to fall,
Nor think he dies with interest in this lady:
Will this content ye?
Pal. Yes. Here, Cousin Arcite,
I'm friends again till that hour.
Arc. I embrace you.
Thes. Are you content, sister?
Emi. Yes: I must, sir;
Else both miscarry.
Thes. Come, shake hands again then;
And take heed, as you're gentlemen, this quarrel
Sleep till the hour prefixed, and hold your course!
Pal. We dare not fail thee, Theseus.
Thes. Come, I'll give ye
Now[1] usage like to princes, and to friends.
When ye return, who wins, I'll settle here;
Who loses, yet I'll weep upon his bier. [*Exeunt.*

ACT IV.

SCENE I.

Enter Gaoler *and a* Friend.

Gaoler. Hear you no more? Was nothing said of me
Concerning the escape of Palamon?
Good sir, remember!
1 Friend. Nothing that I heard;
For I came home before the business
Was fully ended: yet, I might perceive
Ere I departed, a great likelihood
Of both their pardons; for Hippolyta,
And fair-eyed Emily, upon their knees,
Begged with such handsome pity, that the duke,
Methought, stood staggering whether he should follow
His rash oath, or the sweet compassion
Of those two ladies; and, to second them,
That truly noble prince, Perithous —
Half his own heart — set in too, that I hope
All shall be well: neither heard I one question
Of your name, or his 'scape.

Enter Second Friend.

Gaoler. Pray Heaven, it hold so!
2 Friend. Be of good comfort, man! I bring you news,
Good news.
Gaoler. They're welcome.
2 Friend. Palamon has cleared you,
And got your pardon, and discovered how
And by whose means he 'scaped, which was your daughter's,
Whose pardon is procured too; and the prisoner
(Not to be held ungrateful to her goodness)
Has given a sum of money to her marriage,
A large one, I'll assure you.
Gaol. You're a good man,
And ever bring good news.
1 Friend. How was it ended?
2 Friend. Why, as it should be; they that never begged
But they prevailed, had their suits fairly granted.
The prisoners have their lives.
1 Friend. I knew 'twould be so
2 Friend. But there be new conditions, which you'll hear of
At better time.
Gaoler. I hope they're good.
2 Friend. They're honorable;
How good they'll prove, I know not.

Enter Wooer.

1 Friend. 'Twill be known
Wooer. Alas, sir, where's your daughter?
Gaoler. Why do you ask?
Wooer. Oh, sir, when did you see her?
2 Friend. How he looks!
Gaoler. This morning.
Wooer. Was she well? was she in health, sir?
When[2] did she sleep?
1 Friend. These are strange questions.
Gaoler. I do not think she was very well; for, now
You make me mind her, but this very day
I asked her questions, and she answered me
So far from what she was, so childishly,
So sillily, as if she were a fool,
An innocent! — and I was very angry.
But what of her, sir?
Wooer. Nothing but my pity;
But you must know it, and as good by me
As by another that less loves her.
Gaoler. Well, sir?
1 Friend. Not right?
2 Friend. Not well?
Wooer. No, sir; not well:
'Tis too true, she is mad.
1 Friend. It can not be.
Wooer. Believe, you'll find it so.
Gaoler. I half suspected
What you have told me; the gods comfort her!
Either this was her love to Palamon,
Or fear of my miscarrying, on his 'scape,
Or both.
Wooer. 'Tis likely.
Gaoler. But why all this haste, sir?
Wooer. I'll tell you quickly. As I late was angling
In the great lake that lies behind the palace,
From the far shore, thick set with reeds and sedges,
As patiently I was attending sport,
I heard a voice, a shrill one; and, attentive,
I gave my ear; when I might well perceive
'Twas one that sung, and, by the smallness of it,
A boy or woman. I then left my angle
To his own skill; came near, but yet perceived not
Who made the sound, the rushes and the reeds
Had so encompassed it: I laid me down
And listened to the words she sung; for then,
Through a small glade cut by the fishermen,
I saw it was your daughter.
Gaoler. Pray go on, sir!
Wooer. She sung much, but no sense; only I heard her
Repeat this often: "Palamon is gone,
Is gone to th' wood to gather mulberries;
I'll find him out to morrow."
1 Friend. Pretty soul!
Wooer. "His shackles will betray him, he'll be taken;

1 I prefer to read "*new* usage like," &c.

2 We might read with quite as much propriety "*Where* did she sleep."

And what shall I do then? I'll bring a bevy,
A hundred black-eyed maids that love as I do,
With chaplets on their heads, of daffodillies,
With cherry lips, and cheeks of damask roses,
And all we'll dance an antic 'fore the duke,
And beg his pardon." Then she talked of you, sir;
That you must lose your head to-morrow morning,
And she must gather flowers to bury you,
And see the house made handsome: then she sung
Nothing but "Willow, willow, willow;" and between
Ever was, "Palamon, fair Palamon!"
And "Palamon was a tall young man!" The place
Was knee-deep where she sat; her careless tresses,
A wreath of bulrush rounded; 'bout her stuck
Thousand fresh water-flowers of several colors;
That she, methought appeared like the fair nymph
That feeds the lake with waters, or as Iris
Newly dropped down from heaven! Rings she made
Of rushes that grew by, and to 'em spoke
The prettiest posies; "Thus our true love's tied;"
"This you may loose, not me;" and many a one:
And then she wept, and sung again, and sighed,
And with the same breath smiled, and kissed her hand.

2 Friend. Alas, what pity 'tis!

Wooer. I made in to her;
She saw me, and straight sought the flood. I saved [her,
And set her safe to land; when, presently,
She slipped away, and to the city made,
With such a cry, and swiftness, that, believe me,
She left me far behind her. Three, or four,
I saw from far off cross her; one of them
I knew to be your brother; where she stayed,
And fell, scarce to be got away. I left them with her,[1]

Enter Brother, Daughter, *and* Others.

And hither came to tell you. Here they are!

Daugh.
"May you never more enjoy the light," &c.
Is not this a fine song?

Broth. Oh, a very fine one!

Daugh. I can sing twenty more.

Broth. I think you can.

Daugh. Yes, truly can I; I can sing the Broom,
And Bonny Robin. Are not you a tailor?

Broth. Yes.

Daugh. Where's my wedding-gown?

Broth. I'll bring it to-morrow.

Daugh. Do, very rearly;[2] I must be abroad else,
To call the maids, and pay the minstrels;
For I must lose my maidenhead by cocklight;
'Twill never thrive else. [*Sings.*
"Oh, fair, oh, sweet," &c.

Broth. You must e'en take it patiently.

Gaoler. 'Tis true.

Daugh. Good e'en, good men! Pray did you ever [hear
Of one young Palamon?

Gaoler. Yes, wench, we know him.

Daugh. Is't not a fine young gentleman?

Gaoler. 'Tis love!

Broth. By no means cross her; she is then dis- [tempered
Far worse than now she shows.

1 Friend. Yes, he's a fine man.

Daugh. Oh, is he so? You have a sister?

1 Friend. Yes.

Daugh. But she shall never have him; tell her so;
For a trick that I know, you had best look to her,
For if she see him once, she's gone; she's done,
And undone in an hour. All the young maids
Of our town are in love with him; but I laugh at 'em,
And let 'em all alone; is't not a wise course?

1 Friend. Yes.[3]

Daugh. They come from all parts of the dukedom [to him:
I'll warrant you.

Gaoler. She's lost, [she's] past all cure!

Broth. Heaven forbid, man!

Daugh. Come hither; you're a wise man.

1 Friend. Does she know him?

2 Friend. No; would she did!

Daugh. You're master of a ship?

Gaoler. Yes.

Daugh. Where's your compass?

Gaoler. Here.

Daugh. Set it to the north;
And now direct your course to the wood, where Pal- [amon
Lies longing for me; for the tackling
Let me alone: come, weigh, my hearts, cheerly!

All. Owgh, owgh, owgh! 'tis up, the wind is fair,
Top [with] the bowline; out with the mainsail!
Where is your whistle, master?

Broth. Let's get her in.

Gaoler. Up to the top, boy.

Broth. Where's the pilot?

1 Friend. Here.

Daugh. What kenn'st thou?

2 Friend. A fair wood.

Daugh. Bear for it, master; tack about! [*Sings.*
"When Cynthia with her borrowed light," &c.
[*Exeunt.*

SCENE II.

Enter Emilia, *with two pictures.*

Emi. Yet I may bind those wounds up, that must open
And bleed to death for my sake else: I'll choose,
And end their strife; two such young handsome men
Shall never fall for me: their weeping mothers,
Following the dead-cold ashes of their sons,
Shall never curse my cruelty. Good Heaven,
What a sweet face has Arcite! If wise Nature,
With all her best endowments, all those beauties
She sows into the births of noble bodies,
Were here a mortal woman, and had in her
The coy denials of young maids, yet doubtless
She would run mad for this man. What an eye!
Of what a fiery sparkle, and quick sweetness,
Has this young prince! Here Love himself sits [smiling.
Just such another wanton Ganymede
Set Jove afire, and [soon] enforced the god

[1] This scene is a very obvious imitation of the story of Ophelia, though with a less touching termination. But though quite creditable to Fletcher, as an imitation of Shakspeare, the fact that it is an imitation should be conclusive that Shakspeare had no hand in it.

[2] *Rearly*—early. Gay, in his "Shepherd's Week," uses *rear* as a provincial word, in this sense. The original has *rarely.*

[3] We omit some lines here, for the same reason as we have previously stated. The tendency of Fletcher is to destroy his own high merits by a wanton indulgence in pruriency. He loses nothing by occasional omissions; not, however, regulated by over-fastidiousness.

Snatch up the goodly boy, and set him by him
A shining constellation! What a brow,
Of what a spacious majesty, he carries;
Arched like the great-eyed Juno's, but far sweeter;
Smoother than Pelops' shoulder! Fame and Honor,
Methinks, from hence, as from a promontory
Pointed in heaven, should clap their wings and sing
To all the under-world, the loves and fights
Of gods and such men near 'em. Palamon
Is but his foil; to him, a mere dull shadow;
He's swarth and meager, of an eye as heavy
As if he'd lost his mother; a still temper,
No stirring in him, no alacrity;
Of all this sprightly sharpness, not a smile.
Yet these that we count errors, may become him:
Narcissus was a sad boy, but a heavenly.
Oh, who can find the bent of woman's fancy?
I am a fool — my reason is lost in me!
I have no choice, and I have lied so lewdly,
That women ought to beat me. On my knees
I ask thy pardon, Palamon! Thou'rt alone,
And only, beautiful; and these thine eyes,
These the bright lamps of beauty, that command
And threaten love; and what young maid dare cross
What a bold gravity, and yet inviting, ['em?
Has this brown, manly face! Oh, Love, this only
From this hour is complexion. Lie there, Arcite!
Thou art a changeling to him, a mere gipsy,
And this the noble body.—I am sotted,
Utterly lost! My virgin faith has fled me,
For if my brother but e'en now had asked me
Whe'ther I loved, I had run mad for Arcite;
Now, if my sister, more for Palamon. [er;—
Stand both together! Now, come, ask me, broth-
Alas, I know not! Ask me now, sweet sister;
I may[1] go look! What a mere child is fancy,
That, having two fair gawds of equal sweetness,
Can not distinguish, but must cry for both!

Enter a Gentleman.

How now, sir?
Gent. From the noble duke, your brother,
Madam, I bring you news: the knights are come!
Emi. To end the quarrel?
Gent. Yes.
Emi. Would I might end first!
What sins have I committed, chaste Diana,
That my unspotted youth must now be soiled
With blood of princes? and my chastity
Be made the altar, where the lives of lovers
(Two greater and two better never yet
Made mothers' joy) must be the sacrifice
To my unhappy beauty?

Enter THESEUS, HIPPOLYTA, PERITHOUS, *and* Attendants.

Thes. Bring them in,
Quickly, by any means! I long to see them.—
Your two contending lovers are returned,
And with them their fair knights: now, my fair sister,
You must love one of them.
Emi. I had rather both,
So neither for my sake should fall untimely.

Enter Messenger.

Thes. Who saw them?

[1] Qu.? *Must?*

Per. I, awhile.
Gent. And I.
Thes. From whence come you, sir?
Mess. From the knights.
Thes. Pray speak,
You that have seen them, what they are.
Mess. I will, sir,
And truly what I think: six braver spirits
Than these they've brought (if we judge by the out- [side,)
I never saw, nor read of. He that stands
In the first place with Arcite, by his seeming
Should be a stout man, by his face a prince;—
His very looks so say him;—his complexion
Nearer a brown than black; stern, and yet noble,
Which shows him hardy, fearless, proud of dangers;
The circles of his eyes show fair[2] within him,
And, as a heated lion, so he looks;
His hair hangs long behind him, black and shining
Like raven's wings; his shoulders broad and strong;
Armed long and round: and on his thigh a sword
Hung by a curious baldrick, when he frowns
To seal his will with; better, o' my conscience,
Was never soldier's friend.
Thes. Thou hast well described him.
Per. Yet, a great deal short,
Methinks of him that's first with Palamon.
Thes. Pray speak him, friend.
Per. I guess he is a prince too,
And, if it may be, greater; for his show
Has all the ornament of honor in't.
He's somewhat bigger than the knight he spoke of.
But of a face far sweeter; his complexion
Is (as a ripe grape) ruddy; he has felt,
Without doubt, what he fights for, and so, apter
To make this cause his own; in's face appears
All the fair hopes of what he undertakes;
And when he's angry, then a settled valor
(Not tainted with extremes) runs through his body,
And guides his arm to brave things; fear he can not;
He shows no such soft temper; his head's yellow,
Hard-haired and curled, thick twined, like ivy tops,
Not to undo with thunder; in his face
The livery of the warlike maid appears,
Pure red and white, for yet no beard has blessed him;
And in his rolling eyes sits Victory,
As if she ever meant to crown[3] his valor;
His nose stands high, a character of honor,
His red lips, after fights, are fit for ladies.
Emi. Must these men die too?
Per. When he speaks, his tongue
Sounds like a trumpet; all his lineaments
Are as a man would wish them, strong and clean;
He wears a well-steeled axe, the staff of gold;
His age some five-and-twenty.
Mess. There's another,
A little man, but of a tough soul, seeming
As great as any; fairer promises
In such a body yet I never looked on.
Per. Oh, he that's freckle-faced?
Mess. The same, my lord:
Are they not sweet ones?
Per. Yes, they're well.
Mess. Methinks,

[2] *Fair.* So the originals. The modern reading is *far* — implying deep-seated eyes. *Fair* may be received in the sense of *clear*.
[3] *Crown*—the original has *correct*.

Being so few, and well-disposed, they show
Great, and fine art in Nature. He's white-haired,
Not wanton-white, but such a manly color
Next to an auburn; tough, and nimble set,
Which shows an active soul; his arms are brawny,
Lined with strong sinews; to the shoulder-piece
Gently they swell, like women new-conceived,
Which speaks him prone to labor, never fainting
Under the weight of arms; stout-hearted; still;
But, when he stirs, a tiger; he's gray-eyed,
Which yields compassion where he conquers; sharp
To spy advantages, and, where he finds 'em,
He's swift to make 'em his; he does no wrongs,
Nor takes none; he's round-faced, and when he smiles
He shows a lover; when he frowns, a soldier;
About his head he wears the winner's oak,
And in it stuck the favor of his lady;
His age, some six-and-thirty. In his hand
He bears a charging-staff, embossed with silver.

Thes. Are they all thus?

Per. They're all the sons of honor.

Thes. Now, as I have a soul, I long to see them!
Lady, you shall see men fight now.

Hip. I wish it,
But not the cause, my lord: they would show [fight]
Bravely, about the titles of two kingdoms.
'Tis pity love should be so tyrannous.
Oh, my soft-hearted sister, what think you?
Weep not, till they weep blood, wench! It must be.

Thes. You've steeled 'em with your beauty. Honored friend,
To you I give the field; pray order it,
Fitting the persons that must use it!

Per. Yes, sir.

Thes. Come, I'll go visit them: I can not stay—
Their fame has fired me so—till they appear;
Good friend, be royal!

Per. There shall want no bravery.

Emi. Poor wench, go weep; for whosoever wins,
Loses a noble cousin for thy sins. [*Exeunt.*

SCENE III.

Enter GAOLER, WOOER, *and* DOCTOR.

Doctor. Her distraction is more at some time of the moon than at other some, is it not?

Gaoler. She is continually in a harmless distemper; sleeps little, altogether without appetite, save often drinking; dreaming of another world, and a better; and what broken piece of matter soe'er she's about, the name Palamon lards it. That she farces every business withal,—fits it to every question.

Enter DAUGHTER.

Look, where she comes! you shall perceive her behavior.

Daugh. I have forgot it quite; the burden on't was "down-a-down-a;" and penned by no worse man than Giraldo, Emilia's schoolmaster: he's as fantastical too, as ever he may go upon's legs; for in the next world will Dido see Palamon, and then will she be out of love with Æneas.

Doctor. What stuff's here? poor soul!

Gaoler. Even thus all day long.

Daugh. Now for this charm that I told you of; you must bring a piece of silver on the tip of your tongue, or no ferry: then if it be your chance to come where the blessed spirits (as there's a sight now), we maids that have our livers perished, cracked to pieces with love, we shall come there, and do nothing all day long but pick flowers with Proserpine; then will I make Palamon a nosegay; then let him—mark me—then!

Doctor. How prettily she's amiss! note her a little further!

Daugh. Faith, I'll tell you; sometime we go to barley-break, we of the blessed; alas, 'tis a sore life they have i' the other place! If one be mad, or hang, or drown themselves, thither they go; Jupiter bless us!

Doctor. How she continues this fancy! 'Tis not an engrafted madness, but a most thick and profound melancholy.

Daugh. To hear there a proud lady, and a proud city-wife, howl together! I were a beast, an I'd call it good sport![1] [*Sings.*

"I will be true, my stars, my fate," &c.

[*Exit* DAUGHTER.

Gaoler. What think you of her, sir?

Doctor. I think she has a perturbed mind, which I can not minister to.

Gaoler. Alas, what then?

Doctor. Understand you she ever affected any man ere she beheld Palamon?

Gaoler. I was once, sir, in great hope she had fixed her liking on this gentleman, my friend.

Wooer. I did think so too; and would account I had a great pennyworth on't, to give half my state, that both she and I at this present stood unfeignedly on the same terms.

Doctor. That intemperate surfeit of her eye hath distempered the other senses; they may return, and settle again to execute their preordained faculties; but they are now in a most extravagant vagary. This you must do: confine her to a place where the light may rather seem to steal in, than be permitted. Take upon you (young sir, her friend) the name of Palamon; say you come to eat with her, and to commune of love; this will catch her attention, for this

1 We have again been compelled to employ the pruning-knife. Our edition is for general readers, as well as for critical students. The essential difference between Shakspeare and Fletcher makes it necessary to adopt a different course with reference to the two writers. It is not a false reverence for Shakspeare that calls upon an editor to leave his text unchanged; but a just discrimination between the quality of what is offensive in him and in other writers of his age. Coleridge has defined this difference with his usual philosophical judgment: "Even Shakspeare's grossness—that which is really so, independently of the increase in modern times of vicious associations with things indifferent—(for there is a state of manners conceivable so pure, that the language of Hamlet at Ophelia's feet might be a harmless rallying, or playful teazing, of a shame that would exist in Paradise)—at the worst, how diverse in kind is it from Beaumont and Fletcher's! In Shakspeare it is the mere generalities of sex, mere words for the most part, seldom or never distinct images, all headwork, and fancy-drolleries; there is no sensation supposed in the speaker. I need not proceed to contrast this with Beaumont and Fletcher."*

* I see no reason to disturb the opinions or depart from the rule which Mr. Knight has prescribed for himself, in the exclusion of offensive passages. Certainly, the fancy of the gaoler's daughter is not that of Ophelia; and there can be no better illustration of the author's inferiority as an artist, than in the sudden change in her character, from the strong-willed and somewhat coarse rustic, to the creature of such delicate sensibilities as he here endeavors to describe her. It was an after-thought to make her resemble Ophelia. In the first scenes she is totally unlike—indeed, a very good contrast, were it our cue to seek one.

her mind beats upon; other objects, that are inserted 'tween her mind and eye, become the pranks and friskings of her madness; sing to her such green songs of love, as she says Palamon hath sung in prison; come to her, stuck in as sweet flowers as the season is mistress of, and thereto make an addition of some other compounded odors, which are grateful to the sense: all this shall become Palamon, for Palamon can sing, and Palamon is sweet, and every good thing; desire to eat with her, carve for her, drink to her, and still intermingle your petition of grace and acceptance into her favor; learn what maids have been her companions and play-heers;[1] and let them repair to her with Palamon in their mouths, and appear with tokens, as if they suggested for him: it is a falsehood she is in, which is with falsehoods to be combated. This may bring her to eat, to sleep, and reduce what are now out of square in her, into their former law and regimen: I have seen it approved, how many times I know not; but to make the number more, I have great hope in this. I will, between the passages of this project, come in with my appliance. Let us put it in execution; and hasten the success, which, doubt not, will bring forth comfort.

[*Exeunt.*

ACT V.

SCENE I.

Enter THESEUS, PERITHOUS, HIPPOLYTA, *and* Attendants.

Thes. Now let them enter, and before the gods
Tender their holy prayers! Let the temples
Burn bright with sacred fires, and the altars
In hallowed clouds commend their swelling incense
To those above us! Let no due be wanting!
[*Flourish of cornets.*
They have a noble work in hand, will honor
The very powers that love them.

Enter PALAMON, ARCITE, *and their* Knights.

Per. Sir, they enter.
Thes. You valiant and strong-hearted enemies,
You royal germane foes, that this day come
To blow that nearness out that flames between ye,
Lay by your anger for an hour, and, dove-like,
Before the holy altars of your helpers,—
The all-feared gods—bow down your stubborn bodies!
Your ire is more than mortal; so your help be!
And, as the gods regard ye, fight with justice!
I'll leave you to your prayers, and betwixt ye
I part my wishes.
Per. Honor crown the worthiest!
[*Exeunt* THES. *and* Train.
Pal. The glass is running now that can not finish
Till one of us expire: think you but thus;
That were there aught in me which strove to show
Mine enemy in this business, wer't one eye
Against another, arm oppressed by arm,
I would destroy the offender; coz, I would,
Though parcel of myself!—Then from this gather
How I should tender you!
Arc. I am in labor
To push your name, your ancient love, our kindred
Out of my memory; and, i' the self-same place,
To seat something I would confound: so hoist we
The sails that must these vessels port[2] even where
The heavenly Limiter pleases!
Pal. You speak well:
Before I turn, let me embrace thee, cousin!
This I shall never do again.
Arc. One farewell!
Pal. Why, let it be so: farewell, coz!
Arc. Farewell, sir.
[*Exeunt* PAL. *and his* Knights.
Knights, kinsmen, lovers, yea, my sacrifices,
True worshippers of Mars, whose spirit in you
Expels the seeds of fear, and th' apprehension,
Which still is further off it, go with me
Before the god of our profession! There
Require of him the hearts of lions, and
The breath of tigers, yea, the fierceness too!
Yea, the speed also! to go on, I mean,
Else wish we to be snails: you know my prize
Must be dragged out of blood! force and great feat
Must put my garland on, where she will stick
The queen of flowers; our intercession then
Must be to him that makes the camp a cestron[3]
Brimmed[4] with the blood of men; give me your aid,
And bend your spirits toward him!—
[*They kneel.*
Thou mighty one, that with thy power hast turned
Green Neptune into purple;[5] [whose approach][6]
Comets prewarn; whose havoc in vast field
Unearthéd skulls proclaim; whose breath blows down
The teeming Ceres' foison; who dost pluck
With hand armipotent from forth blue clouds
The masoned turrets; that both mak'st and break'st
The stony girths of cities; me, thy pupil,
Young'st follower of thy drum, instruct this day
With military skill, that to thy laud
I may advance my streamer, and by thee
Be styled the lord o'the day! Give me, great Mars,
Some token of thy pleasure!
[*Here they fall on their faces as formerly, and there is heard clanging of armor, with a short thunder, as the burst of a battle, whereupon they all rise, and bow to the altar.*
Oh, great corrector of enormous times,
Shaker of o'er-rank states, thou grand decider
Of dusty and old titles, that healest with blood
The earth when it is sick, and curest the world
Of the plurisy[7] of people; I do take
Thy signs auspiciously, and in thy name
To my design march boldly. Let us go!
[*Exeunt.*

1 *Play-heers*—playfellows.

2 Seward reads "*part*," a reading that seems more obvious without being quite so certain. The *port* at which these vessels must arrive, would seem to be necessarily indicated by the reference to the heavenly "Limiter"—it is to the *limit* of the voyage that he alludes.

3 Ceston I suppose to be the proper word—i. e., "a studded girdle"—a not inappropriate figure descriptive of the ring, or circle of spectators assembled to behold the fight.

4 Some of the old copies read "*primed*" for "*brimmed*."

5 "Making the green one red."

6 The words in brackets are not in the original copies, but were added by Seward. As something is evidently wanting, the addition is judicious.

7 *Plurisy*—used by the old poets for fulness.*

* And yet, as to let blood was to cure pleurisy, the invocation to Mars, for this object, might have no sort of reference to the world's repletion. Mars was the great *bleeder*.

Enter PALAMON *and his* Knights, *with the former observance.*

Pal. Our stars must glister with new fire, or be
To-day extinct: our argument is love,
Which if the goddess of it grant, she gives
Victory too: then blend your spirits with mine,
You, whose free nobleness do make my cause
Your personal hazard! To the goddess Venus
Commend we our proceeding, and implore
Her power unto our party!

[*Here they kneel.*

Hail, sovereign queen of secrets! who hast power
To call the fiercest tyrant from his rage,
To weep unto[1] a girl; that hast the might
Even with an eye-glance to choke Mars's drum,
And turn th' alarm to whispers; that canst make
A cripple flourish with his crutch, and cure him
Before Apollo; that mayst force the king
To be his subjects' vassal, and induce
Stale gravity to dance; the polled[2] bachelor
(Whose youth, like wanton boys through bonfires,
Have skipped thy flame) at seventy thou canst catch,
And make him, to the scorn of his hoarse throat,
Abuse young lays of love. What godlike power
Hast thou not power upon? To Phœbus thou
Add'st flames, hotter than his; the heavenly fires
Did scorch his mortal son, thine him; the huntress,
All moist and cold, some say, began to throw
Her bow away, and sigh; take to thy grace
Me thy vowed soldier! who do bear thy yoke
As 'twere a wreath of roses, yet it is
Heavier than lead itself, stings more than nettles:
I've never been foul-mouthed against thy law;
Ne'er revealed secret, for I knew none; would not
Had I kenned all that were. I never practised
Upon man's wife, nor would the libels read
Of liberal wits; I never at great feasts
Sought to betray a beauty, but have blushed
At simpering sirs that did. I have been harsh
To large confessors, and have hotly asked them
If they had mothers?—I had one, a woman,
And women 'twere they wronged. I knew a man
Of eighty winters (this I told them), who
A lass of fourteen brided; 'twas thy power
To put life into dust; the agéd cramp
Had screwed his square foot round;
The gout had knit his fingers into knots,
Torturing convulsions from his globy eyes
Had almost drawn their spheres, that what was life,
In him, seemed torture; this anatomy
Had, by his young fair pheer, a boy, and I
Believed it was his, for she swore it was,
And who would not believe her? Brief, I am
To those that prate, and have done, no companion;
To those that boast, and have not, a defier;
To those that would, and can not, a rejoicer;[3]
Yea, him I do not love that tells close offices
The foulest way, nor names concealments in
The boldest language: such a one I am [not[4]]
And vow that lover never yet made sigh
Truer than I. Oh, then, most soft sweet goddess,
Give me the victory of this question, which
Is true love's merit,[5] and bless me with a sign
Of thy great pleasure!

[*Here music is heard, doves are seen to flutter; they fall again upon their faces, then on their knees.*

Oh, thou that from eleven to ninety reign'st
In mortal bosoms, whose chase is this [whole] world,
And we in herds thy game, I give thee thanks
For this fair token,—which being laid unto
Mine innocent true heart, arms, in assurance,

[*They bow.*

My body to this business. Let us rise
And bow before the goddess! Time comes on.

[*Exeunt.*

[*Still music of records.*

Enter EMILIA *in white, her hair about her shoulders, a wheaten wreath; one in white holding up her train, her hair stuck with flowers; one before her carrying a silver hind, in which is conveyed incense and sweet odors, which being set upon the altar, her* Maids *standing aloof, she sets fire to it; then they courtesy and kneel.*

Emi. Oh, sacred, shadowy, cold, and constant queen,
Abandoner of revels, mute, contemplative,
Sweet, solitary, white as chaste, and pure
As wind-fanned snow, who, to thy female knights,
Allow'st no more blood than will make a blush,
Which is their order's robe; I here, thy priest,
Am humbled 'fore thine altar. Oh, vouchsafe,
With that thy rare green[6] eye, which never yet
Beheld thing maculate, look on thy virgin!
And, sacred silver mistress, lend thine ear
(Which ne'er heard scurril term, into whose port
Ne'er entered wanton sound) to my petition,
Seasoned with holy fear! This is my last
Of vestal office; I'm bride-habited,
But maiden-hearted; a husband I've appointed,
But do not know him; out of two I should
Choose one, and pray for his success, but I
Am guiltless of election of mine eyes.
Were I to lose one (they are equal precious),
I could doom neither; that which perished should
Go to't unsentenced: therefore, most modest queen,
He, of the two pretenders, that best loves me,
And has the truest title in't, let him

1 Theobald reads "*into*" instead of "unto," which I think the far preferable reading. To weep *unto* a girl seems scarcely to convey the intended idea.

2 Thus the old copy, but that the bachelor should be polled, is a matter of course. Perhaps we should read, the "*bald bachelor*," or the "*poll-bald*" bachelor. Either reading will meet the wants of the sense.

3 I leave this passage as I find it, but would suggest the reading as follows, by which, changing the word "defier" into "desire," it appears to me we compass and supply all its deficiencies:—

"Brief I am,
To those that prate and have done;* no companion
To those that boast, and have not a desire;
To those that would and can not, a rejoicer;"† &c.

* That is, to those that prate only, and do no more than prate.

† That is, doing for them what they desire to have done, and can not do for themselves. The prayer is to Venus. The difficulty is in saying those things it might be grateful to hear, yet which decency would not suffer to be spoken except ambiguously.

4 The sense seems to demand the negative in this place.

5 "Meed," perhaps.

6 A green eye for Diana is something of a novelty. For "rare green," Seward reads "rare sheen," which does not greatly help the matter. Why not "rare seen"—which applied to chastity would be proper enough? But is it not possible that "virgin" has, by the rare faculty which types have of perversion, been converted into those two strangely misplaced words.

Take off my wheaten garland, or else grant
The file and quality I hold, I may
Continue in thy band!
[*Here the hind vanishes under the altar, and in the place ascends a rose-tree, having one rose upon it.*
See what our general of ebbs and flows
Out from the bowels of her holy altar
With sacred act advances! But one rose?
If well inspired, this battle shall confound
Both these brave knights, and I a virgin flower
Must grow alone unplucked.
[*Here is heard a sudden twang of instruments, and the rose falls from the tree.*
The flower is fall'n, the tree descends! Oh, mistress,
Thou here dischargest me; I shall be gathered;
I think so; but I know not thine[1] own will:
Unclasp thy mystery!—I hope she's pleased;
Her signs were gracious.
[*They courtesy, and exeunt.*

SCENE II.

Enter DOCTOR, GAOLER, *and* WOOER (*in habit of* PALAMON).

Doctor. Has this advice I told you
Done any good upon her?
Wooer. Oh, very much:
The maids that kept her company,
Have half persuaded her that I am Palamon;
Within this half-hour she came smiling to me,
And asked me what I'd eat, and when I'd kiss her:
I told her presently, and kissed her twice.
Doctor. 'Twas well done! twenty times had been far better;
For there the cure lies mainly.
Wooer. Then she told me
She'd watch with me to-night, for well she knew
What hour my fit would take me.
Doctor. Let her do so.
Wooer. She'd have me sing.
Doctor. You did so?
Wooer. No.
Doctor. 'Twas very ill done, then:
You should observe her every way.
Wooer. Alas!
I have no voice, sir, to confirm her that way.
Doctor. That's all one, if you [only] make a noise:
Pray bring her in, and let's see how she is.
Gaoler. I will, and tell her Palamon stays for her.
[*Exit.*
Doctor. How old is she?
Wooer. She's eighteen.
Doctor. She may be;
But that's all one, 'tis nothing to our purpose.[2]

Enter GAOLER, DAUGHTER, *and* MAID.

Gaoler. Come; your love Palamon stays for you, child;
And has done this long hour, to visit you.
Daugh. I thank him for his gentle patience;
He's a kind gentleman, and I'm much bound to him.
Did you ne'er see the horse he gave me?
Gaoler. Yes.
Daugh. How do you like him?
Gaoler. He's a very fair one.
Daugh. You never saw him dance?
Gaoler. No.
Daugh. I have often:
He dances very finely, very come[li]ly;
And, for a jig, come cut and long tail to him!
He turns you like a top.
Gaoler. That's fine indeed.
Daugh. He'll dance the morris twenty miles an hour,
And that will founder the best hobby-horse
(If I have any skill) in all the parish:
And gallops to the tune of "Light o'love:"
What think you of this horse?
Gaoler. Having these virtues,
I think he might be brought to play at tennis.
Daugh. Alas, that's nothing.
Gaoler. Can he write and read too?
Daugh. A very fair hand; and casts himself the accounts
Of all his hay and provender: that ostler
Must rise betime that cozens him. You know
The chestnut mare the duke has?
Gaoler. Very well.
Daugh. She's horribly in love with him, poor beast;
But he is like his master, coy and scornful.
Gaoler. What dowry has she?
Daugh. Some two hundred bottles
And twenty strike of oats: but he'll ne'er have her;
He lisps in's neighing, able to entice
A miller's mare; he'll be the death of her.
Doctor. What stuff she utters!
Gaoler. Make courtesy; here your love comes!
Wooer. Pretty soul,
How do you? That's a fine maid! there's a courtesy!
Daugh. Yours to command i' the way of honesty.
How far is't now to the end o' the world, my masters?
Doctor. Why, a day's journey, wench.
Daugh. Will you go with me?
Wooer. What shall we do there, wench?
Daugh. Why, play at stool-ball,
What is there else to do?
Wooer. I am content,
If we shall keep our wedding there.
Daugh. 'Tis true;
For there I will assure you we shall find
Some blind priest for the purpose, that will venture
To marry us, for here they're nice and foolish;
Besides, my father must be hanged to-morrow,
And that would be a blot i' the business.
Are not you Palamon?
Wooer. Do you not know me?
Daugh. Yes; but you care not for me: I have nothing
But this poor petticoat, and two coarse smocks.
Wooer. That's all one; I will have you.
Daugh. Will you surely?[3]
Wooer. Why do you rub my kiss off?
Daugh. 'Tis a sweet one

1 Query: *mine?*

2 Mr. Knight has taken large liberties in lopping off portions of this scene, on the score of its obscenities. It is fortunate that the portions thus exscinded, are as dull as they are vicious. We lose nothing.

3 Here again occurs one of Mr. Knight's omissions, of which he says nothing—indecencies truly, but of the very sort that we find in Hamlet, and scarcely worse. I should not scruple to restore this matter were it at all necessary to the spirit of the scene.

And will perfume me finely 'gainst the wedding.
Is not this your cousin Arcite?
Doctor. Yes, sweetheart;
And I am glad my cousin Palamon
Has made so fair a choice.
Daugh. Do you think he'll have me?
Doctor. Yes, without doubt.
Daugh. Do you think so too?
Gaoler. Yes.
Daugh. We shall have many children.—Lord, how you're grown!
My Palamon I hope will grow, too, finely,
Now he's at liberty; alas, poor chicken,
He was kept down with hard meat, and ill-lodging,
But I will kiss him up again.

Enter a Messenger.

Mess. What do you here?
You'll lose the noblest sight that e'er was seen.
Gaoler. Are they i' the field?
Mess. They are:
You bear a charge there too.
Gaoler. I'll away straight,
I must even leave you here.
Doctor. Nay, we'll go with you;
I will not lose the fight.
Gaoler. How did you like her?
Doctor. I'll warrant you within these three or four days
I'll make her right again. You must not from her,
But still preserve her in this way.
Wooer. I will.
Doctor. Let's get her in.
Wooer. Come, sweet, we'll go to dinner;
And then we'll play at cards.[1]
Daugh. And shall we kiss too?
Wooer. An hundred times.[2]
[*Exeunt.*

SCENE III.

Enter Theseus, Hippolyta, Emilia, Perithous, *and* Attendants.

Emi. I'll no step further.
Per. Will you lose this sight?
Emi. I had rather see a wren hawk at a fly,
Than this decision: every blow that falls
Threats a brave life; each stroke laments
The place whereon it falls, and sounds more like
A bell, than blade: I will stay here:
It is enough my hearing shall be punished
With what shall happen ('gainst the which there is
No deafing), but to hear, not taint mine eye
With dread sights it may shun.
Per. Sir, my good lord,
Your sister will no further.
Thes. Oh, she must:
She shall see deeds of honor in their kind,
Which sometime[3] show well-pencilled: Nature now
Shall make and act the story, the belief
Both sealed with eye and ear. You must be present;
You are the victor's meed, the price and garland
To crown the question's title.
Emi. Pardon me;
If I were there, I'd wink.
Thes. You must be there;
This trial is as 'twere i' the night, and you
The only star to shine.
Emi. I am extinct;
There is but envy in that light, which shows
The one the other. Darkness, which ever was
The dam of Horror, who does stand accursed
Of many mortal millions, may, even now,
By casting her black mantle over both,
That neither could find [th'] other, get herself
Some part of a good name; and many a murder
Set off whereto she's guilty.
Hip. You must go.
Emi. In faith, I will not.
Thes. Why, the knights must kindle
Their valor at your eye. Know, of this war
You are the treasure, and must needs be by
To give the service pay.
Emi. Sir, pardon me;
The title of a kingdom may be tried
Out of itself.
Thes. Well, well, then, at your pleasure!
Those that remain with you could wish their office
To any of their enemies.
Hip. Farewell, sister!
I'm like to know your husband 'fore yourself,
By some small start of time: he whom the gods
Do of the two know best, I pray them, he
Be made your lot!
[*Exeunt* Theseus, Hippolyta, Perithous, &c
Emi. Arcite is gently visaged: yet his eye
Is like an engine bent, or a sharp weapon
In a soft sheath; mercy and manly courage
Are bedfellows in his visage. Palamon
Has a most menacing aspect; his brow
Is graved, and seems to bury what it frowns on;
Yet sometimes 'tis not so, but alters to
The quality of his thoughts; long time his eye
Will dwell upon his object; melancholy
Becomes him nobly; so does Arcite's mirth;
But Palamon's sadness is a kind of mirth,
So mingled, as if mirth did make him sad,
And sadness, merry; those dark[4] humors that
Stick misbecomingly on others, in him[5]
Live in fair dwelling.
[*Cornets. Trumpets sound as to a charge.*
Hark, how yon spurs to spirit do incite
The princes to their proof! Arcite may win me;
And yet may Palamon wound Arcite, to
The spoiling of his figure. Oh, what pity!
Enough for such a chance! If I were by,
I might do hurt; for they would glance their eyes
Toward my seat, and, in that motion, might
Omit a ward, or forfeit an offence,
Which craved that very time; it is much better
[*Cornets. Cry within,* A Palamon!

1 This scene, as it stands in the original, contains impurities of thought far more corrupting than any indelicacies of language alone. We have pursued the same course as in two previous instances.

2 These are two of Mr. Knight's excluded lines, and are only objected to as they are supposed to lead to worse.

3 Seward reads for "sometime show," "Time will show." Perhaps the addition of the letter "*s*" to sometime, will answer the purpose. The duke means to say she will see in reality those deeds of honor which she has only seen in pictures.

4 Other copies read "*darker* humors."

5 Mr. Seward first writes "*on* him," and is followed in this reading by Mr. Knight. I can not doubt that we should say "in him." They are merely grafts on others, in him they are native. It is "*in* him," that they "live in fair dwelling."

I am not there; oh, better never born
Than minister to such harm! — What is the chance?

Enter a Servant.

Serv. The cry's a Palamon.
Emi. Then he has won. 'Twas ever likely:
He looked all grace and success, and he is
Doubtless the prim'st of men. I prithee run,
And tell me how it goes.
[*Shout and cornets; cry,* A Palamon!
Serv. Still Palamon.
Emi. Run and inquire. Poor servant, thou hast lost!
Upon my right side still I wore thy picture,
Palamon's on the left: why so, I know not;
I had no end in't else; chance would have it so.
[*Another cry and shout within, and cornets.*
On the sinister side the heart lies: Palamon
Had the best-boding chance. This burst of clamor
Is sure the end o' the combat.

Enter Servant.

Serv. They said that Palamon had Arcite's body
Within an inch o' the pyramid; that the cry
Was general, a Palamon; but, anon,
The assistants made a brave redemption, and
The two bold tilters at this instant are
Hand to hand at it.
Emi. Were they metamorphosed
Both into one! — Oh, why? There were no woman
Worth so composed a man! Their single share,
Their nobleness peculiar to them, gives
The prejudice of disparity, value's shortness,
[*Cornets. Cry within,* Arcite, Arcite!
To any lady breathing.[1] — More exulting!
Palamon still!
Serv. Nay, now the sound is Arcite.
Emi. I prithee lay attention to the cry;
[*Cornets. A great shout and cry,* Arcite, victory!
Set both thine ears to the business.
Serv. The cry is
Arcite, and victory! Hark! Arcite, victory!
The combat's consummation is proclaimed
By the wind-instruments.
Emi. Half-sights saw
That Arcite was no babe! God's 'lid, his richness
And costliness of spirit looked through him! — could
No more be hid in him than fire in flax,
Than humble banks can go to law with waters,
That drift winds force to raging. I did think
Good Palamon would miscarry; yet I knew not
Why I did think so: our reasons are not prophets,
When oft our fancies are. They're coming off:
Alas, poor Palamon! [*Cornets.*

Enter THESEUS, HIPPOLYTA, PERITHOUS, ARCITE *as* Victor, Attendants, &c.

Thes. Lo, where our sister is in expectation,
Yet quaking and unsettled. Fairest Emilia,
The gods, by their divine arbitrament,
Have given you this knight: he is a good one
As ever struck at head. Give me your hands!
Receive her, you; you him; be plighted with
A love that grows as you decay!
Arc. Emilia,
To buy you I have lost what's dearest to me,
Save what is bought; and yet I purchase cheaply,
As I do rate your value.
Thes. Oh, loved sister,
He speaks now of as brave a knight as e'er
Did spur a noble steed; surely the gods
Would have him die a bachelor, lest his race
Should show i' the world too godlike! His behavior
So charmed me, that methought Alcides was
To him a sow[2] of lead: if I could praise
Each part of him to the all I've spoke, your Arcite
Did not lose by't; for he that was thus good,
Encountered yet his better. I have heard
Two emulous Philomels beat the ear o' the night
With their contentious throats; now one the higher,
Anon the other; then again the first,
And by-and-by out-breasted, that the sense
Could not be judge between them: so it fared
Good space between these kinsmen; till heavens did
Make hardly one the winner. Wear the garland
With joy that you have won! For the subdued,
Give them our present justice, since I know
Their lives but pinch them; let it here be done.
The scene's not for our seeing: go we hence,
Right joyful, with some sorrow! Arm your prize:[3]
I know you will not lose her. Hippolyta,
I see one eye of yours conceives a tear,
The which it will deliver. [*Flourish.*
Emi. Is this winning?
Oh, all you heavenly powers, where is your mercy?
But that your wills have said it must be so,
And charge me live to comfort, thus unfriended,
This miserable prince, that cuts away
A life more worthy from him than all women,
I should and would die too.
Hip. Infinite pity,
That four such eyes should be so fixed on one,
That two must needs be blind for't!
Thes. So it is.
[*Exeunt.*

SCENE IV.

Enter PALAMON *and his* Knights *pinioned,* GAOLER, Executioner, *and* Guard.

Pal. There's many a man alive that hath outlived
The love o' the people; yea, i' the self-same state
Stands many a father with his child: some comfort
We have by so considering; we expire,
And not without men's pity; to live still,
Have their good wishes; we prevent
The loathsome misery of age; beguile
The gout and rheum, that in lag hours attend
For gray approachers; we come tow'rd the gods

1 This passage is very obscure. The first expression is that of a wish that the two should be resolved into one. But the speaker instantly checks herself, exclaiming, "Why should I wish so, when there were no woman worth so composed a man!" The single shade of nobleness peculiar to each, subjects all, however, to the prejudice of disparity, and makes their value fall short of the wonderful standard of excellence which such men might reasonably desire and assert.

2 "*Pig*" of lead would be better understood by the moderns, unless we told them that in the old English the word "sow" was sometimes used to signify "head." The meaning is that Alcides was "leaden-headed to him."

3 *Arm your prize*—offer your arm to the lady you have won.

Young, and unwappened,[1] not halting under crimes
Many and stale; that sure shall please the gods
Sooner than such, to give us nectar with them,
For we are more clear spirits. My dear kinsmen,
Whose lives (for this poor comfort) are laid down,
You've sold them too, too cheap.

1 Knight. What ending could be
Of more content? O'er us the victors have
Fortune, whose title is as momentary
As to us death is certain; a grain of honor
They rot o'erweigh us.

2 Knight. Let us bid farewell;
And with our patience anger tott'ring fortune,
Who, at her certain'st, reels!

3 Knight. Come; who begins?

Pal. Even he that led you to this banquet shall
Taste to you all. Ah-ha, my friend, my friend!
Your gentle daughter gave me freedom once;
You'll see't done now for ever. Pray, how does she?
I heard she was not well; her kind of ill
Gave me some sorrow.

Gaoler. Sir, she's well restored,
And to be married shortly.

Pal. By my short life,
I am most glad on't! 'tis the latest thing
I shall be glad of; prithee tell her so;
Commend me to her, and to piece her portion
Tender her this.

1 Knight. Nay, let's be offerers all!

2 Knight. Is it a maid?

Pal. Verily, I think so;
A right good creature, more to me deserving
Than I can 'quite or speak of!

All Knights. Commend us to her.

[*Give their purses.*

Gaoler. The gods requite you all,
And make her thankful!

Pal. Adieu! and let my life be now as short
As my leave-taking. [*Lies on the block.*

1 Knight. Lead, courageous cousin!

2 Knight. We'll follow cheerfully.

[*A great noise within, crying,* Run, save, hold!

Enter in haste a Messenger.

Mess. Hold, hold! oh, hold, hold, hold![2]

Enter Perithous *in haste.*

Per. Hold, hoa! it is a cursèd haste you made,
If you have done so quickly.—Noble Palamon,
The gods will show their glory in a life
That thou art yet to lead.

Pal. Can that be,
When Venus I've said is false? How do things fare?

Per. Arise, great sir, and give the tidings ear
That are most dearly sweet and bitter!

Pal. What
Hath waked us from our dream?

Per. List then! Your cousin,
Mounted upon a steed that Emily
Did first bestow on him—a black one, owning
Not a hair-worth of white, which some will say
Weakens his price, and many will not buy
His goodness with this note—which superstition
Here finds allowance:—on this horse is Arcite,
Trotting the stones of Athens, which the calkins[3]
Did rather tell than trample; for the horse
Would make his length a mile, if't pleased his rider
To put pride in him:—as he thus went, counting
The flinty pavement, dancing as 'twere to music
His own hoofs made (for, as they say, from iron
Came music's origin), what envious flint,
Cold as old Saturn, and, like him, possessed
With fire malevolent, darted a spark—
Or what fierce sulphur else, to this end made,
I comment not;—the hot horse, hot as fire,
Took toy at this, and fell to what disorder
His power could give his will; bounds, comes on end,
Forgets school-doing, being therein trained,
And of kind manege; pig-like[4] he whines
At the sharp rowel, which he frets at rather
Than any jot obeys; seeks all foul means
Of boisterous and rough jadery, to dis-seat
His lord that kept it bravely: When naught served,
When neither curb would crack, girth break, nor differing plunges
Dis-root his rider whence he grew, but that
He kept him 'tween his legs;—on his hind hoofs,
On end, he stands,
That Arcite's legs being higher than his head,
Seemed with strange art to hang: his victor's wreath
Even then fell off his head; and, presently,
Backward the jade comes o'er, and his full poise
Becomes the rider's load. Yet is he living;
But such a vessel 'tis, that floats but for
The surge that next approaches. He much desires
To have some speech with you. Lo, he appears!

Enter Theseus, Hippolyta, Emilia, Arcite, *in a chair.*

Pal. Oh, miserable end of our alliance!
The gods are mighty!—Arcite, if thy heart,
Thy worthy manly heart, be yet unbroken,
Give me thy last words! I am Palamon,
One that yet loves thee dying.

Arc. Take Emilia,
And with her all the world's joy. Reach thy hand;
Farewell! I've told my last hour. I was false,
Yet never treacherous. Forgive me, cousin!
One kiss from fair Emilia! It is done:
Take her. I die! [*Dies.*

Pal. Thy brave soul seek Elysium!

Emi. I'll close thine eyes, prince; blessed souls be with thee!
Thou art a right good man; and while I live
This day I give to tears.

Pal. And I to honor.

Thes. In this place first you fought; even very here
I sundered you: acknowledge to the gods
Our thanks that you are living.
His part is played, and, though it were too short,

1 *Unwappened.* The originals have *unwappered.* Without knowing exactly the meaning of the word *wappened*, we would receive the epithet here as the opposite to that in Timon—

"That makes the *wappened* widow wed again."*

* *Wappened*, according to Stevens, from *wap*, futuo. *Wapping* is quaking; i. e., "We come before the gods, young and without fear." But, after all, the word may be "unweaponed."

2 Two of these monosyllables may be omitted with perfect propriety, and to the improvement of the rhythm.

3 *Calkins*—hoofs.

4 The image is a very vulgar one, and the line lacks a syllable. "Pigmy-like" might be the more appropriate reading.

He did it well: your day is lengthened, and
The blissful dew of heaven does arrose you;
The powerful Venus well hath graced her altar
And given you your love; our master Mars
Has vouched his oracle, and to Arcite gave
The grace of the contention: so the deities
Have shown due justice. Bear this hence!

Pal. Oh, cousin,
That we should things desire, which do cost us
The loss of our desire! That naught could buy
Dear love, but loss of dear love!

Thes. Never fortune
Did play a subtler game: the conquered triumphs,
The victor has the loss; yet, in the passage,
The gods have been most equal. Palamon,
Your kinsman, hath confessed the right o' the lady
Did lie in you; for you first saw her, and
Even then proclaimed your fancy. He restored her,
As your stolen jewel, and desired your spirit
To send him hence forgiven: the gods my justice
Take from my hand, and they themselves become
The executioners. Lead your lady off;
And call your lovers[1] from the stage of death.
Whom I adopt my friends! A day or two
Let us look sadly, and give grace unto
The funeral of Arcite;—in whose end
The visages of bridegrooms we'll put on,
And smile with Palamon; for whom an hour,
But one hour since, I was as dearly sorry,
As glad of Arcite; and am now as glad,
As for him sorry. Oh, you heavenly charmers,
What things you make of us! For what we lack
We laugh, for what we have are sorry; still
Are children in some kind. Let us be thankful
For that which is, and with you leave disputes
That are above our question! Let's go off,
And bear us like the time! [*Flourish. Exeunt.*

1 *Lovers*—companions, friends.*

* So Mr. Knight; and yet, if written "followers," the sense and measure would be equally improved.

THE END OF THE TWO NOBLE KINSMEN.

INTRODUCTION

TO

THE LONDON PRODIGAL.

This comedy was first published in 1605, with the following title: "The London Prodigall: as it was plaide by the King's Majestie's Servants: By William Shakspeare. London: Printed by T. C., for Nathaniel Butler." T. C. was Thomas Creede, and Nathaniel Butler was the bookseller, who, three years afterward, published King Lear.

"Concerning the origin of this play, having been ever ascribed to Shakspeare, I have not been able to form any probable hypothesis." This is the language of Malone. He adds: "One knows not which most to admire, the impudence of the printer, in affixing our great poet's name to a comedy publicly at his own theatre, of which it is very improbable that he should have written a line, or Shakspeare's negligence of fame, in suffering such a piece to be imputed to him, without taking the least notice of it." Reasoning according to all common modes, one would be apt to admit this latter fact as conclusive of the authorship. It is certainly an argument, to which the mere disparity between this performance and those which the commentators have chosen to adopt exclusively as Shakspeare's, will afford an insufficient obstacle. Schlegel says: "If we are not mistaken, Lessing pronounced this piece to be Shakspeare's, and wished to bring it on the German stage;" and Lessing was one of the soundest of German critics. Tieck, another German, also assigns this comedy to Shakspeare. Hazlitt says: "If Shakspeare's at all, it must be among the sins of his youth." Mr. Knight, while analyzing the plot and materiel, and comparing these with the unquestionable performances of Shakspeare, rejects the play altogether.

Without urging a single word on this subject, we content ourselves with saying that its crudities are equally great as a work of thought and as a work of art. It exhibits a very immature condition of mind on the part of the writer. The invention, the verse, and the philosophy, are equally humble. It was probably the work of a youth — perhaps a boy — and that boy might have been Shakspeare. We know nothing more utterly absurd than this habit of testing the authorship of a work by its intrinsic merits; applying the standards formed in the maturer exhibitions of a great genius, to the crude and feeble performances of his beginning. But we have dwelt upon these generalities already.

The comedy is not wholly devoid of merit. The

ingenuity of the father, in finding excuses for the son's profligacy, is exemplary. The very recklessness and utter profligacy of the son himself, however faulty as a conception of character, has yet a redeeming something in his desperate hardihood. It would seem, too, that the excessive overdrawing of this character was the result of a too great anxiety to bring out that of the weak woman, his wife; whom our author probably sought to make another "Patient Grissil." The scenes in which she appears, and the devotion which she shows, which finally works the miracle in his reformation, are not wanting in force and spirit. Mr. Knight says, harshly: "If Shakspeare had chosen such a plot, in which the sudden repentance of the offender was to compensate for the miseries he had inflicted, he would have made the prodigal retain some sense of honor, some remorse amid his recklessness—something that would have given the assurance that his contrition was not hypocrisy. We have little doubt that the low moral tone of the writer's own mind produced the low morality of the plot and its catastrophe. We see in this play that confusion of principles of which the stage was too long the faithful mirror. In Shakspeare, the partition which separates levity and guilt is never broken down; thoughtlessness and dishonor are not treated with equal indulgence. This is quite argument enough to prove that Shakspeare could not have written this comedy, nor rendered the least assistance in its composition. If it exhibited any traces of his wit or his poetry, we should still reject it upon this sole ground." And if we argued the case with reference only to Shakspeare, as the mature master-mind of ages, rather than with regard to the boy who was just beginning his apprenticeship, we should say exactly the same thing. But this would be very idle. These old plays, if Shakspeare's, are from his "prentice han';" and, with all deference to the commentator, we are inclined to think that the "prentice han'" of a very superior and original genius is much more rude and awkward, for various good reasons, than that of a merely talented person. But we profess to determine nothing in regard to the authorship of the drama before us—only to suggest, that the reasons which render other editors most confident, are, as we think, of no sort of value in this discussion.

THE LONDON PRODIGAL.

PERSONS REPRESENTED.

FLOWERDALE, senior, *a merchant.*
MATTHEW FLOWERDALE, *his son.*
FLOWERDALE, junior, *brother to the merchant.*
Sir LAUNCELOT SPURCOCK.
Sir ARTHUR GREENSHIELD, *a military officer,* } *in love with* Luce.
OLIVER, *a Devonshire Clothier,* } *in love with* Luce.
WEATHERCOCK, *a parasite to* Sir Launcelot Spurcock.
CIVET, *in love with* Frances.
A Citizen.
DAFFODIL, ARTICHOKE, } *servants to* Sir Launcelot Spurcock.
DICK *and* RALPH, *two cheating gamesters.*
RUFFIAN, *a pander.*

DELIA, FRANCES, LUCE, } *daughters to* Sir Launcelot Spurcock.
Citizen's wife.

Sheriff's officers; Lieutenant and Soldiers; Drawers and other Attendants.

SCENE, — LONDON, *and the parts adjacent.*

ACT I.

SCENE I. — London. *A room in* FLOWERDALE, junior's, *house.*

Enter FLOWERDALE, senior, *and* FLOWERDALE, junior.

Flow., sen. Brother, from Venice, being thus disguised,
I come to prove the humors of my son.
How hath he borne himself since my departure,
I leaving you his patron and his guide?

Flow., jun. Faith, brother, so as you will grieve to hear,
And I almost ashamed to report it.

Flow., sen. Why, how is't, brother? What! doth he spend beyond
The allowance that I left him?

Flow., jun. How! beyond that! [Ay] and far more. Why, your exhibition's nothing. He hath spent that and since hath borrowed; protested with oaths; alleged kindred to wring money from me; [entreating] "by the love I bore his father, — by the fortunes [that] might fall upon himself" — to furnish his wants. That done, I have since had his bond, his friend and friend's bond. Although I know, that [what] he spends is yours, yet it grieves me to see the unbridled wildness that reigns over him.[1]

Flow., sen. Brother, what is the manner of his life?
How is the name of his offences? If they do not
Altogether, relish of damnation,
His youth may privilege his wantonness.
I myself ran an unbridled course till thirty; nay, almost till forty: well! you see how I am! For vice once looked into with the eyes of discretion, and well balanced with the weights of reason, the course past seems so abominable, that the landlord of himself, which is the heart of his body,[2] will rather entomb himself in the earth, or seek a new tenant to remain in him;[3] which once settled, how much better are they that in their youth have known all these vices, and left them, than those that know little, and in their age run into them? Believe me, brother, they that die most virtuous, have in their youth lived most vicious; and none knows the danger of the fire more than he that falls into it. But say, how is the course of his life? let's hear his particulars.

Flow., jun. Why, I'll tell you, brother: he is a continual swearer, and a breaker of his oaths; which is bad.

Flow., sen. I grant, indeed, to swear is bad, but in not[4] keeping those oaths is better. For who will set by a bad thing? Nay, by my faith, I hold this rather a virtue than a vice! Well, I pray, proceed.

Flow., jun. He's a mighty brawler, and comes commonly by the worst.

Flow., sen. By my faith, this is none of the worst neither; for if he brawl and be beaten for it, it will in time make him shun it; for what brings man or child more to virtue than correction? What reigns over him else?

Flow., jun. He is a great drinker, and one that will forget himself.

Flow., sen. Oh! best of all! [since] vice should be forgotten. Let him drink on, so he drink not [in] churches. Nay, an this be the worst, I hold it rather a happiness in him than any iniquity. Hath he any more attendants?

[1] Much of this is in a clumsy sort of rhythm, and may have been written originally in verse. The employment of an occasional particle here and there, and the dropping of a syllable, would easily convert it into rhythm again.

[2] That is, the heart of his body is the body's landlord, or ruler, the master of the tenement.

[3] That is, in shame and despair, either commit suicide, or change his character, change his heart, and become another sort of man.

[4] The old copies read, "not in."

Flow., jun. Brother, he is one that will borrow of any man.

Flow., sen. Why, see you,[1] so doth the sea; it borrows of all the small currents in the world, to increase himself.

Flow., jun. Ay, but the sea pays it again, and so will never your son.

Flow., sen. No more would the sea neither, if it were dry as my son.

Flow., jun. Then, brother, I see,
You rather like these vices in your son,
Than any way condemn them.

Flow., sen. Nay, mistake me not, brother,
For though I slur them over now as things
[But] slight and nothing, his crimes being in the bud,
'Twould gall my heart they ever should[2] reign in him.

M. Flow. [*knocking within*]. Ho! who's within; Ho!

Flow., jun. That's your son; he's come
To borrow more money.

Flow., sen. For God's sake give it out
[That] I am dead. See how he'll take it! Say
I've brought you news from his father. I have here drawn
A formal will, as it were from myself,
Which I'll deliver him.

Flow., jun. Go to, brother; no more; I will.

M. Flow. [*within*]. Uncle! where are you, uncle?

Flow., jun. [*aloud*]. Let my cousin[3] in there.

Flow., sen. [*hastily, and in undertones*]. I am a sailor come from Venice, and my name is Christopher.

Enter MATTHEW FLOWERDALE.

Flow. By the Lord, in truth, uncle——

Uncle. In truth would a-served, cousin, without the Lord.

Flow. By your leave, uncle, the Lord is the Lord of truth. A couple of rascals at the gate, set upon me for my purse.

Uncle. You never come, but you bring a brawl in your mouth.

Flow. By my truth, uncle, you must needs lend me ten pound.

Uncle. Give my cousin some small beer here.

Flow. Nay, look you, you turn it to a jest; now, by this light, I should ride to Croydon fair, to meet Sir Launcelot Spurcock; I should have his daughter Luce; and, for scurvy ten pound, a man shall lose nine hundred threescore and odd pounds, and a daily friend beside; by this hand, uncle, 'tis true.

Uncle. Why, anything is true for aught I know.

Flow. To see now! why you shall have my bond, uncle; or Tom White's, James Brock's, or Nick Hall's, as good rapier and dagger men, as any [that] be in England; let's be damned if we do not pay you; the worst of us all will not damn ourselves for ten pound. A pox of ten pound.

Uncle. Cousin, this is not the first time I have believed you.

Flow. Why, trust me now, you know not what may fall: If one thing were but true, I would not greatly care; I should not need ten pound;—but when a man can not be believed,—there's it.

1 Old copy reads "you see."
2 Previous editions, "should ever."
3 Nephew. Cousin formerly was used in the sense of kinsman.

Uncle. Why, what is it, cousin?

Flow. Marry this, uncle, can you tell me if the Kate and Hugh[4] be come home or no?

Uncle. Ay, marry, is't.

Flow. By God! I thank you for that news. What, is't in the pool, can you tell?

Uncle. It is; what of that?

Flow. What?—why then I have six pieces of velvet sent me—I'll give you a piece, uncle: for thus said the letter, a piece of ash-color, a three piled black, a color de roy;[5] a crimson, a sad green, and a purple: yes i'faith.

Uncle. From whom should you receive this?

Flow. From whom? Why, from my father!—With commendations to you, uncle; and thus he writes: "I know," saith he, "thou hast much troubled thy kind uncle, whom, God willing, at my return, I will see amply satisfied."—Amply, I remember, was the very word; so God help me!

Uncle. Have you the letter here?

Flow. Yes, I have the letter here; here is the letter: no—yes, no, let me see! what breeches wore I on Saturday: let me see: o'Tuesday, my calamanco; o'Wednesday, my peach color satin; o'Thursday, my velure;[6] o'Friday, my calamanco again; o'Saturday—let me see, o' Saturday—for in those breeches I wore o'Saturday is the letter: O, my riding breeches, uncle; those that you thought had been velvet—in those very breeches is the letter.

Uncle. When should it be dated?

Flow. Marry, decimo tertio Septembris—no, no, decimo tertio Octobris; ay, Octobris; so it is.

Uncle. Decimo tertio Octobris: and here I receive a letter that your father died in June: how say you, Kester? [*To* FLOW., senior, *as* CHRISTOPHER.

Father. Yes, truly, sir, your father is dead, these hands of mine holp to wind him.

Flow. Dead?

Father. Ay, sir, dead.

Flow. 'Sblood, how should my father come dead?

Fath. I' faith, sir, according to the old proverb,
The child was born, and cried,
Became a man, fell sick, and died.

Uncle. Nay, cousin, do not take't so heavily.

Flow. Nay, I can not weep you extempore: marry, some two or three days hence, I shall weep without any stintance. But I hope he died in good memory.

Fath. Very well, sir, and set down everything in good order; and the Katharine and Hugh you talk of, I came over in; and I saw all the bills of lading; and the velvet that you talk of, there is no such aboard.

Flow. By God! I assure you, then, there is knavery abroad.

Father. I'll be sworn of that: there's knavery abroad, although there were never a piece of velvet in Venice.

Flow. I hope he died in good estate.

Father. To the report of the world he did, and made his will, of which I am the unworthy bearer.

Flow. His will, have you his will?

Father. Yes, sir, and in the presence of your uncle, I was willed to deliver it. [*Delivers the will.*

Uncle. I hope, cousin, now God hath blessed you with wealth, you will not be unmindful of me.

4 Written in the old folio, Katern Hue.
5 Royal-color—something between purple and crimson.
6 Velure is velvet—French, *velours.*

Flow. I'll do reason, uncle; yet, i'faith, I take the denial of this ten pound very hardly.

Uncle. Nay, I denied you not.

Flow. By God, you denied me directly.

Uncle. I'll be judged by this good fellow.

Father. Not directly, sir.

Flow. Why, he said he would lend me none, and that had wont to be a direct denial, if the old phrase hold. Well, uncle, come; we'll fall to the legacies. [*reads.*] In the name of God, Amen.

Item, I bequeath to my brother, Flowerdale, three hundred pounds, to pay such trivial debts as I owe in London.

Item, To my son, Matthew Flowerdale, I bequeath two bale of false dice, videlicit, high men and low men, fulloms, stop-cater-traies,[1] and other bones of function.

Flow. 'Sblood, what doth he mean by this?

Uncle. Proceed, cousin.

Flow. [*reads*]. These precepts I leave him;—let him borrow of his oath—for of his word nobody will trust him. Let him by no means marry an honest woman;—for the other will keep herself. Let him steal as much as he can; that a guilty conscience may bring him to his destinate repentance.—I think he means hanging! An this were his last will and testament, the devil stood laughing at his bed's feet while he made it. 'Sblood, what doth he think to fob off his posterity with paradoxes.

Fath. This he made, sir, with his own hands.

Flow. Ay, well; nay come, good uncle, let me have this ten pound; imagine you have lost it; or were robbed of it; or misreckoned yourself so much: any way, to make it come easily off, good uncle.

Uncle. Not a penny.

Fath. I'faith, lend it him, sir;—I myself have an estate in the city worth twenty pound; all that I'll engage for him;—he saith it concerns him in a marriage.

Flow. Ay, marry doth it; this is a fellow of some sense, this: come, good uncle.

Uncle. Will you give your word for it, Kester?

Fath. I will, sir, willingly.

Uncle. Well, cousin, come to me some hour hence,—you shall have it ready.

Flow. Shall I not fail?

Uncle. You shall not; come or send.

Flow. Nay, I'll come myself.

Fath. By my troth, would I were your worship's man.

Flow. What? wouldst thou serve?

Fath. Very willingly, sir.

Flow. Well, I'll tell thee what thou shalt do;—thou say'st thou hast twenty pound;—go into Burchin lane, and put thyself into clothes;—thou shalt ride with me to Croyden fair.

Fath. I thank you, sir; I will attend you.

Flow. Well, uncle, you will not fail me an hour hence.

Uncle. I will not, cousin.

Flow. What's thy name? Kester?

Fath. Ay, sir.

Flow. Well, provide thyself: uncle, farewell till anon. [*Exit* FLOWERDALE.

Uncle. Brother, how do you like your son?

[1] Quatre-trois.

Fath. I'faith, brother, as a mad, unbridled colt,
Or as a hawk, that never stooped to lure:
The one must be tamèd with an iron bit,
The other must be watched, or still she's wild.[2]
Such is my son, a while let him be so;
For counsel still is folly's deadly foe.
I'll serve his youth, for youth must have his course,
For being restrained, it makes him ten times worse:
His pride, his riot, all that may be named,
Time may recall, and all his madness tamed.

Enter Sir LAUNCELOT, Master WEATHERCOCK, DAFFODIL, ARTICHOKE, LUCE, *and* FRANCES.

Launce. Sirrah, Artichoke, get you home before;
And, as you proved yourself a calf in buying,
Drive home your fellow calves that you have bought.

Art. Yes, forsooth; shall not my fellow Daffodil go along with me?

Launce. No, sir, no; I must have one to wait on me.

Art. Daffodil, farewell, good fellow Daffodil.
You may see, mistress, I'm set up by the halves,
Instead of waiting on you, I'm sent to drive home calves.

Launce. 'Faith, Frank, I must turn away this Daffodil;
He's grown a very foolish, saucy fellow.

Frances. Indeed! la! father, he was so since I had him:
Before, he was wise enough for a foolish[3] serving-man.

Weath. But what say you to me, Sir Launcelot?

Launce. Oh!—
About my daughters; well, I will go forward;
Here's two of them, God save them: but the third,
O, she's a stranger in her course of life:
She hath refused you, Master Weathercock.

Weath. Ay, by the rood, Sir Launcelot, that she hath;
But had she tried me, she'd have found a man
Of me, indeed.

Launce. Nay, be not angry, sir, at her denial,
She hath refused seven of the worshipful'st
And worthiest housekeepers this day in Kent;
Indeed, she will not marry, I suppose.

Weath. The more fool she!

Launce. What! is it folly to love charily?[4]

Weath. No, mistake me not, Sir Launcelot; but
'Tis an old proverb, and you know it well,
That women dying maids, lead apes in hell.

Launce. That is a foolish proverb and a false.

Weath. B'the mass, I think't be, and therefore let it go:
But who shall marry [then] with Mistress Frances?

Frances. By my troth, they are talking of marrying me, sister.

Luce. Peace, let them talk:
Fools may have leave to prattle as they walk.

Daff. Sententious[5] still, sweet mistress,
You have a wit, an 'twere your alabaster.[6]

[2] Or as a hawk,—
—must be watched or still she's wild. *See* the Taming of *a* Shrew, last ed., vol. iii., p. 486. *Steevens.*

[3] Quere? "fool's?"

[4] One of the editions before me reads "charity," another "chastity;" I should prefer "charily," that is, cautiously.

[5] One of the copies before me reads "sentesses," another "sentences."—"Sententious" renders the line at once more significant and musical.

[6] The meaning is obscure. "You have a wit, if it were your alabaster!" that is, fair as alabaster, and as brittle. Something of this sort was probably intended. Hence the rebuke which follows.

Luce. Faith, and thy tongue trips trench-more.[1]
Launce. No, of my knighthood, not a suitor yet:
Alas! God help her, silly girl, a fool, a very fool:
But there's the other black brows, a shrewd girl,
Sh'ath wit at will, and suitors two or three:
Sir Arthur Greenshield one, a gallant knight,
A valiant soldier, but his power but poor.
Then there's young Oliver, the Devonshire lad,
A wary fellow, marry, full of wit,
And rich, by the rood; but there's a third, all air,
Light as a feather, changing as the wind;
Young Flowerdale.
Weath. O, he, sir, he is
A desperate Dick indeed. Bar him your house.
Launce. Fie, sir, not so; he's of good parentage.
Weath. By my say and so he is, a proper man.
Launce. Ay, proper enough, had he good qualities.
Weath. Ay, marry, there's the point, Sir Launcelot:
For there's an old saying:—
Be he rich, or be he poor,
Be he high, or be he low:
Be he born in barn or hall,
'Tis manners make the man and all.
Launce. You are in the right, [good] Master Weathercock.

Enter Monsieur Civet.

Civet. Soul! I think I am sure crossed, or witched with an owl! I have hunted them, inn after inn, booth after booth, yet can not find them; ha, yonder they are; that's she; I hope to God 'tis she; nay, I know 'tis she now, for she treads her shoe a little awry.

Launce. Where is this inn? we are past it, Daffodil.

Daff. The good sign is here, sir, but the black gate is before.

Civet. Save you, sir. I pray, may I borrow a piece of a word with you?

Daff. No pieces, sir.

Civet. Why, then, the whole.
I pray, sir, what may yonder gentlewomen be?

Daff. They may be ladies, sir, if the destinies and mortality work.

Civet. What's *her* name, sir?

Daff. Mistress Frances Spurcock, Sir Launcelot Spurcock's daughter.

Civet. Is she a maid, sir?

Daff. You may ask Pluto, and Dame Proserpine that: I would be loath to be riddled, sir.

Civet. Is she married, I mean, sir?

Daff. The fates know not yet what shoemaker shall make her wedding-shoes.

Civet. I pray where inn you, sir? I would be very glad to bestow the wine of[2] that gentlewoman.

Daff. At the George, sir.

Civet. God save you, sir.

Daff. I pray your name, sir?

Civet. My name is Master Civet, sir.

Daff. A sweet name; God be with you, good Master Civet. [*Exit* Civet.

Launce. Ha! we have spied you, stout St. George? For all
Your dragon, y'had best sell us good wine
That needs no ivy-bush. We'll not sit by it,
As you do on your horse. This room shall serve.
Drawer. . . .

Enter Drawer.

Let me have sack for us old men;
For these [young] girls and knaves, small wines are best.
A pint of sack,—no more!

Drawer. A quart of sack in the Three Tuns. [*Exit.*

Launce. A pint! Draw but a pint. Daffodil
Call [you] for wine to make yourselves[3] drink.

Enter young Flowerdale.

M. Flow. How now! Fie! sit ye in the open room!
Now, good Sir Launcelot, and my kind friend
Worshipful Master Weathercock; what at?—
Your pint!—a quart, for shame!
Launce. Nay, roysterer, by your leave, we will away.
M. Flow. Come, give us some music [first]; we will go dance;
Be gone, Sir Launcelot! what! and fair day too.
Luce.[4] 'Twere foully done to dance within the fair
M. Flow. Nay, if you say so, fairest of all fairs
Then I'll not dance! A pox upon my tailor,
He hath spoiled me a peach-color satin suit,
Cut upon cloth of silver;[5] but, if ever
The rascal serve me such another trick,
I'll give him leave, i'faith, to put me in
The calendar of fools; and you, Sir Launcelot,
You, Master Weathercock, my goldsmith too,
On t'other side [of you]. I bespoke thee, Luce,
A carcanet of gold,[6] and thought thou shouldst
Have had it for the fairing. And [yet] the rogue
Puts me in 'rearages for orient pearl;—
But thou shalt have't by Sunday night, wench.—

Enter Drawer.

Drawer. Sir, here is one that hath sent you a bottle of Rhenish wine, brewed with rose water.[7]

Flow. To me?
Drawer. No, sir, to the knight;
And desires his more acquaintance.
Launce. To me?
What's he that proves so kind?
Daff. I have a trick
To know his name, sir; he hath a month's mind, here,
To Mistress Frances; his name's Master Civet.

1 Trench-more was a boisterous sort of dance to a lively tune, in triple time.

2 Quere: *Upon?*

3 Quere: your *fellows?*

4 This line in two of the copies before me, is ascribed to Sir Launcelot, but it evidently belongs to one of the damsels, Luce or Frances. I think it due to the former.

5 "Cut upon cloth of silver"—that is, with cloth of silver placed under all the *cuts*, openings, or slashes, in it. "Cloth of gold and *cuts*," is mentioned in "Much Ado about Nothing," last ed., vol. ii., p. 322.—*Steevens.*

6 A carcanet was an ornament for the neck formerly worn.—*Malone.* See note on the "Comedy of Errors," last ed., vol. ii., p. 192.—*Steevens.*

7 It was anciently a custom at taverns to send flagons of wine from one room to another, either as a token of friendship or by way of proposal to form an acquaintance. An amusing anecdote of Ben Jonson and the witty Bishop Corbet, has been preserved by which this custom may happily be illustrated. Hearing that Corbet was in the next room, Jonson calls for a quart of *raw* wine and sends it by the tapster, saying: "Sirrah, take this to the gentleman in the next chamber, with my love, and tell him I sacrifice my service to him."—"Friend," says Corbet, "tell the gentleman I thank him for his love; but tell him from me, that he is mistaken in his learning, for that such sacrifices are *burnt* offerings always.

Launce. Call him in, Daffodil.
Flow. O, I know him, sir;
He is a fool, but reasonable rich;
His father's one of these leasemongers, these
Cornmongers, moneymongers, but he never had
The wit to be a whoremonger.

Enter Master CIVET.

Launce. I promise you, sir,
You are at too much charge. [*To* CIVET.
Civet. The charge is small, sir! I thank God,
My father left me wherewithal. If't please you
I've a great mind to this gentlewoman here
I' the way of marriage.
Launce. I thank you, sir;—
Please you to come to Lewsham, my poor house;
You shall be kindly welcome. I knew your father.
He was a wary husband. To pay here, drawer?
Drawer. All's paid, sir; this gentleman hath paid all.
Launce. I'faith, you do us wrong;
But we shall live to make amends ere long.
Master Flowerdale,—is that your man?
M. Flow. Yes, faith; a good old knave.
Launce. Nay, then, I think,
You will turn wise, now you take such a servant.
Come: you'll ride with's to Lewsham? Let's away,
'Tis scarce two hours to the end of day. [*Exeunt.*

ACT II.

SCENE I.—*A Road in* Kent, *near the house of* Sir LAUNCELOT SPURCOCK.

Enter Sir ARTHUR GREENSHIELD, OLIVER, Lieutenant, Soldiers, *and* Recruits.

Arth. Lieutenant, lead your soldiers to the ships,
There let them have their coats; at their arrival
They shall have pay: farewell; look to your charge.
Sol. Ay; we are now sent away, and can not so much as speak with our friends.
Oli. No man what e'er you used a zutch a fashion, thick you can not take your leave of your vreens.
Arth. Fellow, no more; lieutenant, lead them off.
Sol. Well, if I have not my pay and my clothes,
I'll venture a running away, though I hang for't.
Arth. Away, sirrah, charm your tongue.[1]
[*Exeunt* Soldiers.
Oli. Be you a presser, sir?
Arth. I am a commander, sir, under the king.
Oli. Sfoot, man, an you be never such a commander, I shud a-spoke with my vreens before I shud a-gone; so I shud.
Arth. Content yourself, man; my authority
Will stretch to press so good a man as you.
Oli. Press me? I defy ye, press scoundrels, and thy messels[2]: press me, chee scorns thee, i'faith: for, seest thee, here's a worshipful knight [who] knows, cham not to be pressed by thee.

1 So in King Henry—"Charm thy riotous tongue"—in Othello, "Go to; charm your tongue." The phrase was common to the old dramatists.
2 Messel is a leper, but the sense here is, messmates—associates—parties to thy mess.

Enter Sir LAUNCELOT, WEATHERCOCK, *young* FLOWERDALE, *old* FLOWERDALE, LUCE, *and* FRANCES.

Launce. Sir Arthur, welcome to Lewsham, welcome, by my troth. What's the matter, man, [*to Oliver*] why are you vexed?
Oli. Why, man, he would press me.
Launce. O, fie, Sir Arthur, press him?
He is a man of reckoning.
Weath. That he is, Sir Arthur, hath the nobles,
The golden ruddocks[3] he.
Arth. The fitter for the wars: and were he not
In favor with your worships, he should see
That I have power to press so good as he.
Oli. Chill stand to the trial, so chill.
Flow. Ay, marry shall he; press cloth and karsy,[4]
White-pot and drowsen broth:[4] tut, tut, he can not.
Oli. Well, sir, though you see [he] vlouten cloth and karsy, chee a zeen zutch a karsy coat wear out the town sick a zilken jacket, as thick as one you wear.
Flow. Well-fed vlittan vlattan.[5]
Oli. Ay, and well-fed cockney, and bot-bell too:[6] what doest think cham aveard of thy zilken coat? no vear vor thee.
Launce. Nay, come; no more; be all lovers and friends.
Weath. Ay, 'tis best so, good Master Oliver.
Flow. Is your name Master Oliver, I pray you?
Oli. What tit and be tit, an it grieve you.
Flow. No, but I'd gladly know if a man might not have a foolish plot out of Master Oliver to work upon.
Oli. Work thy plots upon me; stand aside; work thy foolish plots upon me; chill so use thee, thou wert never so used since thy dam bound thy head;—work upon me?
Flow. Let him come, let him come.
Oli. Zirrah, zirrah, if it were not for shame, chee would a given thee zutch a whister-poop under the ear, chee would have made thee a vanged another at my feet. Stand aside, let me loose; cham all of a vlaming firebrand; stand aside.
Flow. Well, I forbear you for your friends' sake.
Oli. A vig for all my vreens; dost thou tell me of my vreens?
Launce. No more, good Master Oliver; no more,
Sir Arthur. And maiden, here, in the sight
Of all your suitors, every man of worth,
I'll tell you whom I fainest would prefer
To the hard bargain of your marriage-bed.
Shall I be plain among you, gentlemen?
Arth. Ay, sir, 'tis best.
Launce. Then, sir, first to you,
I do confess you a most gallant knight,
A worthy soldier, and an honest man;
But honesty maintains not a French-hood;
Goes very seldom in a chain of gold;
Keeps a small train of servants; hath few friends.
And, for this wild oats here, young Flowerdale,

3 The golden ruddoch is the red-breast. A cant name for gold pieces.
4 "Cloth and kersey," Devonshire manufactures; *white pot*, a favorite dish in Devonshire; *drowsen broth*, a common drink for servants—herbs boiled up in the grounds of beer.
5 Flowerdale ridicules the man of Kent for his pronunciation of the *f* as *v*.
6 He retorts upon the Londoner.

I will not judge ; God can work miracles,
But he were better make a hundred new,
Than thee a thrifty and an honest one.

Weath. Believe me, he hath hit you there ; he hath touched you to the quick, that he hath.

Flow. Woodcock o' my side ;
Why, Master Weathercock,
You know I am honest, howsoever trifles ——

Weath. Now, by my troth, I know no otherwise.—
Oh ! your old mother was a dame indeed :
Heaven hath her soul, and my wife's too, I trust :
And your good father, honest gentleman,
He's gone a journey as I hear, far hence.

Flow. Ay, God be praiséd, he is far enough ;
He's gone a pilgrimage to Paradise,
And left me to cut capers against care ;
Luce, look on me, that am as light as air.

Luce. I'faith, I like not shadows, bubbles, breath,
I hate a " light o' love," as I hate death.

Launce. Girl, hold thee there : look on this De'nshire lad :
Fat, fair, and lovely, both in purse and person.

Oli. Well, sir, cham as the Lord hath made me, you know me well ivin, cha have threescore pack of karsay at Blackem Hall,[1] and chief credit beside, and my fortunes may be so good as another's, zo it may.

Luce. 'Tis you I love, whatever others say.

Arth. Thanks, fairest.

Flow. What, wouldst thou have me quarrel with him ?

Fath. Do but say he shall hear from you.

Launce. Yet, gentlemen, hows'ever I prefer
This De'nshire suitor, I'll enforce no love ;
My daughter shall have liberty to choose
Whom she likes best : in your lovesuits proceed ;
Not all of you, but only one, must speed.

Weath. You have said well : indeed, right well.

Enter ARTICHOKE.

Arti. Mistress, here's one would speak with you ; my fellow Daffodil hath him in the cellar already ; he knows him ; he met him at Croydon fair.

Launce. Oh, I remember ; a little man.

Arti. Ay, a very little man.

Launce. And yet a proper man.

Arti. A very proper, very little man.

Launce. His name is Monsieur Civet.

Arti. The same, sir.

Launce. Come, gentlemen, if other suitors come,
My foolish daughter will be fitted too :
But my saint Delia, no man dare to move.

[*Exeunt all but young* FLOWERDALE *and* OLIVER, *and old* FLOWERDALE.

Flow. Hark you, sir, a word.

Oli. What han you say to me now ?

Flow. Ye shall hear from me, and that very shortly.

Oli. Is that all ? vare thee well : chee vere thee not a vig. [*Exit* OLIVER.

Flow. What if he should come now ?[2] I am fairly dressed.

Fath. I do not mean that you shall meet with him,
But presently we'll go and draw a will :
Where we will set down land we never saw,
And we will have it of so large a sum,
Sir Launcelot shall entreat you take his daughter :
This being framed, give it to Master Weathercock,
And make Sir Launcelot's daughter heir of all :
And make him swear never to show the will
To any one, until that you be dead.
This done, the foolish changeling Weathercock,
Will straight discourse unto Sir Launcelot,
The form and tenor of your testament.
Ne'er stand to pause of it, be ruled by me :
What will ensue, that you shall quickly see.

Flow. Come, let's about it ; if that a will, sweet Kit,
Can get the wench, I shall renown thy wit.

[*Exeunt.*

SCENE II.—*A Room in* Sir LAUNCELOT's *House.*

Enter DAFFODIL *and* LUCE.

Daff. Mistress ! still froward ? No kind looks unto
Your Daffodil, now, by the gods ——

Luce. Away, you foolish knave, let go my hand.—

Daff. There is your hand, but this shall go with me :
My heart is thine, this is my true love's fee.

[*Takes off her bracelet.*

Luce. I'll have your coat stripped o'er your ears for this,
You saucy rascal.

Enter Sir LAUNCELOT *and* WEATHERCOCK.

Launce. How now, maid, what is the news with you ?

Luce. Your man is something saucy. [*Exit* LUCE.

Launce. Go to, sirrah ; I'll talk with you, anon.

Daff. Sir, I'm a man to be talked with withal ;
I am no horse, I trow :
I know my strength then, no more than so.

Weath. Ay, by the mannikins,[3] good Sir Launcelot,
I saw him t'other day hold up the bucklers,
Like an Hercules ; faith, God-a-mercy, lad, I like thee well.

Launce. I like him well ; go, sirrah, fetch me a cup of wine,
That, ere I part with Master Weathercock,
We may drink down our farewell in French wine.

[*Exit* DAFFODIL.

Weath. I thank you, sir, I thank you, friendly knight ;
I'll come and visit you ; by the mouse-foot I will ;[4]
Meantime, take heed of cutting Flowerdale ;
He is a desperate Dick, I warrant you.

Re-enter DAFFODIL, *with wine.*

Launce. He is, he is ! Fill, Daffodil, some wine,
Ha ! what wears he on his arm ? Fill me !—
My daughter Luce's bracelet ? 'tis the same :
Ha' to you, Master Weathercock.

Weath. I thank you, sir : here, Daffodil, an honest fellow and a tall thou art : Well : I'll take my leave, good knight, and I hope to have you and all your daughters at my poor house ; in good sooth I must.

Launce. Thanks, Master Weathercock,
I shall be bold to trouble you, be sure.

Weath. And welcome, heartily ; — farewell.

[*Exit* WEATH.

1 Blackwell Hall, the great repository of woollen goods in London.

2 Previous editions read, "come more ?"

3 In previous copies " matkins" or " makins."

4 A petty oath that seems to have been in frequent use. Thus, in Colman and Perseda (1549). "By cock and pie and mouse-foot."—*Steevens.*

Launce. Sirrah, I saw my daughter's wrong,[5] and [see] withal,
Her bracelet on your arm. Off with it [sirrah],
And with it my living too. Have I a care
To see my daughter matched with men of worship,
And are you grown so bold? Go from my house
Or I will whip you hence.

Daff. I'll not be whipped, sir: there's your living!
This is a servingman's reward. What care I?
I've means to trust to; I scorn service; ay!

[*Exit* DAFFODIL.

Launce. A lusty knave, but I must let him go.
Our servants must be taught what they should know.

SCENE III.—*Another Room in the same.*

Enter SIR ARTHUR *and* LUCE.

Luce. Sir, as I am a maid, I do affect
You above any suitor that I have,
Although that soldiers scarce know how to love.

Arth. I am a soldier, and a gentleman,
Know what belongs to war, what to a lady:
What man offends me, that my sword shall right:
What woman loves me, I'm her faithful knight.

Luce. I neither doubt your valor nor your love,
But there be some that bear a soldier's form,
That swear by him they never think upon,
Go swaggering up and down from house to house,
Crying, "God pays all;"—— and ——

Arth. Faith, lady, I'll describe you such a man;
Of them there be many which you've spoke of,
That bear the name and shape [alone] of soldiers,
Yet, God knows, very seldom saw the war:
That haunt your taverns and your ordinaries,
Your alehouses sometimes, for all alike
To uphold the brutish humor of their minds,
Being marked down, for the bondmen of despair:
Their mirth begins in wine, but ends in blood,
Their drink is clear, but their conceits are mud.

Luce. Yet these [they tell us] are great gentlemen;

Arth. No soldiers;—they are wretched slaves, [my Luce],
Whose desperate lives doth bring them timeless graves.

Luce. Both for yourself, and for your form of life,
If I may choose, I'll be a soldier's wife. [*Exeunt.*

SCENE IV.

Enter SIR LAUNCELOT *and* OLIVER.

Oli. And tyt trust to it, so then.

Launce. Assure yourself,
You shall be married with all speed we may:
One day shall serve for Frances and for Luce.

Oli. Why che would vain know the time, for providing wedding raiments.

Launce. Why no more but this; first get your assurance made,
Touching my daughter's jointure; that despatched,
We will, in two days, make provision.

Oli. Why, man, chil have the writings made by to-morrow.

Launce. To-morrow be it then; let's meet at the King's Head in Fish street.

Oli. No, fie man, no; let's meet at the Rose at Temple Bar; that will be nearer your counsellor and mine.

Launce. At the Rose be it then, the hour be nine,
He that comes last forfeits a pint of wine.

Oli. A pint is no payment,
Let it be a whole quart, or nothing.

Enter ARTICHOKE.

Arti. Master, here is a man would speak with Master Oliver; he comes from young Master Flowerdale.

Oli. Why chil speak with him, chil speak with him.

Launce. Nay, [good] son Oliver, I'll surely see
What ['tis] young Flowerdale hath sent to you.
Pray God it be no quarrel.

Oli. Why, man, if he quarrel with me, chil give him his hands full.

Enter FLOWERDALE, senior.

Fath. God save you, good Sir Launcelot.

Launce. Welcome, honest friend.

Fath. To you and yours my master wisheth health,
But unto you, sir, this, and this, he sends:
There is the length, sir, of his rapier;
And in that paper shall you know his mind.

Oli. Here, chil meet him, my friend, chil meet him.

Launce. Meet him? you shall not meet the ruffian, fie!

Oli. An I do not meet him, chil give you leave to call
Me Cut. Where is't, sirrah? where is't? where is't?

Fath. The letter showeth both the time and place,
And, if you be a man, then keep your word.

Launce. Sir, he shall not keep his word, he shall not meet.

Fath. Why let him choose; he'll be the better
For a base rascal, and reputed so. [known

Oli. Zirrah, zirrah: and 'twere not an old fellow, and sent after an errand, chid give thee something, but chud be no money: But hold thee, for I see thou art somewhat testern; hold thee; there's vorty shillings; bring thy master a veeld, chil give thee vorty more; look thou bring him, chil maul him, tell him; chil mar his dancing tressels; chil use him, he was ne'er so used since his dam bound his head; chil mar him for capering any more, chy vore thee.

Fath. You seem a man, sir, stout and resolute,
And I will so report, whate'er befall.

Launce. An it fall out ill, assure thy master this,
I'll make him fly the land, or use him worse.

Fath. My master, sir, deserves not this of you,
And that you'll shortly find.

Launce. Thy master is an unthrift, you a knave,
And I'll attach you first, next clap him up;
Or have him bound unto his good behavior.

Oli. I wood you were a sprite if you do him any harm for this: an you do! chil ne'er see you, nor any of yours, while chil have eyes open: what, do you think, chil be abasselled up and down the town for a messel,[1] and a scoundrel? no chy vore you: zirrah, chil come; zay no more; chil come; tell him I defy him.

Fath. Well, sir. [*Exit.*

Launce. Now, gentle son, let me know the place.

Oli. No, chy vore you.

[1] "Wrath," perhaps.

[1] Messel, a leper. He probably means to say that he would be evaded, as if leprous, for his cowardice.

Launce. Let me [but] see the note.

Oli. Nay, chil watch you for zutch a trick. But if chee meet him, zo; if not, zo; chil make him know me, or chil know why I shall not; chil vare the worse.

Launce. What! will you then neglect my daughter's love?
Venture your state and hers, for a loose brawl?

Oli. Why, man, chil not kill him, marry chil veze[1] him too, and again; and zo, God be with you, vather. What, man, we shall meet to-morrow. [*Exit.*

Launce. Who would have thought he had been so desperate?
Come forth, my honest servant, Artichoke.

Enter ARTICHOKE.

Arti. Now, what's the matter? some brawl toward, I warrant you.

Launce. Go get me thy sword bright scoured, thy buckler mended;
Oh! for that knave, that villain Daffodil:
He would have done good service. But to thee.

Arti. Ay, this is the tricks of all you gentlemen, when you stand in need of a good fellow. O for that Daffodil, O, where is he? but if you be angry, and it be but for the wagging of a straw, then out o' doors with the knave; turn the coat over his ears. This is the humor of you all.

Launce. Oh! for that knave, that lusty Daffodil.

Arti. Why there 'tis, now: our year's wages and our vails will scarce pay for broken swords and bucklers that we use in our quarrels. But I'll not fight if Daffodil be o' 't other side; — that's flat.

Launce. 'Tis no such matter, man, get weapons ready,
And be at London ere the break of day:
Watch near the lodging of the De'nshire youth,
But be unseen: and as he goeth out,
As he will go, and early, without doubt —

Arti. What, would you have me draw upon him,
As he goes in the street?

Launce. Not for a world, man;
Into the fields. For to the field he goes,
There to meet the desperate Flowerdale:
Take thou the part of Oliver my son,
For he shall be my son, and marry Luce:
Do'st understand me, knave?

Arti. Ay, sir, I do understand you, but my young mistress might be better provided in matching with my fellow Daffodil.

Launce. No more; [thy fellow] Daffodil's a knave,
A most notorious knave. [*Exit* ARTICHOKE.

Enter WEATHERCOCK.

Master Weathercock, you come in happy time;
The desperate Flowerdale hath writ a challenge:
And who think you must answer it but [he],
The Devonshire man, my son Oliver?

Weath. Marry, I'm sorry for it, good Sir Launcelot,
But if you'll be ruled by me, we'll stay their fury.

Launce. As how, I pray?

Weath. Marry, I'll tell you, by promising young Flowerdale the red-lipped Luce.

Launce. I'll rather follow her unto her grave.

Weath. Ay, Sir Launcelot, I would have thought so too,
But you and I have been deceived in him.
Come read this will, or deed, or what you call it,
I know not: come, your spectacles, I pray.

Launce. Nay, I thank God, I see [it] very well.

Weath. Marry, God bless your eyes, mine have been dim
Almost this thirty years.

Launce. Ha, what is this? what is this? [*Reads.*]

Weath. Nay, there is true love indeed;
He gave it to me but this very morn,
And bade me keep't unseen from any one,
Good youth, to see how men may be deceived.

Launce. Passion of me! What a wretch am I
To hate this loving youth! —
He hath made me, together with my Luce,
He loves so dear, executors of all
His wealth.

Weath. All, all, good man, he hath given you all.

Launce. Three ships, now in the straits, and homeward bound,
Two lordships of two hundred pound a year:
The one in Wales, th' other in Glostershire:
Debts and accounts are thirty thousand pound,
Plate, money, jewels, sixteen thousand more,
Two houses furnished well in Coleman street:
Besides whate'er his uncle leaves to him,
Being of great domains and wealth at Peckham.

Weath. How like you this, good knight? How like you this?

Launce. I have done him wrong; but now I'll make amends.
The De'nshire man shall whistle for a wife;
He marry Luce! Luce shall be Flowerdale's.

Weath. Why that is friendly said, let's ride to London
And straight prevent their match, by promising
Your daughter to that lovely [loving] lad.

Launce. We'll ride to London: — or, it shall not need;
We'll cross to Deptford strand, and take a boat.
Where be these knaves? what, Artichoke; what, fop!

Enter ARTICHOKE.

Arti. Here be the very knaves, but not the merry knaves.

Launce. Here, take my cloak: I'll have a walk to Deptford.

Arti. Sir, we have been scouring of our swords and bucklers for your defence.

Launce. Defence me no defence: let your swords rust;
I'll have no fighting. Ay, let blows alone!
Bid Delia see all things in readiness
Against the wedding. We'll have two at once;
That will save charges, Master Weathercock.

Arti. We'll do it, sir. [*Exeunt.*

ACT III.

SCENE I. — *A walk before the House of* SIR LAUNCELOT.

Enter CIVET, FRANCES, *and* DELIA.

Civ. By my troth this is good luck; I thank God for this. In good sooth I have even my heart's desire: sister Delia, — now I may boldly call you so, for your father hath frank and freely given me his daughter Frank.

[1] Pheeze or feaze him. To take the twist asunder. So in the "Taming of the Shrew"—
"I'll *pheeze* you, i'faith."

Frances. Ay, by my troth, Tom; thou hast my good will too, for, I thank God, I longed for a husband, and would I might never stir, for one whose name was Tom.

Del. Why, sister, now you have your wish.

Civ. You say very true, sister Delia, and I pr'ythee call me nothing but Tom: and I'll call thee sweetheart, and Frank: will it not do well, sister Delia?

Del. It will do very well with both of you.

Frances. But Tom, must I go as I do now when I am married?

Civ. No, Frank, I'll have thee go like a citizen
In a guarded gown, and a French hood.[1]

Frances. By my troth, that will be excellent indeed.

Del. Brother, maintain your wife to your estate,
Apparel you yourself like to your father:
And let her go like to your ancient mother.
He, sparing, got his wealth, left it to you.
Brother, take heed, for pride bids thrift adieu.

Civ. So as my father and my mother went!—
That's a jest indeed; why, she went in
A fringed gown, a single ruff, and white cap.
And my father in a mocado[2] coat,
A pair of red satin sleeves, and a canvass back.

Del. And yet his wealth was full as much as yours.

Civ. My estate, my estate, I thank God, is forty pound a year, in good leases and tenements; besides twenty mark a year at Cuckolds'-Haven; and that comes to us all by inheritance.

Del. That may indeed, 'tis very fitly 'plied.
I know not how it comes, but so't falls out
That those whose fathers have died wondrous rich,
And took no pleasure but to gather wealth,
Thinking of little [but] that they leave behind
For them, they hope, will be of their like mind.—
But it falls out contrary; forty years sparing,
Is scarce three seven years spending; never caring
What will ensue. When all their coin is gone,
And all too late, then thrift is thought upon:
Oft have I heard, that pride and riot kist,
And then repentance cries—For *had I wist.*

Civ. You say well, sister Delia, you say well: but I mean to live within my bounds: for, look you, I have set down my rest thus far, but to maintain my wife in her French hood, and her coach, keep a couple of geldings, and a brace of greyhounds; and this is all I'll do.

Del. And you'll do this with forty pound a year?

Civ. Ay, and a better penny, sister.

Frances. Sister, you forget that at [the] Cuckold's-Haven.

Civ. By my troth well remembered, Frank,
I'll give thee that to buy thee pins.

Del. Keep you the rest for points. Alas the day!
Fools shall have wealth, though all the world say nay:
Come, brother, will you in? dinner stays for us.

Civ. Ay, good sister, with all my heart.

Frances. Ay, by my troth, Tom, for I have a good stomach.

Civ. And I the like, sweet Frank; no, sister, do not think
I'll go beyond my bounds.

Del. God grant you may not. [*Exeunt.*

1 Guards or *facings*. So in Henry IV. we have "velvet *guards* and Sunday *citizens*."

2 A woollen stuff in imitation of velvet. Mock velvet. It is frequently mentioned in the old plays. So in the "Devil's Charter," 1607—"Varlet of velvet, old heart of durance, *moccado* villain!"

SCENE II.—London. *The Street before young* FLOWERDALE'S *House.*

Enter young FLOWERDALE *and his* Father, *with foils in their hands.*

Flow. Sirrah, Kit, tarry thou there; I have spied Sir Launcelot and old Weathercock coming this way; they are hard at hand; I will by no means be spoken withal.

Fath. I'll warrant you; go, get you in.

Enter SIR LAUNCELOT *and* WEATHERCOCK.

Launce. Now, my honest friend, thou dost belong to Master Flowerdale?

Fath. I do, sir.

Launce. Is he within, my good fellow?

Fath. No, sir, he is not within.

Launce. I pr'ythee if he be within, let me speak with him.

Fath. Sir, to tell you true, my master is within, but indeed would not be spoke withal: there be some terms that stand upon his reputation, therefore he will not admit any conference till he hath shook them off.

Launce. I pr'ythee tell him his very good friend Sir Launcelot Spurcock entreats to speak with him.

Fath. By my troth, sir, if you come to take up the matter between my master and the Devonshire man, you do but beguile your hopes, and lose your labor.

Launce. Honest friend, I have not any such thing to him; I come to speak with him about other matters.

Fath. For my master, sir, hath set down his resolution, either to redeem his honor, or leave his life behind him.

Launce. My friend, I do not know any quarrel touching thy master or any other person; my business is of a different nature to him, and I pr'ythee so tell him.

Fath. For howsoever the Devonshire man is,
My master's mind is bloody: that's a round O,[3]
And therefore, sir, entreaties are but vain.

Launce. I have no such thing to him, I tell thee once again.

Fath. I will then so signify to him. [*Exit* Father.

Launce. A sirrah! I see this matter's hotly carried. But I will labor to dissuade him from it.

Enter MATTHEW FLOWERDALE *and his* Father.

Good morrow, Master Flowerdale.

Flow. Good morrow, good Sir Launcelot; Master Weathercock, good morrow; by my troth, gentlemen,
I have been reading over Nick Machiavel;
I find him good to be known, not to be followed:
A pestilent humane fellow! I have made
Certain annotations on him—such as they be!
And how is't, Sir Launcelot? ha? how is't?
A mad world, men can not live quiet in it.

Launce. Master Flowerdale, I do understand there is some jar between the Devonshire man and you.

Fath. They, sir? they are good friends as can be.

Flow. Who? Master Oliver and I? as good friends as can be.

Launce. It is a kind of safety in you to deny it, and a generous silence, which too few are endued withal: but, sir, such a thing I hear, and I could wish it otherwise.

3 A round truth.

Flow. No such thing, Sir Launcelot; o' my reputation, as I am an honest man.

Launce. Now, then, I do believe you, if you do
Engage your reputation there is none.

Flow. Nay, I do not engage my reputation there is not.
You shall not bind me to any condition of hardness;
But if there be anything between us, then there is;
If there be not, then there is not: be, or be not, all's one.

Launce. I do perceive by this, that there is something between you, and I am very sorry for it.

Flow. You may be deceived, Sir Launcelot;—the Italian
Hath a pretty saying, *Questo*—I have forgot it too,
'Tis out of my head [now], but, in my translation,
If't hold, thus: Thou hast a friend, keep him; if a foe, trip him.

Launce. Come, I do see by this there is somewhat between you,
And, before God, I could wish it otherwise.

Flow. Well, what is between us can hardly be altered:
Sir Launcelot, I am to ride forth to-morrow,
That way which I must ride, no man must deny me
The sun; I would not by any particular man,
Be denied common and general passage. If any one
Saith, Flowerdale, thou passest not this way:
My answer is, I must either on or return;
But return is not my word; I must on:
If I can not then make my way, nature
Hath done the last for me, and there's the fine.

Launce. Master Flowerdale, every man hath one tongue,
And two ears. Nature in her building,
Is a most curious workmaster.

Flow. That is as much as to say, a man should hear
More than he should speak.

Launce. You say true, and indeed I have heard more,
Than at this time I will speak.

Flow. You say well.

Launce. Slanders are more common than truths, Master
Flowerdale; but proof is the rule for both.

Flow. You say true. What-do-you-call-him,
Hath't there in his third canton ?[1]

Launce. I have heard you have been wild: I have believed it.

Flow. 'Twas fit, 'twas necessary.

Launce. But I have seen somewhat of late in you,
That hath confirmed in me an opinion of
Goodness toward you.

Flow. Faith, sir, I'm sure I never did you harm:
Some good I've done, either to you or yours,
I'm sure you know not, neither is't my will you should.

Launce. Ay, your will, sir.

Flow. Ay, my will, sir: 'sfoot, do you know aught of my will?
By God, an you do, sir, I am abused.

Launce. Go, Mr. Flowerdale, what I know, I know:
And know you thus much out of my knowledge,
That I [do] truly love you. For my daughter,
She's yours. And if you like a marriage better
Than a brawl, all quirks of reputation set
Aside, go with me presently: and where
You should fight bloody battle, you'll be married
To a [most] lovely lady.

Flow. Nay but, Sir Launcelot?

Launce. If you will not embrace my offer, yet
Assure yourself thus much, I will have order
To hinder your encounter.

Flow. Nay, but hear me, Sir Launcelot.

Launce. Nay, stand not you upon putative honor
'Tis merely unsound, unprofitable, and idle.
Your business is to wed my daughter, therefore
Give me word, I'll go and provide the maid;
Your present resolution, either now
Or never.

Flow. Will you so put me to it?

Launce. Ay, before God, you either take me now,
Or take me never. Else what I thought should be
Our match, shall be our parting, so, fare you well,
For ever.

Flow. Stay: fall out what may,
My love is above all: I will come.

Launce. I [will] expect you, and so fare you well.
[*Exit* Sir LAUNCELOT *and* WEATHERCOCK.

Fath. Now, sir, how shall we do for wedding apparel?

Flow. By the mass, that's true: now help, Kit;
The marriage ended, we'll make amends for all.

Fath. Well, well, no more, prepare you for your bride,
We will not want for clothes, whate'er betide.

Flow. And thou shalt see, when once I have my dower,
In mirth we'll spend full many a merry hour;
As for this wench, I not regard a pin;
It is her gold must bring my pleasures in. [*Exit*

Fath. Is't possible he hath his second living?[2]
Forsaking God, himself to the devil giving:
But that I knew his mother firm and chaste,
My heart would say, my head she had disgraced:
But that her fair mind so foul a deed did shun,[3]
Else would I swear, he never was my son.

Enter Uncle.

Uncle. How now, brother! how do you find your son?

Fath. O brother, heedless as a libertine,
Even grown a master in the school of vice;
One that doth nothing, but invent deceit:
For all the day he humors up and down,
How he the next day might deceive his friend;
He thinks of nothing but the present time:
For one groat ready down, he'll pay a shilling:
But then the lender must needs stay for it.
When I was young, I had the scope of youth,
Both wild, and wanton, careless, desperate:
But such mad strains, as he's possessed withal,
I thought it wonder for to dream upon.

Uncle. I told you so, but you would not believe it.

Fath. Well, I have found it; but one thing comforts me;
Brother, to-morrow he's to be married
To beauteous Luce, Sir Launcelot Spurcock's daughter.

Uncle. Is't possible?

Fath. 'Tis true, and thus I mean to curb him:
Brother, this day, I will you shall arrest him:
If anything will tame him, it must be that,
For he is rank in mischief, chained to a life
That will increase his shame, and kill his wife.

1 Canto is probably the word. Steevens suggests that young Flowerdale means to refer to the third canto of the Faery Queen, in which Abessa slanders the Lady *Una*.

2 That is, his fellow, his equal in depravity.

3 I have transposed these two lines as they occur in other editions.

Uncle. What! arrest him on his wedding-day? That
Were an unchristian, an inhuman part:
How many couple, even for that very day,
Have purchased seven years' sorrow afterward?
Forbear him then to-day;—do it to-morrow;
And this day mingle not his joy with sorrow.
Fath. Brother, I'll have it done this very day,
And, in the view of all, as he comes from church.
Do but observe the course that he will take;
Upon my life he will forswear the debt:
And, for we'll have the sum shall not be slight,
Say that he owes you near three thousand pound:
Good brother, let it be done immediately.
Uncle. Well, brother, seeing you will have it so,
I'll do it, and straight provide the sheriff.
Fath. So, brother, by this means shall we perceive
What ['tis] Sir Launcelot in this pinch will do;
And how his wife doth stand affected to him!
Her love will then be tried to the uttermost;
And all the rest of them. What I will do,
Shall harm him much, and much avail him too. [*Exit.*

SCENE III.—*A High Road near* London.

Enter OLIVER, *and afterward,* Sir ARTHUR GREENSHIELD.

Oli. Cham assured thick be the place that the scoundrel [zo.
Appointed to meet me: if a come, zo; if a come not,
And che war avise, he would make a coystrel[1] on us,
Ched veze him, and che vang him in hand, che would
Hoist him, and give it him too and again, zo chud.
Who been a there! Sir Arthur? chil stay aside.
Arth. I've dogged the De'nshire man into the field,
For fear of any harm that should befall him:
I had an inkling of that yesternight,
That Flowerdale and he should meet this morning:
Though, of my soul, Oliver fears him not,
Yet, for I'd see fair play on either side,
Made me to come, to see their valors tried.
Good morrow to you, Master Oliver.
Oli. God and good morrow.
Arth. What, Master Oliver, are you angry?
Oli. What an it be, tyt an grieven you?
Arth. Not me at all, sir, but I imagine by
Your being here thus armed, you stay for some
That you should fight withal.
Oli. Why an he do, che would not dezire you to take his part.
Arth. No, by my troth, I think you need it not,
For he you look for, I think means not to come.
Oli. No, and che war assure of that, ched veze him in another place.

Enter DAFFODIL.

Daff. O, Sir Arthur, Master Oliver, ah me!
Your love, and yours, and mine, sweet Mistress Luce,
This morn is married to young Flowerdale.
Arth. Married to Flowerdale! Impossible.
Oli. Married, man? che hope thou dost but jest,
To make a vlowten[2] merriment of it.
Daff. O, 'tis too true; here comes his uncle.

[1] Coystrel, from the French *coustillier*, properly the servant of a man-at-arms; hence it became degraded in its signification, and was applied to a low, mean person.
[2] Flouting.

Enter FLOWERDALE, Sheriff, Officers.

Uncle. Good morrow, Sir Arthur; good morrow Master Oliver.
Oli. God and good morn, Mr. Flowerdale. I pray you tellen us, is your scoundrel kinsman married?
Uncle. [Ay], Master Oliver, call him what you will,
But he is married to Sir Launcelot's daughter.
Arth. Unto her?
Oli. Ah! ha the old fellow zerved me thick a trick?
Why, man, he was a promise chil chud a had her;
Is a zitch a vox, chil look to his water che vor him.
Uncle. The music plays; they are coming from the church.
Sheriff, do your office: fellows, stand stoutly to it!

Enter Sir LAUNCELOT SPURCOCK, M. FLOWERDALE, WEATHERCOCK, CIVET, LUCE, FRANCES, FLOWERDALE, senior, and Attendants.

Oli. God give you joy, as the old zaid proverb is, and some zorrow among! You met us well, did you not?
Launce. Nay, be not angry, sir, the fault's in me:
I have done all the wrong—kept him from coming
To the field to you, as I might, sir, for I'm a justice,
And sworn to keep the peace.
Weath. Ay, marry is he, sir,
A very justice, and sworn to keep the peace:
You must not disturb the weddings.
Launce. Nay, never frown nor storm, sir; if you do,
I'll have an order taken for you.
Oli. Well, chil be quiet.
Weath. Master Flowerdale, Sir Launcelot, look you, who's here, Master Flowerdale?
Launce. Master Flowerdale, welcome with all my heart.
Flow. Uncle, this is she—faith! Master under-sheriff,
Arrest me? At whose suit? Draw, Kit!
Uncle. At my suit, sir.
Launce. Why, what's the matter, Master Flowerdale?
Uncle. This is the matter, sir: this unthrift here
Hath cozened you; and [he] hath had of me,
In several sums, three thousand pound.
Flow. Why, uncle!
Uncle. Cousin, you have uncled me,
And if you be not [now] stayed, you will prove
A cozener unto all that know you.
Launce. Why, sir, suppose he be to you in debt
Ten thousand pound, his state to me appears
To be at least three thousand by the year.
Uncle. O, sir, I was too late informed of that plot,
How that he went about to cozen you:
And formed a will, and sent it to your friend there,
Good Master Weathercock, in which was nothing true,
But brags and lies.
Launce. Ha! hath he not such lordships, lands, and ships?
Uncle. Not worth a groat, not worth a halfpenny, he.
Launce. Pray, tell us true; be plain, young Flowerdale.
Flowerda. My uncle 's mad, disposed to do me wrong;
But here's my man, by the Lord, an honest fellow,
And of good credit, knows [that] all is true.
Fath. Not I, sir; I'm too old to lie; I rather know

You forged a will, where every line you writ,
You studied where to quote your lands might lie.

Weath. I pr'ythee, where be they, my honest friend?

Fath. I'faith, nowhere, sir, for he hath none at all.

Weath. Benedict! we are o'erreached, I believe.

Launce. I'm cozened, and my hopeful'st child undone.

Flow. You are not cozened, nor is she undone;
They slander me; by this light, they slander me:
Look you, my uncle here's an usurer,
And would undo me, but I'll stand in law;
Do you but bail me, you shall do no more:
You, brother Civet, Master Weathercock,
Bail me, and let me have my marriage-money,
And we'll ride down, and there your eyes shall see
How my poor tenants there will welcome me.
You shall but bail me, you shall do no more;
And you, you greedy gnat, their bail will serve.

Uncle. Ay, sir, I'll ask no better bail.

Launce. No, sir, you shall not take my bail, nor his,
Nor my son Civet's. I'll not be cheated. Ay!
Shrieve, take your prisoner; I'll not deal with him;
Let's uncle make false dice with his false bones,
I'll not have to do with him: mocked, gulled, and wronged!
Come, girl, though it be late, it falls out well—
Thou shalt not live with him in beggar's hell.

Luce. He is my husband, and high Heaven doth know,
With what unwillingness I went to church,
But you enforced me, you compelled me to it;
The holy man pronounced these words but now:
I must not leave my husband in distress:
Now, I must comfort him, not go with you.

Launce. Comfort a cozener! On my curse forsake him!

Luce. This day you caused me on your curse to take him:
Do not, I pray, my grievéd soul oppress;
God knows my heart doth bleed at his distress!

Launce. O, Master Weathercock, I must confess
I forced her to this match,
Led with opinion his false will was true.

Weath. He hath o'erreached me too.

Launce. She might have lived
Like Delia, in a happy virgin state.

Delia. Father, be patient; sorrow comes too late.

Launce. And on her knees she begged and did entreat,
If she must needs taste a sad marriage-life,
She craved to be Sir Arthur Greenshield's wife.

Arth. You have done her and me the greater wrong.

Launce. O, take her yet.

Arth. Not I.

Launce. Or, Master Oliver,
Accept my child, and half my wealth is yours.

Oli. No, sir, chil break no laws.

Luce. Never fear, she will not trouble you.

Delia. Yet, sister, in this passion
Do not run headlong to confusion:
You may affect him, though not follow him.

Frances. No, sister; hang him, let him go.

Weath. Do, 'faith, Mistress Luce,
Leave him.

Luce. You are three gross fools, let me alone!
I swear, I'll live with him in all his moan.

Oli. But an he have his legs at liberty,
Cham aveard he will never live with you.

Arth. Ay, but he is now in huckster's handling for running away.

Launce. Huswife, you hear how you and I am wronged,
And if you will redress it yet you may:
But if you stand on terms to follow him,
Never come near my sight, nor look on me;
Call me not father; look not for a groat;
For all the portion I will this day give
Unto thy sister Frances.

Frances. How say you to that, Tom? [*To* Civet.
I shall have a good deal;
Besides, I'll be a good wife; and a good wife
Is a good thing I can tell.

Civet. Peace, Frank, I would be sorry to see thy sister cast away, as I am a gentleman.

Launce. What, are you yet resolved?

Luce. Yes, I'm resolved.

Launce. Come then away, or now, or never come.

Luce. This way I turn, go you unto your feast,
And I to weep, that am with grief oppressed.

Launce. For ever fly my sight. Come, gentlemen,
Let's in, I'll help you to far better wives.
Delia, upon my blessing talk not to her;
Base baggage, in such haste to beggary!

Uncle. Sheriff, take your prisoner to your charge.

Flow. Uncle, by God, you have used me very hardly;
By my troth, upon my wedding-day.

[*Exeunt* Sir Launcelot, Civet, *and all but young* Flowerdale, *his* Father, Uncle, Sheriff, *and* Officers.

Luce. O, Master Flowerdale, but hear me speak;
Stay but a little while, good Master Sheriff;
If not for him, for my sake pity him:
Good sir, stop not your ears at my complaint,
My voice grows weak, for women's words are faint.

Flow. Look you, uncle, where she kneels to you.

Uncle. Fair maid, for you, I love you with my heart,
And grieve, sweet soul, thy fortune is so bad,
That thou shouldst match with such a graceless youth;
Go to thy father; think not upon him,
Whom hell hath marked to be the son of shame.

Luce. Impute his wildness, sir, unto his youth,
And think that now's the time he doth repent:
Alas, what good or gain can you receive,
T'imprison him that nothing hath to pay?
And where naught is, the king doth lose his due:
O, pity him, as God shall pity you.

Uncle. Lady, I know his humors all too well,
And nothing in the world can do him good,
But misery itself to chain him with.

Luce. Say that your debts were paid, then is he free.

Uncle. Ay, virgin, that being answered, I have done
But that to him is as impossible,
As 'twere with me to scale the pyramids.
Shrieve, take your prisoner; maiden, fare thee well.

Luce. O, go not yet, good Master Flowerdale:
Take my word for the debt; my word, my bond.

Flow. Ay, by God, uncle, and my bond too.

Luce. Alas, I ne'er ought[1] nothing but I paid it;
And I can work; alas, he can do nothing:
I have some friends perhaps will pity me,
His chiefest friends do seek his misery.

[1] "Ought"—*owed.*

All that I can, or beg, get, or receive,
Shall be for you: O, do not turn away:
Methinks that one with face so reverent;
So well experienced in this tottering world,
Should have some feeling of a maiden's grief:
For my sake, for his father's, your brother's sake,
Ay, for your soul's sake, that doth hope for joy,
Pity my state; do not two souls destroy.

Uncle. Fair maid, stand up; not in regard of him,
But in [deep] pity of thy hapless choice,
I do release him: Master Shrieve, I thank you:
And officers, there is for you to drink.
Maid, take this money, there's a hundred angels;
And, for I will be sure he shall not have it,
Here, Kester, take it you; use't sparingly,
But let not her have any want at all.
Dry your eyes, niece, do not too much lament
For him whose life hath been in riot spent:
If well he useth thee, he gets him friends;
If ill, a shameful end on him depends. [*Exit* UNCLE.

Flow. A plague go with you for an old fornicator:
Come, Kit, the money, come, honest Kit.

Fath. Nay, by my faith, sir, you shall pardon me.

Flow. And why, sir, pardon you? give me the money, you old rascal, or I shall make you.

Luce. Pray, hold your hands, give it him, honest friend.

Fath. If you be so content, with all my heart.

Flow. Content, sir; 'sblood!—she shall be content
Whether she will or no. A rattle-baby come
To follow me!
Go, get you gone to the greasy chuff your father;
Bring me your dowry, or never look on me.

Fath. Sir, she hath forsook her father, and all her friends for you.

Flow. Hang thee, her friends, and father, altogether.

Fath. Yet part with something to provide her lodging.

Flow. Yes, I mean to part with her and you; but if I part with one angel, hang me at a post. I'll rather throw them at a cast of dice, as I have done a thousand of their fellows.

Fath. Nay, then, I will be plain, degenerate boy,
Thou hadst a father would have been ashamed——

Flow. My father was an ass, an old ass.

Fath. Thy father? [Oh! thou] proud licentious villain;
What are you at your foils? I'll foil with you.

Luce. Good sir, forbear him.

Fath. Did not this whining woman hang on me,
I'd teach thee what 't was t'abuse thy father:
Go hang, beg, starve, dice, game, that when all's gone,
Thou may'st after despair and hang thyself.

Luce. O, do not curse him.

Fath. I do not, but to pray for him were vain;
It grieves me that he bears his father's name.

Flow. Well, you old rascal, I shall meet with you:
Sirrah, get you gone; I will not strip the livery
Over your ears, because you paid for it:
But do not use my name, sirrah, do you hear?
Look [that] you do not; you were best.

Fath. Pay me the twenty pound then that I lent [you,
Or give security when I may have it.

Flow. I'll pay thee not a penny;
And for security, I'll give thee none.
Minckins,[1] look you do not follow me;
If you do, beggar, I shall slit your nose.

Luce. Alas, what shall I do?

Flow. Why [not] turn whore? that's a good trade;
And so perhaps I'll see thee now and then.
[*Exit* FLOWERDALE.

Luce. Alas, the day that ever I was born.

Fath. Sweet mistress, do not weep; I'll stick to you.

Luce. Alas, my friend, I know not what to do;
My father and my friends, they have despised me:
And I, a wretched maid, thus cast away,
Know neither where to go, nor what to say.

Fath. It grieves me to[2] the soul to see her tears
Thus stain the crimson roses of her cheeks:
Lady, take comfort, do not mourn in vain,
I have a little living in this town,
The which I think comes to a hundred pound;
All that and more shall be at your dispose;
I'll strait go help you to some strange disguise,
And place you in a service in this town:
Where you shall know all, yet yourself unknown:
Come, grieve no more, where no help can be had,
Weep not for him, that is more worse than bad.

Luce. I thank you, sir. [*Exeunt.*

ACT IV.

SCENE I.—*A Room in* Sir LAUNCELOT SPURCOCK'S *House, in* Kent.

Enter Sir LAUNCELOT SPURCOCK, Sir ARTHUR, OLIVER, WEATHERCOCK, CIVET, FRANCES, *and* DELIA.

Oli. Well, cha' a bin zerved many a sluttish trick,
But such a lerripoop as thick ych was ne'er sarved

Launce. Son Civet, daughter Frances, bear with me,
You see how I 'm pressed down with inward grief,
About that luckless girl. But, 'tis fallen out
With me, as with many families beside,
They are most unhappy, that are most beloved.

Civet. Father, 'tis even so; 'tis fallen out so!
But what the remedy. Set hand to heart,
And let it pass. Here is your daughter Frances,
And I. We'll not say that we will bring forth.
As witty children, but as pretty children
As ever she was; though she had the prick[3]
And praise for a pretty wench. But, father,
Dun[4] is the mouse;—you'll come?

Launce. Ay, son Civet, I'll come.

Civ. And you, Master Oliver?

Oli. Ay, for che a vext out this veast, chil see if a [gan
Make a better veast there.

Civ. And you, Sir Arthur?

Arth. Ay, sir, although my heart be full,
I'll be a partner at your wedding feast.

Civ. And welcome all indeed, and welcome;
Come, Frank, are you ready?

1 Probably a corruption of mannikin, or minikin—a little fellow.
2 Old copies read, "at the soul."
3 "Prick" was the centre of the target in archery. It was consequently the mark shot at. "Pricked and praised" was a common phrase to designate one who was distinguished over all—who had won the prize.
4 "*Dun* is the mouse." That is to say, you can not change the color of the thing now. A proverbial speech, which occurs in Romeo and Juliet: "Tut: dun's the mouse"

Frances. Jeu, how hasty all these husbands are; I pray, father, pray to God to bless me.

Launce. God bless thee, and I do; God make thee Send you both joy, I wish it with wet eyes. [wise;

Frances. But, father, shall not my sister Delia go along with us? She is excellent good at cookery, and such things.

Launce. Yes, marry shall she: Delia, make you ready.

Delia. I'm ready, sir, I will first go to Greenwich,
From thence to my cousin Chesterfield, and so
To London.

Civ. It shall suffice, good sister Delia, it shall suffice; but fail us not, good sister; give order to cooks, and others; for I would not have my sweet Frank to soil her fingers.

Frances. No, by my troth, not I; a gentlewoman, and a married gentlewoman too, to be companion to cooks and kitchen-boys; not I, i'faith; I scorn that.

Civ. Why, I do not mean thou shalt, sweet heart; thou seest I do not go about it: Well, farewell to you. God's pity, Mr. Weathercock! we shall have your company too?

Weath. With all my heart, for I love good cheer.

Civ. Well, God be with you all; come, Frank.

Frances. God be with you, father, God be with you, Sir Arthur, Master Oliver, and Master Weathercock, sister; God be with you all: God be with you, father; God be with you every one.

[*Exeunt* CIVET *and* FRANCES.

Weath. Why, how now, Sir Arthur, all a mort?
Master Oliver, how now, man?
Cheerly, Sir Launcelot, and merrily say,
Who can hold that will away?

Launce. Ay, she is gone indeed, poor girl, undone;
But when they'll be self-willed, children must smart.

Arth. But, that she is wronged, you are the chiefest cause;
Therefore 'tis reason you redress her wrong.

Weath. Indeed you must, Sir Launcelot, you must.

Launce. Must? who can compel me, Master Weath-
I hope I may do what I list. [ercock?

Weath. I grant you may, you may do what you list.

Oli. Nay, but and you be well evisen, it were not good,
By this vrampolness, and vrowardness, to cast away
As pretty a Dowsabel, as ane could chance to see
In a summer's day: chil tell you what chall do,
Chil go spy up and down the town, and see
If I can hear any tale or tidings of her,
And take her away from thick a messel, vor cham
Assured he will but bring her to the spoil;
And so var well; we shall meet at your son Civet's.

Launce. I thank you, sir, I take it very kindly.

Arth. To find her out, I'll spend my dearest blood.
So well I loved her, to effect her good.

[*Exeunt both.*

Launce. O, Master Weathercock, what hap had I
To force my daughter from Master Oliver,
And this good knight, to one that hath no goodness
In's thought?

Weath. Ill luck; but what the remedy?

Launce. Yes, I have almost devised a remedy,
Young Flowerdale is sure a prisoner.

Weath. Sure, nothing more sure.

Launce. And yet perhaps his uncle hath released him.

Weath. It may be very like, no doubt he hath.

Launce. Well, if he be in prison, I'll have warrants
T'attach my daughter till the law be tried,
For I will sue him upon cozenage.

Weath. Marry, you may, and overthrow him too.

Launce. Nay, that's not so; I may chance to be
And sentence passed with him. [scoffed,

Weath. Believe me, so it may; therefore take heed.

Launce. Well howsoever, yet I will have warrants,
In prison, or at liberty, all's one:
You'll help to serve them, Master Weathercock?

[*Exeunt.*

SCENE II.—*A Street in* London.

Enter MATTHEW FLOWERDALE.

Flow. A plague of the devil; the devil take the dice!—the dice, and the devil, and his dam together! Of all my hundred golden angels, I have not left me one denier: a pox of "*come a five*,"[1] what shall I do? I can borrow no more of my credit: there's not any of my acquaintance, man, nor boy, but I have borrowed more or less of; I would I knew where to take a good purse, and go clear away; by this light, I'll venture for it. God's lid, my sister Delia! I'll rob her, by this hand.

Enter DELIA *and* ARTICHOKE.

Delia. I pr'ythee, Artichoke, go not so fast,
The weather's hot, and I am something weary.

Arti. Nay, I warrant you, Mistress Delia, I'll not tire you
With leading, we'll go an extreme moderate pace.

Flow. Stand, deliver your purse.

Arti. O, Lord, thieves, thieves!

[*Exit* ARTICHOKE.

Flow. Come, come, your purse, lady; your purse.

Delia. That voice I have heard often before this time;
What, brother Flowerdale become a thief?

Flow. Ay, plague on't!—thank your father!
But sister, come, your money, come: What!
The world must find me; I was born to live;
'Tis not a sin to steal, when none will give.

Delia. O, God, is all grace banished from thy heart,
Think of the shame that doth attend this fact.

Flow. Shame me no shames; come, give me your purse;
I'll bind you, sister, lest I fare the worse.

Delia. No, bind me not; hold; there is all I have,
And would that money would redeem thy shame.

Enter OLIVER, SIR ARTHUR, *and* ARTICHOKE.

Arti. Thieves, thieves, thieves!

Oli. Thieves! where man? why, how now, Mistress Delia;
Ha' you a liked to been a robbed?

Delia. No, Master Oliver, 'tis Master Flowerdale;
He did but jest with me.

Oli. How, Flowerdale, that scoundrel? sirrah, you meten us well; vang[2] thee that. [*Strikes him.*

Flow. Well, sir, I'll not meddle with you, because I have a charge.

1 "*Come a five!*" was his invocation to the dice;—a pox on it, for he uttered it in vain.

2 *Vang thee that*—"take notice," in the jargon of Devonshire.

Delia. Here, brother Flowerdale, I'll lend you this same money.

Flow. I thank you, sister.

Oli. I wad you were ysplit, an you let the mezel have a penny; but since you can not keep it, chil keep it myself.

Arth. 'Tis pity to relieve him in this sort,
Who makes a triumphant life[1] his daily sport.

Delia. Brother, you see how all men censure you:
Farewell, and I pray God t'amend your life.

Oli. Come, chil bring you along, and you safe enough from twenty such scoundrels as thick an one is. Farewell, and be hanged, zirrah, as I think so thou wilt be shortly. Come, Sir Arthur.

[*Exeunt all but* FLOWERDALE.

Flow. A plague go with you for a kersey rascal!
This De'nshire man I think is made all pork,
His hands made only for to heave up packs;
His heart as fat and big as his face,
As differing far from all brave gallant minds,
As I to serve the hogs, and drink with hinds,
As I am very near now. Well, what remedy?
When money, means, and friends, do grow so small,
Then farewell life, and there's an end of all! [*Exit.*

SCENE III.—*Another Street, before Civet's House.*

Enter FLOWERDALE, senior, LUCE *like a Dutch Frow,* CIVET, *and* FRANCES.

Civ. By my troth, God 'a mercy for this, good Christopher! I thank thee for my maid; like her well: how dost thou like her, Frances?

Frances. In good sadness, Tom, very well, excellent well;
She speaks so prettily.—I pray what's your name?

Luce. My name, forsooth, be called Tanikin.

Frances. By my troth, a fine name: O Tanikin, you are excellent for dressing one's head a new fashion.

Luce. Me sall do everyting about de head.

Civ. What countrywoman is she, Kester?

Fath. A Dutch woman, sir.

Civ. Why, then, she is outlandish, is she not?

Fath. Ay, sir, she is.

Frances. O, then thou canst tell how to help me to cheeks and ears.[2]

Luce. Yes, mistress, wery vell.

Fath. Cheeks and ears! Why, Mistress Frances, why want you cheeks and ears? methinks you have very fair ones.

Frances. Thou art a fool, indeed. Tom, thou knowest what I mean.

Civ. Ay, ay, Kester, 'tis such as they wear o' their heads. I pr'ythee, Kit, have her in, and show her my house.

Fath. I will, sir; come, Tanikin.

Frances. Oh! Tom, you have not bussed me today, Tom.

Civ. No, Frances, we must not kiss afore folks:
God save me, Frank! see yonder: Delia's come;—

Enter DELIA *and* ARTICHOKE.

Welcome, good sister.

Frances. Welcome, sister; how do you like the 'tire of my head?

Delia. Very well, sister.

Civ. I am glad you're come, sister Delia, to give order for supper; they will be here soon.

Arti. Ay, but if good luck had not served, she had not been here now: filching Flowerdale had like to have peppered us; but for Master Oliver, we had been robbed.

Delia. Peace, sirrah! no more.

Fath. Robbed! by whom?

Arti. Marry, by none but Flowerdale; he's turned thief.

Civ. By my faith, but that's not well; but, God be praised
For your escape; will you draw near, my sister?

Fath. Sirrah, come hither; would Flowerdale, he that was my master, have robbed you? I pr'ythee tell me true?

Arti. Yes, faith, even that Flowerdale that was thy master.

Fath. Hold thee, there's a French crown—speak no more of this. [*Aside.*

Arti. Not I; not a word: now do I smell knavery:
In every purse this Flowerdale takes, he's half—
And gives me this to keep counsel: not a word I!

Fath. Why, God ha' mercy!

Frances. Sister, look here; I have a new Dutch maid,
And she speaks so fine, it would do your heart good.

Civ. How do you like her, sister?

Delia. I like your maid well.

Civ. Well, dear sister, will you draw near, and give directions for supper? The guests will be here presently.

Delia. Yes, brother, lead the way; I'll follow you,
[*Exeunt all but* DELIA *and* LUCE.
Hark you, Dutch frow, a word.

Luce. Vat is your vill wit me?

Delia. Sister Luce, 'tis not your broken language,
Nor this same habit, can disguise your face
From I that know you. Pray tell me, what means this?

Luce. Sister, I see you know me, yet be secret:
This borrowed shape that I have ta'en upon me
Is but to keep myself a space unknown,
Both from my father and my nearest friends,
Until I see how time will bring to pass
The desperate course of Master Flowerdale.

Delia. O, he is worse than bad; I pr'ythee leave him,
And let not once thy heart to think on him.

Luce. Do not persuade me now to such a thought;
Imagine yet that he is worse than naught:
Yet one hour's[3] time may all that ill undo
That all his former life did run into.
Therefore, kind sister, do not disclose my state;
If e'er his heart doth turn, 'tis ne'er too late.

Delia. Well, seeing no counsel can remove your mind,
I'll not disclose you, that art wilful blind.

Luce. Delia, I thank you. I now must please her eyes,
My sister Frank, who's neither fair nor wise.
[*Exeunt.*

1 Triumphant life, or triumphant vice? There is something wrong about this passage. Some happy suggestion may make better sense of it to the reader.

2 Malone thinks that this inquiry relates to some fashionable head-dress.

3 The old folio reads "lover's," and it is barely possible that we should ascribe his cure to love rather than time.

ACT V.

SCENE I.—*Street before* CIVET'S *House.*

Enter M. FLOWERDALE, *solus.*

Flow. On goes he that knows no end of his journey! I have passed the very utmost bounds of shifting; I have no course now but to hang myself. I have lived since yesterday, two o'clock, of a spice-cake I had at a burial:[1] and for drink, I got it at an alehouse, among porters—such as will bear out a man, if he have no money indeed,—I mean, out of their companies,—for they are men of good carriage.[2] Who comes here? The two cony-catchers, that won all my money of me. I'll try if they'll lend me any.

Enter DICK *and* RALPH.

What, Master Richard, how do you do? How do'st thou, Ralph? By God! gentlemen, the world grows bare with me: will you do as much as lend me an angel between you both?—you know you won a hundred of me t'other day.

Ralph. How, an angel?
Damn us if we lost not every penny
Within an hour after thou wert gone!

Flow. I pr'ythee lend me so much as will pay for my supper;
I'll pay you again, as I am a gentleman.

Ralph. I'faith, we've not a farthing, not a mite:
I wonder at it, Master Flowerdale,
You will so carelessly undo yourself.
Why, you will lose more money in an hour,
Than any honest man spends in a year.
For shame, betake you to some honest trade,
And live not thus so like a vagabond!
[*Exeunt both.*

Flow. A vagabond, indeed! more villains you:
They give me counsel that first cozened me.
Those devils first brought me to this I am,
And, being thus, the first that do me wrong.
Well, yet I have one friend left me in store:
Not far from hence there dwells a cockatrice,[3]
One that I first put in a satin gown;
And not a tooth that dwells within her head,
But stands me at the least in twenty pound:
Her will I visit, now my coin is gone,
Here, as I take it, dwells the gentlewoman.
What, ho! is Mistress Apricock within?

Enter RUFFIAN.

Ruff. What saucy rascal is't that knocks so bold?
Oh! is it you, old spendthrift? are you here?
One that's turned cozener about the town?
My mistress saw you, and sends this word by me:
Either be packing quickly from the door,
Or you shall have such greeting sent you straight
As you will little like. You had best begone. [*Exit.*

Flow. Why, so, this is as it should be: being poor,
Thus art thou served by a vile, painted whore
Well, since the damnéd crew do so abuse me,
I'll try, of honest men, how they will use me.

Enter an ancient Citizen.

Sir, I beseech you to take compassion of a man; one whose fortunes have been better than at this instant they seem to be: but if I might crave of you so much little portion as would bring me to my friends, I would rest thankful until I had requited so great a courtesy.

Citi. Fie! fie! young man, this course is very bad;
Too many such have we about this city;
Yet, for I have not seen you in this sort,
Nor noted you to be a common beggar—
Hold, there's an angel to bear your charges down:
Go to your friends; do not on this depend;
Such bad beginnings oft have worser end.
[*Exit* Citizen.

Flow. Worser end! Nay, if it fall out no worse than in old angels, I care not! Now, that I have had such a fortunate beginning, I'll not let a six-penny purse escape me. By the mass, here comes another!

Enter a Citizen's Wife, *with* Servant, *and a torch before her.*

God bless you, fair mistress! Now, would it please you, gentlewoman, to look into the wants of a poor gentleman—a younger brother: I doubt not but God will treble restore it back again; one that never before this time demanded penny, halfpenny, nor farthing?

Citi. Wife. Stay, Alexander. Now, by my troth, a very proper man; and 'tis great pity. Hold, my friend; there's all the money I have about me—a couple of shillings: and God bless thee.

Flow. Now God thank you, sweet lady: if you have any friend, or garden-house where you may employ a poor gentleman as your friend, I am yours to command in all secret service.

Citi. Wife. I thank you, good friend; I pr'ythee let me see that again I gave thee; there is one of them a brass shilling: give me them, and here is half-a-crown in gold. [*He gives it her.*
Now out upon thee, rascal! Secret service—what dost thou make of me? It were a good deed to have thee whipped! Now I have my money again, I'll see thee hanged before I give thee a penny. Secret service!—On, good Alexander. [*Exeunt both.*

Flow. This is villanous luck; I perceive dishonesty will not thrive: here comes more! God forgive me! Sir Arthur and Master Oliver! Afore God, I'll speak to them. God save you, Sir Arthur. God save you, Master Oliver.

Oli. Been you there, zirrah? Come, will you taken yourself to your tools, coystrel?

Flow. Nay, Master Oliver, I'll not fight with you; alas! sir, you know it was not my doings; it was only a plot to get Sir Launcelot's daughter: by God, I never meant you harm.

Oli. And where is the gentlewoman thy wife, mezel? Where is she, zirrah, ha?

Flow. By my troth, Master Oliver, sick, very sick; an God is my judge, I know not what means to take for her, good gentlewoman.

1 There was always some refreshment at ancient funerals: rich cake for the mourners, and poor cake (which includes the prodigal's spice-cake) for the populace.

2 A quibble between carrying burdens and demeanor. MALONE.

3 A prostitute.

Oli. Tell me true, is she sick? Tell me true, itch 'vise thee.

Flow. Yes, faith, I tell you true: Master Oliver, if you would do me the small kindness but to lend me forty shillings, so God help me, I will pay you so soon as my ability shall make me able, as I am a gentleman.

Oli. Well, thou zayest thy wife is zick: hold, there's vorty shillings; give it to thy wife; look thou give it her, or I shall so veze thee, thou wert not so vezed this zeven year; look to it.

Arth. I'faith, Master Oliver, it is in vain
To give to him that never thinks of her.

Oli. Well, would che could yvind it.

Flow. I tell you true, Sir Arthur, as I am a gentleman.

Oli. Well, farewell, zirrah. Come, Sir Arthur.
[*Exeunt both.*

Flow. By the Lord, this is excellent!
Five golden angels compassed in an hour:
If this trade hold, I'll never seek a new;—
Welcome, sweet gold, and beggary adieu.

Enter FLOWERDALE, senior, *and* FLOWERDALE, junior.

Uncle. See, Kester, if you can find the house.

Flow. Who's here—my uncle, and my man Kester? By the mass, 'tis they! How do you, uncle? how do'st thou, Kester? By my troth, uncle, you must needs lend me some money; the poor gentlewoman my wife, so God help me, is very sick; I was robbed of the hundred angels you gave me; they are gone.

Uncle. Ay, they are gone, indeed: come, Kester, away.

Flow. Nay, uncle, do you hear? good uncle!

Uncle. Out, hypocrite! I will not hear thee speak.
Come, leave him, Kester.

Flow. Kester, honest Kester!

Fath. Sir, I have naught to say to you.—
Open the door to me. 'Kin, thou hadst best
Lock fast, for there's a false knave [here] without.

Flow. You are an old lying rascal, so you are!
[FLOWERDALE, sen., *and* FLOWERDALE, jun., *go in.*

Enter LUCE *from* CIVET'S *House.*

Luce. Vat is de matter? Vat be you, yonker?

Flow. By this light, a Dutch frow; they say they are called kind; I'll try her.

Luce. Vat be you, yonker? Why do you not speak?

Flow. By my troth, sweetheart, a poor gentleman that would desire of you, if it stand with your liking, the bounty of your purse.

Re-enter FLOWERDALE, senior.

Luce. O hear him, God! so young an armin.[1]

Flow. Armin, sweetheart? I know not what you mean by that; but I am almost a beggar.

Luce. Are you not a married man? Vere been your vife? Here's all I have; take dis.

Flow. What! gold, young frow? This is brave.

Fath. If he have any grace, he'll now repent.
[*Aside.*

Luce. Why speak you not? Vere be your vife?

Flow. Dead, dead, she's dead; 'tis she that hath undone me? Spent me all I had, and kept rascals under my nose to brave me.

Luce. Did you use her vell?

Flow. Use her! there's never a gentlewoman in England could be better used than I did her. I could but coach her; her diet stood me in forty pound a month; but she is dead, and in her grave; my cares are buried.

Luce. Indeed! dat vas not scone.[2]

Fath. He is turned more devil than he was before.
[*Aside.*

Flow. Thou dost belong to Master Civet here:
Dost thou not?

Luce. Yes, me do.

Flow. Why, there's it!
There's not a handful of plate but [it] belongs
To me. God's my judge, if I [but] had
Such a wench as thou, there's never a man
In England would make more of her than I
Would do—so she had any stock?

[*Voice within.*] Why, Tanikin!

Luce. Stay; one doth call. I shall come by-and-by. Again! [*Call within. Exit* LUCE *within.*

Flow. By this hand, this Dutch wench is in love [with me!
Were it not admirable to make her steal
All Civet's plate, and run away [with me]?

Fath. It were beastly! O, Master Flowerdale!
Have you no fear of God, nor conscience?
What do you mean by this vile course you take?

Flow. What do I mean? why, to live: 'tis that I mean.

Fath. To live in this sort? fie upon the course!
Your life doth show, you are a very coward.

Flow. A coward! I pray in what?

Fath. Why, you will borrow sixpence of a boy.

Flow. 'Snails, is there such a cowardice in that? I dare borrow it of a man; ay, and of the tallest man in England,—if he will lend it me: let me borrow it how I can, and let them come by it how they dare. And it is well known, I might have rid out a hundred times if I would; so I might.

Fath. It was not want of will, but cowardice;
There is none that lends to you, but know they gain;
And what is that but only stealth in you?
Delia might hang you now, did not her heart
Take pity of you for her sister's sake.
Go, get you hence, lest ling'ring here your stay,
You fall into their hands you look not for.

Flow. I'll tarry here, till the Dutch frow comes, if all the devils in hell were here.

FLOWERDALE, senior, *goes into* CIVET'S *House. Enter* Sir LAUNCELOT, Master WEATHERCOCK, *and* ARTICHOKE.

Launce. Where is the door? are we not past it, Artichoke?

Arti. By the mass, here's one; I'll ask him. Do you hear, sir? What, are you so proud? Do you hear? which is the way to Master Civet's house? what, will you not speak? O, me! This is filching Flowerdale.

Lance. O, wonderful! is this lewd villain here?
You cheating rogue, you cutpurse, cony-catcher,
What ditch, you villain, is my daughter's grave?
A cozening rascal, that must make a will!

[1] *Armin*—beggar.

[2] *Nicht-schoon*—"not handsome."

Take on him that strict habit; very that;—
When he should turn to angel; 'a dying grace! [will:
I'll father-in-law you, sir; I'll make [you make] a
Speak, villain, where's my daughter? [Speak, I say!]
Poisoned, I warrant you, or knocked o' the head!
And to abuse good Master Weathercock,
With his forged will; and Master Weathercock,
To make[1] my grounded resolution;
Then to abuse the De'nshire gentleman:
Go; away with him to prison.

Flow. Wherefore to prison? Sir, I will not go.

Enter Master CIVET, *his* Wife, OLIVER, Sir ARTHUR, FLOWERDALE, senior *and* junior, *and* DELIA.

Launce. Oh! here's his uncle! Welcome, gentlemen,
Welcome all! Such a cozener gentlemen!
A murderer too, for anything I know;—
My daughter's missing; hath been looked for; can
Be found! — A vild upon thee! [not

Uncle. He is my kinsman, though his life be vile;
Therefore, in God's name, do with him what you will.

Launce. Marry, to prison.

Flow. Wherefore to prison? snick-up;[2] I owe you nothing.

Launce. Bring forth my daugher, then; away with him.

Flow. Go seek your daughter; what do you lay to my charge?

Launce. Suspicion of murder; go, away with him.

Flow. Murder your dogs; I murder your daughter?
Come, uncle; I know you'll bail me.

Uncle. Not I, were there no more,
Than I the gaoler, thou the prisoner.

Launce. Go; away with him.

Enter LUCE.

Luce. O'my life, where will you ha de man?
Vat ha de yonker done?

Weath. Woman, he hath killed his wife.

Luce. His wife, dat is not good; dat is not scone.[3]

Launce. Hang not upon him, huswife; if you do I'll lay you by him.

Luce. Have me no oder way dan you have him!
He tell me dat he love me heartily.

Frances. Lead away my maid to prison; why, Tom, will you suffer that?

Civet. No, by your leave, father, she is no vagrant:
She is my wife's chambermaid, and as true as the skin
Between any man's brows here.

Launce. Go to, you're both fools:
Son Civet, o' my life, this is a plot;
Some straggling counterfeit preferred to you;
No doubt, to rob you of your plate and jewels:
I'll have you led away to prison, trull.

Luce. I am no trull, neither outlandish frow;
Nor he, nor I, shall to the prison go:
Know you me now? Nay, never stand amazed.
Father, I know I have offended you,
And though that duty wills me bend my knee,
To you, in duty and obedience;
Yet this way do I turn, and to him yield
My love, my duty, and my humbleness.

Launce. Bastard in nature, kneel to such a slave?

Luce. O, Master Flowerdale, if too much grief
Have not stopped up the organs of your voice,
Then speak to her that is thy faithful wife;
Or doth contempt of me thus tie thy tongue:
Turn not away, I am no Ethiop,
No wanton Cressid, nor a changing Helen:
But rather one made wretched by thy loss.
What! turnest thou still from me? O, then,
I guess thee wofullest 'mong hapless men.

Flow. I am, indeed, wife;—wonder among wives!
Thy chastity and virtue hath infused
Another soul in me; red with defame,
For, in my blushing cheeks is seen my shame.

Launce. Out, hypocrite! I charge thee, trust him not.

Luce. Not trust him; by the hopes of after bliss,
I know no sorrow can be compared to his.

Launce. Well, since thou wert ordained to beggary,
Follow thy fortune. I defy thee, I——

Oli. Ywood che were so well ydoussed as was ever white
Cloth in tocking mill, an che ha not made me weep.

Fath. If he hath any grace he'll now repent.

Arth. It moves my heart.

Weath. By my troth, I must weep; I can not choose.

Uncle. None but a beast would such a maid misuse.

Flow. Content thyself; I hope to win his favor,
And to redeem my reputation lost:
And gentlemen, believe me, I beseech you;
I hope your eyes shall [soon] behold such change,
As shall deceive your expectation.

Oli. I would che were split now, but che believe him.

Launce. How, believe him?

Weath. By the mackins, I do.

Launce. What do you think that ever he'll have grace?

Weath. By my faith it will go hard.

Oli. Well, che vor ye he is changed; and Master Flowerdale, in hope you been so, hold, there's vorty pound toward your zetting up: what! be not ashamed; vang it man, vang it; be a good husband; loving to your wife: and you shall not want for vorty more, I che vor thee.

Arth. My means are little, but if you'll allow[4] me
I will instruct you in my ablest power:
But to your wife I give this diamond;
And prove true diamond, fair, in all your life.

Flow. Thanks, good Sir Arthur: Master Oliver,
You being my enemy, and grown so kind,
Binds me in all endeavor to restore.

Oli. What! restore me no restorings, man; I have vorty pound more here; vang it: zouth chil devie London else: what, do not think me a mezel or a scoundrel, to throw away my money? che have an hundred pound more to pace of any good spotation: I hope your under and your uncle will vollow my zamples.

Uncle. You have guessed right of me; if he leave
This course of life, he [yet] shall be mine heir. [off

[1] To unmake, rather—to mar.

[2] Malone tells us that "snick-up" is equivalent to the modern phrase, "go hang yourself."

[3] Not handsome—*Nicht-schoon.*

[4] The old copies read, "follow."

Launce. But he shall never get a groat of me!
A cozener, a deceiver; one that killed
His painful father; honest gentleman,
That passed the fearful danger of the sea,
To get him living and maintain him brave.
Weath. What! hath he killed his father?
Launce. Ay, sir, with conceit
Of his vile courses.
Fath. Sir, you are misinformed.
Launce. Why, thou old knave, thou told'st me so thyself.
Fath. I wronged him, then; toward my master's stock
There's twenty nobles for to make amends.
Flow. No, Kest, I've troubled thee, and wronged thee more;
What thou in love giv'st, I in love restore.
Frances. Ha! ha! sister, there you played bo-peep with Tom;
What shall I give her toward her household, sister?
Delia, shall I give her my fan?
Delia. You were best ask your husband.
Frances. Shall I, Tom?
Civet. Ay, do, Frank;
I'll buy thee a new one, with a longer handle.
Frances. A russet one, Tom?
Civet. Ay, with russet feathers.
Frances. Here, sister, there's my fan toward your household,
To keep you warm.[1]
Luce. I thank you, sister.
Weath. Why, this is well; and toward fair Luce's stock,
Here's forty shillings: and forty good shillings more,
I'll give her, marry. Come, Sir Launcelot, I
Must have you friends.
Launce. Not I; all this is counterfeit!
He will consume it, were it a million.
Fath. Sir, what is your daughter's dower worth?
Launce. Had she been married to an honest man,
It had been better than a thousand pound.
Fath. Pay it him, [then] and I'll give you my bond,
To make her jointure better worth than three.
Launce. Your bond, sir! why, what are you?
Fath. One whose word in London, though I say it,
Will pass there for as much as yours.
Launce. Wert not thou late, that unthrift's serving-man?
Fath. Look on me better, now my scar is off;
Ne'er muse, man, at this metamorphosis.
Launce. Master Flowerdale!
Flow. My father! Oh! I shame to look on him.
Pardon, dear father, the follies that are passed.
Fath. Son, son, I do, and joy at this thy change;
And 'plaud thy fortune in this virtuous maid,
Whom Heaven hath sent to thee to save thy soul.
Luce. This addeth joy to joy; high Heaven be praised.
Weath. Welcome from death, good Master Flowerdale.
'Twas said so here, 'twas said so here, good faith.
Fath. I caused that rumor to be spread myself,
Because I'd see the humors of my son,
Which to relate the circumstance is needless:
And, sirrah, see you run no more in that disease;
For he that's once cured of that malady,
Of riot, swearing, drunkenness, and pride,
And falls again into the like distress,—
That fever is deadly;—doth till death, endure:
Such men die mad, as of a calenture.
Flow. Heaven helping me, I'll hate the course as hell.
Uncle. Say it, and do it, cousin, all is well.
Launce. Well, being in hope you'll prove an honest man,
I take you to my favor. Brother Flowerdale,
Welcome with all my heart. I see your care
Hath brought these acts to this conclusion,
And I am glad of it; come, let's in and feast.
Oli. Nay, zost you a while; you promised to make
Sir Arthur and me amends; here is your wisest
Daughter; see which on's she'll have.
Launce. A' God's name, you have my good will; get hers.
Oli. How say you, then, damsel; tyters hate?
Delia. I, sir, am yours.
Oli. Why, then, send for the vicar, and chil have it
Despatched in a trice, so chil.
Delia. Pardon me, sir; I mean [that] I am yours,
In love, in duty, and affection;
But not to love as wife; shall ne'er be said,
Delia was buried married, but a maid.
Arth. Do not condemn yourself for ever [thus],
[Most] virtuous fair; for you were born to love.
Oli. Why, you say true, Sir Arthur; she was ybore to it,
So well as her mother:—but I pray you show us
Some zamples or reasons why you will not marry?
Delia. Not that I do condemn a married life,
For 'tis, no doubt, a sanctimonious thing:
But for the care and crosses of a wife,
The trouble in this world that children bring,
My vow's in heaven, on earth to live alone;
Husbands, however good, I will have none.
Oli. Why, then, chil live a bachelor too! Che zet not a vig by a wife, if a wife zet not a vig by me: come, shall's go to dinner?
Fath. To-morrow I crave your companies in Mark-lane:
To-night we'll frolic in Master Civet's house,
And to each health drink down a full carouse.
[*Exeunt.*

THE END OF THE LONDON PRODIGAL.

1 We must not think too lightly of the gift, toward Luce's housekeeping, of the silly sister Frances. Fans were costly things at the period of our play. Their handles were of considerable length, probably to be used by pages, and were of silver, and inlaid with ornaments.

INTRODUCTION

TO

THOMAS LORD CROMWELL.

The first edition of this play was published in 1602, under the title of the "Chronicle History of Thomas Lord Cromwell." No name or initials, of any author, appear in the titlepage of this edition. "A booke called the Life and Death of the Lord Cromwell, as yt was lately acted by the Lord Chamberleyn his Servantes," was entered on the stationer's books, by William Cotton, on the 11th August, of the same year. In 1613 appeared "The True Chronicle Historie of the whole Life and Death of Thomas Lord Cromwell: as it hath been sundry times publickly acted by the King's Majestie's Servants: Written by W. S." It appears, therefore, that the play was originally performed, and continued to be performed, by the company in which Shakspeare himself was a chief proprietor. Whether this fact can make at all, either one way or the other, in resolving the question of authorship, is a matter which the reader may decide for himself, quite as readily as if he had the assistance of an editor. Shakspeare was in London, and connected with the actors, as a proprietor, up to 1613, the year when this play was first published with the initials W. S.; and we are, therefore, almost at liberty to assume that, if not by himself, and by another having the same initials, he was yet not unwilling that his theatre should derive from the publication all the advantages which might be expected to accrue from his supposed authorship of the piece.

Beyond the initials, in the edition of 1613, there is no external evidence whatever, by which we should ascribe Sir Thomas Cromwell to William Shakspeare. If the question depended upon the intrinsic evidence, assuming, for the standards by which to judge of its qualities, any of the acknowledged and unquestionable plays of his mature genius, we should unhesitatingly reject the claim. There is nothing in the performance to entitle it, as a production of Shakspeare, to the smallest consideration.

Thomas, Lord Cromwell, is a very feeble effort, almost totally deficient in poetry, and lamentably wanting as a work of art. The story is disjointed, rambling, and purposeless; and, but for a something of sedateness in the thought, occasional passages which show good sense, and an appreciation of the general characteristics of humanity, with a very tolerable individualization of the persons of the drama, it would be wholly without a redeeming feature. And yet there are critics who find it in possession of considerable merits, which escape our search. Schlegel, speaking of this play, of "the Yorkshire Tragedy," and of "Sir John Oldcastle," says: "*They are not only unquestionably Shakspeare's, but, in my opinion, they deserve to be classed among his best and maturest works.*" After this judgment, we may well hesitate to speak our own. Schlegel proceeds to describe them as "biographical dramas, and models in this species." Biographical they are, certainly — singularly so, indeed — since, in this play of Sir Thomas, we have almost all the events of his life, from his earliest manhood to his death, crowded into the scene with a rapidity of action which defies all reason and probability, and largely overleaps the usual privileges of the dramatic historian. But to call this play, or either of the others mentioned, a model of its kind, betrays a large liberality in the critic which we can not conscientiously emulate Mr. Knight, at the close of his analysis of this play, remarks, that "it would be a waste of time to attempt to show that Thomas Lord Cromwell could not have been written by Shakspeare." Certainly it would be, if the question were to depend entirely upon the arbitrary requisition of the commentators, that Shakspeare's writings must be all of them of a uniform excellence, determined by standards drawn from our sense of his highest excellences. This, however, is not permitted us. But this point we have considered in another place. It has been suggested, that "W. S." might be the initials of Wentworth Smith, another dramatic writer, of whom little is known, but for whom this play has never been claimed.

It remains to add, that the subject of Sir Thomas Cromwell is derived from Fuller, Stow, Speed, Holingshead, and other English chroniclers. The events are narrated at large, in Fox's Book of Martyrs. The particulars relating to Frescobald, the benevolent Italian, were first published by Bandello, the novelist, in 1554: "Francesco Frescobaldi, fa cortessa ad un straniero, e nè ben remeritato, essendo colui diuenuto contestabile d'Inghilterra." His story is translated by Fox.

THE HISTORY OF THE LIFE AND DEATH OF

THOMAS LORD CROMWELL.

PERSONS REPRESENTED.

DUKE OF NORFOLK.
DUKE OF SUFFOLK.
EARL OF BEDFORD.
Cardinal WOLSEY.
GARDINER, *Bishop of* Winchester.
Sir THOMAS MORE.
Sir CHRISTOPHER HALES.
Sir RALPH SADLER.
Old CROMWELL, *a blacksmith of* Putney.
THOMAS CROMWELL, *his son.*
BANISTER, BOWSER, NEWTON, CROSBY, } English *merchants.*
BAGOT, *a money-broker.*
FRESCOBALD, *a* Florentine *merchant.*
The Governor of the English *factory at* Antwerp.
Governor and other officers of Bolognia.
Master of an hotel in Bolognia.
SEELY, *a publican of* Hounslow.
Lieutenant of the Tower.
Young CROMWELL, *the son of* Thomas.
HODGE, WILL, *and* TOM, *old* Cromwell's *servants.*
Two Citizens.

MRS. BANISTER.
JOAN, *wife to* Seely.

Two Witnesses; a Sergeant-at-arms; a Herald; a Hangman; a Post; Messengers; Officers; Ushers, and Attendants.

SCENE,—*Partly in* LONDON, *and the adjoining Districts; partly in* ANTWERP *and* BOLOGNIA.

ACT I.

SCENE I.—Putney. *The entrance of a Smith's shop.*

Enter HODGE, WILL, *and* TOM.

Hodge. Come, masters, I think it be past five o'clock. Is it not time we were at work? My old master, he'll be stirring anon.

Will. I can not tell whether my old master will be stirring or no; but I am sure I can hardly take my afternoon's nap, for my young Master Thomas. He keeps such a coil in his study, with the sun, and the moon, and the seven stars, that I do verily think he'll read out his wits.

Hodge. He skill of the stars! There's Goodman Car of Fulham (he that carried us to the strong ale, where Goody Trundel had her maid got with child): O, he knows the stars; he'll tickle you Charles's Wain in nine degrees. That same man will tell Goody Trundel when her ale shall miscarry, only by the stars.

Tom. That's a great virtue, indeed; I think Thomas be nobody in comparison to him.

Will. Well, masters, come; shall we to our hammers?

Hodge. Ay, content; first let's take our morning's draught, and then to work, roundly.

Tom. Ay, agreed. Go in, Hodge. [*Exeunt.*

SCENE II.—*The same.*

Enter young CROMWELL.

Crom. Good morrow, morn; I do salute thy brightness!
The night seems tedious to my troubled soul,
Whose black obscurity breeds[1] in my mind
A thousand sundry cogitations:
And now Aurora, with a lively dye,
Adds comfort to my spirit that mounts high;[2]
Too high, indeed, my state being so mean.
My study, like a mineral of gold,
Makes my heart proud, wherein my hope's enrolled;
My books are all the wealth I do possess,
And unto them I have engaged my heart.
Oh, Learning! how divine thou seem'st to me,—
Within whose arms is all felicity.
[*Smiths within hammer.*
Peace with your hammers, leave your knocking there!
You do disturb my study and my rest:—
Leave off, I say:—you mad me with your noise.

Enter HODGE, WILL, *and* TOM, *from within.*

Hodge. Why, how now, Master Thomas, how now, Will you not let us work for you?

Crom. You fret my heart, with making of this noise.

[1] Old copy, "binds." [2] Former copies read, "on high."

Hodge. How! fret your heart? Ay, Thomas, but you'll fret
Your father's purse if you let us from working.
Tom. Ay, this 'tis for to make him a gentleman:
Shall we leave work for your musing? That's well, i'faith;
But here comes my old master, now

Enter old CROMWELL.

Old Crom. You idle knaves, why are you loit'ring now?
No hammers walking,[1] and my work to do?
What, not a heat among your work to-day?
Hodge. Marry, sir, your son Thomas will not let us work at all.
Old Crom. Why, knave, I say, have I thus carked and cared,
And all to keep thee like a gentleman;
And dost thou let my servants at their work,
That sweat for thee, knave—labor thus for thee?
Crom. Father, their hammers do offend my study.
Old Crom. Out of my doors, knave, if thou lik'st it not:
I cry you mercy; are your ears so fine?
I tell thee, knave, these get when I do sleep;
I will not have my anvil stand for thee.
Crom. There's money, father; I will pay your men. [*Throws money among them.*
Old Crom. Have I thus brought thee up unto my cost,
In hope that one day thou'dst relieve my age,
And art thou now so lavish of thy coin,
To scatter it among these idle knaves?
Crom. Father, be patient, and content yourself:
The time will come I shall hold gold as trash:
And here, I speak with a presaging soul,
To build a palace where this cottage stands,
As fine as is King Henry's house at Sheen.
Old Crom. You build a house! You knave, you'll be a beggar!
Now, afore God, all is but cast away,
That is bestowed upon this thriftless lad!
Well, had I bound him to some honest trade,
This had not been; but 'twas his mother's doing,
To send him to the university.
How? Build a house where now this cottage stands,
As fair as that at Sheen?—they shall not hear me! [*Aside.*
A good boy, Tom; I con thee;—thank thee, Tom,
Well said, Tom; Gramercy to ye, Tom!
In to your work, knaves; hence [thou] saucy boy.
[*Exeunt all but young* CROMWELL.
Crom. Why should my birth keep down my mounting spirit?
Are not all creatures subject unto time;
To time who doth abuse the cheated world,
And fills it full of hodge-podge bastardy?
There's legions now of beggars on the earth,
That their original did spring from kings;
And many monarchs now, whose fathers were
The riff-raff of their age; for time and fortune
Wear out a noble train to beggary;
And from the dunghill, minions[2] do advance
To state and mark in this admiring world.
This is but course, which, in the name of fate,

1 Quere: *Working?* 2 Quere: *Millions?*

Is seen as often as it whirls about.
The river Thames, that by our door doth pass,
His first beginning is but small and shallow;
Yet, keeping on his course, grows to a sea.
And likewise Wolsey, the wonder of our age,
His birth as mean as mine, a butcher's son;
Now, who, within this land a greater man?
Then, Cromwell, cheer thee up, and tell thy soul,
That thou may'st live to flourish and control.

Enter old CROMWELL.

Old Crom. Tom Cromwell; what, Tom, I say!
Crom. Do you call, sir?
Old Crom. Here is Master Bowser come to know if you have despatched his petition for the lords of the council, or no.
Crom. Father, I have; please you to call him in.
Old Crom. That's well said, Tom; a good lad, Tom.

Enter Master BOWSER.

Bow. Now, Master Cromwell, have you despatched this petition?
Crom. I have, sir; here it is; please you, peruse it.
Bow. It shall not need; we'll read't as we go by water.
And, Master Cromwell, I have made a motion
May do you good, an if you like of it.
Our secretary at Antwerp, sir, is dead,
And [now] the merchants there have sent to me,
For to provide a man fit for the place:
Now, I do know none fitter than yourself,
If it stand with your liking, Master Cromwell.
Crom. With all my heart, sir; and I much am bound,
In love and duty for your kindness shown.
Old Crom. Body o'me, Tom, make haste, lest somebody get between thee and honor, Tom.[3] I thank you, good Master Bowser, I thank you for my boy; I thank you always; I thank you most heartily, sir: Ho, a cup of beer here for Master Bowser.
Bow. It shall not need, sir: Master Cromwell, will you go?
Crom. I will attend you, sir.
Old Crom. Farewell, Tom; God bless thee, Tom; God speed thee, good Tom. [*Exeunt*

SCENE III.—London. *A Street before* FRESCOBALD'S *House.*

Enter BAGOT.

Bag. I hope this day is fatal unto some,
And by their loss must Bagot seek to gain.
This is the lodge of Master Frescobald,
A liberal merchant and a Florentine,
To whom Banister owes a thousand pound;
A merchant bankrupt, whose father was my master.
What do I care for pity or regard?
He once was wealthy, but he now is fallen,
And I this morning have him got arrested
At suit of this same Master Frescobald;
And, by this means, shall I be sure of coin,
For doing this same good to him unknown:
And, in good time, see where the merchant comes.

3 Old copies, "between thee and *home*."

Enter FRESCOBALD.

Good morrow to kind Master Frescobald.
Fres. Good morrow to yourself, good Master Bagot;
And what's the news, you are so early stirring?
It is for gain; I make no doubt of that.
Bag. 'Tis for the love, sir, that I bear to you.
When did you see your debtor, Banister?
Fres. I promise you, I have not seen the man
This two months day; his poverty is such,
As I do think he shames to see his friends.
Bag. Why then assure yourself to see him straight,
For at your suit I have arrested him,
And here they will be with him presently.
Fres. Arrest him at my suit? You were to blame,
I know the man's misfortunes to be such,
As he's not able for to pay the debt;
And were it known to some, he were undone.
Bag. This is your pitiful heart to think it so;
But you are much deceived in Banister:
Why, such as he will break for fashion sake,
And unto those they owe a thousand pound,
Pay scarce a hundred. O, sir, beware of him,
The man is lewdly given to dice and drabs;
Spends all he hath in harlot's companies;
It is no mercy for to pity him:
I speak the truth of him, for nothing else,
But for the kindness that I bear to you.
Fres. If it be so, he hath deceived me much,
And to deal strictly with such a one as he,
Better severe than too much lenity:
But here is Master Banister himself,
And with him, as I take it, [are] the officers.

Enter BANISTER, *his* Wife, *and two* Officers.

Ban. O, Master Frescobald, you have undone me:
My state was well nigh overthrown before,
Now, altogether downcast by your means.
Mrs. Ban. O, Master Frescobald, pity my husband's case;
He is a man hath lived as well as any,
Till envious fortune and the ravenous sea
Did rob, disrobe, and spoil us of our own.
Fres. Mistress Banister, I envy not your husband,
Nor willingly would I have used him thus:
But that I hear he is so lewdly given,
Haunts wicked company, and hath enough
To pay his debts, yet will not own[1] thereof.
Ban. This is that damned broker, that same Bagot,
Whom I have often from my trencher fed:
Ungrateful villain for to use me thus.
Bag. What I have said to him is naught but truth.
Mrs. Ban. What thou hast said springs from an envious heart!
O! cannibal,[2] that doth eat men alive!
But here, upon my knee, believe me, sir;
And what I speak, so help me God, is true!
We scarce have meat to feed our little babes:
Most of our plate is in that broker's hand,
Which, had we money to defray our debts,
O think, we would not bide that penury!
Be merciful, kind Master Frescobald;
My husband, children, and myself will eat
But one meal a day; the other, will we keep
And sell; in part to pay the debt we owe you.
If ever tears did pierce a tender mind,
Be pitiful;—let me some favor find.
Fres. Go to; I see thou art an envious man.—
Good Mistress Banister, kneel not to me:
I pray rise up; you shall have your desire.
Hold, officers; begone; there's for your pains.
[*Exit* Officers.
You know you owe to me a thousand pound;
[*To* BANISTER.
Here, take my hand; if e'er God make you able,
And place you in your former state again,
Pay me: but, if still [dark] your fortune frown,
Upon my faith, I'll never ask a crown.
I never yet did wrong to men in thrall,
For God doth know what to myself may fall.
Ban. This unexpected favor, undeserved,
Doth make my heart bleed inwardly with joy:
Ne'er may aught prosper with me as[3] my own,
If I forget this kindness you have shown.
Mrs. Ban. My children, in their prayers, both night and day,
For your good fortune and success shall pray.
Fres. I thank you both; I pray go dine with me;
Within these three days, if God give me leave,
I will to Florence, to my native home.
Hold, Bagot, there's a portague[4] to drink,
Although you ill deserved it by your merit;
Give not such cruel scope unto your heart;
Be sure, the ill you do will be requited:
Remember what I say, Bagot; farewell.
Come, Master Banister, you shall with me,
My fare's but simple, but welcome heartily.
[*Exeunt all but* BAGOT
Bag. A plague go with you! would you had eat your last!
Is this the thanks I have for all my pains?
Confusion light upon you all for me!
Where he had wont to give a score of crowns,[4]
Doth he now foist me with a portague?
Well, I will be revenged upon this Banister.
I'll to his creditors; buy the debts he owes,
As seeming that I do it for good will;
I'm sure to have them at an easy rate;
And when 'tis done, in Christendom he stays not,
But I will make his heart to ache with sorrow;—
And if that Banister become my debtor,
By heaven and earth, I'll make his plague the greater.
[*Exit* BAGOT.

ACT II.

Enter Chorus.

Cho. Now, gentlemen, imagine that young Cromwell,
In Antwerp's lieger[5] for the English merchants;
And Banister, to shun this Bagot's hate,
Hearing that he hath got some of his debts,
Is fled to Antwerp, with his wife and children;
Which, Bagot hearing, is gone after them:

1 Former editions read, "be known thereof."
2 "A cannibal," in other copies.
3 Old editions read "is."
4 The portague (Fr. *portugaise*) was a gold coin of Portugal, worth about £4 10*s.* sterling. "Score of *pounds*" may be intended; for, as a correspondent remarks, at £4 10*s.* a *portague* can not be much less than "a score of *crowns*."
5 *Lieger*—ambassador.

And thither sends his bills of debt before,
To be revenged on wretched Banister.
What doth fall out, with patience sit and see,
A just requital of false treachery.

SCENE I.—Antwerp. CROMWELL *in his study, discovered at a table, with bags of money before him, and books of account.*

Crom. Thus far my reckoning doth go straight and even.
But, Cromwell, this same plodding fits not thee;
Thy mind is altogether set on travel,
And not to live thus cloistered, like a nun.
It is not this same trash, that I regard;
Experience is the jewel of my heart.

Enter a Post (*courier*).

Post. I pray, sir, are you ready to despatch me?
Crom. Yes; here's those sums of money you must carry.
You go as far as Frankfort, do you not?
Post. I do, sir.
Crom. Well, pr'ythee, then, make all the haste thou canst,
For there be certain English gentlemen
Are bound for Venice, and may haply want,
An if that you should linger by the way:
But in the hope that you will make good speed,
There are two angels to buy spurs and wands.[1]
Post. I thank you, sir; this will add wings indeed.
Crom. Gold is of power to make an eagle's speed.

Enter Mistress BANISTER.

What gentlewoman is this, that grieves so much?
It seems she doth address herself to me.
Mrs. Ban. God save you, sir; is your name Master Cromwell?
Crom. My name is Thomas Cromwell, gentlewoman.
Mrs. Ban. Know you one Bagot, sir, that's come to Antwerp?
Crom. No, trust me, I ne'er saw the man; but here
Are bills of debt I have received against
One Banister, a merchant fallen into decay.
Mrs. Ban. Into decay, indeed, 'long of that wretch!
I am the wife to woful Banister,
And, by that bloody villain am pursued,
From London, here to Antwerp, where my husband
Lies in the governor's hands; the God of Heaven
He only knows how he will deal with him!
Now, sir, your heart is framed of milder temper,
Be merciful to a distressèd soul,
And God, no doubt, will trebly bless your gain.
Crom. Good Mistress Banister, what I can, I will,
In anything that lies within my power.
Mrs. Ban. O, speak to Bagot, that same wicked wretch;
An angel's voice may move a damnèd devil.
Crom. Why, is he come to Antwerp, as you hear?
Mrs. Ban. I heard he landed some two hours since.
Crom. Well, Mistress Banister, assure yourself,
I will to Bagot speak in your behalf,
And win him to all the pity that I can:

[1] *Wands*—switches.

Meantime, to comfort you, in your distress,
Receive these angels to relieve your need,
And, be assured, that what I can effect,
To do you good, no way will I neglect.
Mrs. Ban. That mighty God that knows each mortal's heart,
Keep you from trouble, sorrow, grief, and smart.
[*Exit* Mistress BANISTER.
Crom. Thanks, courteous woman, for thy hearty prayer!
It grieves my soul to see her misery;
But we that live under the work of fate,
May hope the best, yet know not to what state
Our stars and destinies have us assigned;
Fickle is fortune, and her face is blind. [*Exit.*

SCENE II.—*A Street in* Antwerp.

Enter BAGOT.

Bag. So, all goes well; it is as I would have it!
Banister, he is with the governor,
And shortly shall have gyves upon his heels.
It glads my heart to think upon the slave;
I hope to have his body rot in prison,
And after hear his wife to hang herself,
And all his children die for want of food.
The jewels I have brought with me to Antwerp,
Are reckoned to be worth five thousand pound,
Which scarcely stood me in three hundred pound.
I bought them at an easy kind of rate;—
I care not much which way they came by them,
That sold them me; it comes not near my heart;
And, lest they should be stolen—as sure they are—
I thought it meet to sell them here in Antwerp;
And so have left them in the governor's hand,
Who offers me within two hundred pound
Of all my price;—but now, no more of that.—
I must go see an if my bills be safe,
The which I sent before to Master Cromwell,
That, if the wind should keep me on the sea,
He might arrest him here before I came:
And, in good time, see where he is:

Enter CROMWELL.

God save you, sir.
Crom. And you.—Pray, pardon me, I know you not.
Bag. It may be so, sir; but my name is Bagot;
The man that sent to you the bills of debt.
Crom. Oh, you're the man that pursues Banister?
Here are the bills of debt you sent to me;
As for the man, you best know where he is.
It is reported you've a flinty heart,
A mind that will not stoop to any pity;
An eye that knows not how to shed a tear,
A hand that's always open for reward.
But, Master Bagot, would you be ruled by me,
You should turn all these to the contrary;
Your heart should still have feeling of remorse,
Your mind, according to your state, be liberal
To those that stand in need and in distress;
Your hand to help them that do sink in want,
Rather than with your poise to hold them down;—
For every ill turn, show yourself more kind:—
Thus should I; pardon me, I speak my mind.
Bag. Ay, sir, you speak to hear what I would say;

But you must live, I know, as well as I.
I know this place to be extortionate,
And 'tis not for a man to keep safe here,
But he must lie; cog with his dearest friend,
And, as for pity, scorn it; hate all conscience:
But yet I do commend your wit in this,
To make a show of what I hope you are not;—
But I commend you, and it is well done:
This is the only way to bring you gain.

Crom. Gain! I had rather chain me to an oar,
And, like a slave, there toil out all my life,
Before I'd live so base a slave as thou.
Ay, like a hypocrite, to make a show
Of seeming virtue, and a devil within!
No, Bagot, if thy conscience were as clear,
Ne'er had poor Banister been troubled here.

Bag. Nay, Master Cromwell, be not angry, sir;
I know full well that you are no such man,
But if your conscience were as white as snow,
It will be thought that you are otherwise.

Crom. Will it be thought [that] I am otherwise?
Let them that think so, know they are deceived;
Shall Cromwell live to have his faith misconstr'ed?
Antwerp, for all the wealth within thy town,
I will not stay here full two hours longer.
As good luck serves, my accounts are all made even,
Therefore, I'll straight unto the treasurer.
Bagot, I know you'll to the governor:
Commend me to him; say I'm bound to travel,
To see the fruitful parts of Italy;
And if you ever bore a Christian mind,
Let Banister some favor of you find.

Bag. For your sake, sir, I'll help him all I can—
To starve his heart out e'er he gets a groat— [*aside.*]
So Master Cromwell, do I take my leave,
For I must straight unto the governor.

Crom. Farewell, sir; pray remember what I've said. [*Exit* BAGOT.
No, Cromwell, no; thy heart was ne'er so base,
To live by falsehood or by brokery.
But it falls out well;—I little it repent;
Hereafter, time in travel shall be spent.

Enter HODGE.

Hodge. Your son Thomas, quoth you? I have been Thomas'd. I had thought it had been no such matter to ha' gone by water; for at Putney I'll go you to Parish Garden for two pence; sit as still as may be, without any wagging or jolting in my guts, in a little boat, too: here, we were scarce some four mile in the great green water, but I, thinking to go to my afternoon's nuncheon,[1] as was my manner at home, felt a kind of rising in my guts. At last, one o' the sailors spying of me,—"Be o'good cheer," says he; "set down thy victual, and up with it; thou hast nothing but an eel in thy belly."—Well, to't I went, and to my victuals went the sailors; and, thinking me to be a man of better experience than any in the ship, they asked me what wood the ship was made of? They all swore I told them as right as if I had been acquainted with the carpenter that made it. At last, we grew near land, I grew villanous hungry, and went to my bag. The devil a bit there was; the sailors had tickled me; yet I can not blame them; it was a part of kindness, for I in kindness told them what wood the ship was made of, and they in kindness eat up my victuals; as, indeed, one good turn asketh another. Well, would I could find my Master Thomas, in this Dutch town!—he might put some English beer into my belly.

[1] Luncheon.

Crom. What, Hodge, my father's man! by my hand, welcome:
How doth my father? What's the news at home?

Hodge. Master Thomas! O God, Master Thomas! your hand—glove and all! this is to give you to understand that your father is in health; and Alice Downing here hath sent you a nutmeg; and Bess Make-water a race of ginger; my fellows Will and Tom, have, between them, sent you a dozen of points, and Goodman Toll, of the Goat, a pair of mittens; myself came in person, and this is all the news.

Crom. Gramercy, Hodge, and thou art welcome to me,
But in as ill a time thou comest as may be;
For I am travelling into Italy:—
What say'st thou, Hodge, wilt bear me company?

Hodge. Will I bear thee company, Tom? What tell'st me of Italy? Were it to the farthest part of Flanders, I would go with thee, Tom. I am thine all, in weal and wo, thine own to command. What, Tom, I have passed the rigorous waves of Neptune's blasts. I tell you, Thomas, I have been in danger of the floods; and when I have seen Boreas begin to play the ruffian with us, then would I down on my knees, and call upon Vulcan.

Crom. And why upon him?

Hodge. Because, as this same fellow Neptune, is god of the seas, so Vulcan is lord over the smiths, and therefore, I, being a smith, thought his godhead would have some care yet of me.

Crom. A good conceit; but tell me, hast thou dined yet?

Hodge. Thomas, to speak the truth, not a bit yet I.

Crom. Come, go with me, thou shalt have cheer good store;
And farewell, Antwerp, if I come no more.

Hodge. I follow thee, sweet Tom; I follow thee. [*Exeunt.*

SCENE III.—*Another Street in the same.*

Enter the Governor *of the* English *Factory;* BAGOT, Mr. *and* Mrs. BANISTER, *and two* Officers.

Gov. Is Cromwell gone, then, say you, Master Bagot?
What the dislike, I pray? What was the cause?

Bag. To tell you true, a wild brain of his own;
Such youth as he can't see when they are well:
He is all bent to travel—that's his reason—
And doth not love to eat his bread at home.

Gov. Well, good fortune with him if the man be gone.
We hardly shall find such a man as he,
To fit our turns; his dealings were so honest.
But now, sir, for your jewels that I have,—
What do you say? what, will you take my price?

Bag. O, sir, you offer too much under foot.

Gov. 'Tis but two hundred pound between us, man,
What's that, in payment of five thousand pound?

Bag. Two hundred pound, by'r lady, sir, 'tis great;
Before I got so much it made me sweat.

Gov. Well, Master Bagot, I'll proffer you fairly.
You see this merchant, Master Banister,

Is going now to prison at your suit:
His substance all is gone; what would you have?
Yet, in regard I knew the man in[1] wealth,
Never dishonest dealing, but such mishaps
Hath fallen on him, may light on me or you:—
There is two hundred pound between us two;
We will divide the same; I'll give you one,
On that condition you will set him free.
His state is nothing; that you see yourself;
And where naught is, the king must lose his right.

Bag. Sir, you speak out of your love; [but know]
'Tis foolish love, sir, sure to pity him.
Therefore content yourself, this is my mind;
To do him good, I will not bate a penny.

Ban. This is my comfort, though thou dost no good,
A mighty ebb follows a mighty flood.

Mrs. Ban. O, thou base wretch, whom we have fostered,
Even as a serpent, for to poison us!
If God did ever right a woman's wrong,
To that same God I bend and bow my heart,
To let his heavy wrath fall on thy head,
By whom my hopes and joys are butchered.

Bag. Alas, fond woman, I pr'ythee pray thy worst,
The fox fares better still, when he is cursed.

Enter BOWSER.

Gov. Master Bowser! you're welcome, sir, from England.
What's the best news? and how do all our friends?

Bow. They are all well, and do commend them to you:
There's letters from your brother and your son:
So, fare you well, sir, I must take my leave,
My haste and business do require it so.

Gov. Before you dine, sir? What, go you out of town?

Bow. I'faith, unless I hear some news in town,
I must away; there is no remedy.

Gov. Master Bowser, what is your business?—may I know it?

Bow. You may, sir, and so shall all the city.
The king of late hath had his treasury robbed,
And of the choicest jewels that he had;
The value of them was seven thousand pound,
The fellow that did steal these jewels is hanged,
And did confess that, for three hundred pound,
He sold them to one Bagot, dwelling in London:
Now Bagot's fled, and, as we hear, to Antwerp;
And hither am I come to seek him out;
And they that first can tell me of his news,
Shall have a hundred pound for their reward.

Ban. How just is God to right the innocent!

Gov. Master Bowser, you come in happy time,
Here is the villain Bagot that you seek,
And all those jewels have I in my hands.—
Here, officers, look to him, hold him fast.

Bagot. The devil owed me a shame, and now hath paid it.

Bow. Is this that Bagot? Fellows, bear him hence,
We will not now stand here for his reply;
Lade him with irons, we will have him tried
In England, where his villanies are known.

Bag. Mischief, confusion, light upon you all!
O, hang me, drown me, let me kill myself;
Let go my arms, let me run quick to hell.

Bow. Away; bear him away; stop the slave's mouth. [*Exeunt* Officers, *with* BAGOT.

Mrs. Ban. Thy works are infinite, great God of Heaven!

Gov. I heard this Bagot was a wealthy fellow.

Bow. He was indeed; for when his goods were seized,
Of jewels, coin, and plate, within his house,
Was found the value of five thousand pound,
His furniture worth fully half so much;
Which, being all distrainèd for the king,
He frankly gave it to the Antwerp merchants;
And they again, out of their bounteous mind,
Have, to a brother of their company,
A man decayed by fortune of the seas,
Given Bagot's wealth, to set him up again,
And keep it for him; his name's Banister.

Gov. Good Master Bowser, with this happy news,
You have revived two from the gates of death,
This is that Banister, and this his wife.

Bow. Sir, I am glad my fortune is so good,
To bring such tidings as may comfort you.

Ban. You have given life unto a man deemed dead;
For by these news, my life is newly bred.

Mrs. Ban. Thanks to my God, next to my sovereign king;
And last to you that these good news do bring.

Gov. The hundred pound I must receive, as due
For finding Bagot, I freely give to you.

Bow. And, Master Banister, if so you please,
I'll bear you company, when you cross the seas.

Ban. If it please you, sir, my company is but mean:
Stands with your liking,[2] I will wait on you.

Gov. I am glad that all things do accord so well:
Come, Master Bowser, let us in to dinner;
And Mistress Banister, be merry, woman.
Come, after sorrow now let's cheer your spirit,
Knaves have their due, and you but what you merit.
[*Exeunt.*

ACT III.

SCENE I.—*The principal Bridge at* Florence.

Enter CROMWELL *and* HODGE *in their shirts, and without hats.*

Hodge. Call you this seeing of fashions? Marry would I had stayed at Putney still. Oh! Master Thomas, we are spoiled, we are gone.

Crom. Content thee, man; this is but fortune.

Hodge. Fortune! a plague of this fortune; it makes me go wet-shod; the rogues would not leave me a shoe to my feet: for my hose, they scorned them with their heels; but for my doublet and hat, O, Lord—they embraced me and unlaced me, and took away my clothes, and so disgraced me!

Crom. Well, Hodge, what remedy?
What shift shall we make now?

Hodge. Nay, I know not. For begging I am naught,

[1] The old copies read, "of wealth."

[2] *Stands with your liking.* Elliptical for "If it stands," &c.—*Percy.*

for stealing worse: by my troth I must even fall to my old trade; to the hammer and the horse-heels again; but now, the worst is, I am not acquainted with the humor of the horses in this country; whether they are not coltish; given much to kicking or no: for when I have one leg in my hand, if he should up and lay t'other on my chaps, I were gone; there lay I, there lay Hodge.

Crom. Hodge, I believe thou must work for us both.

Hodge. O, Master Thomas, have not I told you of this? Have not I, many a time and often, said, "Tom, or Master Thomas, learn to make a horse-shoe; it will be your own another day:" this was not regarded. Hark you, Thomas, what do you call the fellows that robbed us?

Crom. The banditti.

Hodge. The banditti, do you call them? I know not what they are called here, but I am sure we will call them plain thieves in England. O, Tom, that we were now at Putney, at the ale there.

Crom. Content thee, man;—here set up these two bills,
And let us keep our standing on the bridge:
The fashion of this country still is such,
If any stranger be oppressed with want,
To write the manner of his misery;
And such as are disposed to succor him,
Will do it. What, Hodge, hast thou set them up?

Hodge. Ay, they are up; God send some to read them, and not only to read them, but also to look on us; and not altogether look on us, but relieve us. Oh! cold, cold, cold!

[CROMWELL *stands at one end of the bridge, and* HODGE *at the other.*

Enter FRESCOBALD.

Frescobald. [*reads*]. What's here?
Two Englishmen robbed by the banditti?
One of them seems to be a gentleman,
'Tis pity that his fortune was so hard,
To fall into the desperate hands of thieves!—
I'll question him of what estate he is.
God save you, sir, are you an Englishman?

Crom. I am, sir, a distressèd Englishman.

Fres. And what are you, my friend?

Hodge. Who I, sir? By my troth, I do not know myself, what I am now; but, sir, I was a smith, sir; a poor farrier of Putney. That's my master, sir, yonder; I was robbed for his sake, sir.

Fres. I see you have been met by the banditti,
And therefore need not ask how came you thus:
But, Frescobald, why dost thou question them
Of their estate, and not relieve their need?
Sirs,—the coin I have about me is not much;
There's sixteen ducats for to clothe yourselves,
There's sixteen more to buy your diet with,
And there's sixteen to pay for your horse-hire:
'Tis all the wealth you see, my purse possesses;
But if you please for to inquire me out,
You shall not want for aught that I can do.
My name is Frescobald, a Florence merchant:
A man that always loved your nation much.

Crom. This unexpected favor at your hands,—
Which God doth know, if e'er I shall requite,
Necessity makes me to take your bounty,
And for your gold can yield you naught but thanks.
Your charity hath helped me from despair;
Your name shall still be in my hearty prayer.

Fres. It is not worth such thanks: come to my house;
Your want shall better be relieved than thus.

Crom. I pray excuse me; this shall well suffice,
To bear my charges to Bolognia,
Whereat a noble earl is much distressed;—
An Englishman, Russel, the earl of Bedford,
Is by the French king sold unto his death.
It may fall out that I may do him good:
To save his life, I'll hazard my heart's blood:
Therefore, kind sir, thanks for your liberal gift,
I must be gone to aid him; there's no shift.

Fres. I'll be no hinderer to so good an act,
Heaven prosper you, in that you go about:
If fortune bring you this way back again,
Pray let me see you; so I take my leave;
All a good man can wish, I do bequeath.

[*Exit* FRESCOBALD.

Crom. All good that God doth send, light on your head;
There's few such men within our climate bred.
How say you now, Hodge? is not this good fortune?

Hodge. How say you? I'll tell you what, Master Thomas; if all men be of this gentleman's mind, let's keep our stand upon this bridge: we shall get more here, with begging, in one day, than I shall with making horseshoes in a whole year.

Crom. No, Hodge, we must be gone unto Bolognia,
There to relieve the noble earl of Bedford;
Where, if I fail not in my policy,
I shall deceive their subtle treachery.

Hodge. Nay, I'll follow you. God bless us from the thieving banditti again. [*Exeunt.*

SCENE II.—Bolognia. *A Room in an Hotel.*

Enter BEDFORD *and his* Host.

Bed. Am I betrayed? was Bedford born to die,
By such base slaves, in such a place as this?
Have I escaped so many times in France,
So many battles have I over-passed,
And made the French stir when they heard my name;
And am I now betrayed unto my death?
Some of their heart's blood first shall pay for it.

Host. They do desire, my lord, to speak with you.

Bed. The traitors do desire to have my blood,
But by my birth, my honor, and my name,—
By all my hopes, my life shall cost them dear.
Open the door; I'll venture out upon them,
And, if I must die, then I'll die with honor.

Host. Alas, my lord, that is a desperate course;
They have begirt you, round about the house.
Their meaning is to take you prisoner,
And so to send your body unto France.

Bed. First shall the ocean be as dry as sand,
Before alive they send me unto France:
I'll have my body first bored like a sieve,
And die as Hector, 'gainst the Myrmidons,
E'er France shall boast, Bedford's their prisoner.
O! treacherous France, that, 'gainst the law of arms,
Hath here betrayed thine enemy to death!
But, be assured, my blood shall be revenged
Upon the best lives that remain in France.

Enter a Servant.

Stand back, or else thou runn'st upon thy death.

Mes. Pardon, my lord, I come to tell your honor,
That they have hired a Neapolitan,
Who, by his oratory, hath promised them,
Without the shedding of one drop of blood,
Into their hands, safe to deliver you;
And therefore craves, none but himself may enter,
And a poor swain that doth attend on him.

Bed. A Neapolitan? bid him come in.
[*Exit* Servant.
Were he as cunning in his eloquence,
As Cicero, the famous man of Rome,
His words would be as chaff against the wind.
Sweet-tongued Ulysses, that made Ajax mad,
Were he;—and his tongue in this speaker's head,
Alive he wins not; 'tis no conquest, dead!

Enter CROMWELL, *in* Neapolitan *habit, and* HODGE.

Crom. Sir, are you the master of the house?

Host. I am, sir.

Crom. By this same token you must leave this [place,
And leave none but the earl and I together,
And this, my peasant, here to tend on us.

Host. With all my heart: God grant you do some good.
[*Exit* Host. CROMWELL *shuts the door.*

Bed. Now, sir, what's your will with me?

Crom. Intends your honor not to yield yourself?

Bed. No, goodman goose, not while my sword doth [last.
Is this your eloquence for to persuade me?

Crom. My lord, my eloquence is for to save you;
I am not, as you judge, a Neapolitan,
But Cromwell, your servant, and an Englishman.

Bed. How! Cromwell? not my farrier's son?

Crom. The same, sir; and am come to succor you.

Hodge. Yes, faith, sir, and I am Hodge, your poor smith; many a time and oft have I shoed your dapple gray.

Bed. And what avails it me, that thou art here?

Crom. It may avail, if you'll be ruled by me.
My lord, you know, the men of Mantua
And these Bolognians are at deadly strife
And they, my lord, both love and honor you.
Could you but get out of the Mantua port,
Then were you safe, despite of all their force.

Bed. Tut, man, thou talk'st of things impossible;
Dost thou not see, that we are round beset?
How then is't possible we should escape?

Crom. By force we can not, but by policy.
Put on the apparel here that Hodge doth wear,
And give him yours: the states they know you not,—
For, as I think, they never saw your face,—
And, at a watch-word, must I call them in,
And will desire, that we two safe may pass
To Mantua, where I'll say my business lies;
How doth your honor like of this device?

Bed. O, wondrous good: but wilt thou venture, Hodge?

Hodge. Will I?
Oh, noble lord, I do accord,
In anything I can;
And do agree to set thee free,
Do fortune what she can.

Bed. Come, then, and change [we] our apparel straight.

Crom. Go, Hodge, make haste, lest they should chance to call.

Hodge. I warrant you, I'll fit him with a suit.
[*Exeunt* BEDFORD *and* HODGE.

Crom. Heaven grant this policy doth take success,
And that the earl may safely 'scape away!
And yet it grieves me for this simple wretch,
For fear lest they should do him violence!
But of two evils best to shun the greatest,
And better is't that he should live in thrall,
Than such a noble earl as this should fall.
Their stubborn hearts, it may be, will relent,
Since he is gone, on whom their hate is bent.

Re-enter BEDFORD *and* HODGE.

My lord, have you despatched?

Bed. How dost thou like us, Cromwell?—is it well?

Crom. O, my good lord, excellent. Hodge, how dost feel thyself?

Hodge. How do I feel myself? why, as a noble man should do! Oh! how I feel honor come creeping on; my nobility is wonderful melancholy. Is it not most gentlemanlike to be melancholy?

Crom. Yes, Hodge; now go [and] sit down in thy [study,
And take [thy] state upon thee.

Hodge. I warrant you, my lord; let me alone to take state upon me: but hark, my lord, do you feel nothing bite about you?

Bed. No, trust me, Hodge.

Hodge. Ay, they know they want their old pasture. 'Tis a strange thing of this vermin, they dare not meddle with nobility.

Crom. Go take thy place, Hodge, while I call them [in.
All is now done. Enter, an if you please.
[*Speaking within.*

Enter the Governor, *and other* States *and* Citizens *of* Bolognia, *and* Officers *with halberds.*

Gov. What, have you won him? will he yield himself?

Crom. I have, an't please you; and the quiet earl
Doth yield himself to be disposed by you.

Gov. Give him the money that we promised him:
So let him go, whither he please himself.

Crom. My business, sir, lies unto Mantua;
Please you to give me a safe conduct thither.

Gov. Go and conduct him to the Mantua port,
And see him safe delivered presently.
[*Exeunt* CROMWELL, BEDFORD, *and* Officers.
Go, draw the curtains, let us see the earl:
O, he is writing, stand apart awhile.

Hodge. [*reads*]. Fellow William, I am not as I have been. I went from you a smith; I write to you as a lord: I am at this present writing, among the Bononian sausages. I do commend my lordship to Ralph and to Roger; to Bridget and to Dorothy, and so to all the youth of Putney.

Gov. Sure these are names of English noblemen,
Some of his special friends to whom he writes:
But stay, he doth address himself to sing.
[HODGE *sings a song.*
My lord, I'm glad you are so frolic and blithe;
Believe me, noble lord, if you knew all,
You'd change your merry vein to sudden sorrow.

Hodge. I change my merry vein? no, thou Bononian, no;

I am a lord, and therefore let me go;
I do defy thee and thy sausages:
Therefore stand off, and come not near my honor.

Gov. My lord, this jesting can not serve your turn.

Hodge. Dost think, thou black Bononian beast,
That I do flout, do jibe, or jest?
No, no, thou bear-pot; know that I,
A noble earl, a lord par-dy. [*A trumpet sounds.*

Gov. What means this trumpet's sound?

Enter a Messenger.

Cit. One is come hither from the states of Mantua.

Gov. What would you with us? Speak, thou man of Mantua!

Mess. Men of Bolognia, this my message is,
To let you know the noble earl of Bedford
Is safe within the town of Mantua,
And wills you send the peasant that you have,
Who hath deceived your expectation;
Or else the states of Mantua have vowed
They will recall the truce that they have made,
And not a man shall stir from forth your town,
That shall return, unless you send him back.

Gov. O, this misfortune, how it mads my heart!
The Neapolitan hath beguiled us all.
Hence with this fool. What should we do with him,
The earl being gone? A plague upon it all!

Hodge. No, I'll assure you, I am no earl, but a smith, sir—
One Hodge, a smith at Putney, sir; one that hath
Gulled you; that hath bored you, sir.

Gov. Away with him; take hence the fool you came for.

Hodge. Ay, sir. I leave the greater fool with you.

Mess. Farewell, Bolognians.[1] Come, friend, along with me.

Hodge. My friend, afore; my lordship will follow thee. [*Exit.*

Gov. Well, Mantua, since by thee the earl is lost,
Within few days I hope to see thee crost. [*Exeunt.*

Enter Chorus.

Cho. Thus far you see how Cromwell's fortune passed.
The earl of Bedford, being safe in Mantua,
Desires Cromwell's company into France,
To make requital for his courtesy:
But Cromwell doth deny the earl his suit,
And tells him that those parts he meant to see,
He had not yet set footing on the land:
And so directly takes his way to Spain—
The earl to France—and so they both do part.
Now, let your thoughts, as swift as is the wind,
Skip some few years that Cromwell spent in travel:
And now imagine him to be in England,
Servant unto the master of the rolls;
Where, in short time, he there began to flourish:
An hour shall show you what few years did cherish. [*Exit.*

SCENE III.—London. *A Room in* Sir CHRISTOPHER HALES' *House. Music plays; then a Banquet. Enter* Sir CHRISTOPHER HALES, CROMWELL, *and two* Servants.

Hales. Come, sirs, be careful of your master's credit;
And as our bounty now exceeds the figure
Of common entertainment, so do you,
With looks as free as is your master's soul,
Give formal welcome to the throngèd tables
That shall receive the cardinal's followers
And the attendants of the great lord chancellor.
But, Cromwell, all my care depends on thee:
Thou art a man, differing from vulgar form,
And by how much thy spirit's ranked 'bove these,
In rules of art, by so much it shines brighter
By travel, whose observance pleads thy[2] merit,
In a most learned yet unaffected[3] spirit.
Good Cromwell, cast an eye of fair regard
'Bout all my house—and what this ruder flesh,
Through ignorance, or wine, do miscreate,
Salve thou with courtesy: if welcome want,
Full bowls and ample banquets will seem scant.

Crom. Sir, whatsoever lies in me, assure you
I will show my utmost duty. [*Exit* CROMWELL.

Hales. About it, then; the lords will straight be here.
Cromwell, thou hast those parts would rather suit
The service of the state than of my house:
I look upon thee with a loving eye,
That one day will prefer thy destiny.

Enter Messenger.

Mess. Sir, the lords be at hand.

Hales. They are welcome; bid Cromwell straight attend us,
And look you all things be in readiness.

The Music plays. Enter Cardinal WOLSEY, Sir THOMAS MORE, GARDINER, CROMWELL, *and* Attendants.

Wol. O, Sir Christopher,
You are too liberal: what, a banquet too?

Hales. My lords, if words could show the ample welcome
That my free heart affords you, I could then
Become a prater: but I now must deal
Like a feast-politician with your lordships;
Defer your welcome till the banquet end,
That it may then salve our defect of fare:
Yet welcome now, and all that tend on you.

Wol. Our thanks to the kind master of the rolls.
Come and sit down;—sit down, Sir Thomas More.
'Tis strange how that we and the Spaniard differ:
Their dinner is our banquet, after dinner,
And they are men of active disposition.
This I gather, that, by their sparing meat,
Their bodies are more fitter for the wars;
And if that famine chance to pinch their maws,
Being used to fast, it breeds in them less pain.

Hales. Fill me some wine; I'll answer Cardinal Wolsey:—
My lord, we English are of more free souls
Than hunger-starved and ill-complexioned Spaniards.
They that are rich, in Spain, spare belly-food,
To deck their backs with an Italian hood,
And silks of Seville: and the poorest snake,
That feeds on lemons, pilchards, and ne'er heated
His palate with sweet flesh, will bear a case
More fat and gallant than his starvèd face.

1 I should be for giving this affectionate parting apostrophe to Hodge, and the rest of the line to the messenger.

2 Elsewhere it reads, "*his* merit."

3 Other editions, "unaffecting."

Pride, the inquisition, and this belly-evil,
Are, in my judgment, Spain's three-headed devil.[1]
More. Indeed, it is a plague unto their nation,
Who stagger after in blind imitation.
Hales. My lords, with welcome,[2] I present your lord-
A solemn health. [ships
More. I love healths well, but when that healths do bring
Pain to the head, and body's surfeiting,
Then cease I healths:
Nay, spill not, friend, for though the drops be small,
Yet have they force, to force men to the wall.
Wol. Sir Christopher, is that your man?
Hales. An it like
Your grace, he is a scholar and a linguist —
One that hath travelled over many parts
Of Christendom, my lord.
Wol. My friend, come nearer. Have you been a traveller?
Crom. My lord,
I've added to my knowledge the Low Countries,
With France, Spain, Germany, and Italy:
And though small gain of profit I did find,
Yet did it please my eye, content my mind.
Wol. What do you think, then, of the several states
And princes' courts that you have travelled [through]?
Crom. My lord, no court with England may compare,
Neither for state, nor civil government:
Lust dwells in France, in Italy, and Spain,
From the poor peasant to the prince's train;
In Germany and Holland, riot serves,
And he that most can drink, he most deserves.
England I praise not, for I here was born,
But that she laughs the others all to scorn.
Wol. My lord, there dwells within that spirit more
Than can be discernèd by the outward eye.
Sir Christopher, will you part with your man?
Hales. I have sought to proffer him unto your lordship,
And now I see he hath preferred himself.
Wol. What is thy name?
Crom. Cromwell, my lord.
Wol. Then, Cromwell, here we make thee of our causes
Solicitor, and nearest next ourself.
Gardiner, give you kind welcome to the man.
[GARDINER *embraces him.*
More. Oh, my lord cardinal, you're a royal winner:
Have got a man, besides your bounteous dinner:
Well may you pray, knight, that we come no more —
If we come often, thou may'st shut thy door.
Wol. Sir Christopher, hadst thou given me half thy lands,
Thou couldst not have pleased me so much as with
This man of thine. My infant thoughts do spell,
Shortly, his fortune shall be lifted higher;
True industry doth kindle honor's fire,
And so, kind master of the rolls, farewell.
Hales. Cromwell, farewell.
Crom. Cromwell takes leave of you
That ne'er will leave to love and honor you. [*Exeunt.*
[*The music plays as they go out.*

[1] The philosophy of Hales is more decidedly true than that of Wolsey. John Bull owes much of his fighting propensity to his beef.
[2] "With welcome"—with permission.

ACT IV.

Enter Chorus.

Cho. Now Cromwell's highest fortunes do begin.
Wolsey, that loved him as he did his life
Committed all his treasure to his hands.
Wolsey is dead; and Gardiner, his man,
Is now created bishop of Winchester.
Pardon, if we omit all Wolsey's life,
Because our play depends on Cromwell's death.
Now sit and see his highest state of all,
His height of rising, and his sudden fall.
Pardon the errors are already past,
And live in hope the best doth come at last:
My hope upon your favor doth depend,
And looks to have your liking ere the end. [*Exit*

SCENE I. — *The same. A public Walk.*

Enter GARDINER, *Bishop of* Winchester, *the Dukes of* Norfolk *and* Suffolk, Sir THOMAS MORE, Sir CHRISTOPHER HALES, *and* CROMWELL.

Norf. Master Cromwell, since Cardinal Wolsey's
His majesty is given to understand [death,
There's certain bills and writings in your hand
That much concern the [present] state of England.
My lord of Winchester, is it not so?
Gar. My lord of Norfolk, we two were whilome fellows,
And Master Cromwell — though our master's love
Did bind us, while his love was to the king
It is no boot now to deny those things
Which may be prejudicial to the state:
And though that God hath raised my fortune higher
Than any way I looked for, or deserved,
Yet may my life no longer with me dwell,
Than I prove true unto my sovereign.
Suff. What say you, Master Cromwell? Have you
[Speak!] ay or no? [those writings?
Crom. Here are the writings, and upon my knees
I give them up unto the worthy dukes
Of Suffolk and of Norfolk.
He was my master, and each virtuous part
That lived in him I tendered with my heart;
But what his head complotted 'gainst the state,
My country's love commands me that to hate.
His sudden death I grieve for, not his fall,
Because he sought to work my country's thrall.
Suff. Cromwell, the king shall hear of this thy
Who, I assure myself, will well reward thee. [duty,
My lord, let's go unto his majesty,
And show these writings which he longs to see.
[*Exeunt* NORFOLK *and* SUFFOLK.

Enter BEDFORD *hastily.*

Bed. How now? who is this? Cromwell? By my soul,
Welcome to England! Thou didst save my life,
Didst thou not, Cromwell?
Crom. If I did so, 'tis greater glory
For me [my lord], that you remember it,
Than for myself [now] vainly to report it.
Bed. Well, Cromwell, now's the time [for grati-
I shall commend thee to my sovereign: [tude:]
Cheer up thyself, for I will raise thy state;
A Russell yet was never found ingrate. [*Exit*

Hales. O how uncertain is the wheel of state![1]
Who lately greater than the cardinal,
For fear and love? And now who lower lies?
Gay honors are but fortune's flatteries;
And whom, this day, pride and promotion[2] swell,
To-morrow envy and ambition quell.
More. Who sees the cobweb tangle the poor fly,
May boldly say the wretch's death is nigh.
Gar. I know his state and proud ambition
Were too, too violent to last o'er long.
Hales. Who soars too near the sun with golden wings,
Melts them;—to ruin his own fortune brings.

Enter the Duke of SUFFOLK.

Suff. Cromwell, kneel down, and, in King Henry's [name,
Arise, Sir Thomas;—thus begins thy fame.

Enter the Duke of NORFOLK.

Norf. Cromwell, the gracious majesty of England,
For the good liking he conceives of thee,
Makes thee the master of the jewel-house;
Chief secretary to himself; and, withal,
Creates thee one of his highness' privy council.

Enter the Earl of BEDFORD.

Bed. Where is Sir Thomas Cromwell? Is he knighted?
Suff. He is, my lord.
Bed. Then, to add honor to
His name, the king creates him lord keeper of
His privy seal,[3] and master of the rolls—
Which you, Sir Christopher, do now enjoy:[4]
The king determines higher place for you.
Crom. My lords,
These honors are too high for my desert.
More. O, content thee, man, who would not choose [it?
Yet thou art wise in seeming to refuse it.
Gar. Here are honors, titles, and promotions!
I fear this climbing will have sudden fall. [*Aside.*][5]
Norf. Then come, my lords, let's all together bring
This new-made counsellor to England's king.
[*Exeunt all but* GARDINER.
Gar. But Gardiner means his glory shall be dimmed!
Shall Cromwell live a greater man than I?
My envy with his honor now is bred:
I hope to shorten Cromwell by the head. [*Exit.*

1 We should probably read it "fate" with more propriety—fate in the sense of fortune.

2 Some of the editions read, "pride and *ambition*," but I see no reason to disturb the text.

3 The rise of Cromwell to the highest honors of the state was certainly sudden, but not quite so rapid as the author has represented. In 1531, he was made a privy counsellor and master of the jewel-house; and the next year clerk of the hanaper and chancellor of the exchequer; in 1534, principal secretary of state and master of the rolls. The following year he was appointed vicar-general over all the spiritualities in England, under the king; on the 2d of July, 1536, lord keeper of the privy seal; and, soon afterward, he was advanced to the dignity of a baron. In 1537, he was created knight of the garter; and, in 1540, earl of Essex and lord high chamberlain of England.—MALONE. Mr. Malone has been at great and unnecessary pains to show that our dramatist was not also a chronologist.

4 The fact was exactly the reverse of what is here stated. Cromwell's predecessor in this office was not Sir Christopher Hales, but Dr. Taylor; and Hales (who was the king's attorney-general) *succeeded* Cromwell in the rolls; not, however, immediately on his advancement to the office of keeper of the privy seal.—MALONE.

5 I add this stage direction, which seems necessary, and is appropriate.

SCENE II.—London. *A Street before* CROMWELL'S *House.*

Enter FRESCOBALD.

Fres. O Frescobald! what shall become of thee?
Where shalt thou go, or whither shalt thou turn?
Fortune, that turns her too-inconstant wheel,
Hath drowned[6] thy wealth and riches in the sea.
All parts abroad, wherever I have been,
Grow weary of me, and deny me succor;
My debtors, they that should relieve my want,
Forswear my money—say they owe me none:
They know my state too mean to bear out law;
And here, in London, where I oft have been,
And have done good to many a wretched man,
Am[7] now most wretched and despised myself.
In vain it is more of their hearts to try:
Be patient, therefore, lay thee down and die!
[*Lies down.*

Enter SEELY *and* JOAN.

Seely. Come, Joan; come, let's see what he'll do for us now. I wis we have done for him, when many a time and often he might have gone a hungry to bed.

Wife. Alas! man, now he is made a lord, he'll never look upon us; he'll fulfil the old proverb: *Set beggars a horseback, and they'll ride!* Ah! well-a-day for my cow! Such as he hath made us come behindhand: we had never pawned our cow else to pay our rent.

Seely. Well, Joan, he'll come this way: and by God's dickers, I'll tell him roundly of it; an if he were ten lords, he shall know that I had not my cheese and my bacon for nothing.

Wife. Do you remember, husband, how he would mounch upon my cheese-cakes? He hath forgot this now; but now we'll remember him.

Seely. Ay, we shall have now three flaps with a fox-tail: but i'faith I'll jibber a joint,[7] but I'll tell him his own. Stay, who comes here? O, stand up; here he comes; stand up.

Enter HODGE, *with a tip-staff;* CROMWELL, *with the mace carried before him; the Dukes of* NORFOLK *and* SUFFOLK, *and* Attendants.

Hodge. Come, away with these beggars here. Rise [up,
Sirrah; come out, good people. Run before,
There, ho! [FRESCOBALD *rises and stands aloof.*

Seely. Ay, we are kicked away now, now we come for our own; the time hath been, he would a looked more friendly upon us. And you, Hodge, we know you well enough, though you are so fine.

Crom. Come hither, sirrah; stay, what men are [these?
My honest host of Hounslow, and his wife?
I owe thee money, father, do I not?

Seely. Ay, by the body of me, dost thou: would thou wouldst pay me; good four pound it is: I have the post o't at home.

Crom. I know 'tis true. Sirrah, give him ten an- [gels;
And look your wife and you do stay to dinner.[8]
And while you live, I freely give to you
Four pound a year, for the four pound I owed you.

6 "Turned," is the old reading. 7 "And" in other copies.

8 Jeopard a joint—that is, risk a limb, for my object.

9 Stowe says (quoted by Malone) that he had himself "often seen at Lord Cromwell's gate more than two hundred persons served twice every day with bread, meat, and drink, sufficient."

Seely. Th'art not changed; th'art old Tom still! — Now, God bless thee, good Lord Tom! Home, Joan, home; I'll dine with my Lord Tom to-day, and thou shalt come next week. Fetch my cow; home, Joan, home.

Wife. Now, God bless thee, my good Lord Tom! Fetch my cow presently. [I'll

[*Exit* JOAN.

Enter GARDINER.

Crom. Sirrah, go to yon stranger: tell him I
Desire him stay to dinner: I must speak
With him. [*To* HODGE.

Gar. My lord of Norfolk, see you this same bubble?
That's a mere puff;[1] but mark the end, my lord;
But mark the end!

Norf. I promise you, I like not something he hath done;
But let that pass; the king doth love him well.

Crom. Good-morrow to my lord of Winchester:
You bear me hard about the abbey lands.

Gar. Have I not reason, when religion 's wronged?
You had no color for what you have done.

Crom. Yes, the abolishing of Antichrist,
And of his popish order, from our realm.
I am no enemy to religion,
But what is done, it is for England's good.
What did they serve for, but to feed a sort
Of lazy abbots and of full-fed friars?
They neither plough nor sow, and yet they reap
The fat of all the land, and suck the poor.
Look, what was theirs is in King Henry's hands:
His wealth before lay in the abbey lands.

Gar. Indeed, these things you have alleged, my lord:
When, God doth know, the infant yet unborn
Will curse the time the abbeys were pulled down.
I pray now where is hospitality?
Where now may poor distressèd people go,
For to relieve their need, or rest their bones,
When weary travel doth oppress their limbs?
And where religious men should take them in,
Shall now be kept back by a mastiff-dog;
And thousand, thousand ——

Norf. O my lord, no more;
Things past redress 'tis bootless to complain.

Crom. What, shall we to the convocation-house?

Norf. We'll follow you, my lord; pray, lead the way.

Enter old CROMWELL, *in the dress of a Farmer.*

Old Crom. How! one Cromwell made lord keeper since I left Putney and dwelt in Yorkshire? I never heard better news: I'll see that Cromwell, or it shall go hard.

Crom. My agèd father here! State set aside.
Father, upon my knee I crave your blessing.
One of my servants go and have him in;
At better leisure will we talk with him.

Old Crom. Now if I die, how happy were the day!
To see this comfort, weeps and rains forth showers of joy. [*Exit old* CROMWELL *with* Servant.

Norf. This duty in him shows a kind of grace. [*Aside.*

[1] In the old editions it reads, "That same puff."

Crom. Go on before, for time draws on apace.

[*Exeunt all but* FRESCOBALD.

Fres. I wonder what this lord would have with me,
His man so strictly gave me charge to stay?
I never did offend him to my knowledge.
Well, good or bad, I mean to bide it all;
Worse than I am now, never can befall.

Enter BANISTER *and his* Wife.

Ban. Come, wife, I take it be almost dinner-time;
For Master Newton and Master Crosby sent to me
Last night, they would come dine with me [to-day],
And take their bond in. — Pray thee, hie thee home,
And see that all things be in readiness.

Mrs. Ban. They shall be welcome; husband, I'll before.
But is not that man Master Frescobald?

[*She runs and embraces him.*

Ban. O Heavens! it is kind Master Frescobald.
Say, sir, what hap hath brought you to this pass?

Fres. The same that brought you to your misery.

Ban. Why would you not acquaint me with your state?
Is Banister, your poor friend, then forgot,
Whose goods, whose love, whose life and all, are yours?

Fres. I thought your usage would be as the rest,
That had more kindness at my hands than you,
Yet looked askance when as they saw me poor.

Mrs. Ban. If Banister could bear so base a heart,
I ne'er would look my husband in the face,
But hate him as I would a cockatrice.

Ban. And well thou might'st, should Banister so deal!
Since that I saw you, sir, my state is mended:
And, for the thousand pound I owe to you,
I have it ready for you, sir, at home;
And though I grieve your fortune is so bad,
Yet, that my hap's to help you, makes me glad.
And now, sir, will it please you walk with me?

Fres. Not yet; I can not: for the lord chancellor
Hath here commanded me to wait on him;
For what, I know not: pray God it be for good.

Ban. Never make doubt of that! I'll warrant you!
He is as kind and noble a gentleman
As ever did possess the place he hath.

Mrs. Ban. My brother is his steward, sir; if you please,
We'll go along and bear you company;
I know we shall not want for welcome there.

Fres. With all my heart! But what's become of Bagot?

Ban. He is hanged for buying jewels of the king's.

Fres. A just reward for one so impious!
The time draws on, sir; will you go along?

Ban. I'll follow you, kind Master Frescobald.

[*Exeunt.*

SCENE III. — *The same. Another Street.*

Enter NEWTON *and* CROSBY.

New. Now, Master Crosby, I see you have a care
To keep your word, in payment of your money.

Cros. By my faith, I have some reason on a bond:
Three thousand pounds is far too much to forfeit;
Yet do I doubt not Master Banister.

New. By my faith, sir, your sum is more than mine;
And yet I am not much behind you, too,
Considering what to-day I paid at court.

Cros. Mass, and 'tis well remembered! What's the reason
That the Lord Cromwell's men wear such long skirts
Upon their coats? They reach down to their hams.
New. I will resolve you, sir; and thus it is:
The bishop of Winchester, that loves not Cromwell —
As great men are envied as well as less —
A while ago there was a jar between them,
And it was brought to my Lord Cromwell's ear,
That Bishop Gardiner would sit on his skirts;
Upon which word he made his men long blue coats,
And, in the court, wore one of them himself:
And, meeting with the bishop — quoth he, My lord,
Here's skirts enough now for your grace to sit on:
Which vexed the bishop to the very heart.
This is the reason why they wear these long coats.[1]
Cros. 'Tis always seen, and mark it for a rule,
That one great man will envy still another;
But 'tis a thing that nothing concerns me.
What, shall we now to Master Banister?
New. Ay, come, we'll pay him royally for our dinner. [*Exeunt.*

SCENE IV.—*A Room in* CROMWELL'S *House.*

Enter the Usher *and the* Sewer.[2] Servants *cross the Stage with Dishes in their hands.*

Usher. Uncover, there, gentlemen. [*To* Attendants.

Enter CROMWELL, BEDFORD, SUFFOLK, *old* CROMWELL, FRESCOBALD, SEELY, *and* Attendants.

Crom. My noble lords of Suffolk and of Bedford,
Your honors are welcome to poor Cromwell's house.
Where is my father? Nay, be covered, father;
Although that duty to these noble men
Doth challenge it, yet I'll make bold with them.
Your head doth bear the calendar of care:
What! Cromwell covered, and his father bare?
It must not be.—Now, sir, to you: is not
Your name Frescobald, and a Florentine?
Fres. My name was Frescobald, till cruel fate
Did rob me of my name and of my state.
Crom. What fortune brought you to this country now?
Fres. All other parts have left me succorless,
Save only this. Because of debts I have,
I hope to gain for to relieve my want.
Crom. Did you not once, upon your Florence bridge,
Help a distressed man, robbed by the banditti?
His name was Cromwell.
Fres. I never made my brain
A calendar of any good I did;
I always loved this nation with my heart.
Crom. I am that Cromwell that you there relieved.
You gave me, for to clothe me, sixteen ducats,
Sixteen to bear my charges by the way,
And sixteen more I had for my horse-hire.
There be those several sums justly returned;
Yet 'twere injustice, serving at my need,
For to repay thee without interest:
Therefore receive of me these several bags;
In each of them there are four hundred marks;
And bring to me the names of all your debtors,
And if they will not see you paid, I will.
O, God forbid that I should see him fall,
That helped me in my greatest need of all.
Here stands my father that first gave me life —
Alas! what duty is too much for him?
This man in time of need did save my life —
I therefore can not do too much for him.
By this old man I oftentimes was fed,
Else might I have gone supperless to bed.
Such kindness have I had of these three men,
That Cromwell no way can repay agen.
Now, in to dinner, for we stay too long,
And, to good stomachs, there's no greater wrong. [*Exeunt.*

SCENE V.—*A Room in the Bishop of* WINCHESTER'S *House.*

Enter GARDINER *and* Servant.

Gar. Sirrah, where be those men I caused to stay?
Ser. They do attend your pleasure, sir, within.
Gar. Bid them come hither, and stay you without; [*Exit* Servant.
For, by these men the fox of this same land,
That makes a goose of better than himself,
Must worried be even to his latest home,
Or Gardiner will fail in his intent.
As for the dukes of Suffolk and of Norfolk,
Whom I have sent for, to come speak with me,
Howsoever outwardly they shadow it,
Yet in their hearts I know they love him not.
As for the earl of Bedford, he's but one,
And dares not gainsay what we do set down.

Enter the two Witnesses.

Now, my good friends, you know I saved your lives,
When by the law you had deservéd death;
And then you promised me, upon your oaths,
To venture both your lives to do me good.
Both Wit. We swore no more than that we will perform.
Gar. I take your words; and that which you must do,
Is service for your God and for your king:
To root a rebel from this flourishing land —
One that's an enemy unto the church;
And therefore must you take your solemn oaths
That you heard Cromwell, the lord chancellor,[3]

1 Whatever might have been the reason, the fact is as here represented. Stowe, who tells us that he remembered Cromwell's household, says that the skirts of his yeomen in livery were large enough for his friends to sit upon them.—MALONE. Is not this story of the bishop sitting on his skirts told of the difference between the duke of Buckingham and Cardinal Wolsey?—PERCY. The story told of the duke of Buckingham and Cardinal Wolsey is somewhat different. The duke one day, holding a basin for the king to wash, as soon as his majesty had done, the cardinal dipped his hands in the same water. The duke, resenting this as an indignity, spilled some of the water in Wolsey's shoes, with which, the cardinal being provoked, threatened him that he would sit on his skirts. Buckingham, the next day, came to court very richly dressed, but without skirts to his doublet, assigning, as a reason, to the king, for this strange omission, his purpose to prevent Wolsey from executing his threat.

2 The sewer, or shewer, was the officer in ancient times who set and removed the dishes, and tasted them.

3 Cromwell was never lord chancellor. It is with equal impropriety that he is called lord keeper in a previous scene, and represented with the mace borne before him. It is by confounding the *great* and *privy* seal that the dramatist fell into his error. The charge brought against him by the bishop of wishing a dagger in the king's heart, is pure invention. Gardiner was his enemy, and contributed to his downfall, but he was neither the only nor the principal enemy. Cromwell's ruin was due to several causes—the jealousy of

Did wish a dagger at King Henry's heart:
Fear not to swear it, for I heard him speak it;
Therefore will shield you from ensuing harms.
Both Wit. If you will warrant us the deed is good,
We'll undertake it.
Gar. Kneel down, and I will here absolve you both.
This crucifix[1] I lay upon your heads,
And sprinkle holy water on your brows:
The deed is meritorious that you do,
And by it shall you purchase grace from Heaven.
1 *Wit.* Now, sir, we'll undertake it, by our souls!
2 *Wit.* For Cromwell never loved one of our sort.
Gar. I know he hath not; and, for both of you,
I will prefer you to some place of worth.
Now get you in, until I call for you,
For presently the dukes mean to be here.
[*Exeunt* Witnesses.
Cromwell, sit fast; thy time's not long to reign:
The abbeys that were pulled down by thy means,
Are now a mean for me to pull thee down;
Thy pride thy own head also lights upon,
For thou art he hath changed religion.
But now no more, for here the dukes are come.

Enter SUFFOLK, NORFOLK, *and the Earl of* BEDFORD.

Suff. Good-even to my lord bishop.
Norf. How fares my lord? what, are you all alone?
Gar. No, not alone, my lords; my mind is troubled:
I know your honors muse wherefore I sent,
And in such haste. What, came you from the king?
Norf. We did, and left none but Lord Cromwell with him.
Gar. O, what a dangerous time is this we live in!
There's Thomas Wolsey—he's already gone;
And Thomas More—he followed after him;
Another Thomas yet there doth remain,
That is far worse than either of those twain;
And if with speed, my lords, we not pursue it,
I fear the king and all the land will rue it.
Bed. Another Thomas? Pray God, it be not Cromwell!
Gar. My lord of Bedford, 'tis that traitor Cromwell.
Bed. Is Cromwell false? My heart will never think it.
Suff. My lord of Winchester, what likelihood,
Or proof, have you, of this his treachery?
Gar. My lord, too much. Call in the men within.

Enter the Witnesses.

These men, my lord, upon their oaths affirm
That they did hear Lord Cromwell, in his garden,
Wishing a dagger sticking at the heart
Of our King Henry;—what is this but treason?
Bed. If it be so, my heart doth bleed with sorrow.
Suff. How say you, friends? What, did you hear these words?
1 *Wit.* We did, an't like your grace.
Norf. In what place was Lord Cromwell when he spake them?
2 *Wit.* In his garden, where we did attend a suit,
Which we had waited for two years and more.
Suff. How long is't since you heard him speak these words?
2 *Wit.* Some half a year since.
Bed. How chance that you concealed it all this time?
1 *Wit.* His greatness made us fear; that was the cause.
Gar. Ay, ay, his greatness, that's the cause indeed:
And to make his treason here more manifest,
He calls his servants to him round about,
Tells them of Wolsey's life, and of his fall:
Says that himself hath many enemies;
And gives to some of them a park, or manor;
To others, leases; lands to other some.
What need he do this in his prime of life,
An if he were not fearful of his death?
Suff. My lord, these likelihoods are very great.
Bed. Pardon me, lords, for I must needs depart;
Their proofs are great, but greater is my heart.
[*Exit* BEDFORD.
Norf. My friends, take heed of that which you have said:
Your souls must answer what your tongues report:
Therefore, take heed; be wary what you do.
2 *Wit.* My lord, we speak no more but truth,
Norf. Let them depart,[2] my lord of Winchester;
Let these men be close kept,
Until the day of trial.
Gar. They shall, my lord. Ho! take in these two men. [*Exeunt* Witnesses, &c.
My lords, if Cromwell have a public trial,
That which we do is void by his denial:
You know the king will credit none but him.
Norf. 'Tis true; he rules the king even as he pleases.
Suff. How shall we do for to attach him, then?
Gar. Marry, thus, my lord; by an act he made himself,
With an intent to entrap some of our lives—
And this it is: If any counsellor
Be convicted of high-treason, he shall
Be executed without public trial.
This act, my lords, he caused the king to make.
Suff. He did, indeed, and I remember it;
And now 'tis like to fall upon himself.
Norf. Let us not slack it; 'tis for England's good;
We must be wary, else he'll go beyond us!
Gar. Well hath your grace said, my good lord of [Norfolk,
Therefore let us to Lambeth presently:
Thither comes Cromwell from the court to-night:
Let us arrest him, send him to the Tower,
And, in the morn, cut off the traitor's head.
Norf. Come, then, about it; let us guard the town;
This is the day that Cromwell must go down.
Gar. Along, my lords. Well, Cromwell is half dead:
He shook my heart, but I will shear his head!
[*Exeunt.*

the nobility, the subversion of the monasteries, and not least, the king's aversion to Anne of Cleves, and his desire to marry Catherine Howard, niece to the duke of Norfolk, who was Cromwell's chief assailant.—*Note of Malone, abridged.*

1 It is supposed that, before the Reformation, the English bishops wore a small crucifix hanging to their outward garments, as in popish countries the bishops do at this day. MALONE.

2 "Let them depart," in one breath, and "let them be kept," in another, denotes a gross corruption of the passage. "*Set* them apart," would be the probable reading, were it not that Norfolk has no motive or desire to purge their testimony. Perhaps the true reading should be—

"Let them be kept, my lord of Winchester,
Close, till the day of trial."

ACT V.

SCENE I.—*A Street in* London.

Enter BEDFORD.

Bed. My soul is like a water [greatly] troubled;
And Gardiner is the man that makes it so.
O, Cromwell, I do fear thy end is near!
Yet I'll prevent their malice if I can:
And, in good time, see where the man doth come,
Who little knows how near's his day of doom.

Enter CROMWELL *with his train;* BEDFORD *makes as though he would speak to him;* CROMWELL *goes on.*

Crom. You're well encountered, my good lord of Bedford:
I see your honor is addressed to talk:—
Pray, pardon me; I am sent for to the king,
And do not know the business yet myself:—
So fare you well, for I must needs be gone.
[*Exit* CROMWELL, *&c.*

Bed. [Be gone] you must; well, what [the] remedy?
I fear too soon you must be gone indeed.
The king hath business;—little dost thou know
Who's busy for thy life: thou think'st not so.

Re-enter CROMWELL, *attended.*

Crom. The second time well met, my lord of Bedford:
I am very sorry that my haste is such;
Lord Marquis Dorset being sick to death,
I must receive of him the privy seal.
At Lambeth, soon, my lord, we'll take our fill.
[*Exit.*

Bed. How smooth and easy is the way to death!

Enter a Messenger.

Mess. My lord, the dukes of Norfolk and of Suffolk,
Accompanied with the bishop of Winchester,
Entreat you to come presently to Lambeth,
On earnest matters that concern the state.

Bed. To Lambeth! so: go fetch me pen and ink;
I and Lord Cromwell there shall talk enough:
Ay, and our last, I fear, an if he come. [*Writes.*
Here, take this letter—bear it to Lord Cromwell:
Bid him to read it; say't concerns him near;
Away! begone! make all the haste you can.
To Lambeth do I go, a woful man. [*Exeunt.*

SCENE II.—*A Street near the Thames.*

Enter CROMWELL, *attended.*

Crom. Is the barge ready? I will straight to Lambeth;
And, if this one day's business once were past,
I'd take my ease to-morrow, after trouble.

Enter Messenger.

How now, my friend, what, wouldst thou speak with me?

Mess. Sir, here's a letter from my lord of Bedford.
[Messenger *gives letter.* CROMWELL *puts it in his pocket.*

Crom. O good, my friend, commend me to thy lord:
Hold, take these angels; drink them for thy pains.

Mess. He doth desire your grace to read it [straight],
Because he says it doth concern you near.

Crom. Bid him assure himself of that: farewell;
To-morrow, tell him, he shall hear from me.—
Set on before there, and away to Lambeth.
[*Exeunt.*

SCENE III.—*Lambeth.*

Enter GARDINER, SUFFOLK, NORFOLK, BEDFORD, Lieutenant *of the* Tower, Sergeant-at-arms, Herald, *and* Halberdiers.

Gar. Halberts, stand close unto the water-side,
Sergeant-at-arms, be you bold in your office;
Herald, deliver [now] your proclamation.

Her. This is to give notice to all the king's subjects, the late Lord Cromwell, lord chancellor of England, vicar-general over the realm, him to hold and esteem as a traitor, against the crown and dignity of England. So, God save the king!

Gar. Amen.

Bed. Amen, and [may God] root thee from the land,
For, whilst thou livest, the truth can never stand.

Nor. Make a lane there, the traitor is at hand.
Keep back Cromwell's men:
Drown them if they come on. Sergeant, your office!

Enter CROMWELL, *attended. The* Halberdiers *make a lane.*

Crom. What means my lord of Norfolk by these words?
Sirs, come along.

Gar. Kill them, if they come on.

Ser. Lord Thomas Cromwell, in King Henry's name,
I do arrest your honor of high treason.

Crom. Sergeant, me of treason!
[CROMWELL's Men *offer to draw.*

Suff. Kill them, if they draw a sword.

Crom. Hold, I charge you,
As you love me, [friends,] draw not a sword,
Who dares accuse Cromwell of treason now?

Gar. This is no place to reckon up your crime,
Your dove-like looks were viewed with serpent's eyes.

Crom. With serpent's eyes, indeed, if[1] thine they were.
But, Gardiner, do thy worst; I fear thee not.
My faith compared with thine, as much shall pass,
As doth the diamond [still] excel the glass:
Attached of treason, no accusers by,
Indeed! what tongue dares speak so foul a lie?

Norf. My lord, my lord, matters are too well known,
And it is time the king had note thereof.

Crom. The king, let me go to him, face to face,
No better trial I desire than that.
Let him but say that Cromwell's faith was feigned,
Then let my honor, and my name be stained;
If e'er my heart against the king was set,
O let my soul in judgment answer it!
Then, if my faith's confirmed with his reason,
'Gainst whom hath Cromwell then committed treason?

Suff. My lord, your matter shall be [quickly] tried,
Meantime, with patience [pray] content yourself.

Crom. Perforce, I must with patience be content:
O, dear friend Bedford, dost thou stand so near?
Cromwell rejoiceth, one friend sheds a tear:
And whither is't? Which way must Cromwell now?

1 "*By* thine," in former copies.

Gar. My lord, you must unto the Tower: lieutenant,
Take him into your charge.
Crom. Well, where you please; but yet, before I part,
Let me confer a little with my men.
Gar. Ay, as you go by water, so you shall.
Crom. I have some business present to impart.
Norf. You may not stay: lieutenant, take your charge.
Crom. Well, well, my lord, you second Gardiner's text.
Norfolk, farewell! thy turn will be the next.
[*Exeunt* CROMWELL *and the* Lieutenant.
Gar. His guilty conscience makes him rave, my lord.
Norf. Ay, let him talk; his time is short enough.
Gar. My lord of Bedford, come; you weep for him,
That would not shed a [single] tear for you.
Bed. It grieves me for to see his sudden fall
Gar. Such success wish I unto traitors all.
[*Exeunt.*

SCENE IV.—London. *A Street.*

Enter two Citizens.

1 *Cit.* Why? can this news be true? is't possible?
The great Lord Cromwell 'rested for high treason,
I hardly will believe it can be so.
2 *Cit.* It is too true, sir; would't were otherwise,
Condition I spent half the wealth I have.
I was at Lambeth, saw him there arrested,
And afterward committed to the Tower.
1 *Cit.* What, was't for treason that he was committed?
2 *Cit.* Kind noble gentleman! I may rue the time:
All that I have, I did enjoy by him;
And, if he die, then all my state is gone.
1 *Cit.* It may be hoped, sir, that he shall not die,
Because the king did favor him so much.
2 *Cit.* O, sir, you are deceived in thinking so:
The grace and favor he had with the king,
Hath caused him have so many enemies:
He that in court secure will keep himself,
Must not be great, for then he is envied at.
The shrub is safe, when as the cedar shakes;
For where the king doth love above compare,
Of others, they as much more envied are.
1 *Cit.* 'Tis pity that this nobleman should fall,
He did so many charitable deeds.
2 *Cit.* 'Tis true; and yet you see, in each estate,
There's none so good, but some one doth him hate;
And they before would smile him in the face,
Will be the foremost to do him disgrace.
What, will you go along unto the court?
1 *Cit.* I care not if I do, and hear the news,
How men will judge what shall become of him.
2 *Cit.* Some men will speak him hardly, some will pity.
Go you to the court? I'll go into the city:
There I am sure to hear more news than you.
1 *Cit.* Why then we soon will meet again. Adieu.
[*Exeunt.*

SCENE V.—*A Room in the* Tower.

Enter CROMWELL.

Crom. Now, Cromwell, hast thou time to meditate,
And think upon thy state, and of the time.
Thy honors came unsought, ay, and unlooked for;
Thy fall is sudden, and unlooked for, too.
What glory was in England that I had not?
Who in this land commanded more than Cromwell?
Except the king, who greater than myself?
But now I see, what after-ages shall,
More great the men, more sudden is their fall.
And now I do remember, th' earl of Bedford
Was very desirous for to speak to me;
And afterward sent unto me a letter,
The which I think I still have in my pocket;
Now may I read it, for I now have leisure,
And this, I take't, it is. [*He reads the letter.*
My lord, come not this night to Lambeth,
For if you do, your state is overthrown;
And much I doubt your life, an if you come:
Then, if you love yourself, stay where you are.
O God, had I but read this [friendly] letter,
Then had I been free from the lion's paw:
Deferring this to read until to-morrow,
I spurned at joy, and did embrace my sorrow.

Enter the Lieutenant *of the* Tower, Officers, *&c.*

Master lieutenant, when's this day of death?
Lieu. Alas, my lord, would I might never see it!
Here are the dukes of Suffolk and of Norfolk,
Winchester, Bedford, and Sir Richard Radcliff,
With others still;—but why they come I know not.
Crom. No matter wherefore; Cromwell is prepared,
For Gardiner has my life and state ensnared.
Bid them come in, or you shall do them wrong,
For here stands he, who some think, lives too long;—
Learning kills learning, and, instead of ink
To dip his pen, Cromwell's heart-blood doth drink.

Enter the Dukes of SUFFOLK *and* NORFOLK; *the Earl of* BEDFORD, GARDINER, *Bishop of* WINCHESTER, Sir RICHARD RADCLIFF, *and* Sir RALPH SADLER.

Norf. Good-morrow, Cromwell. What, so sad?
Crom. One good among you, none of you are bad:
For my part, it best fits me be alone;
Sadness with me, not I with any one.
Have you the king acquainted with my cause?
Norf. We have, and he hath answered us, my lord.
Crom. How shall I come to speak with him myself?
Gar. The king is so advertised of your guilt,
He'll by no means admit you to his presence.
Crom. No way admit me! am I so soon forgot?
Did he but yesterday embrace my neck,
And say that Cromwell was even half himself?
And are his princely ears so much bewitched
With scandalous ignominy, and slanderous speeches,
That now he doth deny to look on me?
Well, lord of Winchester, no doubt but you
Are much in favor with his majesty,
Wilt bear a letter from me to his grace?
Gar. Pardon me, I'll bear no traitor's letters.
Crom. Ha, will you do this kindness then, to tell him,
By word of mouth, what I shall say to you?
Gar. That will I.
Crom. But, on your honor will you?
Gar. Ay, on my honor.
Crom. Bear witness, lords.—
Tell him, when he hath known you,
And tried your faith but half so much as mine,
He'll find you to be the falsest-hearted man
[Living] in England: pray [you] tell him this.
Bed. Be patient, good my lord, in these extremities

Crom. My kind and honorable lord of Bedford,
I know your honor always loved me well:
But, pardon me, this still shall be my theme;
Gardiner's the cause makes Cromwell's so extreme.
Sir Ralph Sadler, I pray a word with you;
You were my man, and all that you possess
Came by my means: sir, to requite all this,
Say, will you take this letter here of me,
And give it with your own hands to the king?
Sad. I kiss your hand, and never will I rest,
Ere to the king this be delivered. [*Exit* SADLER.
Crom. Why then hath Cromwell yet one friend in store.
Gard. But all the haste he makes shall be but vain;
Here's a discharge, sir, for your prisoner,
To see him executed presently:
My lord, you hear the tenure of your life.
Crom. I do embrace it; welcome my last date,
And of this glistering world I take last leave;
And, noble lords, I take my leave of you.
As willingly I go to meet with death,
As Gardiner did pronounce it with his breath:
From treason is my heart as white as snow,
My death procurèd only by my foe:
I pray commend me to my sovereign king,
And tell him in what sort his Cromwell died,
To lose his head before his cause was tried;
But let his grace, when he shall hear my name,
Say only this;—Gardiner procured the same.

Enter young CROMWELL.

Lieut. Here is your son, sir, come to take his leave.
Crom. To take his leave? Come hither, Harry Cromwell;
Mark, boy, the last words that I speak to thee;
Flatter not fortune, neither fawn upon her;
Gape not for state, yet lose no spark of honor;
Ambition, like the plague see thou eschew it;
I die for treason, boy, and never knew it;
Yet, let thy faith as spotless be as mine,
And Cromwell's virtues in thy face shall shine:
Come, go along and see me leave my breath,
And I'll leave thee upon the floor of death.
Son. O father, I shall die to see that wound,
Your blood being spilt will make my heart to swound.
Crom. How, boy, not dare to look upon the axe?
How shall I do then, to have my head struck off?
Come on, my child, and see the end of all,
And after say, that Gardiner was my fall.
Gar. My lord, you speak it of an envious heart,
I have done no more than law and equity.
Bed. O, my good lord of Winchester, forbear;
'Twould better have beseemed you to be absent,
Than, with your words, disturb a dying man.
Crom. Who, me, my lord? no: he disturbs not me;
My mind he stirs not, though his mighty shock
Hath brought more peers' heads down unto the block.
Farewell, my boy; all Cromwell can bequeath,
My hearty blessing!—so, I take my leave.
Hang. I am your deathsman; pray, my lord, forgive me.
Crom. Even with my soul! why, man, thou art my doctor,
And bring'st me precious physic for my soul;
My lord of Bedford, I desire of you,
Before my death, a corporal embrace.
[CROMWELL *embraces him.*
Farewell, great lord; my lord,[1] I do commend
My heart to you; my soul to heaven I send;
This is my joy, that ere my body fleet,
Your honored arms are my true winding-sheet;
Farewell, dear Bedford, my peace is made in heaven;
Thus falls great Cromwell, a poor ell in length,
To rise t'unmeasured height, winged with new strength.
The land of worms,[2] which dying men discover.
My soul is shrined with heaven's celestial cover.
[*Exeunt* CROMWELL, Officers, *&c.*
Bed. Well, farewell. Cromwell! sure the truest friend
That ever Bedford shall possess again!
Well, lords, I fear that when this man is dead,
You'll wish in vain that Cromwell had a head.

Enter Officer, *with* CROMWELL'S *Head.*

Offi. Here is the head of the deceased Cromwell.
Bed. Pray thee go hence, and bear his head away
Unto his corse;—inter them both in clay.

Enter Sir RALPH SADLER.

Sad. How now, my lords? what, is Lord Cromwell dead?
Bed. Lord Cromwell's body now doth want a head.
Sad. O, God! a little speed had saved his life.
Here is a kind reprieve come from the king,
To bring him straight unto his majesty.
Suff. Ay, ay, Sir Ralph, reprieves come now too late.
Gar. My conscience tells me now this deed was ill!
Would Christ that Cromwell were alive again!
Norf. Come, let us to the king, who, well I know,
Will grieve for Cromwell, that his death was so.
[*Exeunt.*

1 Old copy reads, "my *love*."
2 This passage is manifestly corrupt.

THE END OF THE LIFE AND DEATH OF THOMAS LORD CROMWELL.

INTRODUCTION

TO

SIR JOHN OLDCASTLE.

The history of Sir John Oldcastle may be found in Holingshead; but the author of the drama has not been tenacious of his facts. He has used them at pleasure, wherever a perversion of them might heighten the interest of the play, or bring out the character of his hero more impressively. The play before us was entered on the stationer's books, on the 4th of August, 1600, as "The first part of the History of the Life of Sir John Oldcastle — Lord Cobham;" the second part, "with his martyrdom," was entered at the same time; but this was never published. The first part was entered *without* the name of Shakspeare; but of two editions printed in 1600, one of them bears the name of William Shakspeare at full length, in the titlepage, with the addition: "as it hath beene lately acted by the Right Honorable the Earle of Nottingham, Lord High Admiral of England, his Servants." Mr. Knight remarks, of this fact: "In 1594, a play of Shakspeare's might have been acted as we believe Hamlet was, at Henslowe's theatre, which was that of the lord high admiral his servants; but in 1600, a play of Shakspeare's would have unquestionably been acted by the lord chamberlain his servants." This is not conclusive. The interest of Shakspeare, in 1600, undoubtedly lay in the latter theatre; but a former play might have become the property of the manager of another house, at a time when Shakspeare was connected with neither, and thus be entirely out of the author's possession and control, as well to revise, rewrite, or entirely suppress. Recently, however, we find by the Diary of Ph. Henslowe, lately published by the Shakspeare Society, that, on the 16th of October, 1599, he paid "for the first part of the Lyfe of Sir Ihon Oldcastle, and in earnest of the second Pte., for the use of the company, ten pound;" and the money was received by "Thomas Downton," "to pay Mr. Monday, Mr. Drayton, Mr. Wilson, and Mr. Hathaway." This might be considered conclusive, were it not that nothing was more frequent than the production, at rival theatres, of pieces on the same subjects, particularly at the same time, and when the successful run of one piece provoked the cupidity of managers to desire a share in the profits accruing largely to their neighbors. The very employment of no less than four hands, in the preparation of this play, would seem to declare some present emergency. Mr. Knight speaks of it "as a very curious example of the imperfect manner in which it was attempted to imitate the excellence, and to rival the popularity, of Shakspeare's best historical plays, at the time of their original production." Certainly, there are several respects in which Sir John Oldcastle reminds us of Shakspeare. The character of Sir John of Wrotham, the priest, is just such an instance of resemblance, as a feebler or a younger writer would attempt, at the character of Falstaff, who desired at the same time to escape the charge of imitation.

The prologue has been relied upon to prove that Shakspeare had no agency in the piece, since it is supposed in two of the lines to reflect unfavorably upon his own labors :—

"It is no pampered glutton we present,
Nor aged counsellor to youthful sin."

Offence seems to have been taken at the character of Falstaff, who, it appears, had been confounded with Sir John Oldcastle. The employment of this name, openly, at the head of a new piece, might have occasioned some doubts as to the character in which that historical personage would be shown; and the language of the prologue was intended to disarm all apprehensions.

"Let fair truth be graced"—

is the entreaty of the dramatist—

"Since forged invention former time defaced."

This is construed into a sarcasm upon Shakspeare's labors in Falstaff, and is supposed to be conclusive against his share in the production. If a sarcasm, it is a very gentle one. Shakspeare himself judges of Falstaff, through Henry V. and the Chief Justice, much more severely, and in much the same language. Were we, indeed, disposed to make out a case, we might insist upon this prologue as really apologetic, and assume that the play was chiefly written to atone for the supposed wrong done by the author of Sir John Falstaff, to the historical reputation of Sir John Oldcastle. But we take no interest in the question.

It may be well to mention, that the opinion is held by some that the Sir John Falstaff of Shakspeare's Henry IV. was originally *called* Sir John Oldcastle. The character and name, indeed, seem to have been employed frequently by the dramatists. In the old play of "The Famous Victories," according to Mr. Knight, the character of Sir John Oldcastle occurs as a low and ruffianly sort of person. Fuller, in his Church History, has something directly on this subject. "Stage poets," quoth he, "have themselves been very bold with, and others very merry at, the memory of Sir John Oldcastle, whom they have fancied a boon companion, a jovial royster, and a coward to boot. The best is, Sir John Falstaff hath relieved the memory of Sir John Oldcastle, and of late is substituted buffoon in his place." This description of Fuller would seem especially to describe our own Sir John of Shakspeare memory. Mr. Knight adds: "Whether or not Shakspeare's Falstaff was originally called Oldcastle, he was, after the character was fairly established as Falstaff, anxious to vindicate himself from the charge that he had attempted to represent the Oldcastle of history. In the epilogue to the Second Part of Henry IV., we find this passage: "For anything I know, Falstaff shall die of a sweat, unless already he be killed with your hard opinions; for Oldcastle died a martyr, and this is not the man." This would show a consciousness of some necessity to apologize and atone for the past—precisely some such feeling us would prompt the language of the prologue to Sir John Oldcastle;—which is very well written, and in that frank and manly style which distinguishes the poetry of Shakspeare, when he contemplates nothing beyond the actual and direct :—

"The *doubtful* title, gentlemen, prefixed
Upon the argument we have in hand,
May breed suspense, and wrongfully disturb
The peaceful quiet of your settled thoughts:
To stop which scruple, let this brief suffice:
It is no pampered glutton we present,
Nor aged counsellor to youthful sin,
But one," &c.:
"*Let fair truth be graced,*
Since forged invention former time defaced."

"The mode," says Mr. Knight, "in which some of the German critics have spoken of this play, is a rebuke to dogmatic assertions and criticism." We have shown, elsewhere, what Schlegel says concerning these biographical dramas;—how he describes Sir John Oldcastle, Thomas Lord Cromwell, and the Yorkshire Tragedy—putting them all in the same category—as not only unquestionably Shakspeare's, but the best of his works, and models of their species. Teick is equally confident in assigning the authorship of the play before us to Shakspeare. Ulrici, on the contrary, takes a more sober view of the matter. He says: "The whole betrays a poët who endeavored to form himself on Shakspeare's model—nay, even to imitate him—but who stood far below him in mind and talent."

Schlegel's criticism seems wholly valueless in regard to these plays. There is, for example, a monstrous inequality between the play of Cromwell and Oldcastle. To class them together, as equally models, and either as worthy to be ranked among the best of Shakspeare's plays, is sheer absurdity.

But Sir John Oldcastle is a performance of very considerable merit. The poetry is sometimes forcicible and fine, if not rich and generous. It lacks the glow, the fire, and invention, of Shakspeare, when on the wing, but possesses his frankness, impulse, and transparency. When Ulrici speaks of the unknown author of this play as imitating Shakspeare, or modelling himself upon him, he probably confounds two things, in their nature very different. It appears to me that, while the author of Sir John Oldcastle has appropriated certain of Shakspeare's materials, some two or more of his characters, and some of his incidents, he has, neither in the plan of his story, nor in the structure of his verse, imitated any writer. His style of expression seems to be that of a practised writer, confident in his own mode of utterance, and never pausing to pick and choose his phrase in regard to any model. Remark, for instance, the prologue, where we see an instance of ease and freedom in the verse, such as prevails in all the better portions of this play, which conclusively show the habitual writer, and one totally unaffected and unconstrained in the manner of delivering himself. If Shakspeare did not write this play — and we attempt only to furnish the reader with the facts in relation to the question, and not to provide a comment upon them — there are certain portions of it which are quite worthy of his pen. Take, for example, the manner in which the conspirators attempt to inveigle Lord Cobham into their confederacy. The allegory here is well sustained, and very forcibly given :—

"*Cam.* Nay, but the stag which we desire to strike,
Lives not in Cowling: if you will consent,
And go with us, we'll bring you to a forest
Where runs a lusty herd; among the which
There is a stag superior to the rest;
A stately beast, that, when his fellows run,
He leads the race, and beats the sullen earth,
As though he scorned it, with his trampling hoofs;
Aloft he bears his head, and with his breast,
Like a a huge bulwark, counterchecks the wind:
And, when he standeth still, he stretcheth forth
His proud ambitious neck, as if he meant
To wound the firmament with forked horns.
Cob. 'Tis pity such a goodly beast should die.
Cam. Not so, Sir John; for he is tyrannous,
And gores the other deer, and will not keep
Within the limits are appointed him.
Of late he's broke into a several,
Which doth belong to me, and there he spoils
Both corn and pasture. Two of his wild race,
Alike for stealth and covetous encroaching,
Already are removed: if he were dead,
I should not only be secure from hurt,
But with his body make a royal feast."

It is objected to the morality of this part of the play, that Cobham should betray those who had confided their conspiracy to him. I am somewhat doubtful whether this censure is deserved. What was Cobham to do? The friend of the king, a conspiracy is forced upon him, of which he disapproves, which contemplates the king's murder. Is he to suffer it to go forward to completion of its objects? Surely not. If he had sought out the conspirators for their secret, and under false guises had obtained it, then to betray them would have been criminal; but this was not the case. They thrust themselves upon him, assuming that he sympathizes with them, and the safety of the king compels the course which he adopts.

As a play, Sir John Oldcastle lacks unity. It is desultory, and the purposes of the several characters do not work together. The several performances of the parties do not contemplate the denouément. The separate scenes are lively — some of them very impressive — and more than one of the persons of the drama are exceedingly well conceived. Sir John of Wrotham, who is meant to be a Falstaff, with the additional virtue of courage, might have been successful, but that Falstaff stood in his way. Whether drawn by Shakspeare or another, the character of Sir John of Wrotham fails only as it reminds us that we have known Falstaff. It was this knowledge that paralyzed the effort to repaint the character under another name, and with additional attributes. Our "sweet Jack Falstaff," "kind Jack Falstaff," "true Jack Falstaff," "valiant and plump Jack Falstaff," is already sufficiently perfect; and an accumulation of more virtues in his character might only withdraw him in some degree from our sympathies. Sir John of Wrotham is a failure; but we see what he might have been, but for the overwhelming excellence of his predecessor.

SIR JOHN OLDCASTLE.

PART FIRST.

PERSONS REPRESENTED.

KING HENRY THE FIFTH.
Sir JOHN OLDCASTLE, Lord COBHAM.
Lord HERBERT.
Lord POWIS.
The DUKE OF SUFFOLK.
The EARL OF HUNTINGTON.
The EARL OF CAMBRIDGE, Lord SCROOP, Sir THOMAS GREY, } *Conspirators against the king.*
Sir ROGER ACTON, Sir RICHARD LEE, Master BOURN, Master BEVERLEY, MURLEY, *the Brewer of* Dunstable, } *Rebels.*
The BISHOP OF ROCHESTER.
Two Judges of Assize.
Lord-Warden of the Cinque Ports.
Master BUTLER, *Gentleman of the Privy Chamber.*
CHARTRES, *the* French *Agent.*
CROMER, *Sheriff of* Kent.
The Mayor of Hereford.
The Sheriff of Hereford shire.
Sir JOHN, *the Parson of* Wrotham.
Lieutenant of the Tower.
The Mayor and Gaoler of St. Alban's.
A Kentish *Constable and an Ale-man.*
DICK *and* TOM, *Servants to* Murley.
An Irishman.
HARPOOL, *Servant to the Lord* Cobham.
GOUGH, *Servant to* Lord Herbert.
OWEN *and* DAVY, *Servants to* Lord Powis.
CLUN, *Sumner to the Bishop of* Rochester.

Lady COBHAM.
Lady POWIS.
DOLL, *Concubine to* Sir John, *Parson of* Wrotham.
KATE, *the Carrier's Daughter.*

Host, Ostler, Carriers, Soldiers, Beggarmen, Constables, Warders of the Tower, *Bailiffs, Messengers, and Attendants.*

SCENE,—ENGLAND.

PROLOGUE.

The doubtful title, gentlemen, prefixed
Upon the argument we have in hand,
May breed suspence, and wrongfully disturb
The peaceful quiet of your settled thoughts.
To stop which scruple, let this brief suffice;
It is no pampered glutton we present,
Nor agéd counsellor to youthful sin;
But one, whose virtues shine above the rest,
A valiant martyr, and a virtuous peer;
In whose true faith and loyalty expressed
Unto his sovereign, and his country's weal,
We strive to pay that tribute of our love
Your favors merit. Let fair truth be graced,
Since forged invention former time defaced.

ACT I.

SCENE I.—*A Street in* Hereford.

Enter Lord HERBERT, Lord POWIS, OWEN, GOUGH, DAVY, *and others,* followers *of the* Lords Powis *and* HERBERT. *They fight. Enter the* Sheriff *of* Hereford shire *and a* Bailiff.

Sher. My lords, I charge you in his highness' name,
To keep the peace, you and your followers.

Herb. Good master sheriff, look unto yourself.

Pow. Do so, for we have other business.

[*They attempt to fight again.*

Sher. Will ye disturb the judges, and the assize?
Hear the king's proclamation;—ye were best.

Pow. Hold, then; let's hear it.

Herb. But be brief, be brief!

Bail. O—yes.

Davy. Cossone, make shorter O, or shall mar your yes.

Bail. O—yes.

Owen. What, has hur nothing to say but, O yes?

Bail. O—yes.

Davy. O nay; py coss plut, down with hur, down with hur. A Powis! a Powis!

Gough. A Herbert! a Herbert! and down with Powis! [*They fight again.*

Sher. Hold! in the king's name, hold!

Owen. Down with a knave's name, down.

[*The* Bailiff *is knocked down, and the* Sheriff *runs away.*

Herb. Powis, I think thy Welsh and thou do smart.

Pow. Herbert, I think my sword came near thy heart.

Herb. Thy heart's best blood shall pay the loss of mine.

Gough. A Herbert! a Herbert!

Davy. A Powis! a Powis!

As they are fighting, enter the Mayor *of* Hereford, *his* Officers *and* Townsmen, *with Clubs.*

Mayor. My lords, as you are liegemen to the crown,
True noblemen, and subjects to the king,
Attend his highness' proclamation,
Commanded by the judges of assize,
For keeping peace at this assembly.

Herb. Good master mayor of Hereford, be brief.

Mayor. Sergeant, without the ceremonies of "O yes,"
Pronounce aloud the proclamation.

Serg. The king's justices, perceiving what public mischief may ensue this private quarrel, in his majesty's name do straightly charge and command all persons, of what degree soever, to depart this city of Hereford, except such as are bound to give attendance at this assize, and that no man presume to wear any weapon, especially welsh-hooks, forest-bills.

Owen. Haw? No pill nor Wells hoog? ha?

Mayor. Peace, and hear the proclamation.

Serg. And that the lord Powis do presently disperse and discharge his retinue, and depart the city in the king's peace, he and his followers, on pain of imprisonment.

Davy. Haw? pud hur lord Powis in prison? A Powis! A Powis! Cossone, hur will live and tie with hur lord.

Gough. A Herbert! a Herbert!

They fight; Lord Herbert *is wounded, and falls to the ground; the* Mayor *and his followers interpose.* Lord Powis *runs away. Enter two* Judges, *the* Sheriff *and his* Bailiffs *before them.*

1 *Judge.* Where's the lord Herbert? Is he hurt or slain?

Sher. He's here, my lord.

2 *Judge.* How fares his lordship, friends?

Gough. Mortally wounded, speechless; he can not live.

1 *Judge.* Convey him hence, let not his wounds take [air,
And get them[1] dressed with expedition.

[*Exeunt* Lord Herbert *and* Gough.

Master mayor of Hereford, master sh'riff o'the shire,
Commit Lord Powis to safe custody,
To answer the disturbance of the peace,
Lord Herbert's peril, and his high contempt
Of us, and you, the king's commissioners: —
See it be done with care and diligence.

Sher. Please it your lordship, my lord Powis is gone,
Past all recovery.

2 *Judge.* Yet, let search be made,
To apprehend his followers that are left.

Sher. Here are some of them, sirs; lay hold of them.

Owen. Of us? and why? what has hur done, I pray you?

Sher. Disarm them, bailiffs.

Mayor. Officers, assist.

Davy. Hear you, lord shudge, what resson for this?

Owen. Cossone, pe'puse for fighting for our lord?

1 *Judge.* Away with them.

Davy. Harg you, my lord.

Owen. Gough, my lord Herbert's man's a scurvy[2] knave.

Davy. I'se live and tie in good quarrel.

Owen. Pray you do shustice, let awl be prison.

Davy. Prison, no!
Lord shudge, I wool give you pale, good surety.

2 *Judge.* What bail? what sureties?

Davy. Hur cozen ap Rice, ap Evan, ap Morice, ap Morgan, ap Llwellyn, ap Madoc, ap Meredith, ap Griffin, ap Davy, ap Owen, ap Shinken Shones.

2 *Judge.* Two of the most sufficient are enow.

Sher. An't please your lordship, these are all but one.

1 *Judge.* To jail with them, and the Lord Herbert's men.
We'll talk with them, when the assize is done.

[*Exeunt* Bailiffs *with* Owen, Davy, *&c.*

Riotous, audacious, and unruly grooms,
Must we be forced to come from [off] the bench,
To quiet brawls, which every constable
In other civil places can suppress?

2 *Judge.* What was the quarrel that caused all this stir?

Sher. About religion, as I heard, my lord;—
Lord Powis detracted from the power of Rome,
Affirming Wickliffe's doctrine to be true,
And Rome's erroneous: hot reply was made
By the lord Herbert, — they were traitors all
That would maintain it. Powis answerèd; —
They were as true, as noble, and as wise,
As he, — and would defend it with their lives!
He named, for instance, Sir John Oldcastle,
The lord Cobham: Herbert replied again, —
He, thou, and all, are traitors that so hold.
The lie was given, the several factions drawn,
And so enraged, that we could not appease it.

1 *Judge.* This case concerns the king's prerogative
'Tis dangerous to the state and commonwealth.
Gentlemen, justices, master mayor, and sheriff,
It doth behoove us all, and each of us,
In general and particular, to have care
For the suppressing of all mutinies,
And all assemblies, except soldiers' musters,
For the king's preparation unto France.
We hear of secret conventicles made,
And there is doubt of some conspiracies,
Which may break out into rebellious arms
When the king's gone — perchance before he go.
Note, as an instance, this one perilous fray:
What factions might have grown on either part,
To the destruction of the king and realm!
Yet, in my conscience, Sir John Oldcastle is
Innocent of it; only his name was used.
We, therefore, from his highness, give this charge:
You, master mayor, look to your citizens;
You, master sheriff, unto your shire; and you,
As justices, in every one's precinct,
There be no meetings; — when the vulgar sort
Sit on their ale-bench, with their cups and cans,
Matters of state be not their common talk,
Nor pure religion by their lips profaned.
Let us return unto the bench again,
And there examine further of this fray.

Enter a Bailiff *and a* Sergeant.

Sher. Sirs, have ye taken the lord Powis yet?

Bail. No, nor heard of him.

Serg. He's gone far enough.

2 *Judge.* They that are left behind shall answer all.

[*Exeunt.*

1 Previous copies read "get *him* dressed."

2 I substitute here one epithet for another, to avoid a mere brutality.

SCENE II.—Eltham. *An Antechamber in the Palace.*

Enter the Duke of SUFFOLK, *Bishop of* ROCHESTER, BUTLER, *and* Sir JOHN *of* Wrotham.

Suff. Now, my lord Bishop, take free liberty
To speak your mind: what is your suit to us?
Bish. My noble lord, no more than what you know,
And have been oftentimes invested with.
Grievous complaints have passed between the lips
Of envious persons to upbraid the clergy:
Some carping at the livings which we have;
And others spurning at the ceremonies
That are of ancient custom in the church;—
Among the which, Lord Cobham is a chief.
What inconvenience may proceed hereof,
Both to the king and to the commonwealth,
May easily be discerned, when, like a phrensy,
This innovation shall possess their minds.
These upstarts will have followers to uphold
Their damned opinion, more than Harry shall,
To undergo his quarrel 'gainst the French.
Suff. What proof is there against them to be had,
That what you say the law may justify?
Bish. They give themselves the names of protest-
And meet in fields and solitary groves. [ants,
Sir John. Was ever heard, my lord, the like till now,
That thieves and rebels—'sblood! that heretics—
Plain heretics, I'll stand to't to their teeth—
Should have, to color their vile practices,
A title of such worth as protestant?

Enter Messenger *to the Duke of* SUFFOLK, *with a Letter.*

Suff. O, but you must not swear: it ill becomes
One of your coat, to rap out bloody oaths.
Bish. Pardon him, good my lord; it is his zeal—
An honest country prelate, who laments
To see such foul disorders in the church.
Sir John. There's one—they call him Sir John Oldcastle—
He has not his name for naught; for, like a castle,
Doth he encompass them within his walls:
But, till that castle be subverted quite,
We ne'er shall be at quiet in the realm.
Bish. This is our suit, my lord, that he be ta'en
And brought in question for his heresy:
Besides, two letters, brought me out of Wales,
Wherein my lord of Hereford writes to me
What tumult and sedition was begun,
'Bout the Lord Cobham, at the 'sizes there;
For they had much ado to calm the rage—
And that the valiant Herbert there is slain.
Suff. A fire that must be quenched. Well, say no
The king anon goes to the council-chamber, [more;
There to debate of matters touching France.
As he doth pass, I will inform his grace
Concerning your petition. Master Butler,
If I forget, do you remember me.
But. I will, my lord.
Bish. [*Offers the* Duke *a purse*]. Not as a recom-
But as a token of our love to you, [pense,
By me, my lord, the clergy doth present
This purse, and in it full a thousand angels,
Praying your lordship to accept their gift.
Suff. I thank them, my lord bishop, for their love,
But will not take their money;—if you please
To give it to this gentleman, you may.
Bish. Sir, then we crave your furtherance herein.
But. The best I can, my lord of Rochester.
Bish. Nay, pray you take it; trust me, sir, you shall.
Sir John. Were ye all three upon Newmarket heath,
You should not need strain court'sy who should have
Sir John would quickly rid ye of that care. [it:
[*Aside.*
Suff. The king is coming. Fear ye not, my lord;
The very first thing I will break with him
Shall be about your matter.

Enter King HENRY *and the Earl of* HUNTINGTON.

K. Hen. My lord of Suffolk,
Was it not said the clergy did refuse
To lend us money toward our wars in France?
Suff. It was, my lord, but very wrongfully.
K. Hen. I know it was; for Huntington here tells
They have been very bountiful of late. [me
Suff. And still they vow, my gracious lord, to be so,
Hoping your majesty will think on them
As of your loving subjects, and suppress
All such malicious errors as begin
To spot their calling, and disturb the church.
K. Hen. God else forbid! Why, Suffolk, is there,
Any new rupture to disquiet them? [then],
Suff. No new, my lord; the old is great enough,
And so increasing, as, if not cut down,
Will breed a scandal to your royal state,
And set your kingdom quickly in an uproar.
The Kentish knight, Lord Cobham, in despite
Of any law, or spiritual discipline,
Maintains this upstart new religion still;
And divers great assemblies, by his means,
And private quarrels, are commenced abroad,
As, by this letter, more at large, my liege,
Is made apparent.
K. Hen. We do find it here—
There was in Wales a certain fray of late
Between two noblemen. But what of this?
Follows it straight Lord Cobham must be he
Did cause the same? I dare be sworn, good knight,
He never dreamed of any such contention.
Bish. But in his name the quarrel did begin,
About the opinion which he held, my liege.
K. Hen. What if it did? Was either he in place
To take part with them, or abet them in it?
If brabbling fellows, whose enkindled blood
Seeths in their fiery veins, will needs go fight,
Making their quarrels of some words that passed
Either of you, or yours, among your cups,
Is the fault yours? or are ye guilty of it?
Suff. With pardon of your highness, my dread lord
Such little sparks neglected, may, in time,
Grow to a mighty flame. But that's not all:
He doth besides maintain a strange religion,
And will not be compelled to come to mass.
Bish. We do beseech you, therefore, gracious prince,
Without offence unto your majesty,
We may be bold to use authority.
K. Hen. As how?
Bish. To summon him to the arches,[1] [sire],
Where such offences have their punishment.

[1] The court of *Arches*, so called because it was anciently held in the church of St. Mary *le Bow*, Sancta Maria de Arcubus.—MALONE.

K. Hen. To answer personally? — is that your meaning?
Bish. It is, my lord.
K. Hen. How, if he appeal?
Bish. My lord, he can not in such case as this.
Suff. Not where religion is the plea, my lord.
K. Hen. I took it always that ourself stood on't
As a sufficient refuge; unto whom
Not any but might lawfully appeal:
But we'll not argue now upon that point.
For Sir John Oldcastle, whom you do accuse,
Let me entreat you to dispense a while
With your high title of pre-eminence.
Report did never yet condemn him so,
But he hath always been reputed loyal;
And, in my knowledge, I can say thus much,
That he is virtuous, wise, and honorable.
If any way his conscience be seduced
To waver in his faith, I'll send for him,
And school him privately. If that serve not,
Then, afterward, you may proceed against him.
Butler, be you the messenger for us,
And will him presently repair to court.
[*Exeunt* King HENRY, HUNTINGTON, SUFFOLK, *and* BUTLER.
Sir John. How now, my lord? why stand you discontent?
In sooth, methinks the king hath well decreed.
Bish. Ay, ay, Sir John, if he would keep his word:
But I perceive he favors him so much,
As this will be to small effect, I fear.
Sir John. Why, then, I'll tell you what you're best to do:
If you suspect the king will be but cold
In reprehending, send your process too
To serve upon him; so you may be sure
To make him answer it, howsoe'er it fall.
Bish. And well remembered; I will have it so:
A sumner[1] shall be sent about it straight. [*Exit.*
Sir John. Yea, do so. In the mean space this remains,
For kind Sir John of Wrotham, honest Jack.
Methinks the purse of gold the bishop gave
Made a good show; it had a tempting look:
Beshrew me, but my fingers' ends do itch
To be upon those golden ruddocks. Well! —
I am not what the world doth take me for:
If ever wolf were clothéd in sheep's coat,
Then I am he; — old huddle and twang i'faith;
A priest in show, but in plain terms a thief:
Yet, let me tell you too, an honest thief;
One that will take it where it may be spared,
And spend it freely in good fellowship.
I have as many shapes as Proteus had,
That still, when any villany is done,
There may be none suspect it was Sir John.
Besides, to comfort me — for what's this life,
Except the crabbed bitterness thereof
Be sweetened now and then with lechery? —
I have my Doll, my concubine, as 'twere,
To frolic with — a lusty, bouncing girl!
But, whilst I loiter here, the gold may 'scape,
And that must not be so: it is mine own; —
Therefore, I'll meet him on his way to court,
And shrive him of it; there will be the sport. [*Exit.*

1 A *sumner* was an apparitor—in plain, a *summoner* of persons to appear in the spiritual court.

SCENE III. — Kent. *An outer Court before* Lord COBHAM'S *House. A public Road leading to it, and an Alehouse at a little distance.*

Enter four poor People, *some* Soldiers, *some old* Men.

1 Sold. God help! God help! there's law for punishing,
But there's no law for our necessity:
There be more stocks to set poor soldiers in,
Than there be houses to relieve them at.
Old Man. Ay, housekeeping now decays in every place,
Even as Saint Peter writ, still worse and worse.

2 Old Man. Master mayor of Rochester has given command that none shall go abroad out of the parish; and has set down an order, forsooth, of what every poor householder must give for our relief: where there be some 'sessed — I may say to you — had almost as much need to beg as we.

1 Old Man. It is a hard world the while.

2 Old Man. If a poor man ask at door for God's sake, they ask him for a license or a certificate from a justice.

1 Sold. Faith, we have none, but what we bear upon our bodies — our maimed limbs — God help us!

2 Sold. And yet, as lame as I am, I'll with the king into France, if I can but crawl o' shipboard. I had rather be slain in France than starve in England.

1 Old Man. Ha, were I but as lusty as I was at Shrewsbury battle, I would not do as I do: but we are now come to the good Lord Cobham's, the best man to the poor in all Kent.

2 Old Man. God bless him! there be but few such.

Enter Lord COBHAM *with* HARPOOL.

Cob. Thou peevish, froward man, what wouldst thou have?
Har. This pride, this pride, brings all to beggary.
I served your father, and your grandfather; —
Show me such two men now. No, no, your backs,
Your backs, the devil, and pride, have cut the throat
Of all good housekeeping; they were the best
Yeomen's masters that ever were in England.
Cob. Yea, except thou have a crew of filthy knaves
And sturdy rogues still feeding at my gate,
There is no hospitality with thee.

Har. They may sit at the gate well enough, but the devil of anything you give them, except they'll eat stones.

Cob. 'Tis 'long, then, of such hungry knaves as you:
Here, sir's, your retinue; your guests be come:
They know their hours, I warrant you.

1 Old Man. God bless your honor! God save the good Lord Cobham, and all his house!

1 Sold. Good your honor, bestow your blesséd alms
Upon poor men.
Cob. Now, sir, here be your alms-knights:
Now are you as safe as the emperor.
Har. My alms-knights? Nay, they're yours:
It is a shame for you, and I'll stand to't;
Your foolish alms maintains more vagabonds
Than all the noblemen in Kent beside.
Out, you rogues! you knaves, work for your livings.
Alas! poor men, they may beg their hearts out [here],
There's no more charity among [living] men
Than among so many mastiff-dogs. [*Aside.*

What make you here, you needy knaves? Away!
Away, you villains?

2 Sold. Nay, I beseech you, sir, be good to us.

Cob. Nay, nay,
They know thee well enough! I think that all
The beggars in this land are thy acquaintance:
Go, bestow your alms; none will control you, sir.

Har. What should I give them? You are grown so beggarly, that you can scarce give a bit of bread at your door. You talk of your religion so long, that you have banished charity from you. A man may make a flax-shop in your kitchen-chimneys, for any fire there is stirring.

Cob. If thou wilt give them nothing, send them hence:
Let them not stand here starving in the cold.

Har. Who? I drive them hence? If I drive poor men from the door, I'll be hanged! I know not what I may come to myself. God help ye, poor knaves! ye see the world. Well, you had a mother: O, God be with thee, good lady! thy soul's at rest; she gave more in shirts and smocks to poor children, than you spend in your house; and yet you live a beggar too.

Cob. E'en the worst deed that e'er my mother did,
Was in relieving such a fool as thou.

Har. Ay, I am a fool still; with all your wit, you'll die a beggar; go to!

Cob. Go, you old fool, give the poor people something.
Go in, poor men, into the inner court,
And take such alms as there is to be had.

Sold. God bless your honor!

Har. Hang you, rogues, hang you! there's nothing but misery among you; you fear no law, you! [*Exit.*

2 Old Man. God bless you, good Master Ralph!—
God save your life, you are good to the poor still!

Enter Lord Powis, *disguised.*

Cob. What fellow yonder comes along the grove?
Few passengers there be that know this way:
Methinks he stops as though he stayed for me,
And meant to shroud himself among the bushes.
I know the clergy hate me to the death,
And my religion gets me many foes;
And this may be some desperate rogue, suborned
To work me mischief: as it pleaseth God!
If he come toward me, sure I'll stay his coming,
Be he but one man, whatsoe'er he be.

[Lord Powis *advances.*

I have been well acquainted with that face.

Pow. Well met, my honorable lord and friend.

Cob. You are very welcome, sir, whoe'er you be;
But of this sudden, sir, I do not know you.

Pow. I am one that wisheth well unto your honor:
My name is Powis, an old friend of yours.

Cob. My honorable lord and worthy friend,
What makes your lordship thus alone in Kent,
And thus disguiséd in this strange attire?

Pow. My lord, an unexpected accident
Hath at this time enforced me to these parts,
And thus it happ'd: Not yet full five days since
Now, at the last assize at Hereford,
It chanced that the Lord Herbert and myself,
'Mong other things discoursing at the table,
Did fall in speech about some certain points
Of Wickliffe's doctrine 'gainst the papacy,
And the religion catholic maintained
Through the most part of Europe at this day.
This wilful, testy lord, stuck not to say
That Wickliffe was a knave, a schismatic—
His doctrine devilish and heretical;
And whatsoe'er he was maintained the same,
Was traitor both to God and to his country.
Being movéd at his peremptory speech,
I told him some maintained those opinions,
Good men, and truer subjects than Lord Herbert;
And he, replying in comparisons,
Your name was urged, my lord, against his challenge
To be a perfect favorer of the truth.
And, to be short, from words we fell to blows,
Our servants and our tenants taking parts;
Many on both sides hurt: and, for an hour,
The broil by no means could be pacified,
Until the judges, rising from the bench,
Were, in their persons, forced to part the fray.

Cob. I hope no man was violently slain.

Pow. 'Faith, none, I trust, but the Lord Herbert's self
Who is in truth so dangerously hurt,
As it is doubted he can hardly 'scape.

Cob. I am sorry, my good lord, of these ill news.

Pow. This is the cause that drives me into Kent,
To shroud myself with you, so good a friend,
Until I hear how things do speed at home.

Cob. Your lordship is most welcome unto Cobham:
But I am very sorry, my good lord,
My name was brought in question in this matter,
Considering I have many enemies,
That threaten malice, and do lie in wait
To take the 'vantage of the smallest thing.
But you are welcome to repose your lordship,
And keep yourself here secret in my house,
Until we hear how the Lord Herbert speeds.

Enter Harpool.

Here comes my man. Sirrah, what news?

Har. Yonder's one Master Butler, of the privy chamber, is sent unto you from the king.

Pow. Pray God the Lord Herbert be not dead—
And the king, hearing whither I am gone,
Hath sent for me.

Cob. Comfort yourself, my lord, I warrant you.

Har. Fellow, what ails thee? Dost thou quake? dost thou shake? Dost thou tremble? ha?

Cob. Peace, you old fool! Sirrah, convey this gentleman in the back way, and bring the other into the walk.

Har. Come, sir, you're welcome, if you love my lord.

Pow. Gramercy, gentle friend.

[*Exeunt* Powis *and* Harpool.

Cob. I thought as much—that it would not be long
Before I heard of something from the king
About this matter.

Enter Harpool, *with* Butler.

Har. Sir, yonder my lord walks: you see him;
I'll have your men into the cellar the while.

Cob. Welcome, good Master Butler.

But. Thanks, my good lord. His majesty doth commend his love unto your lordship, and wills you to repair unto the court.

Cob. God bless his highness, and confound his enemies! I hope his majesty is well?

But. In good health, my lord.

Cob. God long continue it. Methinks you look
As though you were not well: what ails ye, sir?

But. 'Faith, I have had a foolish, odd mischance,
That angers me. Coming o'er Shooters' hill,
There came one to me like a sailor, and
Asked me money; and whilst I stayed my horse,
To draw my purse, he takes th' advantage of
A little bank, and leaps behind me, whips
My purse away, and with a sudden jerk,
I know not how, threw me at least three yards
Out of my saddle. I never was so robbed
In all my life.

Cob. I am very sorry, sir, for your mischance;
We will send our warrant forth to stay all such
Suspicious persons as shall [here] be found:
Then, Master Butler, we'll attend on you.

But. I humbly thank your lordship; I'll await you.
[*Exeunt.*

ACT II.

SCENE I.—*The same. Before* Lord COBHAM'S *House.*

Enter a Sumner.

Sum. I have the law to warrant what I do; — and though the Lord Cobham be a nobleman, that dispenses not with law. I dare serve a process were he five noblemen. Though we sumners make sometimes a mad slip in a corner with a pretty wench, a sumner must not go always by seeing; a man may be content to hide his eyes where he may feel his profit. Well, this is Lord Cobham's house: if I can not speak with him, I'll clap my citation upon his door; so my lord of Rochester bade me: but methinks here comes one of his men.

Enter HARPOOL.

Har. Welcome, good fellow, welcome: who wouldst thou speak with?

Sum. With my Lord Cobham I would speak, if thou be one of his men.

Har. Yes, I am one of his men, but thou canst not speak with my lord.

Sum. May I send to him, then?

Har. I'll tell thee that, when I know thy errand.

Sum. I will not tell my errand to thee.

Har. Then keep it to thyself, and walk like a knave, as thou camest.

Sum. I tell thee, my lord keeps no knaves, sirrah!

Har. Then thou servest him not, I believe. What lord is thy master?

Sum. My lord of Rochester.

Har. In good time: and what wouldst thou have with my Lord Cobham?

Sum. I come by virtue of a process, to cite him to appear before my lord in the court at Rochester.

Har. [*aside*]. Well, God grant me patience! I could eat this counger.[1] My lord is not at home; therefore it were good, sumner, you carried your process back.

Sum. Why, if he will not be spoken withal, then will I leave it here: and see that he take knowledge of it. [*Fixes the citation on the gate*

Har. 'Zounds! you slave, do you set up your bills here? go to; take it down again. Dost thou know what thou dost? Dost thou know on whom thou servest a process?

Sum. Yes, marry do I: on Sir John Oldcastle, Lord Cobham.

Har. I am glad thou knowest him yet. And sirrah, dost not know that the Lord Cobham is a brave lord, that keeps good beef and beer in his house, and every day feeds a hundred poor people at's gate, and keeps a hundred tall fellows?

Sum. What that's to my process?

Har. Marry, this, sir: is this process parchment?

Sum. Yes, marry, is it.

Har. And this seal wax?

Sum. It is so.

Har. If this be parchment, and this wax, eat you this parchment and this wax, or I will make parchment of your skin, and beat your brains into wax. Sirrah sumner, despatch, devour, sirrah, devour![2]

Sum. I am my lord of Rochester's sumner; I came to do my office, and thou shalt answer it.

Har. Sirrah, no railing; but betake yourself to your teeth. Thou shalt eat no worse than thou bring'st with thee. Thou bring'st it for my lord, and wilt thou bring my lord worse than thou wilt eat thyself?

Sum. Sir, I brought it not my lord to eat.

Har. O, do you *sir* me now? All's one for that; I'll make you eat it, for bringing it.

Sum. I can not eat it.

Har. Can you not? 'Sblood! I'll beat you till you have a stomach. [*Beats him.*

Sum. Oh, hold, hold, good master servingman! I will eat it.

Har. Be champing, be chewing, sir, or I'll chew you, you rogue! Tough wax shows the purest of the honey.

Sum. Tough wax the purest honey! O Lord, sir, oh! oh! [*Eats.*

Har. Feed, feed — 'tis wholesome, rogue, wholesome. Can not you, like an honest sumner, walk with the devil your brother, to fetch in your bailiff's rents, but you must come to a nobleman's house with process? If thy seal were as broad as the lead that covers Rochester church, thou shouldst eat it.

Sum. O, I am almost choked, I am almost choked!

Har. Who's within there? will you shame my lord? Is there no beer in the house? Butler, I say!

Enter Butler.

But. Here, here.

Har. Give him beer. There: tough old sheepskin's bare dry meat! [Sumner *drinks.*

Sum. O, sir, let me go no further: I'll eat my word.

Har. Yea, marry, sir, I mean ye shall eat more than your own word; for I'll make you eat all the words in the process. Why, you drabmonger, can not the secrets of all the wenches in a shire serve your turn, but you must come hither with a citation, with a pox? I'll cite you. — A cup of sack for the sumner!

[1] So written in the old folio. In subsequent editions, "conger." The reader has his choice. The word "counger" seems at one period to have been used for conjurer—it was to conjure. Harpool may be supposed to sneer at the depth and mysteriousness of the sumner. "Conger" was the sea-eel—and might very well apply to a slippery fellow. Either word, accordingly, may be made to answer.

[2] The dramatist owes little in this process to his invention. Nash, one of the early dramatists, tells us that he saw Greene, another of the faculty, "make an *apparitor* eat his citation, wax and all, very handsomely served 'twixt two dishes." The same punishment has been several times employed since.

But. Here, sir, here.

Har. Here, slave, I drink to thee.

Sum. I thank you, sir.

Har. Now, if thou find'st thy stomach well — because thou shalt see my lord keeps meat in's house — if thou wilt go in, thou shalt have a piece of beef to thy breakfast.

Sum. No, I am very well, good master servingman; I thank you, very well, sir.

Har. I am glad on't; then be walking toward Rochester, to keep your stomach warm. And, sumner, if I do know you disturb a good wench within this diocese, if I do not make thee eat her petticoat, if there were four yards of Kentish cloth in't, I am a villain.

Sum. God be wi'ye, master servingman.

[*Exit* Sumner.

Har. Farewell, sumner.

Enter Constable.

Con. Save you, Master Harpool.

Har. Welcome, constable, welcome, constable; — what news with thee?

Con. An't please you, Master Harpool, I am to make hue and cry for a fellow with one eye, that has robbed two clothiers, and am to crave your hinderance to search all suspected places; and they say there was a woman in the company.

Har. Hast thou been at the alehouse? hast thou sought there?

Con. I durst not search in my Lord Cobham's liberty, except I had some of his servants for my warrant.

Har. An honest constable; — call forth him that keeps the alehouse there.

Con. Ho! who's within there?

Ale-Man. Who calls there? Oh, is't you, master constable, and Master Harpool? You're welcome with all my heart. What make you here so early, this morning?

Har. Sirrah, what strangers do you lodge? There is a robbery done this morning, and we are to search for all suspected persons.

Ale-Man. God's-bore, I am sorry for't. I'faith, sir, I lodge nobody but a good, honest priest, called Sir John o' Wrotham, and a handsome woman that is his niece, that he says he has some suit in law for; and as they go up and down to London, sometimes they lie at my house.

Har. What, is she here in thy house now?

Ale-Man. She is, sir. I promise you, sir, he is a quiet man; and because he will not trouble too many rooms, he makes the woman lie every night at his bed's feet.

Har. Bring her forth, constable, bring her forth, let's see her, let's see her.

Ale-Man. Dorothy, you must come down to master constable.

Enter Dorothy.

Doll. Anon forsooth.

Har. Welcome, sweet lass, welcome.

Doll. I thank you, good sir, and master constable also.

Har. A plump girl, by the mass, a plump girl! ha, Doll, ha. Wilt thou forsake the priest, and go with me, Doll?

Con. Ah! well said, Master Harpool, you are a merry old man, i'faith; you will never be old. Now, by the macke,[1] a pretty wench, indeed.

Har. You old mad, merry constable, art thou advised of that? Ha, well said, Doll; fill some ale here.

Doll. [*aside*]. Oh, if I wist this old priest would not stick to me, by Jove, I would ingle[2] this old servingman.

Har. Oh, you old mad colt, i'faith, I'll ferk you: fill all the pots in the house there.

Con. Oh! well said, Master Harpool, you are heart of oak when all's done.

Har. Ha, Doll, thou hast a sweet pair of lips, by the mass.

Doll. Truly, you are a most sweet old man, as ever I saw; by my troth, you have a face able to make any woman in love with you.

Har. Fill, sweet Doll, I'll drink to thee.

Doll. I pledge you, sir, and thank you therefore, and I pray you let it come.

Har. [*embracing her*]. Doll, canst thou love me? a mad, merry lass; would to God I had never seen thee.

Doll. I warrant you, you will not out of my thoughts this twelvemonth; truly, you are as full of favor as any man may be. Ah, these sweet gray locks! by my troth, they are most lovely.

Con. Cud's bores, Master Harpool, I'll have one buss, too.

Har. No licking for you, constable; hands off, hands off.

Con. By'r lady, I love kissing as well as you.

Doll. Oh, you are an odd boy; you have a wanton eye of your own: ah, you sweet, sugar-lipped wanton, you will win as many women's hearts as come in your company.

Enter Sir John, *of* Wrotham.

Sir John. Doll, come hither.

Har. Priest, she shall not.

Doll. I'll come anon, sweet love.

Sir John. Hands off, old fornicator.

Har. Vicar, I'll sit here in spite of thee. Is this stuff for a priest to carry up and down with him?

Sir John. Sirrah, dost thou not know that a good fellow parson may have a chapel of ease, where his parish church is far off?

Har. You whorson-stoned vicar.

Sir John. You old stale ruffian, you lion of Cotswold.[3]

Har. Zounds, vicar, I'll geld you. [*Flies upon him.*

Con. Keep the king's peace.

Doll. Murder, murder, murder!

Ale-Man. Hold, as you are men, hold! for God's sake, be quiet: put up your weapons; you draw not in my house.

Har. You whorson bawdy priest.

Sir John. You old mutton-monger.

Con. Hold, Sir John, hold.

Doll. I pray thee, sweet-heart, be quiet. I was but sitting to drink a pot of ale with him, even as kind a man as ever I met with.

Har. Thou art a thief, I warrant thee.

1 *Macke*—an ancient game at cards.
2 *Ingle*—make a favorite or friend of, &c.
3 That is, "you *Cotswold sheep.*"

Sir John. Then I am but as thou hast been in thy days; let's not be ashamed of our trade; the king has been a thief himself.

Doll. Come, be quiet; hast thou sped?

Sir John. I have, wench; there be crowns i'faith.

Doll. Come, let's be all friends, then.

Con. Well said, Mistress Dorothy.

Har. Thou art the maddest priest that ever I met with.

Sir John. Give me thy hand; thou art as good a fellow. I am a singer, a drinker, a bencher,[1] a wencher; I can say a mass, and kiss a lass: faith, I have a parsonage, and because I would not be at too much charges, this wench serveth me for a sexton.

Har. Well said, mad priest, we'll in and be friends.
[*Exeunt.*

SCENE II.—London. *A Room in the Axe Inn, without Bishop-gate.*

Enter Sir ROGER ACTON, BOURN, BEVERLEY, *and* MURLEY.

Acton. Now, Master Murley, I am well assured
You know our errand, and do like the cause,
Being a man affected as we are.

Mur. Marry God dild[2] ye, dainty my dear! No master, good Sir Roger Acton, Master Bourn, and Master Beverley, gentlemen and justices of the peace; no master I, but plain William Murley, the brewer of Dunstable, your honest neighbor and your friend, if ye be men of my profession.

Bev. Professed friends to Wickliffe; foes to Rome.

Mur. Hold by me, lad; lean upon that staff, good Master Beverley; all of a house. Say your mind, say your mind.

Acton. You know our faction now is grown so great
Throughout the realm, that it begins to smoke
Into the clergy's eyes, and the king's ears;
High time it is that we were drawn to head,
Our general and officers appointed;—
And wars, ye wot, will ask great store of coin.
Able to strengthen our action with your purse,
You are elected for a colonel, sir,
Over a regiment of fifteen bands.

Mur. Phew! paltry, paltry! in and out, to and fro, be it more or less, upon occasion. Lord have mercy upon us, what a world is this! Sir Roger Acton, I am but a Dunstable man, a plain brewer, you know. Will lusty cavaliering captains, gentlemen, come at my calling, go at my bidding? Dainty my dear, they'll do a dog of wax, a horse of cheese, a prick and a pudding. No, no; you must appoint some lord, or knight at least, to that place.

Bourn. Why, Master Murley, you shall be a knight:
Were you not in election to be sheriff?
Have ye not past all offices but that?
Have ye not wealth to make your wife a lady?
I warrant you, my lord, our general
Bestows that honor on you, at first sight.

Mur. Marry God dild ye, dainty my dear:
But tell me who shall be our general.
Where's the lord Cobham, Sir John Oldcastle,
That noble alms-giver, housekeeper virtuous,
Religious gentleman? Come to me there, boys,
Come to me there.

Acton. Why, who but he shall be our general?

Mur. And shall he knight me, and make me colonel?

Acton. My word for that, Sir William Murley, knight.

Mur. Fellow [of] Sir Roger Acton, knight; all fellows, I mean in arms, how strong are we? how many partners? Our enemies beside the king are mighty; be it more or less, upon occasion, reckon our force.

Acton. There are of us our friends and followers,
Three thousand and three hundred at the least:
Of northern lads, four thousand, beside horse;
From Kent there comes, with Sir John Oldcastle
Seven thousand: then, from London issue out,
Of masters, servants, strangers, 'prentices,
Forty odd thousand into Ficket-field,
Where we appoint our special rendezvous.

Mur. Phew! paltry, paltry! in and out, to and fro, Lord have mercy upon us, what a world is this! Where's that Ficket-field, Sir Roger?

Acton. Behind St. Giles in the field, near Holborn.

Mur. Newgate, up Holborn, St. Giles in the field, and to Tyburn; an old say.[3] For the day, for the day?

Acton. On Friday next, the fourteenth day of January.

Mur. Tilly vally, trust me never if I have any liking of that day. Phew! paltry, paltry! Friday, quotha; dismal day; Childermas day this year was Friday.

Bev. Nay, Master Murley, if you observe such days,
We make some question of your constancy,
All days are like to men resolved in right.

Mur. Say amen, and say no more, but say and hold, Master Beverley: Friday next, and Ficket-field, and William Murley and his merry men shall be all one. I have half a score jades that draw my beer-carts, and every jade shall bear a knave, and every knave shall wear a jack, and every jack shall have a scull, and every scull shall show a spear, and every spear shall kill a foe at Ficket-field, at Ficket-field: John and Tom, Dick and Hodge, Ralph and Robbin, Will and George, and all my knaves shall fight like men, at Ficket-field, on Friday next.

Bourn. What sum of money mean you to disburse?

Mur. It may be modestly, decently, and soberly, and handsomely, I may bring five hundred pound.

Acton. Five hundred, man? five thousand's not enough:
A hundred thousand will not pay our men
Two months together. Either come prepared,
Like a brave knight, and martial colonel,
In glittering gold, and gallant furniture,
Bringing in coin, a cartload at the least,
And all your followers mounted on good horse,
Or never come disgraceful to us all.

Bev. Perchance you may be chosen treasurer;
Ten thousand pound's the least that you can bring.

Mur. Paltry, paltry! in and out, to and fro: upon occasion I have ten thousand pound to spend, and ten [more] too. And rather than the bishop shall have his will of me, for my conscience, it shall all go. Flame and flax, flax and flame. It was got with wa-

[1] One who does not scruple to sleep on an ale-bench after his potations. "Thou art so fatwitted," says the prince to Falstaff, "with drinking of old sack, and unbuttoning thee after supper, and *sleeping upon benches* at noon."

[2] *Dild*—a corruption and compound of "do shield"—thus: "do shield"—do-ield,—dild.

[3] *Say* or *saw*—the word is written both ways.

ter and malt, and it shall fly with fire and gunpowder. Sir Roger, a cart-load of money till the axletree crack; myself and my men in Ficket-field on Friday next: remember my knighthood and my place: there's my hand; I'll be there. [*Exit* MURLEY.

Acton. See what ambition may persuade men to,
In hope of honor he will spend himself.

Bourn. I never thought a brewer half so rich.

Bev. Was never bankrupt brewer yet but one,
With using too much malt, too little water.

Acton. That is no fault in brewers now-a-days:
Come, let's away, about our business.
[*Exeunt.*

SCENE III.—*An Audience Chamber in the Palace at* Eltham.

Enter King HENRY, *the Duke of* SUFFOLK, BUTLER, *and* Sir JOHN OLDCASTLE—*he kneels to the* King.

K. Hen. 'Tis not enough, Lord Cobham, to submit;
You must forsake your gross opinion.
The bishops find themselves much injured,
And though, for some good service you have done,
We, for our part, are pleased to pardon you,
Yet they will not so soon be satisfied.

Cob. My gracious lord, unto your majesty,
Next unto God [himself], I owe my life;
And what is mine, either by nature's gift,
Or fortune's bounty, all is at your service.
But for obedience to the pope of Rome,
I owe him none; nor shall his shaveling priests
That are in England, alter my belief.
If, out of Holy Scriptures they can prove
That I am in an error, I will yield,
And gladly take instruction at their hands:
But otherwise, I do beseech your grace,
My conscience may not be encroached upon.

K. Hen. We would be loath to press our subjects' bodies,
Much less their souls, the dear redeemêd part
Of Him that is the ruler of us all:
Yet let me counsel you, that might command;
Do not presume to tempt them with ill words,
Nor suffer any meetings to be had
Within your house, but, to the uttermost,
Disperse the flocks of this new gathering sect.

Cob. My liege, if any breath that dares come forth,
And say my life in any of these points
Deserves th'attainder of ignoble thoughts:
Here stand I, craving no remorse at all,
But even the utmost rigor may be shown.

K. Hen. Let it suffice we know your loyalty.
What have you there?

Cob. A deed of clemency,
Your highness' pardon for Lord Powis' life,
Which I did beg, and you, my noble lord,
Of gracious favor did vouchsafe to grant.

K. Hen. But yet it is not signêd with our hand.

Cob. Not yet, my liege.

K. Hen. The fact, you say, was done
Not of prepensed[1] malice, but by chance.

Cob. Upon mine honor so, no otherwise.

K. Hen. [*signs the pardon*]. There is his pardon; bid him make amends,
And cleanse his soul to God for his offence:
What we remit, is but the body's scourge.—

Enter Bishop of ROCHESTER.

How now, lord bishop?

Bishop. Justice, dread sovereign!
As thou art king, so grant I may have justice.

K. Hen. What means this exclamation? Let us know.

Bishop. Ah, my good lord, the state is much abused,
And our decrees most shamefully profaned.

K. Hen. How? and by whom?

Bishop. Even by this heretic,
This Jew, this traitor to your majesty.

Cob. Prelate, thou liest, even in thy greasy maw,
Or whosoever twits me with the name
Either of traitor or of heretic.

K. Hen. Forbear, I say: and bishop, show the cause
From whence this late abuse hath been derived.

Bishop. Thus, mighty king. By general consent
A messenger was sent to cite this lord
To make appearance in the consistory:
And, coming to his house, a ruffian slave,
One of his daily followers, met the man,
Who knowing him to be a paritor,
Assaults him first, and after, in contempt
Of us and our proceedings, makes him eat
The written process, parchment, seal, and all:
Whereby, this matter never was brought forth,
And we but scorned for our authority.

K. Hen. When was this done?

Bishop. At six o'clock this morning

K. Hen. And when came you to court?

Cob. Last night, my liege

K. Hen. By this, it seems, he is not guilty of it,
And you have done him wrong to accuse him so.

Bishop. But it was done, my lord, by his appointment
Or else his man durst not have been so bold.

K. Hen. Or else you durst be bold to interrupt
And fill our ears with frivolous complaints.
Is this the duty you do bear to us?
Was't not sufficient we did pass our word
To send for him; but you, misdoubting it,
Or, which is worse, intending to forestall
Our regal power, must likewise summon him?
This savors of ambition, not of zeal,
And rather proves you malice his estate,
Than any way that he offends the law.
Go to, we like it not: and he, your officer,
Had his desert for being insolent,
That was employed so much amiss herein.
So, Cobham, when you please, you may depart.

Cob. I humbly bid farewell unto my liege.
[*Exit* COBHAM.

K. Hen. Farewell. [*Enter* HUNTINGTON.
What's now the news by Huntington?

Hunt. Sir Roger Acton, and a crew, my lord,
Of bold seditious rebels, are in arms,
Intending reformation of religion,
And with their army they intend to pitch
In Ficket-field, unless they be repulsed.

K. Hen. So near our presence? Dare they be so bold?
And will proud war and eager thirst of blood,
Whom we had thought to entertain far off,
Press forth upon us in our native bounds?

[1] *Pretensed* in the old copy; and as this word anciently was made to signify intended or designed, it still might answer. But malice prepense or prepensed malice seems most legitimate.

Must we be forced to handsel our sharp blades
In England here, which we prepared for France?
Well, in God's name be it. What's their number, say,
Or who's the chief commander of this rout?
Hunt. Their number is not known as yet, my lord,
But 'tis reported, Sir John Oldcastle
Is the chief man, on whom they do depend.
K. Hen. How? the lord Cobham?
Hunt. Yes, my gracious lord.
Bishop. I could have told your majesty as much
Before he went, but that I saw your grace
Was too much blinded by his flattery.
Suff. Send post, my lord, to fetch him back again.
But. Traitor unto his country! how he smoothed
And seemed as innocent as truth itself?
K. Hen. I can not think it yet he would be false;
But, if he be, no matter; — let him go:
We'll meet both him and them unto their wo.
[*Exeunt* King HENRY, SUFFOLK, HUNTINGTON, *and* BUTLER.
Bish. This falls out well; and at the last, I hope
To see this heretic dying in a rope. [*Exit.*

ACT III.

SCENE I. — *An Avenue leading to* Lord COBHAM'S *House in* Kent.

Enter Earl of CAMBRIDGE, Lord SCROOP, Sir THOMAS GREY, *and* CHARTRES.

Scroop. Once more, my lord of Cambridge, make rehearsal
How you do stand entitled to the crown: —
The deeper shall we print it in our minds,
And every man the better be resolved,
When he perceives his quarrel to be just.
Cam. Then thus, Lord Scroop, Sir Thomas Grey, and you,
Monsieur de Chartres, agent for the French: —
This Lionel, duke of Clarence (as I said),
Third son of Edward (England's king) the Third,
Had issue — Philippa, his sole daughter and heir;
Which Philippa afterward was given in marriage
To Edmund Mortimer, the earl of March,
And by him had a son called Roger Mortimer;
Which Roger likewise had of his descent,
Edmund and Roger, Ann and Eleanor,
Two daughters and two sons; but of these, three
Died without issue. Ann, that did survive,
And now was left her father's only heir,
My fortune 'twas to marry, being also,
By my grandfather, of King Edward's line:
So of his surname I am called, you know,
Richard Plantagenet. My father was
Edward, the duke of York, and son and heir
To Edmund Langley, Edward the Third's fifth son.
Scroop. So that it seems your claim comes by your [wife,
As lawful heir to Roger Mortimer,
The son of Edmund, which did marry Philippa,
Daughter and heir to Lionel, duke of Clarence.
Cam. True; for this Harry, and his father both,
Harry the Fourth, as plainly doth appear,
Are false intruders, and usurp the crown.
For when young Richard was at Pomfret slain,
In him the title of Prince Edward died,
That was the eldest of King Edward's sons.
William of Hatfield, and their second brother
Death in his nonage had before bereft:
So that my wife, derived from Lionel,
Third son unto King Edward, ought succeed[1]
And take possession of the diadem
Before this Harry or his father-king,
Who fetch their title but from Lancaster,
Fourth of that royal line. And being thus,
What reason is't but she should have her right?
Scroop. I am resolved: our enterprise is just.
Grey. Harry shall die, or else resign his crown.
Char. Perform but that, and Charles, the king of [France,
Shall aid you, lords, not only with his men,
But send you money to maintain your wars:
Five hundred thousand crowns he bade me proffer,
If you can stop but Harry's voyage for France.
Scroop. We never had a fitter time than now,
The realm in such division as it is.
Cam. Besides, you must persuade you there is due
Vengeance for Richard's murder, which, although
It be deferred, yet will it fall at last,
And now as likely as another time.
Sin hath had many years to ripen in,
And now the harvest can not be far off,
Wherein the weeds of usurpation
Are to be cropped and cast into the fire.
Scroop. No more, Earl Cambridge; here I plight [my faith
To set up thee and thy renownéd wife.
Grey. Grey will perform the same, as he is knight.
Char. And, to assist ye, as I said before,
Chartres doth 'gage the honor of his king.
Scroop. We lack but now Lord Cobham's fellow- [ship,
And then our plot were absolute indeed.
Cam. Doubt not of him, my lord; his life pursued
By the incensed clergy, and, of late,
Brought in displeasure with the king — assures
He may be quickly won unto our faction.
Who hath the articles were drawn at large
Of our whole purpose?
Grey. That have I, my lord.
Cam. We should not now be far off from his house;
Our serious conference hath beguiled the way:
See where his castle stands; give me the writing.
When we are come unto the speech of him,
Because we will not stand to make recount
Of that which hath been said, here he shall read
Our minds at large, and what we crave of him.

Enter Lord COBHAM.

Scroop. A ready way. Here comes the man him-self,
Booted and spurred: it seems he hath been riding.
Cam. Well met, Lord Cobham.
Cob. My lord of Cambridge,
Your honor is most welcome into Kent,
And all the rest of this fair company.
I am new come from London, gentle lords;
But will ye not take Cowling[2] for your host,[3]
And see what entertainment it affords?
Cam. We were intended to have been your guests:
But now this lucky meeting shall suffice
To end our business, and defer that kindness.

1 "*Proceed*" is the word in the old copy, and was no doubt so in the original, but only in the sense of *succeed* or *follow*, so that the present word is the proper one.
2 Cowling was the name of Lord Cobham's seat in Kent.
3 Query: *post?*

Cob. Business, my lord? what business should let
You to be merry? We have no delicates;
Yet this I'll promise you: a piece of venison,
A cup of wine, and so forth—hunters' fare;
And, if you please, we'll strike the stag; ourselves
Shall fill our dishes with his well-fed flesh.

Scroop. That is indeed the thing we all desire.

Cob. My lords, and you shall have your choice with me.

Cam. Nay, but the stag which we desire to strike
Lives not in Cowling: if you will consent,
And go with us, we'll bring you to a forest
Where runs a lusty herd: among the which
There is a stag superior to the rest;
A stately beast, that, when his fellows run,
He leads the race, and beats the sullen earth
As though he scorned it with his trampling hoofs;
Aloft he bears his head, and with his breast,
Like a huge bulwark, counter-checks the wind;
And, when he standeth still, he stretcheth forth
His proud ambitious neck, as if he meant
To wound the firmament with forkèd horns.

Cob. 'Tis pity such a goodly beast should die.

Cam. Not so, Sir John, for he is tyrannous,
And gores the other deer, and will not keep
Within the limits are appointed him.
Of late he's broke into a several,
Which doth belong to me, and there he spoils
Both corn and pasture. Two of his wild race,
Alike for stealth and covetous encroaching,
Already are removed;—if he were dead,
I should not only be secure from hurt,
But with his body make a royal feast.

Scroop. How say you, then? will you first hunt with us?

Cob. 'Faith, lords, I like the pastime; where's the place?

Cam. Peruse this writing: it will show you all,
And what occasion we have for the sport.
[*Presents the paper.*

Cob. [*Reads*]. Call ye this hunting, lords? Is this the stag
You fain would chase—Harry, our most dread king?
So may we make a banquet for the devil,
And, in the stead of wholesome meat, prepare
A dish of poison to confound ourselves!

Cam. Why so, Lord Cobham? See you not our claim?
And how imperiously he holds the crown?

Scroop. Besides, you know yourself is in disgrace,
Held as a recreant, and pursued to death.
This will defend you from your enemies,
And 'stablish your religion through the land.

Cob. [*Aside*]. Notorious treason! yet I will conceal
My secret thoughts, to sound the depth of it.
My lord of Cambridge, I do see your claim,
And what good may redound unto the land
By prosecuting of this enterprise.
But where are men? where's power and furniture
To order such an action? We are weak;
Harry, you know's a mighty potentate.

Cam. Tut, we are strong enough; you are beloved,
And many will be glad to follow you;
We are the like, and some will follow us;
There's hope from France: here's an embassador
That promiseth both men and money too.
The commons likewise, as we hear, pretend
A sudden tumult: we will join with them.

Cob. Some likelihood, I must confess, to speed:
But how shall I believe this in plain truth?
You are, my lords, such men as live in court,
And have been highly favored of the king,
Especially Lord Scroop, whom oftentimes
He maketh choice of for his bed-fellow;
And you, Lord Grey, are of his privy council;
Is not this a train laid to entrap my life?

Cam. Then perish may my soul! What! think you so?

Scroop. We'll swear to you.

Grey. Or take the sacrament.

Cob. Nay, you are noblemen, and I imagine,
As you are honorable by birth and blood,
So you will be in heart, in thought, in word.
I crave no other testimony but this:
That you would all subscribe, and set your hands
Unto this writing which you gave to me.

Cam. With all our hearts. Who hath any pen and ink?

Scroop. My pocket should have one: O, here it is.

Cam. Give it me, Lord Scroop. There is my name.

Scroop. And there is mine.

Grey. And mine.

Cob. Sir, let me crave
That you would likewise write your name with theirs,
For confirmation of your master's words,
The king of France.

Char. That will I, noble lord.

Cob. So, now, this action is well knit together,
And I am for you. Where's our meeting, lords?

Cam. Here, if you please, the tenth of July next.

Cob. In Kent? Agreed. Now let us in to supper;
I hope your honors will not away to-night.

Cam. Yes, presently, for I have far to ride,
About soliciting of other friends.

Scroop. And we would not be absent from the court,
Lest thereby grow suspicion in the king.

Cob. Yet taste a cup of wine before ye go.

Cam. Not now, my lord, we thank you: so farewell. [*Exeunt* SCROOP, GREY, CAMBRIDGE, *and* CHARTRES.

Cob. Farewell, my noble lords!—my noble lords!
My noble villains, base conspirators!
How can they look his highness in the face,
Whom they so closely study to betray?
But I'll not sleep until I make it known:
This head shall not be burdened with such thoughts,
Nor in this heart will I conceal a deed
Of such impiety against my king.
Madam, how now?

Enter Lady COBHAM, Lord POWIS, Lady POWIS, *and* HARPOOL.

Lady Cob. You're welcome home, my lord.
Why seem you so unquiet in your looks?
What hath befallen you that disturbs your mind?

Lady Pow. Bad news, I am afraid, touching my husband.

Cob. Madam, not so: there is your husband's pardon.
Long may ye live, each joy unto the other!

Lady Pow. So great a kindness, as I know not how
To make reply: my sense is quite confounded.

Cob. Let that alone; and, madam, stay me not,
For I must back unto the court again,
With all the speed I can. Harpool, my horse.

Lady Cob. So soon, my lord? what, will you ride all night?

Cob. All night or day: it must be so, sweet wife;
Urge me not why, or what my business is,
But get you in. Lord Powis, bear with me.
And, madam, think your welcome ne'er the worse;
My house is at your use. Harpool, away!

Har. Shall I attend your lordship to the court?

Cob. Yea, sir; your gelding mount you presently. [*Exit* COBHAM.

Lady Cob. I pr'ythee, Harpool, look unto thy lord;
I do not like this sudden posting back.

Pow. Some earnest business is afoot, belike;
Whate'er it be, pray God be his good guide.

Lady Pow. Amen, that hath so highly us bestead.

Lady Cob. Come, madam, and my lord, we'll hope the best;
You shall not into Wales till he return.

Pow. Though great occasion be we should depart,
Yet, madam, will we stay, to be resolved
Of this unlooked-for, doubtful accident. [*Exeunt.*

SCENE II.—*A Road near* Highgate.

Enter MURLEY *and* Followers.

Mur. Come, my hearts of flint, modestly, decently, soberly, and handsomely; no man afore his leader: follow your master, your captain, your knight that shall be, for the honor of mealmen, millers, and maltmen. Dun is the mouse. Dick and Tom, for the credit of Dunstable, ding down the enemy to-morrow. Ye shall not come into the field like beggars. Where be Leonard and Lawrence, my two loaders? Lord have mercy upon us, what a world is this! I would give a couple of shillings for a dozen of good feathers for ye, and forty pence for as many scarfs to set you out withal. Frost and snow! a man has no heart to fight till he be brave.

Dick. Master, we are no babes, our town footballs can bear witness; this little 'parel we have shall off, and we'll fight naked before we run away.

Tom. Nay, I'm of Lawrence' mind for that, for he means to leave his life behind him; he and Leonard, your two loaders, are making their wills, because they have wives; now, we bachelors bid our friends scramble for our goods if we die. But, master, pray let me ride upon Cut.

Mur. Meal and salt, wheat and malt, fire and tow, frost and snow! why, Tom, thou shalt. Let me see: here are you; William and George are with my cart; and Robin and Hodge holding my own two horses; proper men, handsome men, tall men, true men.

Dick. But, master, master, methinks you are mad to hazard your own person, and a cartload of money too.

Tom. Yea, and master, there's a worse matter in't: if it be, as I heard say, we go fight against all the learned bishops, that should give us their blessing, and if they curse us, we shall speed ne'er the better.

Dick. Nay, by'r lady, some say the king takes their part; and, master, dare you fight against the king?

Mur. Fie! paltry, paltry; in and out, to and fro, upon occasion; if the king be so unwise to come there, we'll fight with him too.

Tom. What if ye should kill the king.

Mur. Then we'll make another.

Dick. Is that all? Do ye not speak treason?

Mur. If we do, who dare trip us? We come to fight for our conscience and for honor. Little know you what is in my bosom; look here, mad knaves, a pair of gilt spurs.

Tom. A pair of golden spurs? Why do you not put them on your heels? Your bosom's no place for spurs.

Mur. Be't more or less upon occasion, Lord have mercy upon us. Tom, thou'rt a fool, and thou speak'st treason to knighthood. Dare any wear gold or silver spurs, till he be a knight? No, I shall be knighted to-morrow, and then they shall on. Sirs, was it ever read in the church-book of Dunstable, that ever malt-man was made knight?

Tom. No; but you are more; you are meal-man, malt-man, miller, corn-master, and all.

Dick. Yea, and half a brewer too and the devil and all for wealth. You bring more money with you than all the rest.

Mur. The more's my honor. I shall be a knight to-morrow. Let me 'spose my men;—Tom upon Cut, Dick upon Hob, Hodge upon Ball, Ralph upon Sorrel, and Robin upon the fore-horse.

Enter ACTON, BOURN, *and* BEVERLEY.

Tom. Stand; who comes there?

Acton. All friends, good fellow.

Mur. Friends and fellows, indeed, Sir Roger.

Acton. Why, thus you show yourself a gentleman,
To keep your day, and come so well prepared.
Your cart stands yonder guarded by your men,
Who tell me it is laden well with coin;
What sum is there?

Mur. Ten thousand pound, Sir Roger; and modestly, decently, soberly, and handsomely, see what I have here, against I be knighted.

Acton. Gilt spurs? 'Tis well.

Mur. Where's our army, sir?

Acton. Dispersed in sundry villages about;
Some here with us in Highgate, some at Finchley
Tot'nam, Enfield, Edmunton, Newington,
Islington, Hogsdon, Pancras, Kensington;
Some nearer Thames, Ratcliff, Blackwall, and Bow
But our chief strength must be the Londoners,
Which, ere the sun to-morrow shine,
Will be near fifty thousand in the field.

Mur. Marry, God dild ye, dainty my dear; but upon occasion, Sir Roger Acton, doth not the king know of it, and gather his power against us?

Acton. No, he's secure at Eltham.

Mur. What do the clergy?

Acton. They fear extremely, yet prepare no force.

Mur. In and out, to and fro; bully my boykin, we shall carry the world afore us. I vow, by my worship, when I am knighted, we'll take the king napping, if he stand on their part.

Acton. This night we few in High-gate will repose;
With the first cock we'll rise and arm ourselves,
To be in Ficket-field by break of day,
And there expect our general, Sir John Oldcastle,

Mur. What if he comes not?

Bourn. Yet our action stands;
Sir Roger Acton may supply his place.

Mur. True, Master Bourn, but who shall make me knight?

Bev. He that hath power to be our general.

Act. Talk not of trifles; come, let us away,
Our friends of London long till it be day. [*Exeunt.*

SCENE III.—*A High Road in* Kent.

Enter Sir JOHN *of* Wrotham, *and* DOLL.

Doll. By my troth, thou art as jealous a man as lives.

Sir John. Canst thou blame me, Doll? thou art my lands, my goods, my jewels, my wealth, my purse; none walks within forty miles of London, but supplies thee as truly, as the parish does the poor man's box.

Doll. I am as true to thee as the stone is in the wall, and thou knowest well enough I was in as good doing, when I came to thee, as any wench need to be: and therefore thou hast tried me,—that thou hast: and I will not be kept as I have been, that I will not.

Sir John. Doll, if this blade hold, there's not a pedlar walks with a pack, but thou shalt as boldly choose of his wares, as with thy ready money in a merchant's shop; we'll have as good silver as the king coins any.

Doll. What, is all the gold spent you took the last day from the courtier?

Sir John. 'Tis gone, Doll, 'tis flown; merrily come, merrily gone; he comes a-horseback that must pay for all; we'll have as good meat as money can get, and as good gowns as can be bought for gold: be merry, wench; the malt-man comes on Monday.

Doll. You might have left me at Cobham, until you had been better provided for.

Sir John. No, sweet Doll, no; I like not that; yon old ruffian is not for the priest: I do not like a new clerk should come in the old belfrey.

Doll. Thou art a mad priest, i'faith.

Sir John. Come, Doll, I'll see thee safe at some alehouse here at Cray, and the next sheep that comes, shall leave behind his fleece. [*Exeunt.*

SCENE IV.—Blackheath.

Enter King HENRY, *disguised;* SUFFOLK, *and* BUTLER.

K. Hen. My lord of Suffolk, post away for life,
And let our forces, of such horse and foot,
As can be gathered up by any means,
Make speedy rendezvous in Tothill-fields.
It must be done this evening, my good lord;
This night the rebels mean to draw to head
Near Islington; which, if your speed prevent not—
If once they should unite their several forces—
Their power is almost thought invincible.
Away, my lord, I will be with you soon.

Suff. I go, my sovereign, with all happy speed.

K. Hen. Make haste, my lord of Suffolk, as you love us. [*Exit* SUFFOLK.
Butler, post you to London with all speed:
Command the mayor and sheriffs, on their allegiance,
The city-gates be presently shut up,
And guarded with a strong sufficient watch,
And not a man be sufferèd to pass,
Without a special warrant from ourself.
Command the postern by the tower be kept,
And proclamation, on the pain of death,
That not a citizen stir from his doors,
Except such as the mayor and sheriffs shall choose
For their own guard, and safety of their persons:
Butler, away, have care unto thy[1] charge.

[1] Written, "*my* charge," elsewhere.

But. I go, my sovereign.

K. Hen. Butler!

But. My lord?

K. Hen. Go down by Greenwich, and command a boat,
At the Friars-bridge attend my coming down.

But. I will, my lord. [*Exit* BUTLER.

K. Hen. 'Tis time, I think, to look unto rebellion,
When Acton doth expect unto his aid,
No less than fifty thousand Londoners.
Well, I'll to Westminster in this disguise,
To hear what news is stirring in these brawls.

Enter Sir JOHN *of* Wrotham, *and* DOLL.

Sir John. Stand, true-man, says a thief.

K. Hen. Stand, thief, says a true man: how if a thief?

Sir John. Stand, thief, too.

K. Hen. Then, thief or true-man, I must stand, I see,
Howsoe'er the world wags, trade of thieving yet
Will never down. What art thou?

Sir John. A good fellow.

K. Hen. And so am I, too; I see that thou dost know me.

Sir John. If thou be a good fellow, play the good fellow's part; deliver thy purse without more ado.

K. Hen. I have no money.

Sir John. I must make you find some before we part. If you have no money, you shall have ware; as many sound blows as your skin can carry.

K. Hen. Is that the plain truth?

Sir John. Sirrah, no more ado; come, come; give me the money you have. Despatch, I can not stand all day.

K. Hen. Well, if thou wilt needs have it, there it is: just the proverb, one thief robs another. Where the devil are all my old thieves? Falstaff, that villain, is so fat, he can not get on's horse; but methinks Poins and Peto should be stirring hereabouts.

Sir John. How much is there on't, o'thy word?

K. Hen. A hundred pound in angels, on my word.
The time has been I would have done as much
For thee, if thou hadst past this way, as I
Have now.

Sir John. Sirrah, what art thou? thou seem'st a gentleman.

K. Hen. I am no less; yet a poor one now, for thou hast all my money.

Sir John. From whence cam'st thou?

K. Hen. From the court at Eltham.

Sir John. Art thou one of the king's servants?

K. Hen. Yes, that I am, and one of his chamber.

Sir John. I am glad thou'rt no worse: thou may'st the better spare thy money. I think thou might'st get a poor thief his pardon if he should have need.

K. Hen. Yes, that I can.

Sir John. Wilt thou do so much for me, when I shall have occasion?

K. Hen. Yes, faith will I, so it be for no murder.

Sir John. Nay, I am a pitiful thief; all the hurt I do a man, I take but his purse: I'll kill no man.

K. Hen. Then, on my word, I'll do't.

Sir John. Give me thy hand on the same.

K. Hen. There 'tis.

Sir John. Methinks the king should be good to

thieves, because he has been a thief himself, although I think now he be turned a true man.

K. Hen. 'Faith, I have heard, indeed, he has had an ill name that way in his youth: but how canst thou tell that he has been a thief?

Sir John. How? because he once robbed me before I fell to the trade myself, when that foul villanous guts, that led him to all that roguery, was in his company there; that Falstaff.

K. Hen. [*aside*]. Well, if he did rob thee then, thou art but even with him, now, I'll be sworn. Thou knowest not the king now, I think, if thou sawest him?

Sir John. Not I, i'faith.

K. Hen. [*aside*]. So it should seem.

Sir John. Well, if old King Harry had lived, this king, that is now, had made thieving the best trade in England.

K. Hen. Why so?

Sir John. Because he was the chief warden of our company. It's pity that e'er he should have been a king, he was so brave a thief. But, sirrah, wilt remember my pardon, if need be?

K. Hen. Yes, faith, will I.

Sir John. Wilt thou? well, then, because thou shalt go safe, for thou may'st hap (being so early) be met with again before thou come to Southwark, if any man when he should bid thee good morrow, bid thee stand, say thou but *Sir John*, and they will let thee pass.

K. Hen. Is that the word? then let me alone.

Sir John. Nay, sirrah, because I think, indeed, I shall have some occasion to use thee, and as thou comest oft this way, I may light on thee another time, not knowing thee, here, I'll break this angel; take thou half of it; this is a token betwixt thee and me.

K. Hen. God-a-mercy: farewell. [*Exit.*

Sir John. O, my fine golden slaves! here's for thee, wench, i'faith. Now, Doll, we will revel in our bever,[1] this is a tythe pig of my vicarage. God-a-mercy, neighbor Shooter's Hill, you ha' paid your tythe honestly. Well, I hear there is a company of rebels up against the king, got together in Ficket-field, near Holborn, and as it is thought, here in Kent, the king will be there to-night in his own person. Well, I'll to the king's camp, and it shall go hard, if there be any doings, but I'll make some good boot among them. [*Exeunt.*

ACT IV.

SCENE I.—*A Field near* London. King HENRY'S *Camp.*

Enter King HENRY, *disguised;* SUFFOLK, HUNTINGTON, *and* Attendants, *with torches.*

K. Hen. My lords of Suffolk and of Huntington,
Who scouts it now? or who stand sentinels?
What men of worth? what lords do walk the round?

Suff. May't please your highness—

K. Hen. Peace, no more of that:—
The king's asleep, wake not his majesty,
With terms or titles; he's at rest in bed.
Kings do not use to watch themselves; they sleep,
And let rebellion and conspiracy
Revel and havoc in the commonwealth.
Is London looked unto?

Hunt. It is, my lord:
Your noble uncle, Exeter, is there,—
Your brother Gloster, and my lord of Warwick;
Who, with the mayor and the aldermen,
Do guard the gates, and keep good rule within.
The earl of Cambridge and Sir Thomas Grey
Do walk the round; Lord Scroop and Butler scout;
So, though it please your majesty to jest,
Were you in bed, you well might take your rest.

K. Hen. I thank ye, lords: but you do know of old,
That I have been a perfect night-walker.
London, you say, is safely looked unto,
Alas, poor rebels, there your aid must fail;
And the lord Cobham, Sir John Oldcastle,
Quiet in Kent. Acton, you are deceived:
Reckon again; you count without your host.
To-morrow you shall give account to us;
Till when, my friends, this long, cold winter's night,
How can we spend? King Harry is asleep,
And all his lords; these garments tell us so;
All friends at football, fellows all in field.
Harry, and Dick, and George. Bring us a drum,
Give us square dice; we'll keep this court of guard,
For all good fellows' companies that come.
Where's that mad priest ye told me was in arms
To fight, as well as pray, if need required?

Suff. He's in the camp, and if he knew of this,
I undertake he would not long be hence.

K. Hen. Trip Dick, trip George. [Here] I must have the dice:
What do we play at?[2]

Suff. Passage,[3] if ye please.

Hunt. Set round, then: so; at all.

K. Hen. George, you are out.
Give me the dice;—I pass for twenty pound;—
Here's to our lucky passage into France.

Hunt. Harry, you pass, indeed, for you sweep all.

Suff. A sign King Harry shall sweep all in France.

Enter Sir JOHN *of* Wrotham.

Sir John. Edge ye, good fellows; take a fresh gamester in.

K. Hen. Master parson, we play nothing but gold?

Sir John. And, fellow, I tell thee that the priest hath gold, gold! what? ye are but beggarly soldiers to me; I think I have more gold than all you three.

Hunt. It may be so, but we believe it not.

K. Hen. Set, priest, set: I pass for all that gold.

Sir John. Ye pass, indeed.

K. Hen. Priest, hast any more?

Sir John. More? what a question's that?
I tell thee, I have more than all you three.
At these ten angels.

K. Hen. I wonder how thou comest by all this gold.
How many benefices hast thou, priest?

1 *Bever* was the intermediate refreshment between breakfast and dinner. The term is now used among harvestmen and other laborers. It is a meal between meals.

2 This sentence, in the old copies, is given to Huntington.

3 *Passage* was a game at tables—so Steevens. But this tells us nothing. Passage was a game at dice, played with three dice, and with only two persons. The caster throws continually till he has thrown doublets under ten, and then he is out, and loses; or doublets above ten, and then he passes and wins; high runners are most requisite for this game, such as will rarely run any other chance than four, five, or six, by which means, if the caster throws doublets, he scarcely can throw out.

Sir John. 'Faith, but one. Dost wonder how I come by gold? I wonder rather how poor soldiers should have gold: for I'll tell thee, good fellow, we have every day tithes, offerings, christenings, weddings, burials; and you poor snakes come seldom to a booty. I'll speak a proud word: I have but one parsonage; Wrotham; 'tis better than the bishopric of Rochester; there's ne'er a hill, heath, nor down, in all Kent, but 'tis in my parish; Barrham-down, Cobham-down, Gad's-hill, Wrotham-hill, Black-heath, Cocks'-heath, Birchen-wood — all pay me tithe. Gold, quoth-a? ye pass not for that.

Suff. Harry, you are out; now, parson, shake the dice.

Sir John. Set, set; I'll cover ye; at all. A plague on't, I am out: the devil, and dice, and a wench; who will trust them?

Suff. Say'st thou so, priest? set fair; at all for once.

K. Hen. Out, sir; pay all.

Sir John. Sir, pay me angel gold;
I'll none of your cracked French crowns nor pistolets,
Pay me fair angel gold, as I pay you.

K. Hen. No cracked French crowns [do you say]? I hope to see
More cracked French crowns ere long.

Sir John. Thou mean'st of Frenchmen's crowns, when the king's in France.

Hunt. Set round; at all.

Sir John. Pay all: this is some luck.

K. Hen. Give me the dice; 'tis I must shred the priest. At all, Sir John.

Sir John. The devil and all is yours. At that. 'Sdeath! what casting's this?

Suff. Well thrown, Harry, i'faith.

K. Hen. I'll cast better yet.

Sir John. Then I'll be hanged. Sirrah, hast thou not given thy soul to the devil for casting?

K. Hen. I pass for all.

Sir John. Thou passest all that e'er I played with-
Sirrah, dost thou not cog, nor foist, nor slurr? [al:

K. Hen. Set, parson, set; the dice die in my hand.
When, parson, when? what, can ye find no more?
Already dry? was't you bragged of your store?

Sir John. All's gone but that.

Hunt. What, half a broken angel?

Sir John. Why, sir, 'tis gold.

K. Hen. Yea, and I'll cover it.

Sir John. The devil give ye good on't! I am blind.
You have blown me up.

K. Hen. Nay, tarry, priest; you shall not leave us
Do not these pieces fit each other well? [yet:

Sir John. What if they do?

K. Hen. Thereby begins a tale:—
There was a thief, in face much like Sir John,
But 'twas not he — that thief was all in green —
Met me last day on Black-heath, near the park;
With him a woman. I was all alone
And weaponless; my boy had all my tools,
And was before, providing me a boat.
Short tale to make, Sir John — the thief, I mean —
Took a just hundred pound in gold from me.
I stormed at it, and swore to be revenged
If e'er we met; he, like a lusty thief,
Brake with his teeth this angel just in two,
To be a token at our meeting next,
Provided I should charge no officer
To apprehend him, but at weapon's point
Recover that, and what he had beside.
Well met, Sir John: betake ye to your tools,
By torchlight; for, master parson, you are he
That had my gold.

Sir John. 'Zounds! I won it in play, in fair square play, of the keeper of Eltham-park; and that I will maintain with this poor whyniard. Be you two honest men to stand and look upon us and let us alone, and neither part?

K. Hen. Agreed; I charge ye do not budge a foot.
Sir John, have at ye!

Sir John. Soldier, 'ware your sconce.

As they are preparing to engage, enter BUTLER, *and draws his sword to part them.*

But. Hold, villain, hold! My lords, what do ye
To see a traitor draw against the king? [mean,

Sir John. The king? God's will! I'm in a proper pickle.

K. Hen. Butler, what news? why dost thou trouble us?

But. Please it, your majesty, it is break of day,
And as I scouted near to Islington,
The gray-eyed morning gave me glimmering
Of armèd men coming down Highgate-hill,
Who, by their course, are coasting hitherward.

K. Hen. Let us withdraw, my lords; prepare our
To charge the rebels, if there be such cause. [troops
For this lewd priest, this devilish hypocrite,
That is a thief, a gamester, and what not,
Let him be hanged up for example's sake.

Sir John. Not so, my gracious sovereign. I confess I am a frail man — flesh and blood as other are; but set my imperfections aside, ye have not a taller man, nor a truer subject to the crown and state, than Sir John of Wrotham is.

K. Hen. Will a true subject rob his king?

Sir John. Alas! 'twas ignorance and want, my gracious liege.

K. Hen. 'Twas want of grace. Why, you should
To season others with good document; [be as salt
Your lives, as lamps to give the people light;
As shepherds, not as wolves to spoil the flock:
Go hang him, Butler.

But. Didst thou not rob me?

Sir John. I must confess I saw some of your gold; but, my dread lord, I am in no humor for death: God wills that sinners live: do not you cause me to die.
Once in their lives the best may go astray,
And if the world say true, yourself, my liege,
Have been a thief.

K. Hen. I do confess I have,
But I repent and have reclaimed myself.

Sir John. So will I do, if you will give me time.

K. Hen. Wilt thou? My lords, will you be sureties?

Hunt. That, when he robs again, he shall be hanged.

Sir John. I ask no more.

K. Hen. And we will grant thee that.
Live and repent, and prove an honest man;
Which, when I hear, and safe return from France,
I'll give thee living: till when, take thy gold,
But spend it better than at cards or wine,
For better virtues fit that coat of thine.

Sir John. Vivat rex, et currat lex. My liege, if ye have cause of battle, ye shall see Sir John bestir himself in your quarrel. [*Exeunt.*

SCENE II.—*A Field of Battle near* London.

Alarum. Enter King HENRY, SUFFOLK, HUNTINGTON; Sir JOHN *bringing in* ACTON, BEVERLEY, *and* MURLEY, *Prisoners.*

K. Hen. Bring in those traitors, whose aspiring minds
Thought to have triumphed in our overthrow.
But now ye see, base villains, what success
Attends ill actions wrongfully attempted.
Sir Roger Acton, thou retain'st the name
Of knight, and shouldst be more discreetly tempered
Than join with peasants; gentry is divine,
But thou hast made it more than popular.

Acton. Pardon, my lord; my conscience urged me to it.

K. Hen. Thy conscience! then thy conscience is corrupt,
For in thy conscience thou art bound to us,
And in thy conscience thou shouldst love thy country;
Else what's the difference betwixt a Christian
And the uncivil manners of the Turk?

Bev. We meant no hurt unto your majesty,
But reformation of religion.

K. Hen. Reform religion? was it that you sought?
I pray who gave you that authority?
Belike, then, we do hold the sceptre up,
And sit within the throne but for a cipher.
Time was, good subjects would make known their grief,
And pray amendment, not enforce the same,
Unless their king were tyrant; which I hope
You can not justly say that Harry is.
What is that other?

Suff. A malt-man, my lord,
And dwelling in Dunstable, as he says.

K. Hen. Sirrah, what made you leave your barley-broth,
To come in armor thus against your king?

Mur. Fie! paltry, paltry, to and fro, in and out upon occasion, what a world is this! Knighthood, my liege; 'twas knighthood brought me hither; they told me I had wealth enough to make my wife a lady.

K. Hen. And so you brought those horses which we saw
Trapped all in costly furniture, and meant
To wear these spurs when you were knighted once?

Mur. In and out upon occasion, I did.

K. Hen. In and out upon occasion, therefore,
You shall be hanged, and in the stead of wearing
These spurs upon your heels, about your neck
They shall bewray your folly to the world.

Sir John. In and out upon occasion, that goes hard.

Mur. Fie! paltry, paltry, to and fro. Good my liege, a pardon; I am sorry for my fault.

K. Hen. That comes too late: but tell me, went there none
Beside Sir Roger Acton, upon whom
You did depend to be your governor?

Mur. None, my lord, but Sir John Oldcastle.

K. Hen. Bears he a part in this conspiracy?

Acton. We looked, my lord, that he would meet us here.

K. Hen. But did he promise you that he would come?

Acton. Such letters we received forth of Kent.

Enter the Bishop of ROCHESTER.

Bish. Where is my lord the king? Health to your grace.
Examining, my lord, some of these rebels,
It is a general voice among them all,
That they had never come into this place,
But to have met their valiant general,
The good Lord Cobham, as they title him:
Whereby, my lord, your grace may now perceive
His treason is apparent, which before
He sought to color by his flattery.

K. Hen. Now, by my royalty, I would have sworn,
But for his conscience, which I bear withal,
There had not lived a more true-hearted subject.

Bish. It is but counterfeit, my gracious lord,
And therefore may it please your majesty
To set your hand unto this precept here,
By which we'll cause him forthwith to appear,
And answer this by order of the law.

K. Hen. Not only that, but take commission
To search, attach, imprison, and condemn,
This most notorious traitor as you please.

Bish. It shall be done, my lord, without delay.
So now I hold, Lord Cobham, in my hand,
That which shall finish thy disdainéd life.
[*Aside and exit.*

K. Hen. I think the iron age begins but now,
Which learnéd poets have so often taught,
Wherein there is no credit to be given
To either words, or looks, or solemn oaths:
For if there were, how often hath he sworn,
How gently tuned the music of his tongue,
And with what amiable face beheld he me,
When all, God knows, was but hypocrisy!

Enter COBHAM.

Cob. Long life and prosperous reign unto my lord!

K. Hen. Ah! villain, canst thou wish prosperity,
Whose heart includeth naught but treachery?
I do arrest thee here myself, false knight,
Of treason capital against the state.

Cob. Of treason, mighty prince? your grace mistakes,
I hope it is but in the way of mirth.

K. Hen. Thy neck shall feel it is in earnest shortly!
Dar'st thou intrude into our presence, knowing
How heinously thou hast offended us?
But this is thy accustoméd deceit.
Now, thou perceivest thy purpose is in vain,
With some excuse or other thou wilt come
To clear thyself of this rebellion.

Cob. Rebellion, good my lord? I know of none.

K. Hen. If you deny it, here is evidence:
See you these men? You never counselled
Nor offered them assistance in their wars?

Cob. Speak, sirs; not one, but all: I crave no favor!
Have ever I been conversant with you?
Or written letters to encourage you?
Or kindled but the least or smallest part
Of this your late unnatural rebellion?
Speak, for I dare the uttermost you can.

Mur. In and out upon occasion, I know you not.

K. Hen. No? didst thou not say that Sir John Oldcastle
Was one with whom you purposed to have met?

Mur. True, I did say so, but in what respect?—
Because I heard it was reported so.

K. Hen. Was there no other argument but that?

Acton. To clear my conscience ere I die, my lord,
I must confess we have no other ground,

But only rumor to accuse this lord,
Which now I see was merely fabulous.
K. Hen. The more pernicious you to taint him, then,
Whom you know was not faulty, yea or no.
Cob. Let this, my lord, which I present your grace,
Speak for my loyalty. Read these articles,
And then give sentence of my life or death.
K. Hen. Earl Cambridge, Scroop, and Grey, corrupted
With bribes from Charles of France, either to win
My crown from me, or secretly contrive
My death by treason! Is't possible?
Cob. There is the platform—and their hands, my lord,
Each severally subscribed to the same.
K. Hen. Oh, never-heard-of, base ingratitude!
Even those I hug within my bosom most,
Are readiest evermore to sting my heart.
Pardon me, Cobham, I have done thee wrong;
Hereafter I will live to make amends.
Is, then, their time of meeting so near at hand?
We'll meet with them but little for their ease,
If God permit. Go, take these rebels hence:
Let them have martial law; but as for thee,
Friend to thy king and country, still be free!
[*Exeunt* King HENRY *and* COBHAM.
Mur. Be it more or less, what a world is this!
Would I had continued still of the order of knaves,
And ne'er sought knighthood, since it costs so dear.
Sir Roger, I may thank you for it all.
Acton. Now 'tis too late to have it remedied,
I pr'ythee, Murley, do not urge me with it.
Hunt. Will you away, and make no more to-do?
Mur. Fie! paltry, paltry, to and fro, as occasion serves; if you be so hasty, take my place.
Hunt. No, good sir knight, e'en take it for yourself.
Mur. I could be glad to give my betters place.
[*Exeunt.*

SCENE III.—*A Room in* Lord COBHAM'S *House in* Kent.[1]

Enter CAMBRIDGE, SCROOP, *and* GREY. *They sit down at a Table.* King HENRY, COBHAM, *and other* Lords, *listening at the door.*

Cam. In mine opinion, Scroop hath well advised:
Poison will be the only aptest mean,
And fittest for our purpose, to despatch him.
Grey. But yet there may be doubt in the delivery;
Harry is wise, and therefore, earl of Cambridge,
I judge that way not so convenient.
Scroop. What think ye, then, of this? I am his bedfellow,
And unsuspected nightly sleep with him.
What if I venture in those silent hours,
When sleep hath sealéd up all mortal eyes,
To murder him in bed? How like ye that?
Cam. Herein consists no safety for yourself,
And you disclosed, what shall become of us?
But this day, as ye know, he will aboard—
The wind's so fair—and set away for France:
If, as he goes, or entering in the ship,
It might be done—then were it excellent.
Grey. Why, any of these, or if you will, I'll cause
A present sitting of the council, wherein
I will pretend some matter of such weight,
As needs must have his royal company;
And so despatch him in his council-chamber.
Cam. Tush! yet I hear not anything to purpose.
I wonder that Lord Cobham stays so long;—
His counsel in this case would much avail us.
Scroop. What, shall we rise thus, and determine nothing?
[*The* King *advances with his* Lords.
K. Hen. That were a shame, indeed: no, sit again,
And you shall have my counsel in this case.
If you can find no way to kill the king,
Then you shall see how I can furnish ye.
Scroop's way, by poison, was indifferent,
But yet, being bedfellow to the king,
And unsuspected, sleeping in his bosom,
In mine opinion that's the likelier way;
For such false friends are able to do much,
And silent night is treason's fittest friend.
Now, Cambridge, in his setting hence for France,
Or by the way, or as he goes aboard,
To do the deed—that was indifferent too,
But somewhat doubtful.
Marry, Lord Grey came very near the point—
To have the king at council, and there murder him,
As Cæsar was among his dearest friends.
Tell me, oh tell me, you bright honor's stains,
For which of all my kindnesses to you
Are ye become thus traitors to your king,
And France must have the spoil of Harry's life?
All. Oh! pardon us, dread lord.
K. Hen. How! pardon ye? that were a sin indeed.
Drag them to death, which justly they deserve:
And France shall dearly buy this villany,
So soon as we set footing on her breast.
God have the praise for our deliverance!—
And next, our thanks, Lord Cobham, unto thee,
True, perfect mirror of nobility. [*Exeunt.*

SCENE IV.—Kent. *Court before* Lord COBHAM'S *House.*

Enter Bishop of ROCHESTER, Lord Warden *of the* Cinque Ports, CROMER, Lady COBHAM, *and* Attendants.

Bish. I tell ye, lady, 'tis not possible
But you should know where he conveys himself;
And you have hid him in some secret place.
Lady Cob. My lord, believe me, as I have a soul,
I know not where my lord, my husband, is.
Bish. Go to, go to; you are a heretic,
And will be forced by torture to confess,
If fair means will not serve to make you tell.
Lady Cob. My husband is a noble gentleman,
And need not hide himself for any fact
That e'er I heard of; therefore wrong him not.
Bish. Your husband is a dangerous schismatic,
Traitor to God, the king, and commonwealth;
And therefore, Master Cromer, sheriff of Kent,
I charge you take her to your custody,
And seize the goods of Sir John Oldcastle
To the king's use: let her go in no more,
To fetch so much as her apparel out;
There is your warrant from his majesty.
Lord War. Good my lord bishop, pacify your wrath
Against the lady.

[1] This scene, in previous editions, made the opening scene of the fifth act, but improperly, as it would then have shown Cobham arrested by the bishop before having assisted at the detection of the conspirators. I have transposed several of the scenes in the fourth and fifth acts, which were out of place in old editions.

Bish. Then let her confess
Where Oldcastle, her husband, is concealed.
Lord War. I dare engage mine honor and my life,
Poor gentlewoman, she is ignorant
And innocent of all his practices
If any evil by him be practised.
Bish. If, my lord warden? Nay, then I charge you
That all the cinque-ports whereof you are chief,
Be laid forthwith, that he escape us not.
Show him his highness' warrant, master sheriff.
Lord War. I am sorry for the noble gentleman.
Bish. Peace! here he comes: now do your office, sir.

Enter COBHAM *and* HARPOOL.

Cob. Harpool, what business have we here in hand?
What makes the bishop and the sheriff here?
I fear my coming home is dangerous:
I would I had not made such haste to Cowling.
Har. Be of good cheer, my lord: if they be foes,
We'll scramble shrewdly with them; if they be friends,
They are welcome.
Crom. Sir John Oldcastle, Lord Cobham, in the king's name, I arrest you of high-treason.
Cob. Treason, Master Cromer?
Har. Treason, master sheriff? what treason?
Cob. Harpool, I charge thee stir not, but be quiet.
Do ye arrest me of treason, master sheriff?
Bish. Yea, of high-treason, traitor, heretic!
Cob. Defiance in his face that calls me so!
I am a loyal gentleman; as true
Unto his highness as my proudest enemy.
The king shall witness my late faithful service,
For safety of his sacred majesty.
Bish. What thou art, the king's hand shall testify:
Show him, lord warden.
Cob. Jesu defend me!
Is't possible your cunning could so temper
The princely disposition of his mind,
To sign the damage of a loyal subject?
Well, the best is, it bears an antedate,
Procured by my absence and your malice.
But I, since that, have showed myself as true
As any churchman that dare challenge me.
Let me be brought before his majesty:
If he acquit me not, then do your worst.
Bish. We are not bound to do kind offices
For any traitor, schismatic, or heretic:
The king's hand is our warrant for our work,
Who is departed on his way for France,
And at Southampton doth repose this night.
Har. O that thou and I were within twenty miles of it, on Salisbury plain! I would lose my head if thou brought'st thy head hither again. [*Aside.*
Cob. My lord warden o' the cinque-ports, and lord of Rochester, ye are joint commissioners: favor me so much on my expense, to bring me to the king.
Bish. What, to Southampton?
Cob. Thither, my good lord;
And if he do not clear me of all guilt,
And all suspicion of conspiracy,
Pawning his princely warrant for my truth —
I ask no favor, but extremest torture.
Bring me, or send me to him, good my lord;
Good my lord warden, master sheriff, entreat.
[*They both entreat for him.*
Come hither, lady; nay, sweet wife, forbear
To heap one sorrow on another's neck.
'Tis grief enough falsely to be accused,
And not permitted to acquit myself:
Do not thou, with thy kind, respective tears,
Torment thy husband's heart that bleeds for thee,
But be of comfort. God hath help in store
For those that put assurèd trust in him.
Dear wife, if they commit me to the Tower,
Come up to London to your sister's house;
That, being near me, you may comfort me.
One solace find I settled in my soul —
That I am free from treason's very thought:
Only my conscience, for the gospel's sake,
Is cause of all the troubles I sustain.
Lady Cob. O, my dear lord, what shall betide of us?
You to the Tower, and I turned out of doors;
Our substance seized unto his highness' use,
Even to the garments 'longing to our backs.
Har. Patience, good madam, things at worst will mend,
And if they do not, yet our lives may end.
Bish. Urge it no more; for if an angel spake,
I swear by sweet Saint Peter's blessed keys,
First goes he to the Tower, then to the stake!
Crom. But, by your leave, this warrant doth not stretch
To imprison her.
Bish. No, turn her out of doors,
Even as she is, and lead him to the Tower,
With guard enough, for fear of rescuing.
Lady Cob. O God requite thee, thou blood-thirsty man!
Cob. May it not be, my lord of Rochester? —
Wherein have I incurred your hate so far
That my appeal unto the king's denied?
Bish. No hate of mine, but power of holy church,
Forbids all favor to false heretics.
Cob. Your private malice, more than public power,
Strikes most at me; but with my life it ends.
Har. [*aside*]. O that I had the bishop in that fear
That once I had his sumner — by ourselves!
Crom. My lord, yet grant one suit unto us all,
That this same ancient servingman may wait
Upon my lord, his master, in the Tower.
Bish. This old iniquity, this heretic,
That, in contempt of our church discipline,
Compelled my sumner to devour his process?
Old ruffian past-grace, upstart schismatic,
Had not the king prayed us to pardon you,
You had fried for't, you grizzled heretic!
Har. 'Sblood! my lord bishop, you wrong me; I am neither heretic nor puritan, but of the old church. I'll swear, drink ale, kiss a wench, go to mass, eat fish all Lent, and fast Fridays with cakes and wine, fruit and spicery; — shrive me of my old sins afore Easter, and begin new before Whitsuntide.
Crom. A merry, mad, conceited knave, my lord.
Har. That knave was simply put upon the bishop.
Bish. Well, God forgive him, and I pardon him:
Let him attend his master in the Tower,
For I in charity wish his soul no hurt.
Cob. God bless my soul from such cold charity!
Bish. To th' Tower with him; and when my leisure serves
I will examine him of articles.
Look, my lord warden, as you have 't in charge,
The sheriff, perform his office.
Lord War. Ay, my lord.
[*Exeunt* Lord Warden, CROMER, *and* Lord COBHAM.

Enter, from Lord COBHAM's *House,* Sumner *with Books.*

Bish. What bring'st thou here? what!—books of heresy?

Sum. Yea, my lord, here's not a Latin book,
No, not so much as Our Lady's psalter;
Here's the *Bible,* the *Testament,* the *Psalms* in metre,
The *Sick Man's Salve,* the *Treasury of Gladness*—
All English; no, not so much but the almanac's English.

Bish. Away with them! to the fire with them, Clun!
Now fie upon these upstart heretics!
All English! burn them, burn them quickly, Clun!

Har. But do not, sumner, as you'll answer it; for I have there English books, my lord, that I'll not part withal for your bishopric: *Bevis of Hampton, Owlglass,* the *Friar and the Boy, Ellen of Rumming, Robin Hood,*[1] and other such godly stories, which, if ye burn, by this flesh I'll make ye drink their ashes in Saint Marget's ale. [*Exeunt Bishop of* ROCHESTER, Lady COBHAM, HARPOOL, *and* Sumner.

ACT V.

SCENE I.—*The entrance of the* Tower.

Enter the Bishop of ROCHESTER, *attended.*

1 *Serv.* Is it your honor's pleasure we shall stay,
Or come back in the afternoon to fetch you?

Bish. Now have ye brought me here unto the Tower,
You may go back unto the porter's lodge,
Where, if I have occasion to employ you,
I'll send some officer to call you to me.
Into the city go not, I command you:
Perhaps I may have present need to use you.

2 *Serv.* We will attend your honor here without.

3 *Serv.* Come, we may have a quart of wine at the Rose at Barking, and come back an hour before he'll go.

1 *Serv.* We must hie us, then.

3 *Serv.* Let's away. [*Exeunt.*

Bish. Ho, master lieutenant!

Enter Lieutenant *of the* Tower.

Lieut. Who calls there?

Bish. A friend of yours.

Lieut. My lord of Rochester! your honor's welcome.

Bish. Sir, here is my warrant from the council,
For conference with Sir John Oldcastle,
Upon some matter of great consequence.

Lieut. Ho, Sir John!

Har. [*within*]. Who calls there?

Lieut. Harpool, tell Sir John, my lord of Rochester
Comes from the council to confer with him.
I think you may as safe without suspicion
As any man in England, as I hear,
For it was you most labored his commitment.

Bish. I did, and naught repent it, I assure you.

Enter Lord COBHAM *and* HARPOOL.

Master lieutenant, I pray you, give us leave,
I must confer here with Sir John a little.

Lieut. With all my heart, my lord. [*Ex.* Lieut.

[1] This was all the popular literature of that day. The servingman of my Lord Cobham had quite a comprehensive library.

Har. [*aside*]. My lord, be ruled by me, take this occasion,
While it is offered, and, upon my life
Your lordship will escape.

Cob. No more, I say:
Peace, lest he should suspect it.

Bish. Sir John,
I come to you from the lords o' the council
To know if you do yet recant your errors.

Cob. My lord of Rochester, on good advice,
I see my error; but yet understand me;
I mean not error in the faith I hold,
But error in submitting to your pleasure.
Therefore, your lordship, without more ado,
Must be a means to help me to escape.

Bish. What mean'st thou, heretic?
Dar'st thou but lift thy hand against my calling?

Cob. No, not to hurt you for a thousand pound.

Har. Nothing but to borrow your upper garment a little: not a word more; peace, for waking the children. There, put them on; despatch, my lord; the window that goes out into the leads is sure enough: as for you, I'll bind you surely in the inner room. [*Carries the* Bishop *in, and returns.*

Cob. This is well begun; God send us happy speed,
Hard shift you see men make in time of need.
[*Puts on the* Bishop's *cloak.*

Re-enter the Bishop of ROCHESTER's Servants.

1 *Serv.* I marvel that my lord should stay so long.

2 *Serv.* He hath sent to seek us, I dare lay my life.

3 *Serv.* We come in good time; see where he is coming.

Har. I beseech you, good my lord of Rochester,
Be favorable to my lord and master.

Cob. The inner rooms be very hot and close,
I do not like this air here in the Tower.

Har. His case is hard, my lord.—You shall safely[2] get out of the Tower, but I will down upon them: in which time get you away. Hard under Islington wait my coming: I will bring my lady ready with horses to get hence. [*Aside.*]

Cob. Fellow, go back again unto thy lord,
And counsel him.—

Har. Nay, my good lord of Rochester,
I'll bring you to St. Alban's, through the woods,
I warrant you.

Cob. Villain, away.

Har. Nay, since I am past the Tower's liberty,
You part not so. [*He draws.*

Cob. Clubs, clubs, clubs.

1 *Serv.* Murther, murther, murther.
[*They set upon* HARPOOL.

2 *Serv.* Down with him.

Har. Out, you cowardly rogues. [COBHAM *escapes.*

Enter Lieutenant *of the* Tower, *and* Warder.

Lieut. Who is so bold as dare to draw a sword
So near unto the entrance of the Tower?

1 *Serv.* This ruffian, servant to Sir John Oldcastle,
Was like to have slain my lord.

Lieut. Lay hold on him.

Har. Stand off, if you love your puddings.

[2] Subsequent editions read "scarcely."—Harpool is a little confused. It may be scarcely, or safely, but either word requires you to make allowances for the disorder of the sentence.

Bish. [*within*]. Help, help, help, master lieutenant; help!
Lieut. Who's that within? some treason in the Tower,
Upon my life;—look in; who's that who calls?
[*Exit one of the* Warders *within, and re-enter with the Bishop of* ROCHESTER, *bound.*
Lieut. Without your cloak, my lord of Rochester?
Har. There, now I see it works; then let me speed,
For now's the fittest time to 'scape away.
[*Exit* HARPOOL.
Lieut. Why do you look so ghastly and affrighted?
Bish. Oldcastle, that foul traitor and his man,
When you had left me to confer with him,
Took, bound, and stript me, as you see me now,
And left me lying in this inner chamber;—
And so departed.
1 *Serv.* And I——
Lieut. And you now say that the lord Cobham's man
Did here set on you, like to murder you?
1 *Serv.* And so he did.
Bish. It was upon his master then he did,
That, in the brawl, the traitor might escape.
Lieut. Where is this Harpool?
2 *Serv.* Here he was, even now.
Lieut. Fled!—Where? can you tell?
Bish. They are both escaped!
Lieut. Since it so happens that he is escaped,
I am glad you are a witness of the same:
It might have else been laid unto my charge,
That I had been consenting to the fact.
Bish. Come!
Search shall be made for him with expedition,
The haven's laid that he shall not escape,
And hue and cry continue throughout England,
To find this damnéd, dangerous heretic. [*Exeunt.*

SCENE II.—*A High Road near* St. Alban's.

Enter Sir JOHN *of* Wrotham, *and* DOLL.

Sir John. Come, Doll, come; be merry, wench. Farewell, Kent; we are not for thee. Be lusty, my lass. Come! for Lancashire. We must nip the bung,[1] for these crowns.

Doll. Why, is all the gold spent already, that you had the other day?

Sir John. Gone, Doll, gone; flown, spent, vanished; the devil, drink, and dice, have devoured all.

Doll. You might have left me in Kent, till you had been better provided.

Sir John. No, Doll, no; Kent's too hot, Doll, Kent's too hot; the weathercock of Wrotham will crow no longer; we have plucked him; he has lost his feathers;—I have pruned him bare; left him thrice; he is moulted; he is moulted, wench.

Doll. I might have gone to service, again; old Master Harpool told me he would provide me a mistress.

Sir John, Peace, Doll, peace; come, mad wench, I'll make thee an honest woman; we'll into Lancashire to our friends; the truth is, I'll marry thee; we want but a little money, and money we will have, I warrant thee: stay, who comes here? some Irish villain, methinks, that has slain a man, and now is rifling of him. Stand close, Doll; we'll see the end.

1 *Bung*—a pickpocket.

Enter an Irishman, *with his dead* Master. *He lays him down and rifles him.*

Irish. Alas, poe master, Sir Richard Lee: be St. Patrick, I'se rob and cut dy trote, for dy shain, and dy mony, and dy gold ring. Be me truly, I'se love de well, but now dow be kill, dow be bastely[2] knave.

Sir John. Stand, sirrah, what art thou?

Irish. Be St. Patrick, mester, I'se poor Irishman; I'se a leufter.[3]

Sir John. Sirrah, sirrah, you're a damned rogue; you have killed a man here, and rifled him of all that he has. 'Sblood, you rogue, deliver, or I'll not leave you so much as a hair above your shoulders, you whorson Irish dog. [*Robs him.*

Irish. We's me! Be St. Patrick, I'se kill my mester for his shain and his ring, and now's be rob of all. Me's undo.

Sir John. Avaunt, you rascal; go, sirrah; be walking! Come, Doll, the devil laughs when one thief robs another. Come, wench, we'll to St. Alban's, and revel in our bower, my brave girl.

Doll. O, thou art old[4] Sir John, when all's done, i'faith. [*Exeunt.*

SCENE III.—St. Alban's. *The Entrance of a Carrier's Inn.*

Enter Host *and* Irishman.

Irish. Be me tro', mester, I'se poor Irishman. I'se want ludging; I'se have no mony; I'se starve and cold; good mester, give hur some meat; I'se famish and tie.

Host. 'Faith, fellow, I have no lodging, but what I keep for my guests. As for meat, thou shalt have as much as there is; and if thou wilt lie in the barn there's fair straw, and room enough.

Irish. I'se tank my mester, heartily.

Host. Ho, Robin!

Enter ROBIN.

Robin. Who calls?

Host. Show this poor Irishman to the barn;—go, sirrah. [*Exeunt.*

Enter Carrier *and* KATE.

Car. Who's within, here?—who looks to the horses? Uds heart, here's fine work: the hens in the maunger, and the hogs in the litter. A bots 'found you all! here's a house well looked to, i'faith.

Kate. Mas gaff Club, I'se very cawd.

Car. Get in, Kate, get in to the fire, and warm thee. John Ostler!

Enter Ostler.

Ost. What, gaffer Club! welcome to St. Alban's! How do all our friends in Lancashire?

Car. Well, God-a-mercy, John!—How does Tom? Where is he?

Ostl. Tom's gone from hence; he's at the Three Horse-loaves, at Stony-Stratford. How does old Dick Dun?

Car. Uds heart, old Dun has bin moyr'd in a slough in Brick-hill lane: a plague 'found it! yonder's such abomination-weather as was never seen.

2 I have substituted one epithet here, for another, in order to avoid a sheer brutality.

3 What a "leufter" is, nobody can say at this day. "Leuterer" was a thief, a vagabond. The Irishman is probably willing to confess himself both, that he may escape the more heinous charge of murder.

4 Query: *bold?*

Ostl. Ud's heart! thief! 'a shall have one half peck of pease and oats more for that, as I am John Ostler; he has been ever as good a jade as ever travelled.

Car. 'Faith, well said, old Jack; thou art the old lad still.

Ostl. Come, gaffer Club, unload, unload, and get in to supper. [*Exeunt.*

SCENE IV.—*The same. A Room in the Carrier's Inn.*

Enter Host, Lord COBHAM, *and* HARPOOL.

Host. Sir, you are welcome to this house, and to such as is here, with all my heart: but I fear your lodging will be the worst. I have but two beds, and they are both in one chamber, and the carrier and his daughter lie in the one, and you and your wife must lie in the other.

Cob. 'Faith, sir, for myself I do not greatly press,[1]
My wife is weary, and would be at rest,
For we have travelled very far to-day;
We must be content with such as you have.

Host. But I can not tell what to do with your man.

Har. What? hast thou never an empty room in thy house for me?

Host. Not a bed, in troth. There came a poor Irishman, and I lodged him in the barn, where he has fair straw, although he have nothing else.

Har. Well, mine host, I pry'thee help me to a pair of clean sheets, and I'll go lodge with him.

Host. By the mass, that thou shalt; as good a pair of hempen sheets were never lain in: come. [*Exeunt.*

SCENE V.—*The same. A Street.*

Enter Mayor, Constable, *and* Watch.

Mayor. What! have you searched the town?

Con. All the town, sir; we have not left a house unsearched that uses to lodge.

Mayor. My lord of Rochester was then deceived,
Or ill-informed of Sir John Oldcastle:
Or, if he came this way, he's past the town;
He could not else have 'scaped you in the search.

Con. The privy watch hath been abroad all night,
And not a stranger lodgeth in the town
But he is known; only a lusty priest
We found in bed with a young, pretty wench,
That says she is his wife, yonder at the Shears:
But we have charged the host with his forthcoming
To-morrow morning.

Mayor. What think you best to do?

Con. Faith, master mayor, here's a few straggling houses beyond the bridge, and a little inn, where carriers use to lodge, although I think surely he would never lodge there: but we'll go search, and the rather, because there came notice to the town the last night of an Irishman, that had done a murder, whom we are to make search for.

Mayor. Come, then, I pray you, and be circumspect. [*Exeunt.*

SCENE VI.—*The same. Before the Carrier's Inn.*

Enter Constable *and* Officer.

Con. First beset the house, before you begin to search.

Offi. Content; every man take a several place. [*Noise within*

Voice [*within*]. Keep; keep; strike him down there; down with him!

Enter from the Inn, the Mayor *and* Constable, *with the* Irishman *in* HARPOOL's *apparel.*

Con. Come, you villanous heretic, tell us where your master is.

Irish. Vat mester?

Mayor. Vat mester, you counterfeit rebel? This shall not serve your turn.

Irish. Be Sent Patrick, I ha' no mester.

Con. Where's the lord Cobham, Sir John Oldcastle, that lately escaped out of the Tower?

Irish. Vat lort Cobham?

Mayor. You counterfeit; this shall not serve you; we'll torture you; we'll make you confess where that arch heretic is. Come, bind him fast.

Irish. Ahone, ahone, ahone, a cree!

Con. Ahone! you crafty rascal? [*Exeunt.*

SCENE VII.—*The same. The Yard of the Inn.*

Enter Lord COBHAM, *in his nightgown.*

Cob. Harpool!
I hear a marvellous noise about the house:—
God warrant us, I fear we are pursued!
What! Harpool!

Har. [*within*]. Who calls, there?

Cob. 'Tis I!
Dost thou not hear a noise about the house?

Har. Yes, marry do I. Zounds, I can not find my hose. This Irish rascal that lodged with me all night, hath stolen my apparel, and has left me nothing but a lousy mantle, and a pair of brogues. Get up, get up!
And if the carrier and his wench be 'sleep,
Change you with him, as he[2] hath done with me,
And see if we can 'scape. [*Exit* Lord COBHAM.

SCENE VIII.—*The same. Noises at intervals, about the House. Then enter* HARPOOL, *in the* Irishman's *apparel, the* Mayor, Constable, *and* Officers, *meeting him.*

Con. Stand close; here comes the Irishman that did
The murder;—by all tokens this is he!

Mayor. And perceiving the house beset, would get [away.
Stand, sirrah!

Har. What art thou that bidd'st me stand?

Con. I am the officer, and am come to search for
An Irishman;—such a villain as thyself;—
Thou'st murdered a man, this last night, by the highway.

Har. 'Sblood, constable, art mad? am I an Irishman?

Mayor. Sirrah, we'll find you an Irishman, before
We part.—Lay hold upon him.

Con. Make him fast! Oh! bloody rogue!
[*The* Officers *seize him.*

Enter Lord *and* Lady COBHAM, *in the habits of the* Carrier *and his* Daughter.

Cob. What, will these ostlers sleep all day?

1 "Pass," in the old editions.

2 The Irishman.

Good morrow, good morrow. Come, wench, come: Saddle, saddle; now, afore God, two fair days, ha?

Con. Who goes there?

Mayor. O 'tis the Lancashire carrier, let them pass.

Cob. What, will nobody open us the gates here? Come, let's into stable to look to our capons.

[*Exeunt* Lord *and* Lady COBHAM.

Car. [*within*]. Host! why, ostler! zooks! here's such abomination company of boys: A pox of this pigstye at the house end; it fills all the house full of fleas. Ostler, ostler!

Enter Ostler.

Ostl. Who calls there? what would you have?

Car. [*within*]. Zooks! do you rob your guests?
Do you lodge rogues, and slaves, and scoundrels, ha?
They ha' stolen our clothes, here: why, ostler?

Ostl. A murrain choke you! what a bawling you keep!

Enter Host.

Host. How now? What would the carrier have?
Look up, there!

Ostl. They say the man and the woman that lay by them have stolen their clothes.

Host. What, are the strange folks up, that came in yesternight?

Con. What, mine host, up so early?

Host. What, master mayor, and master constable?

May. We are come to seek for some suspected persons,
And such as here we found have apprehended.

Enter Carrier *and* KATE, *in* Lord *and* Lady COBHAM'S *Apparel.*

Con. Who comes here?

Car. Who comes here? A plague 'found 'em! You bawl, quoth-a? odds heart, I'll forswear your house: you lodged a fellow and his wife by us, that ha' run away with our 'parel, and left us such gewgaws here! Come, Kate; come to me; thou's dizard i'faith.

Mayor. Mine host, know you this man?

Host. Yes, master mayor, I'll give my word for him.
Why, neighbor Club, how comes this gear about?

Kate. Now a foul on't! I can not make this gewgaw stand on my head.

Con. How came this man and woman thus attired?

Host. Here came a man and woman hither this last night,
Which I did take for substantial people,
And lodged all in one chamber by these folks:
Methinks they have been so bold to change apparel,
And gone away this morning ere these rose.

Mayor. It was that traitor Oldcastle that thus
Escaped us; make hue and cry yet after him;
Keep fast that trait'rous rebel, his servant there:
Farewell, mine host.

Car. Come, Kate Owdham, thou and I'se trimly dizard.

Kate. I'faith, neam Club, I'se wot ne'er what to do; I'se be so flouted and so shouted at; but, by the mess, I'se cry. [*Exeunt.*

SCENE IX.—*A Wood near* St. Alban's.

Enter Lord *and* Lady COBHAM, *disguised.*

Cob. Come, madam, happily escaped. Here let us sit;
This place is far remote from any path;
And here awhile our weary limbs may rest
To take refreshing, free from the pursuit
Of envious Rochester.

Lady Cob. But where, my lord,
Shall we find rest for our disquiet minds?
There dwell untamèd thoughts that hardly stoop
To such abasement of disdainèd rags:
We were not wont to travel thus by night,
Especially on foot.

Cob. No matter, love;
Extremities admit no better choice;
And, were it not for thee, say froward time
Imposed a greater task, I would esteem it
As lightly as the wind that blows upon us.
But, in thy sufferance, I am doubly tasked;—
Thou wast not wont to have the earth thy stool,
Nor the moist dewy grass thy pillow, nor
Thy chamber [walls] to be the wide horizon.

Lady Cob. How can it seem a trouble, having you,
A partner with me, in the worst I feel?
No, gentle lord, your presence would give ease
To death itself, should he now seize upon me:

[*She produces some bread and cheese and a bottle.*

Behold what my foresight hath undertaken
For fear we faint;—these are but homely cates;
Yet, sauced with hunger, they may seem as sweet
As greater dainties we were wont to taste.

Cob. Praise be to Him, whose plenty sends both this
And all things else our mortal bodies need!
Nor scorn we this poor feeding, nor the state
We now are in; for what is it on earth,—
Nay, under heaven,—continues at a stay?
Ebbs not the sea, when it hath overflown?
Follows not darkness, when the day is gone?
And see we not, sometimes, the eye of heaven
Dimmed with o'er-flying clouds? There's not that work
Of careful nature, or of cunning art,
How strong, how beauteous, or how rich it be,
But falls in time to ruin. Here, gentle madam,
In this one draught, I wash my sorrow down.

[*Drinks.*

Lady Cob. And I, encouraged with your cheerful speech,
Will do the like.

Cob. Pray God, poor Harpool come!
If he should fall into the bishop's hands,
Or not remember where we bade him meet us,
It were the thing of all things else, that now
Could breed revolt in this new peace of mind.

Lady Cob. Fear not, my lord, he's witty to devise,
And strong to execute a present shift.

Cob. That Power be still his guide hath guided us.
My drowsy eyes wax heavy; early rising,
Together with the travel we have had,
Makes me that I could gladly take a nap,
Were I persuaded we might be secure.

Lady Cob. Let that depend on me: whilst you do sleep,
I'll watch, that no misfortune happen us.

Cob. I shall, dear wife, but too much trouble thee.

Lady Cob. Urge not that;
My duty binds me, and your love commands.
I would I had the skill, with tunèd voice,
To draw on sleep with some sweet melody.
But imperfection, and unaptness[1] too,

[1] The impropriety of drawing attention to their place of shelter.

Are both repugnant: fear inserts[1] the one,
The other nature hath denied me use.
But what talk I of means, to purchase that
Is freely happened? Sleep, with gentle hand,
Hath shut his eyelids. O, victorious labor,
How soon thy power can charm the body's sense!
And now thou likewise climb'st unto my brain,
Making my heavy temples stoop to thee.
Great God of heaven, from danger keep us free!
[*Falls asleep.*

Enter Sir RICHARD LEE *and his* Servants.

Lee. A murder cruelly[2] done, and in my ground?
Search carefully: if anywhere it were,
This obscure thicket is the likeliest place. [*Exit* Servant, *who re-enters, bearing a dead body.*

Serv. Sir, I have found the body stiff with cold,
And mangled cruelly with many wounds.

Lee. Look, if thou know'st him; turn his body up:
Alack, it is my son! my son and heir,
Whom, two years since, I sent to Ireland,
To practise there the discipline of war;
And coming home—for so he wrote to me—
Some savage heart, some bloody, devilish hand,
Either in hate, or thirsting for his coin,
Hath here sluiced out his blood. Unhappy hour!
Accursèd place! but most inconstant fate,
That had reserved him from the bullet's fire,
And suffered him to 'scape the wood-kernes'[3] fury,
Didst here ordain the treasure of his life,
Even here within the arms of tender peace,
To be consumed by treason's wasteful hand!
And, which is most afflicting to my soul,
That this his death and murder should be wrought
Without the knowledge by whose means 'twas done.

2 *Serv.* Not so, sir; I have found the authors of it.
See where they sit, and in their bloody fists
The fatal instruments of death and sin.

Lee. Just judgment of that Power, whose gracious eye,
Loathing the sight of such a heinous fact,
Dazzled their senses with benumbing sleep,
Till their unhallowed treachery was known!—
Awake, ye monsters!—murderers, awake!
Tremble for horror; blush, you can not choose,
Beholding this inhuman deed of yours.

Cob. What mean you, sir, to trouble weary souls,
And interrupt us of our quiet sleep?

Lee. O, devilish! Can you boast unto yourselves
Of quiet sleep, having, within your hearts,
The guilt of murder waking, that with cries
Deafs the loud thunder, and solicits Heaven
With more than mandrakes' shrieks,[4] for your offence?

Lady Cob. What murder? You upbraid us wrongfully.

Lee. Can you deny the fact? See you not here
The body of my son by you misdone?
Look on his wounds, look on his purple hue:
Do we not find you where the deed was done?
Were not your knives fast closèd in your hands?
Is not this cloth an argument besides,
Thus stained and spotted with his innocent blood?
These speaking characters, were there nothing else
To plead against ye, would convict you both.—

1 "*Insists*," perhaps.
2 "Closely" is the word in previous copies.
3 The *kerne* was the Irish light-armed foot-soldier.
4 The mandrake, or mandragora, provoked many superstitions. It was said to shriek when torn up.

To Hertford with them, where the 'size is now:
Their lives shall answer for my son's lost life.

Cob. As we are innocent, so may we speed.

Lee. As I am wronged, so may the law proceed.
[*Exeunt.*

SCENE X.—St. Alban's.

Enter the Bishop of ROCHESTER, Constable *of* St. Alban's, *with* Sir JOHN, DOLL, *and the* Irishman *in* HARPOOL'S *Apparel.*

Bish. What intricate confusion have we here?
Not two hours since, we apprehended one
In habit Irish, but in speech not so;
And now you bring another, that in speech
Is Irish, but in habit English: yea,
And more than so—the servant of that heretic,
Lord Cobham.

Irish. Fait, me be no servant of de Lort Cobham; me be Mackshane of Ulster.

Bish. Otherwise called Harpool of Kent: go to, sir;
You can not blind us with your broken Irish.

Sir John. Trust me, lord bishop, whether Irish or English,
Harpool or not Harpool, I leave to the trial:
But sure I am, this man by face and speech,
Is he that murdered young Sir Richard Lee.
I met him presently upon the fact,
And that he slew his master for that gold,
Those jewels, and that chain, I took from him.

Bish. Well, our affairs do call us back to London,
So that we can not prosecute the cause
As we desire to do; therefore we leave
The charge with you, to see they be conveyed
To Hertford 'sizes: both this counterfeit
And you, Sir John of Wrotham, and your wench,
For you are culpable as well as they,
Though not for murder, yet for felony.
But since you are the means to bring to light
This graceless murder, you shall bear with you
Our letters to the judges of the bench,
To be your friends in what they lawf'ly may.

Sir John. I thank your lordship. [*Exeunt.*

SCENE XI.—Hertford. *A Hall of Justice.*

Enter Gaoler *and* Servants, *bringing forth* Lord COBHAM *in irons.*

Gaol. Bring forth the prisoners; see the court prepared;
The justices are coming to the bench:
So, let him stand; away and fetch the rest.
[*Exit* Servant.

Cob. O, give me patience to endure this scourge,
Thou that art fountain of this virtuous stream!
And though contempt, false witness, and reproach,
Hang on these iron gyves, to press my life
As low as earth, yet strengthen me with faith,
That I may mount in spirit above the clouds!

Re-enter Gaoler's Servant, *bringing in* Lady COBHAM *and* HARPOOL.

Here comes my lady. Sorrow, 'tis for her—
Thy wound is grievous; else I scoff at thee.
What! and poor Harpool? art thou i'th' briars too?

Har. I'faith, my lord, I am in, get out how I can.

Lady Cob. Say, gentle lord—for now we are alone
And may confer—shall we confess in brief
Of whence and what we are, and so prevent
The accusation is commenced against us?

Cob. What will that help us? Being known, sweet love,
We shall for heresy be put to death,
For so they term the religion we profess.
No, if we die, let this our comfort be,
That of the guilt imposed our souls are free.
Har. Ay, ay, my lord! Harpool is so resolved;
I reck of death the less, in that I die
Not by the sentence of that envious priest.
Lady Cob. Well, be it, then, according as Heaven please.

Enter the Judge *of Assize and* Justices, Mayor *of* St. Alban's, Lord *and* Lady Powis, *and* Sir Richard Lee; *the* Judge *and* Justices *take their places on the Bench.*

Judge. Now, master mayor, what gentleman is that
You bring with you before us to the bench?
May. ['Tis] the Lord Powis, if it like your honor,
And this his lady, travelling toward Wales;
Who — for they lodged last night within my house,
And my lord bishop did lay wait for such —
Were very willing to come on with me,
Lest, for their sakes, suspicion we might wrong.
Judge. We cry your honor mercy, good my lord;
Will't please you take your place? Madam, your ladyship
May here, or where you will, repose yourself,
Until this business now in hand be past.
Lady Pow. I will withdraw into some other room,
So that your lordship and the rest be pleased.
Judge. With all our hearts: attend the lady there.
Pow. [*aside to his* Wife]. Wife, I have eyed yon pris'ners all this while,
And my conceit doth tell me 'tis our friend
The noble Cobham and his virtuous lady.
Lady Pow. I think no less. Are they [my lord, do you think]
Suspected for this murder?
Pow. What it means
I can not tell, but we shall know anon:
Meantime, as you pass by them, ask the question;
But do it secret, so you be not seen,
And make some sign, that I may know your mind.
Lady Pow. My Lord Cobham? Madam? [*As she passes over the stage by them.*]
Cob. No Cobham now, nor madam, as you love us,
But John of Lancashire, and Joan his wife.
Lady Pow. O tell, what is it that our love can do
To pleasure you, for we are bound to you?
Cob. Nothing but this, that you conceal our names;
So, gentle lady, pass; — for, being spied ——
Lady Pow. My heart I leave, to bear part of your grief. [*Exit* Lady Powis.
Judge. Call the prisoners to the bar. Sir Richard Lee,
What evidence can you bring against these people,
To prove them guilty of the murder done?
Lee. This bloody towel, and these naked knives:
Besides, we found them sitting by the place
Where the dead body lay within a bush.
Judge. What answer you why law should not proceed
According to this evidence given in,
To tax ye with the penalty of death?
Cob. That we are free from murder's very thought,
And know not how the gentleman was slain.
1 *Just.* How came this linen cloth so bloody, then?
Lady Cob. My husband, hot with travelling, my lord,
His nose gushed out a-bleeding; that was it.
2 *Just.* But how came your sharp-edgéd knives unsheathed?
Lady Cob. To cut such simple victual as we had.
Judge. Say we admit this answer to these articles,
What made you in so private, dark a nook,
So far remote from any common path,
As was the thick where the dead corpse was thrown?
Cob. Journeying, my lord, from London, from the term,
Down into Lancashire, where we do dwell —
And what with age and travel, being faint,
We gladly sought a place where we might rest,
Free from resort of other passengers; —
And so we strayed into that secret corner.
Judge. These are but ambages[1] to drive off time,
And linger justice from her purposed end.

Enter Constable *with the* Irishman, Sir John, *and* Doll.

But who are these?
Const. Stay judgment, and release these innocents,
For here is he whose hand hath done the deed
For which they stand indicted at the bar:
This savage villain, this rude Irish slave —
His tongue already hath confessed the fact,
And here is witness to confirm as much.
Sir John. Yes, my good lord, no sooner had he slain
His loving master for the wealth he had,
But I upon the instant met with him:
And what he purchased with the loss of blood,
With strokes I presently bereaved him of;
Some of the which is spent; the rest remaining,
I willingly surrender to the hands
Of old Sir Richard Lee, as being his;
Besides, my good lord judge, I greet your honor
With letters from my lord of Rochester. [*Delivers a letter.*
Lee. Is this the wolf whose thirsty throat did drink
My dear son's blood? Art thou the curséd snake
He cherished, yet with envious, piercing sting,
Assailedst him mortally? Wer't not that the law
Stands ready to revenge thy cruelty,
Traitor to God, thy master, and to me,
These hands should be thy executioner!
Judge. Patience, Sir Richard Lee, you shall have justice.
The fact is odious: therefore take him hence,
And, being hanged until the wretch be dead,
His body after shall be hanged in chains,
Near to the place where he did act the murder.
Irish. Pr'ythee, lord shudge, let me have mine own clothes, my strouces[2] there, and let me be hanged in a wyth, after my country the Irish fashion.
Judge. Go to, away with him. [*Exit* Gaoler *with* Irishman.
And now, Sir John,
Although by you this murder came to light,
Yet upright law will not hold you excused,
For you did rob the Irishman; by which
You stand attainted here of felony:
Besides, you have been lewd, and many years
Led a lascivious, unbeseeming life.
Sir John. Oh, but Sir John repents, and he will mend.

1 "Ambages"—evasions, subterfuges, circumlocutions, and sometimes circumstances.
2 Trowsers.

Judge. In hope thereof, together with the favor
My lord of Rochester entreats for you,
We are contented that you shall be proved.
Sir John. I thank your lordship.
Judge. These other falsely here
Accused, and brought in peril wrongfully,
We in like sort do set at liberty.
Lee. And for amends,
Touching the wrong unwittingly I've done,
I give these few crowns.
Judge. Your kindness merits praise, Sir Richard
So let us hence. [Lee:
[*Exeunt all but* Powis *and* Cobham.
Pow. But Powis still must stay.
There yet remains a part of that true love
He owes his noble friend, unsatisfied
And unperformed; which first of all doth bind me
To gratulate your lordship's safe delivery:
And then entreat, that since, unlooked for thus
We here are met, your honor will vouchsafe
To ride with me to Wales, where, through my power
Though not to quittance those great benefits
I have received of you—yet both my house,
My purse, my servants, and what else I have,
Are all at your command. Deny me not:
I know the bishop's hate pursues you so,
As there's no safety in abiding here.
Cob. 'Tis true, my lord, and God forgive him for it!
Pow. Then let us hence. You shall be straight provided
Of lusty geldings: and once entered Wales,
Well may the bishop hunt—but, 'spite his face,
He never more shall have the game in chase!
[*Exeunt.*

THE END OF SIR JOHN OLDCASTLE.

INTRODUCTION

TO

THE PURITAN; OR, THE WIDOW OF WATLING STREET.

"*A booke called the Comedie of the Puritan Wydowe*" was entered at Stationers' hall, by G. Eld, August 6, 1607. The first published edition was made in the same year, under the following title: "The Puritaine, or the Widdow of Watling Streete: acted by the children of Paules: written by W. S." It was included in the third edition of Shakspeare's works, and was ascribed to Shakspeare, by Gildon, in 1702. The English critics, of recent times, have uniformly rejected the pretension. Malone supposes this play to have been written by one William Smith, who is known as the author of three plays — the Palsgrave, the Hector of Germany, and the Freeman's Honor. Mr. Steevens remarks that, "though Shakspeare has ridiculed the *Puritans*, in his '*All's Well that Ends Well*,' and '*Twelfth Night*,' yet he seems not to have had the smallest share in the present comedy. The author of it, however, was well acquainted with *his* plays, as appears from resemblances already pointed out." Schlegel, with more indulgence, and perhaps much less discrimination, is of opinion that Shakspeare wrote it. To account for its manifest discrepancy with the acknowledged writings of Shakspeare, he most absurdly supposes that the great dramatist, for once in his life, conceived the idea of writing a play in the manner of Ben Jonson. Mr. Knight properly remarks, that, to investigate this supposed imitation, would "bring us to the conclusion that 'The Puritan' is as unlike Ben Jonson as it is unlike Shakspeare." He adds, justly: "If it possesses little of the wit, the buoyancy, the genial good humor, the sparkling poetry, the deep philosophy, and the universal characterization, of Shakspeare, it wants, in the same degree, the nice discrimination of shades of character, the sound judgment, the careful management of the plot, the lofty and indignant satire, the firm and gorgeous rhetoric, of Jonson." But all this, we must repeat, relates only to the *superior* works of these two masters. I am not prepared to regard the "Puritan" as much, if anything, below the inferior writings of Ben Jonson — the "New Inn," for example — in all that relates to structure, invention, and comic situation. No such comparison can be made with Shakspeare, who, in the very meanest of his acknowledged and unquestioned writings, is so infinitely beyond this performance, as to make any attempt at comparison impertinent.

But the very maturity and continued strength, which everywhere exist in Shakspeare, are among the arguments which prompt the belief in unacknowledged works from his pen; since, we can scarcely suppose him to have reached such an exquisite perfection of his powers at a single bound, or to have retained them to the last chapter of a tolerably advanced life, without diminution or decay. But this belongs to the general argument.

The estimate of Mr. Knight, in regard to the merits of "The Puritan," may well take the place of our own. He says: "As a comedy of manners, 'The Puritan' is at once feeble and extravagant. The author can not paint classes, in painting individuals. 'The Puritan' is a misnomer. We have no representation of the formal manners of that class. The family of the Widow of Watling street is meant to be puritanical; but it is difficult to discover wherein they differ from the rest of the world, except in the coarse exhibition of the loose morality of one of their servants, who professes to lie, though he swears not, and is willing to steal, if the crime is called by some gentler name. Yet the comedy is not without spirit and interest. The events are improbable, and some of the intrigues superfluous; but the action seldom lingers; and, if the characters seem unnatural, they are sufficiently defined to enable us to believe that such characters did exist, and might have been copied from the life by the author." Referring to the scene in the house of the gentleman who rescues Pyeboard from the hands of the bailiffs, by becoming accessory to the stratagem of the prisoner, Mr. Knight remarks: "There is, no doubt, considerable truth in this picture; but it is not such truth as we find in Shakspeare; it belongs to the temporary and the personal, not to the permanent and the universal. Such is the characteristic merit of the whole comedy, whatever merit it has."

Of this character, Pyeboard, we are told by the Rev. Mr. Dyce, in his valuable edition of Peele's works, that George Pyeboard and George Peele have the same meaning — "*peel* signifying a *board* with a long handle, with which bakers put things in and out of the oven." It would seem, then, that George Peel sat for the portrait of the profligate scholar, to the unknown dramatist. Peele was a man of profligate habits, and has published, in one of his tracts, two stories of his own tricks, which remind us of a couple of the stratagems in "The Puritan."

THE PURITAN;

OR,

THE WIDOW OF WATLING STREET.

PERSONS REPRESENTED.

Sir GODFREY PLUS, *brother-in-law to the* Widow Plus.
EDMOND, *son to the* Widow.
Sir OLIVER MUCKHILL, *a rich city knight, and suitor to the* Widow.
Sir JOHN PENNYDUB, *a country knight, and suitor to* Mary.
Sir ANDREW TIPSTAFF, *a courtier, and suitor to* Frances.
GEORGE PYEBOARD, *a scholar.*
The Sheriff of London.
Captain IDLE, *a highwayman.*
PULTOCK, RAVENSHAW, } *sheriff's servants.*
DOGSON, *a catchpole.*
Corporal OATH, *a vain-glorious fellow.*
NICHOLAS ST. ANTLINGS, SIMON ST. MARY-OVERIES, FRAILTY, } *servants to* Lady Plus, *and* Sir Godfrey.
PETER SKIRMISH, *an old soldier.*
A Nobleman.
A Gentleman Citizen.

Lady PLUS, *a citizen's widow.*
FRANCES *and* MARY, *her two daughters.*

Sheriff's Officers, Keeper of the Marshalsea *Prison, Musicians, and Attendants.*

SCENE,—LONDON.

ACT I.

SCENE I.—*A Garden behind the* Widow's *House.*

Enter the Widow PLUS, FRANCES, MARY, Sir GODFREY, *and* EDMOND, *all in mourning;* EDMOND *in a cyprus hat.*[1] *The* Widow *wringing her hands, and bursting out into passion, as newly come from the burial of her husband.*

Wid. Oh, that ever I was born, that ever I was born!

Sir God. Nay, good sister, dear sister, sweet sister, be of good comfort; show yourself a woman now or never.

Wid. Oh, I have lost the dearest man, I have buried the sweetest husband that ever lay by woman.

Sir God. Nay, give him his due, he was indeed an honest, virtuous, discreet, wise man. He was my brother, as right as right.

Wid. O, I shall never forget him, never forget him; he was a man so well given to a woman. Oh!

Sir God. Nay, but kind sister, I could weep as much as any woman; but, alas, our tears can not call him again: methinks you are well read, sister, and know that death is as common as Homo, a common name to all men.——A man shall be taken when he's making water.——Nay, did not the learned parson, Master Pigman, tell us, e'en now, that all flesh is frail.—We are born to die.—Man has but a time: with such like deep and profound persuasions? as he is a rare fellow you know, and an excellent reader And, for example (as there are examples abundance) did not Sir Humphrey Bubble die t'other day? There's a lusty widow! Why, she cried not above half an hour. For shame! for shame! Then followed him old Master Fulsome, the usurer: there's a wise widow; why she cried ne'er a whit at all.

Wid. O rank not me with those wicked women; I had a husband outshined 'em all.

Sir God. Ay, that he did, i'faith; he outshined 'em all.

Wid. Dost thou stand there and see us all weep, and not once shed a tear for thy father's death? oh, thou ungracious son and heir thou!

Edm. Troth, mother, I should not weep, I'm sure; I am past a child, I hope, to make all my old schoolfellows laugh at me; I should be mocked, so I should; pray, let one of my sisters weep for me, I'll laugh as much for her another time?

Wid. O thou past-grace thou! Out of my sight, thou graceless imp! thou grievest me more than the death of thy father. O, thou stubborn only son! Hadst thou such an honest man to thy father—that would deceive all the world to get riches for thee—and canst thou not afford a little salt water? He that so wisely did quite overthrow the right heir of these lands, which now you respect not: up every morning betwixt four and five; so duly at Westminster hall every term-

[1] In plain terms, a hat with a band of crape around it—a mourning hat. The proper spelling should be, "cypress."

time, with all his cards and writings, for thee, thou wicked Absalom. — O, dear husband!

Edm. Weep, quotha? I protest I am glad he's churched; — for now he's gone, I shall spend in quiet.

Frances. Dear mother, pray cease; half your tears suffice; —
'Tis time for you to take truce with your eyes: —
Let me weep now.

Wid. O, such a dear knight, such a sweet husband have I lost, have I lost. — If blessed be the corse the rain rains upon,[1] he had it pouring down.

Sir God. Sister, be of good cheer. We are all mortal ourselves; I come upon you freshly; I ne'er speak without comfort. Hear me, what I shall say: — my brother has left you wealthy; you're rich.

Wid. Oh!

Sir God. I say, you're rich: you are also fair.

Wid. Oh!

Sir God. Go to, you are fair; you can not smother it; beauty will come to light. Nor are your years so far entered with you, but that you will be sought after, and may very well answer another husband. The world is full of fine gallants; choice enow, sister; for what should we do with all our knights, I pray?[2] but to marry rich widows, wealthy citizens' widows; lusty, fair-browed ladies? Go to, be of good comfort, I say; leave sobbing and weeping. — Yet my brother was a kind-hearted man. — I would not have the elf see me now [*aside*]. — Come, pluck up a woman's heart! Here stand your daughters, who be well estated, and at maturity will also be inquired after with good husbands: so all these tears shall be soon dried up, and a better world than ever. — What, woman? you must not weep still! he's dead, he's buried — yet I can not choose but weep for him.[3]

Wid. Marry again! — Let me be buried quick, then!
And that same part o' the choir whereon I tread,
To such intent, O may it be my grave!
And that the priest may turn his wedding-prayers,
Even with a breath, to funeral dust and ashes;
O, out of a million of millions, I should ne'er find such a husband; he was unmatchable — unmatchable: nothing was too hot, nor too dear for me.[4] I could not speak of that one thing that I had not. Besides, I had keys of all, kept all, received all, had money in my purse, spent what I would, went abroad when I would, came home when I would, and did all what I would. O, my sweet husband! I shall never have the like.

Sir God. Sister, never say so. He was an honest brother of mine; and so; and you may light upon one as honest again, or one as honest again may light upon you; — that's the properer phrase, indeed.

Wid. Never! — O, if you love me, urge it not:
O, may I be the by-word of the world, [*kneels.*
The common talk at table in the mouth
Of every groom and waiter, if ever more
I entertain the carnal suit of man.

Mary. I must kneel down, for fashion, too.

Frances. And I, whom never man as yet hath scaled,
Even in this depth of general sorrow, vow
Never to marry, to sustain such loss,
As a dear husband seems to be, once dead.

Mary. I loved my father well, too; but to say,
Nay vow, I would not marry for his death,
Sure I should speak false latin, should I not?
I'd as soon vow never to come in bed:
Tut! women must live by the quick, and not by the dead.

Wid. Dear copy of my husband, let me kiss thee:
[*Kisses her* Husband's *picture.*
How like him is this model! this brief picture
Quickens my tears: my sorrows are renewed
At this fresh sight.

Sir God. Sister ——

Wid. Away!
All honesty with him is turned to clay!
O my sweet husband! O ——

Frances. My dear father!
[*Exeunt* Widow *and* FRANCES.

Mary. Here's a puling, indeed! I think my mother weeps for all the women that ever buried husbands; for if from time to time all the widowers' tears in England had been bottled up, I do not think all would have filled a three-halfpenny bottle. Alas! a small matter bucks a handkerchief;[5] and sometimes the spittle stands too nigh Saint Thomas-a-Waterings.[6] Well, I can mourn in good sober sort as well as another; but where I spend one tear for a dead father, I could give twenty kisses for a quick husband.
[*Exit* MARY.

Sir God. Well, go thy ways, old Sir Godfrey, and thou may'st be proud on't, thou hast a kind, loving sister-in-law. How constant, how passionate, how full of April the poor soul's eyes are! Well, I would my brother knew on't: he should then know what a kind wife he hath left behind him. Truth, an 'twere not for shame that the neighbors at the next garden should hear me betwixt joy and grief, I should even cry outright. [*Exit* Sir GODFREY.

Edm. So; a fair riddance! My father's laid in dust; his coffin and he is like a whole meat-pie, and the worms will cut him up shortly. Farewell, old dad, farewell! I'll be curbed in no more. I perceive a son and heir may quickly be made a fool, an he will be one; but I'll take another order. — Now, she would have me weep for him, forsooth; and why? Because he cozened the right heir, he being a fool, and bestowed those lands on me his eldest son; and therefore I must weep for him: ha! ha! Why, all the world knows, as long as 'twas his pleasure to get me, 'twas his duty to get for me. I know the law on that point: no attorney can gull me. Well, my uncle is an old ass, and an admirable coxcomb. I'll rule the roast myself; I'll be kept under no more; I know what I may do well enough, by my father's copy; the law's in mine own hands now. Nay, now I know my strength, I'll be strong enough for my mother, I warrant you. [*Exit.*

1 The old proverb has it, "Happy the bride that the sun shines on; blessed the corse the clouds rain on."

2 Malone suggests that this may have been meant as a sneer at the multitude of knights made by King James soon after his succession.

3 The same expression occurs in Hamlet, spoken by Ophelia.

4 This is unsatisfactorily explained by some of the commentators to be a proverbial phrase. I should prefer to suppose it an error of the press. It may properly read, "too *good*, nor too dear."

5 That is, wets. Washings were called "buckings."

6 A pun upon the word hospital, of which 'spital is a contraction.

SCENE II.—*A Street.*

Enter PYEBOARD *and* SKIRMISH.

Pye. What's to be done now, old lad of war? Thou that wert wont to be as hot as a turnspit, as nimble as a fencer, and as lousy as a schoolmaster—now thou art put to silence like a sectary.—War sits now like a justice of peace, and does nothing. Where be your muskets, calivers, and hot-shots? In Long-lane, at pawn, at pawn? Now keys are your only guns: key-guns, key-guns, and bawds the gunners—who are your sentinels in peace, and stand ready charged to give warning with hems, hums, and pocky coughs. Only your chambers are licensed to play upon you, and drabs enow to give fire to 'em.

Skir. Well, I can not tell, but I am sure it goes wrong with me; for since the ceasure of the wars, I have spent above a hundred crowns out of purse. I have been a soldier any time this forty years; and now I perceive an old soldier and an old courtier have both one destiny, and in the end turn both into hobnails.

Pye. Pretty mystery for a beggar, for indeed a hobnail is the true emblem of a beggar's shoe-sole.

Skir. I will not say but that war is a bloodsucker, and so; but in my conscience—as there is no soldier but has a piece of one, though it be full of holes like a shot ancient[1]—no matter, 'twill serve to swear by—in my conscience, I think some kind of peace has more hidden oppressions, and violent, heady sins, though looking of a gentle nature, than a professed war.

Pye. Troth, and for mine own part, I am a poor gentleman and a scholar: I have been matriculated in the university; wore out six gowns there; seen some fools, and some scholars; some of the city, and some of the country; kept order; went bareheaded over the quadrangle; eat my commons with a good stomach, and battled with discretion;—at last, having done many sleights and tricks to maintain my wit in use—as my brain would never endure me to be idle—I was expelled the university, only for stealing a cheese out of Jesus college.[2]

Skir. Is't possible?

Pye. O, there was one Welshman—God forgive him!—pursued it hard, and never left, till I turned my staff toward London; where, when I came, all my friends were pit-holed, gone to graves, as, indeed, there was but a few left before. Then was I turned to my wits; to shift in the world; to tower among sons and heirs, and fools, and gulls, and ladies' eldest sons; to work upon nothing; to feed out of flint; and ever since has my belly been much beholden to my brain.[3] But now to return to you, old Skirmish: I say as you say; and, for my part, wish a turbulency in the world; for I have nothing in the world but my wits, and I think they are as mad as they will be: and to strengthen your argument the more, I say that an honest war is better than a bawdy peace. As touching my profession: the multiplicity of scholars, hatched and nourished in the idle calms of peace, makes 'em like fishes, one devour another; and the community of learning has so played upon affections, that thereby almost religion is come about to phantasy, and discredited by being too much spoken of in so many and mean mouths. I myself, being a scholar and a graduate, have no other comfort by my learning but the affection of my words; to know how, scholar-like, to name what I want, and can call myself a beggar both in Greek and Latin. And, therefore, not to cog with peace, I'll not be afraid to say, 'tis a great breeder, but a bad nourisher; a great getter of children, which must either be thieves or rich men, knaves or beggars.

Skir. Well, would I had been born a knave, then, when I was born a beggar! for, if the truth was known, I think I was begot when my father had never a penny in his purse.

Pye. Puh! faint not, old Skirmish; let this warrant thee: *facilis descensus Averni*—'tis an easy journey to a knave; thou may'st be a knave when thou wilt; and peace is a good madam to all other professions, and an arrant drab to us. Let us handle her accordingly, and, by our wits, thrive in despite of her; for, since the lawyer lives by quarrels, the courtier by smooth good-morrows, and every profession makes itself greater by imperfections: why not we, then, by shifts, wiles, and forgeries? And, seeing our brains are the only patrimonies, let's spend with judgment; not like a desperate son and heir, but like a sober and discreet templar—one that will never march beyond the bounds of his allowance. And, for our thriving means, thus: I myself will put on the deceit of a fortune-teller.

Skir. A fortune-teller? Very proper.

Pye. And you a figure-caster, or a conjurer.

Skir. A conjurer?

Pye. Let me alone; I'll instruct you, and teach you to deceive all eyes but the devil's.

Skir. O, ay; for I would not deceive him, an I could choose, of all others.

Pye. Fear not, I warrant you. And so, by these means, we shall help one another to patients: as the condition of the age affords creatures enow for cunning to work upon.

Skir. O wondrous! new fools and fresh asses.

Pye. O fit, fit, excellent! [*Suddenly.*

Skir. What now, in the name of conjuring?

Pye. My memory greets me happily with an admirable subject to graze upon. The lady-widow, who of late I saw weeping in her garden for the death of her husband: sure she's but a waterish soul, and half on't by this time is dropped out of her eyes. Device well managed may do good upon her: it stands firm; my first practice shall be there.

Skir. You have my voice, George.

Pye. She's a gray gull to her brother, a fool to her only son, and an ape to her youngest daughter. I overheard them severally, and from their words I'll derive my device; and thou, old Peter Skirmish, shalt be my second in all sleights.

Skir. Ne'er doubt me, George Pyeboard; only, you must teach me to conjure.

Pye. Puh! I'll perfect thee, Peter.

1 Shot in the sense of cannon. In Henry IV., we have "an old-faced ancient."

2 The commentators assume, from the accumulation of college phrases, that the author must have been an academic. I need not remark that phrases in French and Latin are to be picked up just as easily by those who have studied neither language.

3 An ingenious commentator, determined on proving this play to have been written by Shakspeare, might adduce these passages to show his history. "Pit-holed" might be a quibble upon a favorite part of the theatre as well as a burial-place.

IDLE, *pinioned, and attended by a Guard of* Sheriff's Officers, *passes over the Stage.*

How now? what's he?

Skir. O George! this sight kills me! 'Tis my sworn brother, Captain Idle!

Pye. Captain Idle?

Skir. Apprehended for some felonious act or other. He has started out; has made a night on't; lacked silver; I can not but commend his resolution; he would not pawn his buff jerkin: I would either some of us were employed, or might pitch our tents at usurers' doors, to kill the slaves as they peep out at the wicket.

Pye. Indeed, they are our ancient enemies: they keep our money in their hands, and make us to be hanged for robbing of 'em. But come, let's follow after to the prison, and know the nature of his offence; and what we can stead him in, he shall be sure of it: and I'll uphold it still, that a charitable knave is better than a soothing[1] puritan.

[*Exeunt.*

SCENE III. — *A Street.*

Enter NICHOLAS ST. ANTLINGS,[2] SIMON ST. MARY-OVERIES,[3] *and* FRAILTY, *in black, scurvy Mourning-Coats, and Books at their Girdles, as coming from Church. To them* Corporal OATH.

Nich. What, Corporal Oath! I am sorry we have met with you; next our hearts, you are the man that we are forbidden to keep company withal. We must not swear, I can tell you, and you have the name for swearing.

Sim. Ay, Corporal Oath, I would you would do so much as forsake us; we can not abide you; we must not be seen in your company.

Frail. There is none of us, I can tell you, but shall be soundly whipped for swearing.

Corp. Why, how now? we three[4] puritanical scrape-shoes — flesh o' Good Fridays! a hand.

All. Oh! [*Shakes them by the hand.*

Corp. Why, Nicholas Saint Antlings, Simon Saint Mary-Overies, has the de'il possessed you, that you swear no better? You half-christened catomites, you ungodmothered varlets![5] does the first lesson teach you to be proud, and the second to be coxcombs — proud coxcombs — not once to do duty to a man of mark?

Frail. A man of mark, quoth'a? I do not think he can show a beggar's noble.[6]

Corp. A corporal, a commander, one of spirit, that is able to blow you up all dry with your books at your girdles.

Nich. We are not taught to believe that, sir, for we know the breath of man is weak.

[OATH *breathes on* FRAILTY.

Frail. Foh! you lie, Nicholas! for here's one strong enough. Blow us up, quoth'a! he may well blow me above twelvescore off on him: I warrant, if the wind stood right, a man might smell him from the top of Newgate to the leads of Ludgate.

Corp. Sirrah, thou hollow book of wax-candle[7] ——

Nich. Ay, you may say what you will, so you swear not.

Corp. I swear by the ——

Nich. Hold, hold, good Corporal Oath; for if you swear once, we shall fall down in a swoon presently.

Corp. I must and will swear, you quivering coxcombs! My captain is imprisoned, and by Vulcan's leather cod-piece point ——

Nich. O, Simon, what an oath was there!

Frail. If he should chance to break it, the poor man's breeches would fall down about his heels; for Venus allows but one point to his hose.[8]

Corp. With these, my bully-feet, I will thump ope the prison-doors, and brain the keeper with the begging-box, but I'll set my honest, sweet Captain Idle at liberty.

Nich. How, Captain Idle? my old aunt's son, my dear kinsman, in Cappadochio?

Corp. Ay, thou church-peeling, thou holy-paring, religious-outside, thou! If thou hadst any grace in thee, thou wouldst visit him, relieve him, swear to get him out.

Nich. Assure you, corporal, indeed, la! 'tis the first time I heard on't.

Corp. Why, do't now, then, marmozet. Bring forth thy yearly wages: let not a commander perish.

Sim. But if he be one of the wicked, he shall perish.

Nich. Well, corporal, I'll e'en along with you, to visit my kinsman: if I can do him any good, I will; but I have nothing for him. Simon Saint Mary-Overies and Frailty, pray make a lie for me to the knight my master, old Sir Godfrey.

Corp. A lie? may you lie, then?

Frail. O, ay, we may lie, but we must not swear.

Sim. True, we may lie with our neighbor's wife, but we must not swear we did so.

Corp. O, an excellent tag of religion!

Nich. O, Simon, I have thought upon a sound excuse; it will go current. Say that I am gone to a fast.[9]

Sim. To a fast? Very good.

Nich. Ay, to a fast; say, with Master Fullbelly, the minister.

Sim. Master Fullbelly? An honest man: he feeds the flock well, for he's an excellent feeder.

[*Exeunt* OATH *and* NICHOLAS.

Frail. O, ay; I have seen him eat a whole pig, and afterward fall to the pettitoes.

[*Exeunt* SIMON *and* FRAILTY.

SCENE IV. — *A Room in the* Marshalsea *Prison.*

Enter IDLE; *to him afterward* PYEBOARD *and* SKIRMISH.

Pye. [*within*]. Pray turn the key.

Skir. [*within*]. Turn the key, I pray.

1 Quere: *sobbing?*

2, 3 The names of well-known churches.

4 So in Twelfth Night: "Did you ever see the picture of *We three?*" A common sign in the time of Shakspeare, &c., consisting of *two* men in fools' coats. The spectator, or inquirer concerning its meaning, was supposed to make the *third.*—STEEVENS.

5 The puritans objected to the practice of having godfathers and godmothers in baptism.—PERCY.

6 A quibble between *mark*, an ancient coin, and *mark*, a sign of distinction; and between *noble*, a coin, and *noble*, the opposite of beggar.

7 I suppose alluding to the rolls of wax-candle coiled up in the form of a book.—PERCY.

8 Points were the metal hooks by which the breeches and waistcoat were anciently held together. A similar pleasantry occurs in Henry IV., thus:—

"Their points being broken,
Down fell their hose."

9 A fast—a gaol—a lock-up-fast-enough.

Capt. Who should these be? I almost know their voices! [*Enter* PYEBOARD *and* SKIRMISH] O, my friends! you are welcome to a smelling-room here; you newly took leave of the air: is it not a strange savor?

Pye. As all prisons have smells of sundry wretches, who, though departed, leave their scents behind 'em. By gold, captain, I am sincerely sorry for thee.

Capt. By my troth, George, I thank thee; but, pish! what must be must be.

Skir. Captain, what do you lie in for? is't great? What's your offence?

Capt. Faith, my offence is ordinary — common — a highway: and I fear me my penalty will be ordinary and common too, a halter.

Pye. Nay, prophesy not so ill; it shall go hard, but I'll shift for thy life.

Capt. Whether I live or die, thou'rt an honest George. I'll tell you: silver flowed not with me, as it had done. For now the tide runs to bawds and flatterers. I had a start out, and by chance set upon a fat steward, thinking his purse had been as pursy as his body; and the slave had about him but the poor purchase of ten groats. Notwithstanding, being descried, pursued, and taken, I know the law is so grim in respect of many desperate, unsettled soldiers, that I fear me I shall dance after their pipe for't.

Skir. I am twice sorry for you, captain: first, that your purchase was so small, and now that your danger is so great.

Capt. Pish! the worst is but death. Have you a pipe of tobacco about you?

Skir. I think I have hereabouts.

[*Gives tobacco;* Captain *blows a pipe.*

Capt. Here's a clean gentleman, too, to receive.[1]

Pye. Well, I must cast about some happy sleight:
Work, brain, that ever didst thy master right.

Corp. [*within*]. Keeper, let the key be turned.

[OATH *and* NICHOLAS *knock within.*

Nich. [*within*]. Ay, I pray, master keeper, give's a cast of your office. [*Enter* OATH *and* NICHOLAS.

Capt. How now? more visitants? What! Corporal Oath?

Pye. and Skir. Corporal!

Corp. In prison, honest captain? This must not be.

Nich. How do you, captain kinsman?

Capt. Good coxcomb! What makes that pure, starched fool here?

Nich. You see, kinsman, I am somewhat bold to call in, and see how you do. I heard you were safe enough; and I was very glad on't, that it was no worse.

Capt. This is a double torture, now. This fool, by the book,
Doth vex me more than my imprisonment.
What meant you, corporal, to hook him hither?

Corp. Who, he? he shall relieve thee, and supply thee: I'll make him do't.

Capt. Fie! what vain breath you spend! He supply? I'll sooner expect mercy from a usurer when my bond's forfeited; sooner kindness from a lawyer when my money's spent; nay, sooner charity from the devil, than good from a puritan. I'll look for relief from him when Lucifer is restored to his blood,[2] and in heaven again.

Nich. I warrant my kinsman's talking of me, for my left ear burns most tyrannically.[3]

Pye. Captain Idle! what's he there? He looks like a monkey upward, and a crane downward.

Capt. Pshaw! a foolish cousin of mine. I must thank God for him.

Pye. Why, the better subject to work a 'scape upon. Thou shalt e'en change clothes with him, and leave him here, and so ——

Capt. Pish! I published him e'en now to my corporal; he will be damned ere he do me so much good. Why, I know a more proper, a more handsome device than that, if the slave would be sociable. Now, goodman Fleerface!

Nich. O, my cousin begins to speak to me now; I shall be acquainted with him again, I hope.

Skir. Look! what ridiculous raptures take hold of his wrinkles!

Pye. Then what say you to this device — a happy one, captain?

Capt. Speak low, George. Prison-rats have wider ears than those in malt-lofts.

Nich. Cousin, if it lay in my power, as they say, to do ——

Capt. 'Twould do me an exceeding pleasure indeed, that; but ne'er talk further on't; the fool will be hanged ere he do't. [*To the* Corporal.

Corp. Pox! I'll thump him to't.

Pye. Why, do but try the fopster, and break it to him bluntly.

Capt. And so my disgrace will dwell in his jaws, and the slave slaver out our purpose to his master; for would I were but as sure on't as I am sure he will deny to do't.

Nich. I would be heartily glad, cousin, if any of my friendships, as they say, might — stand, ha —

Pye. Why, you see he offers his friendship foolishly to you already.

Capt. Ay, that's the hell on't; I would he would offer it wisely.

Nich. Verily and indeed, la! cousin ——

Capt. I have took note of thy fleers a good while. If thou art minded to do me good — as thou gap'st upon me comfortably, and giv'st me charitable faces — which, indeed, is but a fashion in you all that are puritans — wilt soon as[4] night steal me thy master's chain?

Nich. Oh, I shall swoon!

Pye. Corporal, he starts already.

Capt. I know it to be worth three hundred crowns; and, with the half of that, I can buy my life at a broker's, at second hand, which now lies in pawn to the law. If this thou refuse to do, being easy and nothing dangerous, in that thou art held in good opinion of thy master, why, 'tis a palpable argument thou hold'st my life at no price, and these thy broken and unjointed offers are but only created in thy lip: now born, and now buried; foolish breath only! What, wilt do't? Shall I look for happiness in thy answer?

Nich. Steal my master's chain, quoth'a? No, it shall ne'er be said that Nicholas Saint Antlings committed bird-lime!

Capt. Nay, I told you as much, did I not? Though he be a puritan, yet he will be a true man.

Nich. Why, cousin, you know 'tis written, *Thou shalt not steal.*

1 A clear pipe to receive it in.
2 That is, to his rank—to his family honors.
3 So in Hamlet, "most tyrannically."
4 "*At*" in former editions.

Capt. Why, and fool, *Thou shalt love thy neighbor*, and help him in extremities.

Nich. Mass, I think it be, indeed; in what chapter's that, cousin?

Capt. Why, in the first of charity, the second verse.

Nich. The first of charity, quoth'a? That's a good jest; there's no such chapter in my book!

Capt. No, I knew 'twas torn out of thy book, and that makes so little in thy heart.

Pye. [*Takes* NICHOLAS *aside*]. Come, let me tell you, you are too unkind a kinsman, i'faith; the captain loving you so dearly—ay, like the pomewater of his eye[1]—and you to be so unconformable.[2] Fie, fie!

Nich. Pray, do not wish me to be hanged. Anything else that I can do: had it been to rob, I would ha' don't; but I must not steal. That's the word, the literal, *Thou shalt not steal;* and would you wish me to steal, then?

Pye. No, i'faith, that were too much, to speak truth. Why, wilt thou nym it from him?

Nich. That I will.

Pye. Why, enough, bully. He will be content with that, or he shall have none. Let me alone with him now. Captain, I have dealt with your kinsman in a corner; a good, kind-natured fellow, methinks: go to, you shall not have all your own asking; you shall 'bate somewhat on't; he is not contented absolutely, as you would say, to steal the chain from him; but, to do you a pleasure, he will nym it from him.

Nich. Ay, that I will, cousin.

Capt. Well, seeing he will do no more, as far as I see, I must be contented with that.

Corp. Here's no notable gullery!

Pye. Nay, I'll come nearer to you, gentlemen. Because we'll have only but a help and a mirth on't, the knight shall not lose his chain neither, but be only laid out of the way some one or two days.

Nich. Ay, that would be good, indeed, kinsman.

Pye. For I have a further reach, to profit us better, by the missing of't only, than if we had it outright, as my discourse shall make it known to you. When thou hast the chain, do but convey it out at a back door into the garden, and there hang it close in the rosemary bank, but for a small season; and, by that harmless device, I know how to wind Captain Idle out of prison: the knight thy master shall get his pardon and release him, and he satisfy thy master with his own chain, and wondrous thanks on both hands.

Nich. That were rare indeed, la! Pray, let me know how.

Pye. Nay, 'tis very necessary thou shouldst know, because thou must be employed as an actor.

Nich. An actor? Oh no, that's a player, and our parson rails against players mightily, I can tell you, because they brought him drunk upon the stage once—as he will be horribly drunk.

Corp. Mass! I can not blame him, then; poor church-spout!

Pye. Why, as an intermeddler, then?

Nich. Ay—that, that.

Pye. Give me audience, then. When the old knight thy master has raged his fill for the loss of the chain, tell him thou hast a kinsman in prison of such exquisite art, that the devil himself is French lackey to him, and runs bareheaded by his horse's belly, when he has one—whom he will cause, with most Irish dexterity,[3] to fetch his chain, though 'twere hid under a mine of sea-coal, and ne'er make spade or pickaxe his instruments. Tell him but this, with further instructions thou shalt receive from me, and thou showest thyself a kinsman, indeed.

Corp. A dainty bully.

Skir. An honest book-keeper.

Corp. And my three-times-thrice-honey-cousin.

Nich. Nay, grace of God, I'll rob him on't suddenly, and hang it in the rosemary bank; but I bear that mind, cousin, I would not steal anything, methinks, for mine own father.

Skir. He bears a good mind in that, captain.

Pye. Why, well said. He begins to be an honest fellow, i'faith.

Corp. In truth he does.

Nich. You see, cousin, I am willing to do you any kindness, always saving myself harmless.

Capt. Why, I thank thee; fare thee well; I shall requite it. [*Exit* NICHOLAS.

Corp. 'Twill be good for thee, captain, that thou hast such an egregious ass to thy cousin.

Capt. Ay, is not that a fine fool, corporal?
But, George, thou talk'st of art and conjuring:
How shall that be?

Pye. Puh! be't not your care:
Leave that to me and my directions.
Well, captain, doubt not thy delivery now,
Even with the 'vantage, man, to gain by prison,
As my thoughts prompt me. Hold on, brain, and plot!
I aim at many cunning, far events,
All which I doubt not but to hit at length.
I'll to the widow with a quaint assault:—
Captain, be merry.

Capt. Who, I? Kerry merry buff jerkin.

Pye. Oh, I am happy in more sleights, and one
Will knit strong in another.—Corporal Oath—

Corp. Ho! bully.

Pye. And thou, old Peter Skirmish; I have a necessary task for you both.

Skir. Lay't upon us, George Pyeboard.

Corp. Whate'er it be, we'll manage it.

Pye. I would have you two maintain a quarrel before the lady-widow's door, and draw your swords i'th' edge of the evening.—Clash a little—clash, clash.

Corp. Fuh!
Let us alone to make our blades ring noon,
Though it be after supper.

Pye. I know you can;
And out of that false fire, I doubt not but to raise strange belief.—And, captain, to countenance my device the better, and grace my words to the widow, I have a good plain satin suit, that I had of a young reveller t'other night; for words pass not regarded now a-days, unless they come from a good suit of clothes; which the fates and my wits have bestowed upon me. Well, Captain Idle, if I did not highly love thee, I would ne'er be seen within twelve score of[4] a

1 The apple of his eye. Pomewater is a kind of apple. But it must not be forgotten that Pyeboard is a scholar.

2 Written "uncomfortable" in previous editions.

3 With the agility of a running footman. In the time of Queen Elizabeth and King James I., many noblemen had Irish running footmen in their service.—MALONE.

4 *Yards*, understood.

prison; for I protest, at this instant, I walk in great danger of small debts. I owe money to several hostesses, and you know such gills will quickly be upon a man's jack.

Capt. True, George.

Pye. Fare thee well, captain. Come, corporal and ancient. Thou shalt hear more news next time we greet thee.

Corp. More news? Ay, by yon Bear at Bridge-foot, in the evening[1] shalt thou.

[*Exeunt* PYEBOARD, SKIRMISH, *and* OATH.

Capt. Enough; my friends, farewell!
This prison shows as ghosts did part in hell.[2]

[*Exit.*

ACT II.

SCENE I.—*A Room in the* Widow's *House.*

Enter MARY.

Mary. Not marry! forswear marriage! Why, all women know 'tis as honorable a thing as to lie with a man; and I, to spite my sister's vow the more, have entertained a suitor already, a fine gallant knight of the last feather.[3] He says he will coach me too; and well appoint me; allow me money to dice withal; and many such pleasing protestations he sticks upon my lips.—Indeed, his short-winded father i'the country is wondrous wealthy; a most abominable farmer; and therefore he may dote in time.[4] Troth, I'll venture upon him. Women are not without ways enough to help themselves: if he prove wise and good as his word, why I shall love him, and use him kindly; and if he prove an ass, why, in a quarter of an hour's warning I can transform him into an ox;—there comes in my relief again.

Enter FRAILTY.

Frail. O, Mistress Mary, Mistress Mary.

Mary. How now? what's the news?

Frail. The knight, your suitor, Sir John Pennydub.

Mary. Sir John Pennydub? where? where?

Frail. He's walking in the gallery.

Mary. Has my mother seen him yet?

Frail. O no; she's spitting in the kitchen.[5]

Mary. Direct him hither softly, my good Frailty. I'll meet him half way.

Frail. That's just like running a tilt; but I hope he'll break nothing this time.[6] [*Exit.*

Enter Sir JOHN PENNYDUB.

Mary. 'Tis happiness my mother saw him not.
O welcome, good Sir John.

Penny. I thank you 'faith.—
Nay, you must stand me till I kiss you: 'tis
The fashion everywhere i'faith, and I
Came from the court even now.

Mary. Nay, the fates forefend
That I should anger the fashion?

Penny. Then, not forgetting the sweet of new ceremonies, I first fall back; then, recovering myself, make my honor to your lip thus; and then accost it.

[*Kisses her.*

Mary. Trust me, very pretty and moving; you're worthy of it, sir. O my mother, my mother! now she is here, we'll steal into the gallery.

[*Exeunt* Sir JOHN *and* MARY.

Enter Widow *and* Sir GODFREY.

Sir God. Nay, sister, let reason rule you;—do not play the fool;—stand not in your own light; you have wealthy offers, large tenderings; do not withstand your good fortune. Who comes a-wooing to you, I pray? No small fool; a rich knight o' the city, Sir Oliver Muckhill; no small fool, I can tell you. And, furthermore, as I heard late by your maid-servants (as your maid-servants will say to me anything, I thank 'em) both your daughters are not without suitors; ay, and worthy ones too; one a brisk courtier, Sir Andrew Tipstaff, suitor afar off to your eldest daughter, and the third a huge wealthy farmer's son, a fine young country knight; they call him Sir John Pennydub; a good name, marry; he may have it coined when he lacks money. What blessings are these, sister?

Wid. Tempt me not, Satan.

Sir God. Satan! do I look like Satan? I hope the devil's not so old as I, I trow.

Wid. You wound my senses, brother, when you name
A suitor to me. Oh, I can't abide it;—
I take in poison when I hear one named.

Enter SIMON.

How now, Simon? where is my son Edmond?

Sim. Verily, madam, he is at vain exercise; dripping in the Tennis-court.

Wid. At Tennis-court? Oh, now his father's gone, I shall have no rule with him; Oh wicked Edmond! I might well compare this with the prophecy in the chronicle, though far inferior. As Harry of Monmouth won all, and Harry of Windsor lost all, so Edmond of Bristow, that was the father, got all, and Edmond of London, that's his son now, will spend all.

Sir God. Peace, sister, we'll have him reformed; there's hope of him yet, though it be but a little.

Enter FRAILTY.

Frail. Forsooth, madam; there are two or three archers at door would very gladly speak with your ladyship.

Wid. Archers?

Sir God. Your husband's fletcher,[7] I warrant.

Wid. Oh,
Let them come near, they bring home things of his;
Troth, I should ha' forgot them. How now, villain!
Which be those archers?

[1] The old copies read, "in *heaven*."

[2] Doubtless, a meaning may be conjured out of the passage, but the idea of the author contracted to the limits of the line, compasses a volume of obscurity. Perhaps it might be something clearer to read "*do* part," or even "depart in hell."

[3] Of the latest fashion.

[4] I have left the reading in the old folio as it was. In other copies it is made to read, "do it in time," that is, provide me with what he promises. But the reference is to the old father, whose *dotage* would set the son free to do what he pleased.

[5] Superintending *the spit* or roasting machine.

[6] Comparison drawn from the tourney. The knights meeting midway in the encounter, and splintering lances.

[7] *Arrow-maker*—probably one who put on the feather.

Enter Sir ANDREW TIPSTAFF, Sir OLIVER MUCKHILL, *and* Sir JOHN PENNYDUB.

Frail. Why, do you not see 'em before you? Are not these archers? — what do you call 'em — shooters?[1] Shooters and archers are all one, I hope.

Wid. Out, ignorant slave.

Sir Oliver. Nay, pray be patient, lady; —
We come in way of honorable love.

Sir And. } *Sir John.* } We do.

Sir Oliver. To you.

Sir And. } *Sir John.* } And to your daughters.

Wid. O, why will you offer me this, gentlemen? Indeed, I will not look upon you. When the tears are scarce out of mine eyes, not yet washed off from my cheeks; and my dear husband's body scarce so cold as the coffin, — what reason have you to offer it? I am not like some of your widows, that will bury one in the evening, and be sure to have another ere morning. Pray away; pray take your answers, good knights; an you be sweet knights; I have vowed never to marry; — and so have my daughters, too!

Sir John. Ay, two of you have, but the third's a good wench!

Sir Oliver. Lady, a shrewd answer, marry. The best is, 'tis but the first; and he's a blunt wooer that will leave for one sharp answer.

Sir And. Where be your daughters, lady? I hope they'll give us better encouragement.

Wid. Indeed, they'll answer you so? take it on my word they'll give you the very same answer verbatim, truly, la.

Sir John. Mum: Mary's a good wench still; I know what she'll do?

Sir Oliver. Well, lady, for this time we'll take our leaves
Hoping for better comfort.

Wid. O never, never: an I live these thousand years, an you be good knights, do not hope; 'twill be all vain, vain. —— Look you, put off all your suits, an you come to me again.

[*Exeunt* Sir JOHN *and* Sir GODFREY.

Frail. Put off all their suits, quotha? Ay, that's the best wooing of a widow indeed, when a man's nonsuited; that is, when he's a-bed with her.

Sir Oliver. Sir Godfrey, here's twenty angels more.
Work hard for me; there's life in't yet.[2]

Sir God. Fear not, Sir Oliver Muckhill; I'll stick close for you: leave all with me. [*Exit* Sir OLIVER.

Enter PYEBOARD.

Pye. By your leave, lady widow.

Wid. What, another suitor now?

Pye. A suitor! no, I protest, lady, if you'd give me yourself, I'd not be troubled with you.

Wid. Say you so, sir? then you're the better welcome, sir.

Pye. Nay, Heaven bless me from a widow, unless I were sure to bury her speedily!

Wid. Good bluntness. Well, your business, sir?

Pye. Very needful; if you were in private once.

Wid. Needful? Brother, pray leave us: and you, sir.

[*Exit* Sir GODFREY.

Frail. I should laugh now, if this blunt fellow should put them all beside the stirrup, and vault into the saddle himself. I have seen as mad a trick.

[*Exit* FRAILTY.

Wid. Now, sir? — here's none but we. — [*Enter* Daughters.] — Daughters, forbear.

Pye. O no,
Pray let them stay; for what I have to speak
Importeth equally to them as you?

Wid. Then you may stay.

Pye. I pray bestow on me a serious ear,
For what I speak is full of weight and fear.

Wid. Fear?

Pye. Ay, if't pass unregarded and uneffected.
Else, peace and joy: — I pray attention, widow.
I have been a mere stranger for these parts that you live in, nor did I ever know the husband of you, and father of them, but I truly know, by certain spiritual intelligence, that he is in purgatory.

Wid. Purgatory! tuh; that word deserves to be spit upon. I wonder that a man of sober tongue, as you seem to be, should have the folly to believe there's such a place.

Pye. Well, lady, in cold blood I speak it; I assure you that there is a purgatory, in which place I know your husband to reside, and wherein he is like to remain, till the dissolution of the world, till the last general bonfire: when all the earth shall melt into nothing, and the seas scald their finny laborers: so long is his abidance, unless you alter the property of your purpose, together with each of your daughters theirs; that is, the purpose of single life in yourself and your eldest daughter, and the speedy determination of marriage in your youngest.

Mary. How knows he that? what, has some devil told him?

Wid. Strange he should know our thoughts — Why? But daughter, have you purposed speedy marriage?

Pye. You see she tells you ay, she says nothing. Nay, give me credit as you please; I am a stranger to you, and yet you see I know your determinations, which must come to me metaphysically, and by a supernatural intelligence.

Wid. This puts amazement on me.

Frances. Know our secrets?

Mary. I had thought to steal a marriage. Would his tongue
Had dropped out when he blabbed it.

Wid. But, sir, my husband was too honest a dealing man, to be now in any purgatories.

Pye. O do not load your conscience with untruths,
'Tis but mere folly now to gild him o'er,
That has past but for copper. Praises here,
Can not unbind him there. Confess but truth;
I know he got his wealth with a hard gripe:
Oh, hardly, hardly!

Wid. This is most strange of all, how knows he that?

Pye. He would eat fools and ignorant heirs clean up;
And had his drink from many a poor man's brow,
Even as their labor brewed it. He would scrape
Riches to him most unjustly. The very dirt
Between his nails was ill got; — not his own!
Oh! I groan to speak of it. The thought makes me shudder! — shudder! —

Wid. It quakes me too, now I think on't. [*aside.*

1 Shooters—*suitors.*

2 So Lear: "Then there's life in it."—*Steevens.* And Sir Toby Belch in Twelfth Night: "There's life in it, man."

Sir, I am much grieved, that you a stranger, should
So deeply wrong my dead husband!

Pye. Oh?

Wid. A man that would keep church so duly; rise early before his servants, and even, for religious haste, go ungartered, unbuttoned, nay, sir reverence, untrussed, to morning prayer?

Pye. Oh, uff.[1]

Wid. Dine quickly upon high-days, and when I had great guests, would even shame me, and rise from the table, to get a good seat at an afternoon sermon.

Pye. There's the devil, there's the devil! True: he thought it sanctity enough, if he had killed a man, so it had been done in a pew;—or undone his neighbor, so it had been near enough to the preacher. Oh!—a sermon's a fine short cloak of an hour long, and will hide the upper part of a dissembler.—Church! ay, he seemed all church, and his conscience was as hard as the pulpit.

Wid. I can no more endure this.

Pye. Nor I, widow,
Endure to flatter.

Wid. Is this all your business with me?

Pye. No, lady, 'tis but the induction to't.
You may believe my strains; I strike all true;—
And if your conscience wonld leap up to your tongue,
Yourself would affirm it; and that you shall perceive
I know of things to come, as well as I do
Of what is present, a brother of your husband's
Shall shortly have a loss.

Wid. A loss? marry Heaven forfend!
Sir Godfrey, my brother!

Pye. Nay, keep in your wonders, till I have told you the fortunes of you all—which are more fearful, if not happily prevented. For your part and for your daughters', if there be not once this day some blood shed before your door, whereof the human creature dies, of you two the elder shall run mad.

Wid.
Frances. } Oh!

Mary. That's not I yet.

Pye. And with most impudent prostitution show
Your naked bodies to the view of all beholders.

Wid. Our naked bodies? fie, for shame!

Pye. Attend me!—and your younger daughter be
Stricken dumb!

Mary. Dumb? out, alas! 'tis the worst pain of all for a woman. I'd rather be mad, or run naked, or anything. Dumb!

Pye. Give ear: ere the evening fall upon hill, bog, and meadow, this my speech shall have past probation, and then shall I be believed accordingly.

Wid. If this be true, we are all shamed, all undone.

Mary. Dumb! I'll speak as much as ever I can possibly before evening.

Pye But if it so come to pass (as for your fair sakes I wish it may) that this presage of your strange fortunes be prevented by that accident of death and bloodshedding which I before told you of, take heed, upon your lives, that two of you which have vowed never to marry, seek out husbands with all present speed, and you the third, that have such a desire to outstrip chastity, look you meddle not with a husband.

Mary. A double torment.

Pye. The breach of this keeps your father in purgatory; and the punishments that shall follow you in this world would with horror kill the ear should hear them related.

Wid. Marry? why, I vowed never to marry.

Frances. And so did I.

Mary. And I vowed never to be such an ass, but to marry. What a cross fortune's this!

Pye. Ladies, though I be a fortune-teller, I can not better fortunes; you have them from me as they are revealed to me: I would they were to your tempers, and fellows with your bloods; that's all the bitterness I would you.

Wid. Oh! 'tis a just vengeance for my husband's hard purchases.

Pye. I wish you to bethink yourselves, and leave them.

Wid. I'll to Sir Godfrey, my brother, and acquaint him with these fearful presages.

Frances. For, mother, they portend losses to him.

Wid. O, ay; they do, they do.
If any happy issue crown thy words,
I will reward thy cunning.

[*Exeunt* Widow *and* FRANCES.

Pye. 'Tis enough, lady; I wish no higher.

Mary. Dumb? and not marry? worse:
Neither to speak, nor kiss, a double curse!

[*Exit* MARY.

Pye. So, all this comes well about yet. I play the fortune-teller as well as if I had had a witch to my grannam: for, by good happiness, being in my hostess's garden, which neighbors the orchard of the widow, I laid the hole of mine ear to a hole in the wall, and heard 'em make these vows, and speak those words, upon which I wrought these advantages; and, to encourage my forgery the more, I may now perceive in 'em a natural simplicity which will easily swallow an abuse, if any covering be over it; and, to confirm my former presage to the widow, I have advised old Peter Skirmish the soldier to hurt Corporal Oath upon the leg;—and, in that hurry, I'll rush amongst 'em—and, instead of giving the corporal some cordial to comfort him, I'll pour into his mouth a potion of a sleepy nature, and make him seem as dead: for the which the old soldier being apprehended, and ready to be borne to execution, I'll step in, and take upon me the cure of the dead man, upon pain of dying the condemned's death. The corporal will wake at this minute, when the sleepy force hath wrought itself, and so shall I get myself into a most admired opinion, and, under the pretext of that cunning, beguile as I see occasion. And if that foolish Nicholas Saint Antlings keep true time with the chain, my plot will be sound, the captain delivered, and my wits applauded amongst scholars and soldiers for ever. [*Exit.*

SCENE II.—*A Garden.*

Enter NICHOLAS, *with the Chain.*

Nich. O, I have found an excellent advantage to take away the chain. My master put it off e'en now, to 'say on a new doublet,[2] and I sneaked it away by

[1] It might be preferable to suppose here what the printers call an *out*, and read "stuff!" as the proper epithet, of which "uff" seems not only the meaning, but a part.

[2] "'Say on"—that is, essay to do on or don a new doublet.

little and little, most puritanically! We shall have good sport anon, when he has missed it, about my cousin the conjurer. The world shall see I'm an honest man of my word: for now I'm going to hang it between heaven and earth amongst the rosemary-branches. [*Exit.*

ACT III.

SCENE I.— *The Street before the* Widow's *House.*

Enter SIMON *and* FRAILTY.

Frail. Sirrah, Simon Saint Mary-Overies, my mistress sends away all her suitors, and puts fleas in their ears.

Sim. Frailty, she does like an honest, chaste, and virtuous woman; for widows ought not to wallow in the puddle of iniquity.

Frail. Yet, Simon, many widows will do't, whatsoe'er comes on't.

Sim. True, Frailty; their filthy flesh desires a conjunction copulative. What strangers are within, Frailty?

Frail. There's none, Simon, but Master Pilfer the tailor; he's above, with Sir Godfrey, 'praising[1] of a doublet: and I must trudge anon to fetch Master Suds the barber.

Sim. Master Suds's a good man: he washes the sins of the beard clean.

Enter SKIRMISH.

Skir. How now, creatures? what's o'clock?

Frail. Why, do you take us to be jacks o' the clock-house?[2]

Skir. I say again to you, what's o'clock?

Sim. Truly, la! we go by the clock of our conscience. All worldly clocks we know go false, and are set by drunken sextons.

Skir. Then what is't o'clock in your conscience? Oh, I must break off: here comes the corporal.—

Enter Corporal.

Hum! hum! What is't o'clock?

Corp. O'clock? why, past seventeen!

Frail. Past seventeen? Nay, he has met with his match now: Corporal Oath will fit him.

Skir. Thou dost not balk or baffle me, dost thou? I am a soldier. Past seventeen!

Corp. Ay, thou art not angry with the figures, art thou? I will prove it unto thee: twelve and one is thirteen, I hope; two, fourteen; three, fifteen; four, sixteen; and five, seventeen: then, past seventeen. I will take the dial's part in a just cause.

Skir. I say 'tis but past five, then.

Corp. I'll swear 'tis past seventeen, then. Dost thou not know numbers? Canst thou not cast?

Skir. Cast? Dost thou speak of my casting i'th' street?[3] [*They draw and fight.*

Corp. Ay, and in the market-place.

Sim. Clubs! clubs! clubs! [SIMON *runs away.*

Frail. Ay, I knew, by their shuffling, clubs would be trump. Mass! here's the knave, an he can do any good upon 'em. Clubs! clubs! clubs! [*Exit* FRAILTY

Enter PYEBOARD.

Corp. O, villain! thou hast opened a vein in my leg.

Pye. How now? For shame, for shame! put up, put up.

Corp. By yon blue welkin, 'twas out of my part, George, to be hurt on the leg.

Enter Officers.

Pye. Oh, peace, now. I have a cordial here to comfort thee.

Offi. Down with 'em, down with 'em; lay hands upon the villain!

Skir. Lay hands on me?

Pye. I'll not be seen among 'em now. [*Exit* PYEBOARD.

Corp. I'm hurt, and had more need to have a sur- [geon
Lay hands upon me, than rough officers.

Offi. Go, carry him to be dressed, then: [*Exeunt some with* OATH.
This mutinous soldier shall along with me
To prison.

Skir. To prison? where's George?

Offi. Away with him! [*Exeunt* Officers *with* SKIRMISH.

SCENE II.— *The same.*

Enter PYEBOARD.

Pye. So!
All lights as I would wish. The amazed widow
Will plant me strongly now in her belief,
And wonder at the virtue of my words:
For the event turns those presages from them,
Of being mad and dumb, and begets joy
Mingled with admiration. These empty creatures,
Soldier and corporal, were but ordained
As instruments for me to work upon.
Now to my patient: here's his potion. [*Exit* PYEBOARD.

SCENE III.—*An Apartment in the* Widow's *House.*

Enter the Widow, FRANCES, *and* MARY.

Wid. O wondrous happiness, beyond our thoughts!
O lucky, fair event! I think our fortunes
Were blest even in our cradles: we are 'quitted
Of all those shameful, violent presages
By this rash, bleeding chance. Go, Frailty, run, and [know
Whether he be yet living, or yet dead,
That here before my door received his hurt.

Frail. Madam, he was carried to the superior; but if he had no money when he came there, I warrant he's dead by this time. [*Exit* FRAILTY.

Frances. Sure that man is a rare fortune-teller!— never looked upon our hands, nor upon any mark about us; a wondrous fellow, surely.

Mary. I am glad I have the use of my tongue yet, though of nothing else. I shall find the way to marry, too, I hope, shortly.

Wid. O, where's my brother Sir Godfrey? I would he were here, that I might relate to him how prophetically the cunning gentleman spoke in all things.

1 Appraising.
2 Figures formerly placed in the great clocks of churches, which, by mechanism, struck the hours.
3 To "cast in the street" was a cant phrase for vomiting. Hence the insult conveyed by the word *casting*.

Enter Sir GODFREY, *in a rage.*

Sir God. O, my chain, my chain! I have lost my chain. Where be these villains, varlets?

Wid. Oh! he has lost his chain.

Sir God. My chain, my chain!

Wid. Brother, be patient; hear me speak. You know I told you that a cunning-man told me that you should have a loss, and he has prophesied so true—

Sir God. Out! he's a villain to prophesy of the loss of my chain. 'Twas worth above three hundred crowns. Besides, 'twas my father's, my father's father's, my grandfather's huge grandfather's.[1] I had as lief ha' lost my neck as the chain that hung about it. O, my chain, my chain!

Wid. Oh, brother, who can be guarded against a misfortune? 'Tis happy 'twas no more.

Sir God. No more? O goodly, godly sister, would you had me lost more? My best gown, too, with the cloth of gold lace? my holyday gaskins, and my jerkin set with pearl? No more!

Wid. Oh, brother, you can read——

Sir God. But I can not read where my chain is. What strangers have been here? You let in strangers, thieves, and catchpoles. How comes it gone? There was none above with me but my tailor, and my tailor will not steal, I hope.

Mary. No, he's afraid of a chain.

Enter FRAILTY.

Wid. How now, sirrah? the news?

Frail. O, mistress, he may well be called a corporal now, for his corpse is as dead as a cold capon's.

Wid. More happiness.

Sir God. Sirrah, what's this to my chain? where's my chain, knave?

Frail. Your chain, sir?

Sir God. My chain is lost, villain.

Frail. I would he were hanged in chains that has it, then. For me, alas! sir, I saw none of your chain since you were hung with it yourself.

Sir God. Out, varlet!—it had full three thousand links:
I have oft told it over at my prayers—
Over and over;—full three thousand links.

Frail. Had it so, sir? Sure it can not be lost, then. I'll put you in that comfort.

Sir God. Why? why?

Frail. Why, if your chain had so many links, it can not choose but come to light.[2]

Enter NICHOLAS.

Sir God. Delusion! Now, long Nicholas, where is my chain?

Nich. Why, about your neck, is't not, sir?

Sir God. About my neck, varlet? my chain is lost; 'tis stolen away; I'm robbed.

Wid. Nay, brother, show yourself a man.

Nich. If it be only lost or stole, if he would be patient, mistress, I could bring him to a cunning kinsman of mine, that would fetch it again with a sesarara.[3]

Sir God. Canst thou? I will be patient: say, where dwells he?

Nich. Marry, he dwells now, sir, where he would not dwell an he could choose—in the Marshalsea, sir; but he's an excellent fellow if he were out: has travelled all the world over, he, and been in the seven-and-twenty provinces. Why, he would make it be fetched, sir, if it were rid a thousand mile out of town.

Sir God. An admirable fellow! What lies he for?

Nich. Why, he did but rob a steward of ten groats t'other night, as any man would ha' done, and there he lies for't.

Sir God. I'll make his peace. A trifle! I'll get his pardon,
Besides a bountiful reward. I'll about it;
But see the clerks; the justice will do much:
I will about it straight. Good sister, pardon me;
All will be well, I hope, and turn to good:
The name of conjurer has laid my blood. [*Exeunt.*

SCENE IV.—*A Street.*

Enter PUTTOCK, RAVENSHAW, *and* DOGSON.

Put. His hostess where he lies will trust him no longer. She hath feed me to arrest him. And If you will accompany me—because I know not of what nature the scholar is, whether desperate or swift[4]—you shall share with me, Sergeant Ravenshaw. I have the good angel to arrest him.[5]

Rav. Troth, I'll take part with thee, then, sergeant; not for the sake of the money so much, as for the hate I bear to a scholar. Why, sergeant, 'tis natural in us, you know, to hate scholars—natural, because they will publish our imperfections, knaveries, and conveyances upon scaffolds and stages.

Put. Ay, and spitefully too. Troth, I have wondered how the slaves could see into our breasts so much, when our doublets are buttoned with pewter.

Rav. Ay, and so close without yielding. Oh, they're parlous fellows; they will search more with their wits than a constable with all his officers.

Put. Whist, whist, whist, yeoman Dogson, yeoman Dogson.

Dog. Ha? what says sergeant?

Put. Is he in the 'pothecary's shop still?

Dog. Ay, ay!

Put. Have an eye, have an eye.

Rav. The best is, sergeant, if he be a true scholar he wears no weapon, I think.

Put. No, no, he wears no weapon.

Rav. Mass, I am right glad of that: it has put me in better heart. Nay, if I clutch him once, let me alone to drag him if he be stiff-necked—I have been one of the six myself, that has dragged as tall men of their hands, when their weapons have been gone, as ever bastinadoed a sergeant. I have done I can tell you.

Dog. Sergeant Puttock, Sergeant Puttock.

Put. Ho!

Dog. He's coming out single.

Put. Peace, peace, be not too greedy; let him play a little, let him play a little; we'll jerk him up of a sudden. I ha' fished in my time.

Rav. Ay, and caught many a fool, sergeant.

Enter PYEBOARD.

Pye. I parted now from Nich'las: the chain's couched,

[1] A *huge* grandfather is no more than a *great*-grandfather.
[2] A link was a torch or light.
[3] *Certiorari* is probably intended—"to be made more certain"—the term and tenor of a law-writ. In our forest regions, the vulgar corruption makes it a "*sashirary.*"
[4] That is, whether he will stand and fight, or run.
[5] He means the coin of that name.

And the old knight has spent his rage upon't.
The widow holds me in great admiration
For cunning art: 'mongst joys I'm even lost,
For my device can no way now be crossed; —
And now I must to prison, to the captain,
And there —

Put. I arrest you, sir.

Pye. Oh! I spoke truer than I was aware;
I must to prison, indeed.

Put. They say you're a scholar, — Nay, sir:—yeoman Dogson, have care to his arms. — You'll rail against sergeants, and stage 'em? You'll tickle their vices?

Pye. Nay, use me like a gentleman; I'm little less.

Put. You a gentleman! that's a good jest, i'faith. Can a scholar be a gentleman, when a gentleman will not be a scholar? Look upon your wealthy citizen's sons, whether they be scholars or no, that are gentlemen by their fathers' trades. A scholar a gentleman!

Pye. Nay, let fortune drive all her stings into me, she can not hurt that in me. A gentleman is *accidens inseparabile* to my blood.

Rav. A rablement! nay, you shall have a bloody rablement upon you, I warrant you.

Put. Go, yeoman Dogson, before, and enter the action i'th' counter. [*Exit* DOGSON.

Pye. Pray do not handle me cruelly; I'll go
Whither you please to have me.

Put. Oh, he's tame; let him loose, sergeant.

Pye. Pray, at whose suit is this?

Put. Why, at your hostess's suit, where you lie; — Mistress Conyburrow's, for bed and board, — the sum four pound, five shillings, and five pence.

Pye. I know the sum too true, yet I presumed
Upon a further day. Well, 'tis my stars;
And I must bear it now, though never harder.
I swear now, my device is crossed indeed.
Captain must lie by't:[1] this is deceit's seed.

Put. Come, come away.

Pye. Pray, give me so much time as to knit my garter,
And I'll away with you.

Put. Well, we must be paid for this waiting upon you; this is no pains to attend thus.[2]

[PYEBOARD *pretends to tie his garter.*

Pye. I am now wretched and miserable; I shall never recover of this disease. Hot iron gnaw their fists! They have struck a fever into my shoulder, which I shall ne'er shake out again, I fear me, till, with a true *habeas corpus*, the sexton remove me. Oh, if I take prison once, I shall be pressed to death with actions; but not so happily as speedily; perhaps I may be forty year a pressing till I be a thin old man; that, looking through the grates, men may look through me. All my means confounded, what shall I do? Have my wits served me so long, now to give me the slip, like a trained servant, when I have most need of 'em? No device to keep my poor carcass from these puttocks? — Yes, happiness! have I a paper about me now?
Yes, two; I'll try it, it may hit;
Extremity is touchstone unto wit.
Ay! Ay! [*Answering* Officer.

Put. 'Sfoot, how many yards are in thy garters, that thou art so long a tying of them? Come away, sir.

Pye. Troth, sergeant, I protest, you could never have took me at a worse time; for now, at this instant, I have no lawful picture[3] about me.

Put. 'Slid, how shall we come by our fees, then?

Rav. We must have fees, sirrah.

Pye. I could have wished, i'faith, that you had took me half an hour hence for your own sake, for I protest if you had not crossed me, I was going in great joy to receive five pound of a gentleman, for the device of a mask here, drawn in this paper. But now, come, I must be contented; 'tis but so much lost, and answerable to the rest of my fortunes?

Put. Why, how far hence dwells that gentleman?

Rav. Ay, well said, sergeant; 'tis good to cast about for money.

Put. Speak, if it be not far——

Pye. We are but a little past it; the next street behind us.

Put. 'Slid, we have waited upon you grievously already; if you'll say you'll be liberal when you have it; give us double fees, and spend upon us; why, we'll show you that kindness, and go along with you to the gentleman.

Rav. Ay, well said still, sergeant; urge that.

Pye. Troth, if it will suffice, it shall all be among you; for my part I'll not pocket a penny; my hostess shall have her four pound, five shillings, and bate me the five pence, and the other fifteen shillings I'll spend upon you.

Rav. Why now thou art a good scholar.

Put. An excellent scholar, i'faith; has proceeded very well o' late. Come, we'll along with you.

[*Exeunt* PUTTOCK, RAVENSHAW, *and* PYEBOARD. *The latter knocks at the door of a* Gentleman's *house, at the inside of the stage.*

SCENE V.—*A Gallery in a* Gentleman's *House.*

Enter a Servant.

Serv. Who knocks? who's at door? We had need of a porter.

Pye. [*within*]. A few friends here — pray is the gentleman your master within?

Serv. Yes; is your business to him?

[*Opens the door; enter* PYEBOARD, PUTTOCK, RAVENSHAW, *and* DOGSON.

Pye. Ay, he knows it when he sees me:
I pray you, have you forgot me?

Serv. Ay, by my troth, sir; pray, come near; I'll in and tell him of you. Please you to walk here in the gallery till he comes. [*Exit* Servant.

Pye. We will attend his worship. — Worship, I think; for so much the posts at his door should signify,[4] and the fair coming in, and the wicket; else, I neither knew him nor his worship; but 'tis happiness he is within doors, whatsoe'er he be. If he be not too much a formal citizen, he may do me good [*aside*]. Sergeant and yeoman, how do you like this house? Is't not most wholesomely plotted?[5]

Rav. Troth, prisoner, an exceeding fine house.

Pye. Yet I wonder how he should forget me; — for

1 Or *lose* by it.
2 That is, there is neither pain nor penalty which compels us to this servility.

3 Lawful *coin*. The picture of his majesty.
4 *Posts* at the door, in Queen Elizabeth's time, were signs of a justice of the peace and sheriff.
5 Laid out—the ground-*plot*, the garden.

he ne'er know me [*aside*]. No matter, what is forgot in you will be remembered in your master.
A pretty comfortable room this, methinks:
You have no such rooms in prison now?

Put. Oh, dog-holes to't.

Pye. Dog-holes, indeed. I can tell you, I have great hope to have my chamber here shortly, nay, and diet too; for he's the most free-heartedst gentleman where he takes: you would little think it? And what a fine gallery were here for me to walk and study, and make verses.

Put. O, it stands pleasantly for a scholar.

Enter Gentleman.

Pye. Look what maps, and pictures, and devices, and things, neatly, delicately! Mass, here he comes; he should be a gentleman; I like his beard well.—All happiness to your worship.

Gent. You're kindly welcome, sir.

Put. A simple salutation.

Rav. Mass, it seems the gentleman makes great account of him.

Pye. [*aloud*]. I have the thing here for you, sir.
[*Takes the* Gentleman *aside.*
I beseech you, conceal me, sir; I'm undone else [*aside*]. I have the mask here for you, sir [*aloud*].—Look you, sir [*aside*]. I beseech your worship, first pardon my rudeness, for my extremes make me bolder than I would be. I am a poor gentleman, and a scholar, and am now most unfortunately fallen into the hands of unmerciful officers, arrested for debt, which, though small, I am not able to compass, by reason I am destitute of lands, money, and friends; so that if I fall into the hungry swallow of the prison, I am like utterly to perish, and with fees and extortions be pinched clean to the bone. Now, if ever pity had interest in the blood of a gentleman, I beseech you, vouchsafe but to favor that means of my escape which I have already thought upon.

Gent. Go forward.

Put. I warrant he likes it rarely.

Pye. In the plunge of my extremities, being giddy, and doubtful what to do, at last it was put into my laboring thoughts, to make a happy use of this paper; and to blear their unlettered eyes, I told them there was a device for a mask drawn in't, and that (but for their interception) I was going to a gentleman to receive my reward for't. They, greedy at this word, and hoping to make purchase of me, offered their attendance, to go along with me. My hap was to make bold with your door, sir, which my thoughts showed me the most fairest and comfortablest entrance; and I hope I have happened right upon understanding and pity. May it please your good worship, then, but to uphold my device, which is to let one of your men put me out at a back-door, and I shall be bound to your worship for ever.

Gent. By my troth, an excellent device.

Put. An excellent device, he says; he likes it wonderfully.

Gent. O' my faith, I never heard a better.

Rav. Hark, he swears he never heard a better, sergeant.

Put. O, there's no talk on't; he's an excellent scholar, and especially for a mask.

Gent. Give me your paper, your device. I was never better pleased in all my life: good wit, brave wit, finely wrought! come in, sir, and receive your money, sir. [*Exit within.*

Pye. I'll follow your good worship.—You heard how he liked it, now?

Put. Puh, we knew he could not choose but like it. Go thy ways; thou art a fine witty fellow, i'faith; thou shalt discourse it to us at the tavern, anon; wilt thou?

Pye. Ay, ay, that I will. Look, sergeant, here are maps and pretty toys; be doing, in the meantime; I shall quickly have told out the money, you know.

Put. Go, go, little villain; fetch thy chink; I begin to love thee;—I'll be drunk to-night in thy company.

Pye. This gentleman I may well call a part
Of my salvation, in these earthly evils,
For he has saved me from three hungry devils.
[*Exit* PYEBOARD.

Put. Sirrah, sergeant, these maps are pretty painted things, but I could ne'er fancy them yet;—methinks they're too busy, and full of circles and conjurations; they say all the world's in one of them, but I could ne'er find the counter in the poultry.[1]

Rav. I think so. How could you find it? for you know it stands behind these houses.

Dog. Mass, that's true; then we must look o' the backside for't: 'sfoot, here's nothing; all's *bare.*

Rav. I warrant thee *that* stands for the counter;—for you know there's a company of *bare* fellows there.

Put. 'Faith, like enough, sergeant; I never marked so much before. Sirrah sergeant and yeoman, I should love these maps out o' cry now, if we could see men peep out of door in 'em. Oh, we might have 'em in a morning to our breakfast so finely, and ne'er knock our heels to the ground a whole day for 'em.

Rav. Ay, marry, sir, I'd buy one then myself. But this talk is by the way. Where shall's sup to-night? Five pound received,—let's talk of that. I have a trick worth all. You two shall bear him to th' tavern, whilst I go close with his hostess, and work out of her. I know she would be glad of [half] the sum, to finger [the] money; because she knows 'tis but a desperate debt, and full of hazard. What will you say if I bring it to pass, that the hostess shall be contented with one half for all, and we to share t'other fifty shillings, bullies?

Put. Why, I would call thee king of sergeants, and thou shouldst be chronicled in the counter-book for ever.

Rav. Well, put it to me; we'll make a night on't, i'faith.

Dog. 'Sfoot, I think he receives more money, he stays so long.

Put. He tarries long, indeed. May be, I can tell you, upon the good liking on't the gentleman may prove more bountiful.

Rav. That would be rare; we'll search him.

Put. Nay, be sure of it; we'll search him, and make him light enough.

Enter Gentleman.

Rav. Oh, here comes the gentleman. By your leave, sir.

Gen. Give[2] you god den sirs,—Would you speak with me?

[1] The *prison*, so called.—MALONE. [2] In other copies "*god.*"

Put. No, not with your worship, sir; only we are bold to stay for a friend of ours that went in with your worship.

Gen. Who? Not the scholar?

Put. Yes, e'en he, an it please your worship.

Gen. Did he make you stay for him! he did you wrong, then: why, I can assure you he's gone above an hour ago.

Rav. How, sir?

Gen. I paid him his money, and my man told me he went out at back-door.

Put. Back-door?

Gen. Why, what's the matter?

Put. He was our prisoner, sir; we did arrest him.

Gen. What! he was not? You the sheriff's officers?
You were to blame, then!
Why did you not make known to me as much?
I could have kept him for you. I protest,
He received all of me in Britain gold,
Of the last coining.

Rav. Vengeance dog him with't!

Put. 'Sfoot, has he gulled us so?

Dog. Where shall we sup now, sergeants?

Put. Sup, Simon, now! eat porridge for a month. Well, we can not impute it to any lack of good will in your worship; — you did but as another would have done; 'twas our hard fortunes to miss the purchase; but if ever we clutch him again, the counter shall charm him.

Rav. The hole shall rot him.[1]

Dog. Amen. [*Exeunt* Sergeants.

Gent. So: —
Vex out your lungs without doors; I am proud
It was my hap to help him. It fell fit: —
He went not empty neither for his wit.
Alas! poor wretch, I could not blame his brain,
To labor his delivery, to be free
From their unpitying fangs; I'm glad it stood
Within my power to do a scholar good. [*Exit.*

SCENE VI. — *A Room in the* Marshalsea *Prison.*

Enter Captain IDLE; *to him* PYEBOARD, *in disguise.*

Capt. How now? who's that? what are you?

Pye. The same that I should be, captain.

Capt. George Pyeboard? honest George! Why com'st thou in half-faced and muffled so?

Pye. Oh, captain, I thought we should ne'er have laughed again, never spent frolic hour again.

Capt. Why? why?

Pye. I, coming to prepare thee, and with news
As happy as thy quick delivery,
Was traced out by the scent — arrested, captain.

Capt. Arrested, George?

Pye. Arrested! guess, how many dogs do you think I had upon me?

Capt. Dogs? I say, I know not.

Pye. Almost as many as George Stone, the bear:[2]
Three at once, three at once.

Capt. How didst thou shake 'em off, then?

Pye. The time is busy, and calls upon our wits:
Let it suffice —
Here I stand safe, and 'scaped by miracle:
Some other hour shall tell thee, when we'll steep
Our eyes in laughter. Captain, my device
Leans to thy happiness; for, ere the day
Be spent to th' girdle,[3] thou shalt [sure] be free.
The corporal's in's first sleep; the chain is missed;
Thy kinsman has expressed thee,[4] and the old knight
With palsy hams[5] now labors thy release.
What rests, is all in thee to conjure, captain.

Capt. Conjure? 'Sfoot! George, you know the devil o' conjuring I can conjure.

Pye. The devil o' conjuring? Nay, by my say, I'd not have thee do so much, captain, as the devil, a-conjuring. Look here: I have brought thee a circle, ready charactered and all.

Capt. 'Sfoot! George, art in thy right wits? Dost know what thou say'st? Why dost talk to a captain of conjuring? Didst thou ever hear of a captain conjure in thy life? Dost call't a circle? 'Tis too wide a thing, methinks. Had it been a lesser circle, then I knew what to have done.

Pye. Why, every fool knows that, captain. Nay, then I'll not cog with you, captain; if you'll stay and hang, the next sessions, you may.

Capt. No, by my faith, George. Come, come; let's to conjuring.

Pye. But if you look to be released (as my wits have took pain to work it, and all means wrought to further it), besides, to put crowns in your purse; to make you a man of better hopes; and, whereas, before you were a captain or poor soldier, to make you now a commander of rich fools — which is truly the only best purchase peace can allow you — safer than highways, heath, or cony-groves, and yet a far better booty; for your greatest thieves are never hanged, never hanged: for why? they're wise, and cheat within doors; and we geld fools of more money in one night than your false-tailed gelding[6] will purchase in a twelve-month's running — which confirms the old beldam's saying: *He's wisest that keeps himself warmest;* that is, he that robs by a good fire.

Capt. Well opened, i'faith, George; thou hast pulled that saying out of the husk.

Pye. Captain Idle, 'tis no time now to delude or delay. The old knight will be here suddenly. I'll perfect you, direct you, tell you the trick on't: 'tis nothing.

Capt. 'Sfoot! George, I know not what to say to't Conjure? I shall be hanged ere I conjure.

Pye. Nay, tell not me of that, captain; you'll ne'er conjure after you're hanged, I warrant you. Look you, sir: a parlous matter, sure! first, to spread your circle upon the ground; then, with a little conjuring ceremony (as I'll have a hackney-man's wand silvered o'er a-purpose for you); then, arriving in the circle, with a huge word, and a great trample — as, for instance, have you never seen a stalking, stamping player, that will raise a tempest with his tongue, and thunder with his heels?[7]

Capt. O yes, yes, yes; often, often.

Pye. Why, be like such a one. For anything will blear the old knight's eyes; for you must note that

1 One of the worst apartments in the counter-prison.
2 A famous bear exhibited at Paris garden, and called after his owner.

3 To the horizon.
4 Acted thy wishes.
5 That is, bending. He is seeking, soliciting on thy behalf.
6 A highwayman's horse, the tail of which is removable at the will of the owner.
7 "A robustious, periwig-pated fellow," &c.—*Hamlet.*

he'll ne'er dare to venture into the room, only perhaps peep fearfully through the keyhole, to see how the play goes forward.

Capt. Well, I may go about it when I will; — but mark the end on't: I shall but shame myself, i'faith, George. Speak big words, and stamp and stare, and he look in at keyhole! Why, the very thought of that would make me laugh outright, and spoil all. Nay, I'll tell thee, George, when I apprehend a thing once, I am of such a laxative laughter, that, if the devil himself stood by, I should laugh in his face!

Pye. Puh! that's but the babe of a man, and may easily be hushed — as, to think upon some disaster, some sad misfortune, as the death of thy father i'th' country.

Capt. 'Sfoot! that would be the more to drive me into such an ecstasy, that I should ne'er lin[1] laughing else.

Pye. Why, then, think upon going to hanging.

Capt. Mass! that's well remembered: now I'll do well, I warrant thee; ne'er fear me now. But how shall I do, George, for boisterous words and horrible names?

Pye. Puh! any fustian invocations, captain, will serve as well as the best, so you rant them out well; or you may go to a 'pothecary's shop, and take all the words from the boxes.

Capt. Troth, and you say true, George: there's strange words enow to raise a hundred quack-salvers, though they be ne'er so poor when they begin. But here lies the fear on't: how, if in this false conjuration, a true devil should pop up indeed?

Pye. A true devil, captain? why, there was ne'er such a one. Nay, i'faith, he that has this place, is as false a knave as our last church-warden.

Capt. Then he's false enough o' conscience, i'faith, George.

[Prisoners *cry within.*] Good gentlemen over the way, send your relief; good gentlemen over the way, good Sir Godfrey! —

Pye. He's come, he's come!

Enter Sir GODFREY, EDMOND, *and* NICHOLAS.

Nich. Master, that's my kinsman yonder, in the buff jerkin. Kinsman, that's my master yonder, i'th' taffaty hat. Pray, salute him entirely.

[Sir GODFREY *and* IDLE *salute, and* PYEBOARD *salutes* EDMOND.

Sir God. Now, my friend —

[Sir GODFREY *and* IDLE *converse apart.*

Pye. May I partake your name, sir?

Edm. My name is Master Edmond.

Pye. Master Edmond? Are you not a Welshman, sir?

Edm. A Welshman? why?

Pye. Because master is your Christian name, and Edmond your surname.

Edm. O no; I have more names at home: Master Edmond Plus is my full name at length.

Pye. O, cry you mercy, sir.

Capt. [*aside to* Sir GODFREY]. I understand that you are my kinsman's good master, and, in regard of that, the best of my skill is at your service. But had you fortuned a mere stranger, and made no means to me by acquaintance, I should have utterly denied to have been the man; both by reason of the act of parliament against conjurers and witches,[2] as also because I would not have my art vulgar, trite, and common.

Sir God. I much commend your care there, good captain conjurer; and that I will be sure to have it private enough, you shall do't in my sister's house — mine own house I may call it, for both our charges therein are proportioned.

Capt. Very good, sir. What may I call your loss, sir?

Sir God. O, you may call't a great loss, a grievous loss, sir: as goodly a chain of gold, though I say it, that wore it — how say'st thou, Nicholas?

Nich. O, 'twas as delicious a chain of gold, kinsman, you know——

Sir God. You know? did you know't, captain?

Capt. Trust a fool with secrets! [*Aside*]. Sir, he may say I know. His meaning is, because my art is such, that by it I may gather a knowledge of all things——

Sir God. Ay, very true.

Capt. A pox of all fools! The excuse stuck upon my tongue like ship-pitch upon a mariner's gown, not to come off in haste. [*Aside.*] — By'r lady, knight, to lose such a fair chain of gold were a foul loss. Well, I can put you in this good comfort on't, if it be between heaven and earth, knight, I'll have it for you.

Sir God. A wonderful conjurer! O, ay; 'tis between heaven and earth, I warrant you: it can not go out of the realm. I know 'tis somewhere about the earth.

Capt. Ay, nigher the earth than thou wot'st of.

[*Aside.*

Sir God. For, first, my chain was rich: and no rich thing shall enter into heaven, you know.

Nich. And as for the devil, master, he has no need on't, for you know he has a great chain of his own.

Sir God. Thou say'st true, Nicholas, but he has put off that now; that lies by him.

Capt. I'faith, knight, in few words, I presume so much upon the power of my art, that I could warrant your chain again.

Sir God. O dainty captain!

Capt. Marry, it will cost me much sweat. I were better go to sixteen hot-houses.

Sir God. Ay, good man, I warrant thee.

Capt. Beside great vexation of kidney and liver.

Nich. O, 'twill tickle you hereabouts, cousin, because you have not been used to't.

Sir God. No? Have you not been used to't, captain?

Capt. Plague of all fools still! [*Aside.*] Indeed, knight, I have not used it a good while, and therefore 'twill strain me so much the more, you know.

Sir God. O, it will, it will!

Capt. What plunges he puts me to! Were not this knight a fool, I had been twice spoiled now. That captain's worse than accursed that has an ass to his kinsman. 'Sfoot! I fear he will drivel it out before I come to't. [*Aside.*] Now, sir, to come to the point indeed, you see I stick here in the jaw of the Marshalsea, and can not do't.

Sir God. Tut, tut — I know thy meaning. Thou wouldst say thou'rt a prisoner. I tell thee thou art none.

[1] "Lin"—to stop, to cease.

[2] An act passed in the first year of James I. (1604).

Capt. How, none? Why, is not this the Marshalsea?

Sir God. Wilt hear me speak? I heard of thy rare conjuring:—
My chain was lost; I sweat for thy release,
As thou shalt do the like at home for me.—
Keeper!

Enter Keeper.

Keep. Sir!

Sir God. Speak, is not this man free?

Keep. Yes, at his pleasure, sir, the fees discharged.

Sir God. Go, go; I'll discharge them, I.

Keep. I thank your worship. [*Exit* Keeper.

Capt. Now, trust me, you are a dear knight. Kindness unexpected! O, there's nothing to a free gentleman. I will conjure for you, sir, till froth come through my buff jerkin.

Sir God. Nay, then thou shalt not pass with so little a bounty, for, at the first sight of my chain again, forty-five angels shall appear unto thee.

Capt. 'Twill be a glorious show, i'faith, knight, a very fine show; but are all these of your own house? are you sure of that, sir?

Sir God. Ay, ay; no, no: what's he yonder talking with my wild nephew? Pray Heaven, he give him good counsel.

Capt. Who, he? He's a rare friend of mine, an admirable fellow, knight — the finest fortune-teller!

Sir God. O, 'tis he, indeed, that came to my lady-sister, and foretold the loss of my chain. I am not angry with him now, for I see 'twas my fortune to lose it. — By your leave, master fortune-teller, I had a glimpse of you at home, at my sister's the widow's. There you prophesied of the loss of a chain. Simply, though I stand here, I was he that lost it.

Pye. Was it you, sir?

Edm. O' my troth, nuncle, he's the rarest fellow — has told me my fortune so right; I find it so right to my nature!

Sir God. What is't? God send it a good one.

Edm. O, 'tis a passing good one, nuncle: for he says I shall prove such an excellent gamester in my time, that I shall spend all faster than my father got it.

Sir God. There's a fortune, indeed!

Edm. Nay, it hits my humor so pat.

Sir God. Ay, that will be the end on't. Will the curse of the beggar prevail so much, that the son shall consnme that foolishly which the father got craftily? Ay, ay, ay; 'twill, 'twill, 'twill.

Pye. Stay, stay, stay! [Pyeboard *opens an almanac, and takes* Idle *aside.*

Capt. Turn over, George.

Pye. June, July; here, July: that's the month:— Sunday thirteen, yesterday fourteen, to-day fifteen.

Capt. Look quickly for the fifteenth day. If, within the compass of these two days there would be some boisterous storm or other, it would be the best; I'd defer him off till then. Some tempest, an it be thy will.

Pye. Here's the fifteenth day. [*Reads.*] *Hot and fair.*

Capt. Puh! would it had been hot and foul.

Pye. The sixteenth day; that's to-morrow. *The morning, for the most part, fair and pleasant.*

Capt. No luck.

Pye. But about high noon, lightning and thunder.

Capt. Lightning and thunder? Admirable! best of all! I'll conjure to-morrow just at high noon, George.

Pye. Happen but true to-morrow, almanac, and I'll give thee leave to lie all the year after.

Capt. Sir, I must crave your patience, to bestow this day upon me, that I may furnish myself strongly. I sent a spirit into Lancashire t'other day, to fetch back a knave-drover, and I look for his return this evening. To-morrow morning, my friend here and I will come and breakfast with you.

Sir God. O, you shall be most welcome.

Capt. And about noon, without fail, I purpose to conjure.

Sir God. Midnoon will be a fit time for you.

Edm. Conjuring? do you mean to conjure at our house to-morrow, sir?

Capt. Marry, do I, sir; 'tis my intent, young gentleman.

Edm. By my troth, I'll love you while I live, for't. O rare! Nicholas, we shall have conjuring to-morrow.

Nich. Puh! ay; I could have told you of that.

Capt. La, he could have told him of that! Fool, coxcomb, could you? [*Aside.*]

Edm. Do you hear me, sir? I desire more acquaintance of you. You shall earn some money of me, now I know you can conjure; but can you fetch any that is lost?

Capt. Oh, anything that's lost.

Edm. Why, look you, sir; I tell't you as a friend and a conjurer: I should marry a 'pothecary's daughter, and 'twas told me she lost her maidenhead at Stony-Stratford. Now if you'll do but so much as conjure for't, and make all whole again——

Capt. That I will, sir.

Edm. By my troth, I thank you, la.

Capt. A little merry with your sister's son, sir.

Sir God. Oh, a simple young man, very simple. Come, captain; and you, sir: we'll e'en part with a gallon of wine till to-morrow breakfast.

Capt. and Pye. Troth, agreed, sir.

Nich. Kinsman, scholar!

Pye. Why, now thou art a good knave, worth a hundred Brownists.

Nich. Am I, indeed? la, I thank you heartily, la! [*Exeunt.*

ACT IV.

SCENE I. — *An Apartment in the* Widow's *House.*

Enter Mary *and* Sir John Pennydub.

Sir John. But I hope you will not serve a knight so, gentlewoman, will you? to cashier him, and cast him off at your pleasure! What, do you think I was dubbed for nothing? No, by my faith, lady's daughter——

Mary. Pray, Sir John Pennydub, let it be deferred a while; I have as much heart to marry as you can have; but, as the fortune-teller told me——

Sir John. Pox o' th' fortune-teller! Would Derrick[1] had been his fortune seven year ago — to cross my love thus! Did he know what case I was in?—

[1] Derrick was the name of the common hangman at this period.

Why, this is able to make a man drown himself in his father's fish-pond.

Mary. And then he told me, moreover, Sir John, that the breach of it kept my father in purgatory.

Sir John. In purgatory? Why, let him purge out his heart there; what have we to do with that?—there's physicians enow there to cast his water:[1] is that any matter to us now? can he hinder our love? Why, let him be hanged, now he's dead. Well, have I rid post day and night, to bring you merry news of my father's death, and now——

Mary. Thy father's death? Is the old farmer dead?

Sir John. As dead as his barn-door, Moll.

Mary. And you'll keep your word with me now, Sir John, that I shall have my coach and my coachman?

Sir John. Ay, i'faith.

Mary. And two white horses with black feathers to draw it?

Sir John. Two.

Mary. A guarded lackey[2] to run before it, and pied liveries to come trashing[3] after't?

Sir John. Thou shalt, Moll.

Mary. And to let me have money in my purse to go whither I will?

Sir John. All this.

Mary. Then come; whatsoe'er comes on't, we'll be made sure together before the maids o'th' kitchen. [*Exeunt.*

SCENE II.—*A Room in the* Widow's *House, with a door at the side, leading to another Apartment.*

Enter Widow, FRANCES, *and* FRAILTY.

Wid. How now? where's my brother Sir Godfrey? Went he forth this morning?

Frail. O no, madam; he's above at breakfast, with Sir Reverence, a conjurer.

Wid. A conjurer? what manner of fellow is he?

Frail. Oh, a wondrous rare fellow, mistress; very strongly made upward, for he goes in a buff jerkin. He says he will fetch Sir Godfrey's chain again, if it hang between heaven and earth.

Wid. What! he will not? Then he's an excellent fellow, I warrant. How happy were that woman, to be blest with such a husband! A cunning man! how does he look, Frailty? Very swartly, I warrant—with black beard, scorched cheeks, and smoky eyebrows.

Frail. Foh! he's neither smoke-dried, nor scorched, nor black, nor nothing. I tell you, madam, he looks as fair to see to as one of us. I do not think but, if you saw him once, you'd take him to be a Christian.

Frances. So fair, and yet so cunning? That's to be wondered at, mother.

Enter Sir OLIVER MUCKHILL *and* Sir ANDREW TIPSTAFF.

Sir Oli. Bless you, sweet lady.

Sir And. And you, fair mistress. [*Exit* FRAILTY.

Wid. Coades, what do you mean, gentlemen? Fie, did I not give you your answers?

Sir Oli. Sweet lady!

Wid. Well, I will not stick with you for a kiss: Daughter, kiss the gentleman for once.

Frances. Yes, forsooth.

Sir And. I'm proud of such a favor.

Wid. Truly, la! Sir Oliver, you are much to blame to come again when you know my mind so well delivered—as a widow could deliver a thing.

Sir Oli. But I expect a further comfort, lady.

Wid. Why la you now! did I not desire you to put off your suit quite and clean when you came to me again? How say you? Did I not?

Sir Oli. But the sincere love which my heart bears to you——

Wid. Go to, I'll cut you off. And, Sir Oliver, to put you in comfort, afar off, my fortune is read me: I must marry again.

Sir Oli. O blest fortune!

Wid. But not as long as I can choose; nay, I'll hold out well.

Sir Oli. Yet are my hopes now fairer.

Enter FRAILTY.

Frail. O, madam, madam!

Wid. How now? what's the haste? [FRAILTY *whispers her.*

Sir And. I'faith, Mistress Frances, I'll maintain you gallantly. I'll bring you to court; wean you among the fair society of ladies, poor kinswomen of mine, in cloth of silver; besides, you shall have your monkey, your parrot, your musk-cat, and your——

Frances. It will do very well.

Wid. What, does he mean to conjure here, then? How shall I do to be rid of these knights?—Please you, gentlemen, to walk a while i'th' garden, to gather a pink or a gilliflower?

Both. With all our hearts, lady, and 'count us favored. [*Exeunt* Sir ANDREW, Sir OLIVER, *and* FRAILTY; *the* Widow *and* FRANCES *go into the adjoining room.*

Sir God. [*within*]. Step in, Nicholas; look, is the coast clear?

Nich. [*within*]. Oh, as clear as a cat's eye, sir?

Sir God. Then enter, captain conjurer.

Enter Sir GODFREY, Captain IDLE, PYEBOARD, EDMOND, *and* NICHOLAS.

Now, how like you your room, sir?

Capt. O, wonderful convenient.

Edm. I can tell you, captain, simply though it lies here, 'tis the fairest room in my mother's house; as dainty a room to conjure in, methinks—why, you may bid, I can not tell how many devils, welcome in't; my father has had twenty in't at once.

Pye. What, devils?

Edm. Devils? no, deputies, and the wealthiest men he could get.

Sir God. Nay, put by your chats now; fall to your business roundly. The fescue of the dial is upon the Christ-cross of noon.[4] But oh, hear me, captain; a qualm comes o'er my stomach.

Capt. Why, what's the matter, sir?

Sir God. O, how if the devil should prove a knave, and tear the hangings?

1 Medical divination from the inspection of urine.

2 A "guarded lackey" was one whose liveries were *faced* or guarded.

3 "Trashing" really means *trailing*, in this connexion. It is a term derived from the mode of breaking dogs who were too eager in the chase, by a long rope, which trashed or trailed along the ground, and impeded his movements.

4 "Fescue," the *pointer*.

Capt. Foh! I warrant you, Sir Godfrey.

Edm. Ay, nuncle, or spit fire upo' the ceiling?

Sir God. Very true, too; for 'tis but thin plastered, and 'twill quickly take hold o' the laths; and if he chance to spit downward too, he will burn all the boards.

Capt. My life for yours, Sir Godfrey.

Sir God. My sister is very curious and dainty of this room, I can tell you; and, therefore, if he must needs spit, I pray desire him to spit i'th' chimney.

Pye. Why, assure you, Sir Godfrey, he shall not be brought up with so little manners, to spit and spawl o' the floor.

Sir God. Why, I thank you; good captain, pray, have a care. [IDLE *and* PYEBOARD *retire to the upper end of the room.*] Ay, fall to your circle; we'll not trouble you, I warrant you. Come, we'll into the next room; and, because we'll be sure to keep him out there, we'll bar up the door with some of the godly's zealous works.

Edm. That will be a fine device, nuncle; and, because the ground shall be as holy as the door, I'll tear two or three rosaries in pieces, and strew the pieces about the chamber. Oh, the devil already! [*Lightning and thunder.*

Pye. 'Sfoot! captain, speak somewhat, for shame: it lightens and thunders before thou wilt begin. Why, when —

Capt. Pray, peace, George; thou'lt make me laugh anon, and spoil all. [*Lightning and thunder.*

Pye. Oh, now it begins again; now, now, now, captain!

Capt. *Rhumbos-ragdayon, pur, pur, colucundrion, hoisplois!*

Sir God. [*at the door*]. O, admirable conjurer! has fetched thunder already.

Pye. Hark, hark! Again, captain!

Capt. *Benjamino, gaspois-kay-gofgothoteron-umbrois!*

Sir God. [*at the door*]. Oh, I would the devil would come away quickly; he has no conscience, to put a man to such pain!

Pye. Again.

Capt. *Flowste kak opumpos-dragone-leloomenos-hodge podge!*

Pye. Well said, captain.

Sir God. [*at the door*]. So long a coming? O, would I had ne'er begun it, now, for I fear me these roaring tempests will destroy all the fruits of the earth, and tread upon my corn [*thunder*] — oh — i'th' country!

Capt. *Gog de gog, hobgoblin hunchs hounslow hockley te coom park!*

Wid. [*at the door*]. O, brother, brother, what a tempest i'th' garden! Sure there's some conjuration abroad.

Sir God. [*at the door*]. 'Tis at home, sister.

Pye. By-and-by, I'll step in, captain.

Capt. *Nunck-nunck, rip-gascoines, ips, drip-dropite!*

Sir God. [*at the door*]. He drips and drops, poor man; alas! alas!

Pye. Now, I come!

Capt. O, *sulphure sootface!* ——

Pye. Arch-conjurer, what wouldst thou with me?

Sir God. [*at the door*]. Oh, the devil, sister, i'th' dining-chamber! Sing, sister; I warrant you that will keep him out: quickly, quickly, quickly!

Pye. So, so, so: I'll release thee. Enough, captain, enough. Allow us some time to laugh a little; they're shuddering and shaking by this time, as if an earthquake were in their kidneys.

Capt. Sirrah George, how was't, how was't? did I do't well enough?

Pye. Woult believe me, captain? better than any conjurer; for here was no harm in this, and yet their horrible expectations satisfied well. You were much beholden to thunder and lightning at this time; it graced you well, I can tell you.

Capt. I must needs say so, George. Sirrah, if we could have conveyed hither cleanly a cracker, or a fire-wheel, it had been admirable.

Pye. Blurt, blurt! There's nothing remains to put thee to pain now, captain.

Capt. Pain? I protest, George, my heels are sorer than a Whitsun morris-dancer's.

Pye. All's past now; — only to reveal that the chain's i'th' garden, where, thou know'st, it has lain these two days.

Capt. But I fear that fox Nicholas has revealed it already.

Pye. Fear not, captain; you must put it to th' venture now. Nay, 'tis time: call upon 'em, take pity on 'em; for I believe some of 'em are in a pitiful case by this time.

Capt. Sir Godfrey! Nicholas — kinsman! 'Sfoot! they're fast at it still, George. Sir Godfrey!

Sir God. [*at the door*]. Oh! is that the devil's voice? how comes he to know my name?

Capt. Fear not, Sir Godfrey; all's quieted.

Enter Sir GODFREY, *the* Widow, FRANCES, *and* NICHOLAS.

Sir God. What! is he laid?

Capt. Laid: and has newly dropped your chain i' th' garden.

Sir God. I'th' garden? in our garden?

Capt. In your garden.

Sir God. O, sweet conjurer! whereabouts there?

Capt. Look well about a bank of rosemary.

Sir God. Sister, the rosemary-bank! Come, come: there's my chain, he says.

Wid. Oh, happiness! run, run! [*Exeunt* Widow, Sir GODFREY, FRANCES, *and* NICHOLAS.

Edm. [*at the door*]. Captain conjurer!

Capt. Who? Master Edmond?

Edm. Ay, Master Edmond. May I come in safely without danger, think you?

Capt. Puh! long ago; it is all as 'twas at first: Fear nothing; pray, come near. How now, man?

Edm. Oh! this room's mightily hot, i'faith. 'Slid! my shirt sticks to my belly already. What a steam the rogue has left behind him! Foh! this room must be aired, gentlemen; it smells horribly of brimstone. Let's open the windows.

Pye. I'faith, Master Edmond, 'tis but your conceit.

Edm. I would you could make me believe that, i'faith. Why, do you think I can not smell his savor from another? Yet I take it kindly from you, because you would not put me in a fear, i'faith. O' my troth, I shall love you for this the longest day of my life.

Capt. Puh! 'tis nothing, sir: love me when you see more.

Edm. Mass, now I remember: I'll look whether he has singed the hangings or no.

Pye. Captain, to entertain a little sport till they

come, make him believe you'll charm him invisible. He's apt to admire anything, you see. Let me alone to give force to't.

Capt. Go, retire to yonder end, then.

Edm. I protest you are a rare fellow, are you not?

Capt. O, Master Edmond, you know but the least part of me yet. Why now, at this instant, I could flourish my wand thrice o'er your head, and charm you invisible.

Edm. What! you could not? Make me walk invisible, man? I should laugh at that, i'faith; troth, I'll requite your kindness, an you'll do't, good captain conjurer.

Capt. Nay, I should hardly deny you such a small kindness, Master Edmond Plus. Why, look you, sir, 'tis no more but this, and thus again — and now you are invisible.

Edm. Am I, i'faith? who would think it?

Capt. You see the fortune-teller yonder, at farther end o'th' chamber? Go toward him, do what you will with him — he shall ne'er find you.

Edm. Say you so, I'll try that, i'faith.— [*Jostles him.*

Pye. How now, captain? who's that jostled me?

Capt. Jostled you? I saw nobody.

Edm. Ha, ha, ha! — say 'twas a spirit. [*Aside to* IDLE.

Capt. Shall I? — May be some spirits that haunt the circle. [EDMOND *pulls* PYEBOARD's *nose.*

Pye. O, my nose, again! Pray conjure them, captain.

Edm. Troth, this is excellent. I may do any knavery now and never be seen. — And now I remember me, Sir Godfrey, my uncle abused me t'other day, and told tales of me to my mother. — Troth, now I'm invisible, I'll hit him a sound wherrit o'th' ear, when he comes out o'th' garden. — I may be revenged on him now finely.

Enter Sir GODFREY, Widow, *and* FRANCES.

Sir God. I have my chain again; my chain's found again. O, sweet captain! O, admirable conjurer! [EDMOND *strikes him.*] O, what mean you by that, nephew?

Edm. Nephew? I hope you do not know me, uncle?

Wid. Why did you strike your uncle, son?

Edm. Why, captain, am I not invisible?

Capt. A good jest, George! Not now you are not, sir!
Why, did not you see me when I did uncharm you?

Edm. Not I, by my troth, captain. Then pray you pardon me, uncle. I thought I had been invisible when I struck you.

Sir God. So, you would do't? Go, — you're a foolish boy,
And were I not o'ercome with greater joy,
I'd make you taste correction.

Edm. Correction! puh. — No, neither you nor my mother [now] shall think to whip me as you have done.

Sir God. Captain, my joy is such, I know not how to thank you; let me embrace you. O, my sweet chain! gladness e'en makes me giddy. Rare man! 'twas just i'th' rosemary bank, as if one should have laid it there. O, cunning, cunning!

Wid. Well, seeing my fortune tells me I must marry, let me marry a man of wit, a man of parts Here's a worthy captain, and 'tis a fine title truly, la, to be a captain's wife. A captain's wife! it goes very finely; beside, all the world knows that a worthy captain is a fit companion to any lord; then why not a sweet bedfellow for any lady? — I'll have it so. —

Enter FRAILTY.

Frail. O, mistress—gentlemen — there's the bravest sight coming along this way.

Wid. What brave sight?

Frail. O, one going to burying, and another going to hanging.

Wid. A rueful sight!

Pye. 'Sfoot, captain, I'll pawn my life the corporal's coffined, and old Skirmish the soldier going to execution; and 'tis now about the time of his waking. Hold out a little longer, sleepy potion, and we shall have excellent admiration; for I'll take upon me the cure of him. [*Exeunt.*

SCENE III. — *The Street before the* Widow's *House.*

Enter from the House, Sir GODFREY, *the* Widow, IDLE, PYEBOARD, EDMOND, FRAILTY, *and* NICHOLAS. *A Coffin, with* Corporal OATH *in it, brought in. Then enter* SKIRMISH, *bound and led by* Officers, *the* Sheriff, *&c., attending.*

Frail. O, here they come, here they come!

Pye. Now must I close secretly with the soldier, prevent his impatience, or else all's discovered.

Wid. O, lamentable seeing, these were those brothers, that fought and bled before our door.

Sir God. What! they were not, sister?

Skir. George, look to't, I'll 'peach at Tyburn else.

Pye. Mum. — Gentles all, vouchsafe me audience,
And you especially, good master sheriff:
Yon man is bound to execution, because
He wounded this that now lies coffined [here].

Sher. True, true; he shall have the law, — and I know the law.

Pye. But, under favor, master sheriff: if this man had been cured and safe again, he should have been released, then?

Sher. Why, make you question of that, sir?

Pye. Then I release him freely, and will take upon me the death that he should die, if, within a little season, I do not cure him to his proper health again.

Sher. How, sir? recover a dead man?
That were most strange of all!
[FRANCES *approaches* PYEBOARD.

Frances. Sweet sir, I love you dearly, and could wish
My best part yours! — O do not undertake
Such an impossible venture!

Pye. Love you me? then for your sweet sake I'll do't:
Let me entreat the corpse be set down [here].

Sher. Bearers, set down the coffin. — This is wonderful, and worthy Stow's Chronicle.

Pye. I pray bestow the freedom of the air upon our wholesome art. — Mass, his cheeks begin to receive natural warmth: nay, good corporal, wake betime, or I shall have a longer sleep than you. — 'Sfoot, if he should prove dead indeed now, he were fully revenged upon me for making a property of him; yet I had rather run upon the ropes, than have the rope like a tetter run upon me. O, he stirs! — he stirs again! —! look, gentlemen, he recovers! he starts! he rises!

Sher. Oh, oh, defend us! — Out, alas!

Pye. Nay, pray be still; you'll make him more giddy else. — He knows nobody yet.

Corp. Zounds! where am I? covered with snow? I marvel?

Pye. Nay, I knew he would swear the first thing he did, as soon as he came to life again.

Corp. 'Sfoot, hostess — some hot porridge. — Oh! oh! lay on a dozen of fagots in the moon parlor, there.

Pye. Lady, you must needs take a little pity of him, i'faith, and send him into your kitchen fire.

Wid. O, with all my heart, sir; Nicholas and Frailty, help to bear him in.

Nich. Bear him in, quotha! pray call out the maids. I shall ne'er have the heart to do't, indeed, la.

Frail. Nor I neither. I can not abide to handle a ghost, of all men.

Corp. 'Sblood, let me see, where was I drunk last night? hah ——

Wid. O, shall I bid you once again, take him away?

Frail. Why, we're as fearful as you, I warrant you — oh ——

Wid. Away, villains, bid the maids make him a caudle presently to settle his brain—or a posset of sack; quickly, quickly.

[*Exeunt* NICHOLAS *and* FRAILTY, *pushing in the* Corporal.

Sher. Sir, whatsoe'er you are, I do more than admire you.

Wid. O, ay, if you knew all, master sheriff, as you shall do, you would say then, that here were two of the rarest men within the walls of Christendom.

Sher. Two of 'em? O wonderful! Officers, I discharge you; set him free; all's in tune.

Sir God. Ay, and a banquet ready by this time, master sheriff, to which I most cheerfully invite you, and your late prisoner there. See you this goodly chain, sir? Mum! no more words; 'twas lost and is found again. Come, my inestimable bullies, we'll talk of your noble acts in sparkling charnico,[1] and, instead of a jester, we'll have the ghost i'th' white sheet sit at upper end o'th' table.

Sher. Excellent! merry man, i'faith.

[*Exeunt all but* FRANCES.

Frances. Well, seeing I'm enjoined to love and marry,
My foolish vow thus I cashier to air
Which first begot it.—Now, love, play thy part;
The scholar reads his lecture in my heart. [*Exit.*

ACT V.

SCENE I.—*The Street before the* Widow's *House.*

Enter EDMOND *and* FRAILTY.

Edm. This is the marriage-morning for my mother and my sister.

Frail. O me, Master Edmond! we shall have rare doings.

1 *Charnico*—a sweet wine of Lisbon.

Edm. Nay, go, Frailty, run to the sexton; you know my mother will be married at Saint Antlings. Hie thee; 'tis past five; bid them open the church door; my sister is almost ready.

Frail. What, already, Master Edmond?

Edm. Nay, go; hie thee. First run to the sexton, and run to the clerk; and then run to Master Pigman, the parson; and then run to the milliner; and then run home again.

Frail. Here's run, run, run.——

Edm. But hark, Frailty.

Frail. What, more yet?

Edm. Have the maids remembered to strew the way to the church.

Frail. Foh! an hour ago: I helped 'em myself.

Edm. Away, away, away; away then.

Frail. Away, away, away; away then.

[*Exit* FRAILTY.

Edm. I shall have a simple father-in-law, a brave captain, able to beat all our street, Captain Idle. Now my lady mother will be fitted for a delicate name; my lady Idle, my lady Idle! the finest name that can be for a woman; and then the scholar, Master Pyeboard, for my sister Frances, that will be, Mistress Frances Pyeboard; Mistress Frances Pyeboard! They'll keep a good table, I warrant you. Now all the knights' noses are put out of joint; they may go to a bone-setter's now.

Enter Captain IDLE, PYEBOARD, *and* Attendants.

Hark, hark! O, who comes here with two torches before them? my sweet captain and my fine scholar? O, how bravely they are shot up in one night! They look like fine Britons now methinks. Here's a gallant change, i'faith. 'Slid, they have hired men, and all, by the clock.

Capt. Master Edmond; kind, honest, dainty Master Edmond.

Edm. Foh, sweet captain father-in-law! a rare perfume, i'faith.

Pye. What, are the brides stirring? May we steal upon 'em, thinkst thou, Master Edmond?

Edm. Foh! they're e'en upon readiness, I can assure you; for they were at their torch e'en now; by the same token I tumbled down the stairs.

Pye. Alas, poor Master Edmond.

Enter Musicians.

Capt. O, the musicians! I pry'thee, Master Edmond, call 'em in, and liquor 'em a little.

Edm. That I will, sweet captain father-in-law, and make each of them as drunk as a common fidler.

[*Exeunt.*

SCENE II.—*The same.*

Enter MARY *in a balcony above. To her below* Sir JOHN PENNYDUB.

Sir John. Whew! Mistress Moll, Mistress Moll.

Mary. Who's there?

Sir John. 'Tis I.

Mary. Who? Sir John Pennydub? O, you're an early cock, i'faith. Who would have thought you to be so rare a stirrer?

Sir John. Pry'thee, Moll, let me come up.

Mary. No, by my faith, Sir John; I'll keep you

down; for you knights are very dangerous, if once you get above.

Sir John. I'll not stay, i'faith.

Mary. I'faith, you shall stay; for, Sir John, you must note the nature of the climates: your northern wench in her own country may well hold out till she be fifteen; but if she touch the south once, and come up to London, here the chimes go presently after twelve.

Sir John. O, thou'rt a mad wench, Moll, but I pr'ythee make haste, for the priest is gone before.

Mary. Do you follow him; I'll not be long after.

[*Exeunt.*

SCENE III.—*A Room in* Sir OLIVER MUCKHILL'S *House.*

Enter Sir OLIVER MUCKHILL, Sir ANDREW TIPSTAFF, *and* SKIRMISH.

Sir Oli. O, monstrous, unheard-of forgery!

Sir And. Knight, I never heard of such villany, in our own country, in my life.

Sir Oli. Why, 'tis impossible. Dare you maintain your words?

Skir. Dare we? Even to their weazen-pipes. We know all their plots; they can not squander with us; they have knavishly abused us; made only properties of us to advance themselves upon our shoulders: but they shall rue their abuses. This morning they are to be married.

Sir Oli. 'Tis too true. Yet if the widow be not too much besotted on sleights and forgeries, the revelation of their villanies will make 'em loathsome. And, to that end—be it in private to you—I sent late last night to an honorable personage, to whom I am much indebted in kindness, as he is to me, and therefore presume upon the payment of his tongue, and that he will lay out good words for me; and, to speak truth, for such needful occasions only, I preserve him in bond; and sometimes he may do me more good here in the city, by a free word of his mouth, than if he had paid one half in hand, and took doomsday for t'other.

Sir And. In troth, sir, without soothing be it spoken,
You have published much judgment in these few [words.

Sir Oli. For you know, what such a man utters will be thought effectual, and to weighty purpose; and therefore into his mouth we'll put the approved theme of their forgeries.

Skir. And I'll maintain it, knight, if she'll be true.

Enter a Servant.

Sir Oli. How now, fellow?

Serv. May it please you, sir, my lord is newly lighted from his coach.

Sir Oli. Is my lord come already? His honor's [early.
You see he loves me well. Up before seven?
Trust me, I have found him night-capped at eleven:
There's good hope yet; come, I'll relate all to him.

[*Exeunt.*

SCENE IV.—*A Street; Church in the Distance.*

Enter Captain IDLE, PYEBOARD, Sir GODFREY, *and* EDMOND; *the* Widow *in bridal Dress;* Sir JOHN PENNYDUB, MARY *and* FRANCES, NICHOLAS, FRAILTY, *and other* Attendants. *To them a* Nobleman, Sir OLIVER MUCKHILL, *and* Sir ANDREW TIPSTAFF.

Noble. By your leave, lady!

Wid. My lord, your honor is most chastely welcome.

Noble. Madam, though I came now from court, I come not to flatter you. Upon whom can I justly cast this blot, but upon your own forehead, that know not ink from milk?—such is the blind besotting in the state of an unheaded woman that's a widow. For it is the property of all you that are widows (a handful excepted) to hate those that honestly and carefully love you, to the maintenance of credit, state, and posterity; and strongly to dote on those that only love you to undo you. [They who] regard you least, are best regarded; who hate you most, are best beloved. And if there be but one man amongst ten thousand millions of men that is accursed, disastrous, and evilly-planeted—whom fortune beats most, whom God hates most, and all societies esteem least—that man is sure to be a husband. Such is the peevish moon that rules your bloods. An impudent fellow best woos you, a flattering lip best wins you; or, in mirth, who talks roughliest, is most sweetest. Nor can you distinguish truth from forgeries, mists from simplicity: witness these two deceitful monsters, that you have entertained for bridegrooms!

Wid. Deceitful——

Pye. All will out.

Capt. 'Sfoot! who has blabbed, George? that foolish Nicholas!

Noble. For, what they have besotted your easy blood withal, were nought but forgeries: the fortune-telling for husbands, and the conjuring for the chain; Sir Godfrey, hear the falsehood of all: nothing but mere knavery, deceit, and cozenage.

Wid. O, wonderful! Indeed, I wondered that my husband, with all his craft, could not keep himself out of purgatory.

Sir God. And I more wondered that my chain should be gone, and my tailor had none of it.

Mary. And I wondered most of all that I should be tied from marriage, having such a mind to't. Come, Sir John Pennydub, fair weather on our side: the moon has changed since yesternight.

Pye. The sting of every evil is within me!

Noble. And that you may perceive I feign not with you, behold their fellow-actor in these forgeries, who, full of spleen and envy at their so sudden advancements, revealed all their plot in anger.

[SKIRMISH *comes forward.*

Pye. Base soldier, to reveal us!

Wid. Is't possible we should be blinded so, and our eyes open?

Noble. Widow, will you now believe that false, which too soon you believed true?

Wid. Oh, to my shame, I do.

Sir God. But, under favor, my lord, my chain was truly lost, and strangely found again.

Noble. Resolve him of that, soldier.

Skir. In few words, knight, then, thou wert the arch-gull of all.

Sir God. How, sir?

Skir. Nay, I'll prove it: for the chain was but hid in the rosemary-bank all this while, and thou got'st him out of prison to conjure for it, who did it admirably, fustianly: for indeed what needed any other, when he knew where it was?

Sir God. O, villany of villains! but how came my chain there?

Skir. Where's *Truly la, indeed la*[1]—he that will not swear, but lie—he that will not steal, but rob—pure Nicholas Saint Antlings?

Sir God. O, villain! one of our society—
Deemed always holy, pure, religious:
A puritan a thief! when was't ever heard?
Sooner we'll kill a man than steal, thou know'st.
Out, slave! I'll rend my lion from thy back
With mine own hands.

Nich. Dear master! oh!

Noble. Nay, knight, dwell in patience.
And now, widow, being so near the church, 'twere great pity, nay, uncharity, to send you home again without a husband:—
Draw near, you of true worship, state, and credit,
That should not stand so far off from a widow,
And suffer forgèd shapes to come between you:
Not that in these I blemish the true title
Of a captain, or blot the fair margent of a scholar;
For I honor worthy and deserving parts in the one,
And cherish fruitful virtues in the other.—
Come, lady, and you, virgin, bestow your eyes and your purest affections upon men of estimation, both in court and city, that have long wooed you, and both with their hearts and wealth sincerely love you.

Sir God. Good sister, do; sweet little Franke, these are men of reputation: you shall be welcome at court—a great credit for a citizen, sweet sister——

Noble. Come, her silence does consent to't.

Wid. I know not with what face——

Noble. Poh! poh! with your own face: they desire no other.

Wid. Pardon me, worthy sirs, I and my daughter,
Have wronged your loves.

Sir Oli. 'Tis easily pardoned, lady,
If you vouchsafe it now.

Wid. With all my soul.

Frances. And I, with all my heart.

Mary. And I, Sir John, with soul, heart, lights, and all.

Sir John. They are all mine, Moll.

Noble. Now, lady,
What honest spirit but will applaud your choice,
And gladly furnish you with hand and voice?—
A happy change, which makes e'en heaven rejoice.
Come, enter in your joys; you shall not want
For fathers now; I doubt it not, believe me,
But that you shall have hands enough to give me.[2]

[*Exeunt.*

1 The exclamations of Nicholas.

2 Some of the copies read, "give ye," but the original reading, which is here followed, seems more proper, and accords with the wants of the rhyme. The last section of the sentence is meant to suggest the applauses of the audience. It is their "hands enough" which the speaker anticipates.

THE END OF THE PURITAN; OR, THE WIDOW OF WATLING STREET.

INTRODUCTION

TO

THE YORKSHIRE TRAGEDY.

"A Yorkshire Tragedy—not so new, as lamentable and true: written by W. Shakspeare." This was the title of the original edition of the play which follows, printed in 1608. Upon a subsequent titlepage, we have "All's One, or, One of the four Plaies in one, called a Yorkshire Tragedy." We may receive "All's One" as the general title of four short plays, represented in the same day, and standing in the place of a regular tragedy or comedy. Of the four plays thus presented, it is to be remarked, that "The Yorkshire Tragedy" is the only one which appears to have been published. This was entered, on the 2d of May, 1608, on the stationers' registers, as "A booke The Yorkshire Tragedy, written by Wylliam Shakespere." The publisher of the play, Thomas Pavyer, in 1605, entered "A Ballad of lamentable Murther done in Yorkshire, by a Gent. upon two of his owne Children, sore wounding his Wyfe and Nurse." The fact upon which the ballad and the tragedy are founded, is thus related in Stow's Chronicle, under the year 1604: "Walter Calverly, of Calverly, Yorkshire, esquire, murdered two of his young children, stabbed his wife into the body, with full purpose to have murdered her, and instantly went from his house to have slain his youngest child, at nurse, but was prevented: for which fact, at his trial in York, he stood mute, and was judged to be pressed to death; according to which judgment he was executed, at the castle of York, the 5th of August."

"Concerning this play," says Mr. Malone, "I have not been able to form any decided opinion. The arguments produced by Mr. Steevens, in support of its authenticity, appear to me to have considerable weight. If its date were not so precisely ascertained, little doubt would remain, in my mind at least, upon the subject. I find it, however, difficult to believe that Shakspeare could have written Macbeth, King Lear, and the Yorkshire Tragedy, at nearly the same period." There would be more force in this objection, could we be sure *when* these several plays of Shakspeare were written; but most of the attempts to ascertain the dates of their original production have only tended to make the facts more doubtful. Besides, even were they productions of the same period, there would be nothing in the inequality of the pieces to urge against the argument, when we make the usual allowances for the inferiority of subject, and the differing mental moods, or different bodily condition of the writer. This short play was evidently written for an emergency — to grasp a popular occasion, and make use of an event fresh in the public mind, by which it had been greatly possessed and excited. Very unlike Shakspeare, in every essential particular, it is yet possible that he wrote it, in nightgown and slippers, scene by scene, to meet the wants of the actors. The demands of a theatre, the hurried competition of rival houses, might readily prompt him to this drudgery, as an aside from his usual labors, at the very moment that he was most busy, on his most glorious achievement. I attach but little importance to the scruple of Mr. Malone.

Dr. Farmer has something after the same fashion. "The Yorkshire Tragedy," saith he, "hath been frequently called Shakspeare's earliest attempt in the drama; but, most certainly, it was not written by our poet at all. The fact on which it is built, was perpetrated no sooner than 1605 — much too late for so mean a performance from the hand of Shakspeare."

"I confess," says Mr. Steevens, in a very elaborate note, "I have always regarded this little drama as a genuine but a hasty production of our author." This opinion he sustains by a series of generalities, which most readers can readily conceive for themselves.

A writer in the Retrospective Review, analyzing the Yorkshire Tragedy, says: "There is no reason why Shakspeare should *not* have written it, any more than why he should." To this Mr. Knight answers: "The reason why Shakspeare should not have written it is, we think, to be deduced from the circumstance that he, who had never even written a comedy in which the scene is placed in his own country in his own times, would very unwillingly have gone out of his way to dramatize a real incident of horror, occurring in Yorkshire in 1604, which of necessity could only have been presented to the *senses* of an audience, as a *fact* admitting of very little elevation by a poetical treatment, which might seize upon their imaginations." We really see very little in this argument, which depends wholly on an assumption. Certainly, there is nothing in it to oppose to the suggestion of that policy, on the part of a manager, which would be apt to consult the tastes of his audience, rather than his own, and which, whatever might be his poetical nature, would scarcely suffer this to interfere with his interests. Besides, Mr. Knight has not taken all the *facts* into this connexion. Though the event took place in 1604, its freshness had been preserved by ballads. These were popular, and the play is probably neither more nor less than the amplification of a ballad.

The Retrospective Review further says: "If he [Shakspeare] *had* written it, on the principle of merely dramatizing the known fact, he would not have done it much better than it is here done; and there were many of his contemporaries who could have done it quite as well." — "We agree," says Mr. Knight, "with this assertion. If the Yorkshire Tragedy had been done better than it is — that is, if the power of the poet had more prevailed in it — it would not have answered the purpose for which it was intended; it would, in truth, have been a mistake in art. Shakspeare would not have committed this mistake. But then, we doubt whether he would have consented at all to have had a circle drawn around him by the antipoetical, within which his mastery over the spirits of the earth and of the air was unavailing."

All this seems to us a mere waste of speculation. To say what Shakspeare would have done, as a poet, is one thing; but Mr. Knight can hardly venture to say that, as a manager, largely interested in the success of his theatre, Shakspeare would have been so tenacious of his particular tastes as to have rejected a popular topic, solely because of its poverty and rudeness. This is surely exceedingly gratuitous. If Shakspeare wrote the piece at all, upon which I do not propose to decide, this alone would have been the motive. It certainly would not have been a favorite study of the artist. One fact is indisputable, however: the play was entered in the stationers' books, and published by the press, with the name of William Shakspeare, at full length, in 1608; not only while Shakspeare was living, but while he was connected with the London theatres — and the publication remained, and still remains, without alteration or contradiction.

This is one of those facts which, it appears to me, no editor can possibly reject or set aside, by a reference to the mere general inferiority of this piece to the other productions of the supposed author. The truth is, the nature of the subject rendered it unsusceptible of any high poetical embellishments, if only because it was one which did not, and could not, commend itself to the tastes and affections of the poet. As a domestic sketch, though one mainly of horror, it has yet considerable merit. The patience and gentleness of the wife are well contrasted with the insane brutality, and the passionate selfishness, of the husband; and, in the selection and distribution of his material — the choice of the subject itself being kept from sight — the author shows equal good taste and discretion. Mr. Knight is of opinion that it belongs to the numerous performances of Thomas Heywood, whom Charles Lamb has called "a sort of prose Shakspeare;" and, if not Shakspeare's, it is most likely to have been Heywood's. Indeed, regarding the intrinsic evidence only, we should at once prefer the claims of Heywood to those of any of his contemporaries.

A YORKSHIRE TRAGEDY.

PERSONS REPRESENTED.

Husband.
Master of a college.
A Knight (a Magistrate).
Several Gentlemen.
OLIVER, } *servants.*
RALPH,
SAMUEL,
Other servants, officers, a little boy, &c.
Wife.
Maid-Servant.

SCENE I.—*An old House in* Yorkshire. Servants' *Hall.*

Enter OLIVER *and* RALPH.

Oli. Sirrah Ralph, my young mistress is in such a pitiful passionate humor for the long absence of her love—

Ralph. Why, can you blame her? Why, apples hanging longer on the tree than when they are ripe, makes so many fallings; viz., mad wenches, because they are not gathered in time, are fain to drop of themselves, and then 'tis common, you know, for every man to take them up.

Oli. Mass, thou say'st true, 'tis common indeed! But, sirrah, is neither our young master returned, nor our fellow Sam come from London?

Ralph. Neither of either, as the puritan bawd says. 'Slid, I hear Sam. Sam's come; here he is; tarry; come, i'faith: now my nose itches for news.

Oli. And so does mine elbow.

Sam. [*within*]. Where are you, there? Boy, look you walk my horse with discretion. I have rid him simply:[1] I warrant his skin sticks to his back with very heat. If he should catch cold and get the cough of the lungs, I were well served, were I not?

Enter SAMUEL.

What, Ralph and Oliver!

Both. Honest fellow Sam, welcome, i'faith. What tricks hast thou brought from London?

Sam. You see I am hanged after the truest fashion: three hats, and two glasses bobbing upon them; two rebato wires[2] upon my breast, a cap-case by my side, a brush at my back, an almanac in my pocket, and three ballads in my codpiece.[3] Now am I[4] the true picture of a common servingman.

Oli. I'll swear thou art; thou may'st set up when thou wilt: there's many a one begins with less, I can tell thee, that proves a rich man ere he dies. But what's the news from London, Sam?

Ralph. Ay, that's well said; what's the news from London, sirrah? My young mistress keeps such a puling for her love.

Sam. Why, the more fool she; ay, the more ninnyhammer she.

Oli. Why, Sam, why?

Sam. Why, he is married to another long ago.

Both. I'faith? You jest.

Sam. Why, did you not know that till now? why, he's married, beats his wife, and has two or three children by her. For you must note, that a woman bears the more when she is beaten.[5]

Ralph. Ay, that's true, for she bears the blows.

Oli. Sirrah Sam, I would not for two years' wages my young mistress knew so much; she'd run upon the left hand of her wit, and ne'er be her own woman again.

Sam. And I think she was blest in her cradle, that he never came in her bed. Why, he has consumed all, pawned his lands, and made his university brother stand in wax for him:[6] there's a fine phrase for a scrivener. Puh! he owes more than his skin is worth.

Oli. Is't possible?

Sam. Nay, I'll tell you, moreover, he calls his wife whore, as familiarly as one would call Moll and Doll; and his children bastards, as naturally as can be.—But what have we here? I thought 'twas something pulled down my breeches; I quite forgot my two poking-sticks: these came from London. Now, anything is good here that comes from London.

Oli. Ay, far-fetched, you know, Sam.—But speak in your conscience, i'faith; have not we as good poking-sticks i'the country as need to be put in the fire?

Sam. The mind of a thing is all; the mind of a thing is all; and as thou saidst even now, far-fetched are the best things for ladies.

Oli. Ay, and for waiting-gentlewomen too.

Sam. But, Ralph, what, is our beer sour this thunder?

Ralph. No, no, it holds countenance yet.

1 I am inclined to think that the proper word here is *sinfully*, and not "simply," which would seem purposeless.

2 "Rebato" was the name of an ancient head-dress. The wires were used to distend the hair or lace.—PERCY.

3 A protuberance in the breeches, sometimes used as a pincushion. An article of the same name, and used for a like purpose, was worn by women about the breast.

4 Written elsewhere, "Nay, I am," &c.

5 The old proverb has it, "A woman and a walnut-tree bear the better for being thrashed."

6 Give bond—sign and *seal* for him.

Sam. Why, then follow me; I'll teach you the finest humor to be drunk in: I learned it at London last week.

Both. I'faith? Let's hear it, let's hear it.

Sam. The bravest humor! 'twould do a man good to be drunk in it: they call it knighting in London, when they drink upon their knees.[1]

Both. I'faith, that's excellent.

Sam. Come, follow me; I'll give you all the degrees of it in order. [*Exeunt.*

SCENE II.—*A Room in* Calverly Hall.

Enter Wife.

Wife. What will become of us? All will away:
My husband never ceases in expense,
Both to consume his credit and his house;
And 'tis set down by Heaven's just decree,
That riot's child must needs be beggary.
Are these the virtues that his youth did promise?
Dice and voluptuous meetings, midnight revels,
Taking his bed with surfeits; ill beseeming
The ancient honor of his house and name?
And this not all, but that which kills me most,
When he recounts his losses and false fortunes,
The weakness of his state so much dejected,
Not as a man repentant, but half mad
His fortunes can not answer his expense,
He sits, and sullenly locks up his arms;
Forgetting heaven, looks downward; which makes [him
Appear so dreadful that he frights my heart:
Walks heavily, as if his soul were earth;
Not penitent for those his sins are past,
But vexed his money can not make them last:
A fearful melancholy, ungodly sorrow!
O, yonder he comes; now in despite of ills
I'll speak to him, and I will hear him speak,
And do my best to drive it from his heart.

Enter Husband.

Hus. Pox o' the last throw! It made five hundred angels
Vanish from my sight. I am damned, I'm damned!
The angels have forsook me. Nay, it is
Certainly true; for he that has no coin
Is damned in this world; he is gone, he's gone.

Wife. Dear husband!

Hus. O! most punishment of all, I have a wife.

Wife. I do entreat you, as you love your soul,
Tell me the cause of this your discontent.

Hus. A vengeance strip thee naked! thou art the [cause,
The effect, the quality, the property;—
Thou, thou, thou! [*Exit.*

Wife. Bad turned to worse! A[2] beggary of the soul
As of the body. And so much unlike
Himself at first, as if some vexing[3] spirit
Had got his form upon him. He comes again!

Re-enter Husband.

He says I am the cause: I never yet
Spoke less than words of duty and of love.

Hus. If marriage be honorable, then cuckolds are honorable, for they can not be made without marriage. Fool! what meant I to marry to get beggars? Now must my eldest son be a knave or nothing; he can not live upon the fool, for he will have no land to maintain him. That mortgage sits like a snaffle upon mine inheritance, and makes me chew upon iron. My second son must be a promoter,[4] and my third a thief, or an under-putter;[5] a slave pander. Oh, beggary, beggary, to what base uses dost thou put a man![6] I think the devil scorns to be a bawd; he bears himself more proudly, has more care of his credit.—Base, slavish, abject, filthy poverty!

Wife. Good sir, by all our vows I do beseech you,
Show me the true cause of your discontent.

Hus. Money, money, money; and thou must supply me.

Wife. Alas, I am the least cause of your discon- [tent;
Yet what is mine, either in rings or jewels,
Use to your own desire; but I beseech you,
As you're a gentleman by many bloods,
Though I myself be out of your respect,
Think on the state of these three lovely boys
You have been father to.

Hus. Puh! bastards, bastards, bastards; begot in tricks, begot in tricks.

Wife. Heaven knows how these words wrong me: but I may
Endure these griefs among a thousand more.
O, call to mind your lands already mortgaged,
Yourself wound into debts, your hopeful brother,
At th' university, in bonds for you,
Like to be seized upon; and——

Hus. Have done, thou harlot,
Whom, though for fashion-sake I married,
I never could abide. Think'st thou, thy words
Shall kill my pleasures? Fall off to thy friends;
Thou and thy bastards beg; I will not bate
A whit in humor. Midnight, still I love you,
And revel in your company! Curbed in?
Shall it be said in all societies,
That I broke custom? that I flagged in money?
No, those thy jewels I will play as freely
As when my state was fullest.

Wife. Be it so.

Hus. Nay, I protest—and take that for an earnest,— [*Spurns her.*
I will for ever hold thee in contempt,
And never touch the sheets that cover thee,
But be divorced in bed, till thou consent
Thy dowry shall be sold, to give new life
Unto those pleasures which I most affect.

Wife. Sir, do but turn a gentle eye upon me,
And what the law shall give me leave to do,
You shall command.

Hus. Look it be done. Shall I want dust,
And, like a slave, wear nothing in my pockets
[*Holds his hands in his pockets.*
But my bare hands, to fill them up with nails?
O much against my blood, let it be done!

1 As the person to be knighted always knelt to receive the honor.

2 The old folio reads, "*both* beggary of the soul *as* of the body." Subsequent editors, in amending the grammar of the sentence, have converted "*as*" into "*and*," and thus, it appears to me, though rendering the line grammatically correct, have lessened something of the euphony and force of the sentence. "*A* beggary of the soul *as* of the body," seems to reconcile both objects.

3 Previous editions have it "vexed."

4 *Promoter*—informer.

5 Or *putour*—a leecher—a whoremonger.

6 "To what base uses we may return, Horatio!"—*Hamlet.*

I was never made to be a looker-on,
A bawd to dice; I'll shake the drabs myself,
And make them yield. I say, look it be done.
Wife. I take my leave: it shall. [*Exit.*
Hus. Speedily, speedily.
I hate the very hour I chose a wife:
A trouble, trouble! Three children, like three evils,
Hang on me. Fie, fie, fie! Strumpet and bastards!

Enter three Gentlemen.

Strumpet and bastards!
1 *Gent.* Still do these loathsome thoughts jar on your tongue!
Yourself to stain the honor of your wife,
Nobly descended! Those whom men call mad,
Endanger others; but he's more than mad
That wounds himself; whose own words do proclaim
Scandals unjust, to soil his better name.
It is not fit; I pray [you, sir,] forsake it.
2 *Gent.* Good sir, let modesty reprove you[r speech].
3 *Gent.* Let honest kindness sway so much with you.
Hus. Good den; I thank you, sir; and how do you?
Adieu! I am glad to see you! And farewell
Instructions! — admonitions! [*Exeunt* Gentlemen.

Enter a Servant.

How now, sirrah? What would you?
Serv. Only to certify you, sir, that my mistress was met by the way, by them who were sent for her up to London by her honorable uncle, your worship's late guardian.
Hus. So, then she is gone, sir; and so may you be;
But let her look the thing be done she wots of,
Or hell will stand more pleasant than her home.
[*Exit* Servant.

Enter a Gentleman.

Gent. Well or ill met, I care not.
Hus. No, nor I.
Gent. I am come with confidence to chide you.
Hus. Who? me?
Chide me? Do't finely, then; let it not move me:
For if thou chidest me angry, I shall strike.
Gent. Strike thine own follies, for 'tis they deserve
To be well beaten. We are now in private;
There's none but thou and I. Thou art fond and peevish;
An unclean rioter; thy lands and credit
Lie now both sick of a consumption:
I am sorry for thee. That man spends with shame,
That with his riches doth consume his name;
And such art thou.
Hus. Peace!
Gent. No, thou shalt hear me further.
Thy father's and forefathers' worthy honors,
Which were our country monuments, our grace,
Follies in thee begin now to deface.
The spring-time of thy youth did fairly promise
Such a most fruitful summer to thy friends,
It scarce can enter into men's beliefs
Such dearth should hang upon thee. We that see it
Are sorry to believe it. In thy change,
This voice into all places will be hurled —
Thou and the devil have deceived the world.
Hus. I'll not endure thee.
Gent. But, of all the worst,
Thy virtuous wife, right honorably allied,
Thou hast proclaimed a strumpet.
Hus. Nay, then I know thee;
Thou art her champion, thou; her private friend;
The party you wot on.
Gent. O, ignoble thought!
I am past my patient blood. Shall I stand idle,
And see my reputation touched to death?
Hus. It has galled you, this; has it?
Gent. No, monster; I will prove
My thoughts did only tend to virtuous love.
Hus. Love of her virtues? there it goes.
Gent. Base spirit,
To lay thy hate upon the fruitful honor
Of thine own bed.
[*They fight, and the* Husband *is hurt.*
Hus. Oh!
Gent. Wilt thou yield it yet?
Hus. Sir, sir, I have not done with you.
Gent. I hope [not] nor ne'er shall be.[1]
[*They fight again.*
Hus. Have you got tricks? Are you in cunning with me?[2]
Gent. No, plain and right:
He needs no cunning that for truth doth fight.
[Husband *falls down.*
Hus. Hard fortune! am I levelled with the ground?
Gent. Now, sir, you lie at mercy.
Hus. Ay, you slave.
Gent. Alas, that hate should bring us to our grave!
You see, my sword's not thirsty for your life:
I am sorrier for your wound than you yourself.
You're of a virtuous house; show virtuous deeds;
'Tis not your honor, 'tis your folly bleeds.
Much good has been expected in your life;
Cancel not all men's hopes: you have a wife,
Kind and obedient; heap not wrongful shame
On her and your posterity; let only sin be sore,
And by this fall, rise, never to fall more.—
And so I leave you. [*Exit.*
Hus. Has the dog left me, then,
After his tooth has left[3] me? O, my heart
Would fain leap after him. Revenge, I say;
I'm mad to be revenged. My strumpet wife! —
It is thy quarrel that rips thus my flesh,
And makes my breast spout[4] blood; but thou shalt bleed.
Vanquished? got down? unable even to speak?
Surely 'tis want of money makes men weak:
Ay, 'twas that o'erthrew me: I'd ne'er been down else. [*Exit.*

SCENE III.—*Another Room, in the same.*

Enter Wife, *in a riding-suit, and a* Servant.

Serv. 'Faith, mistress, if it might not be presumption
In me to tell you so, for his excuse
You had small reason, knowing his abuse.
Wife. I grant I had [small reason]; but, alas,

1 In former copies the line runs thus; —
"I hope, nor ne'er shall *do*."
2 "An I had thought him so valiant," &c., "so *cunning in fence*," &c.— *Twelfth Night.*
3 "Left" is not the word here—perhaps "*ript.*"
4 Other copies read, "*spit.*"

Why should our faults at home be spread abroad ?
'Tis grief enough within doors. At first sight,
Mine uncle could run o'er his prodigal life,
As perfectly, as if his serious eye
Had numbered all his follies : [all he knew :]
Knew of his mortgaged lands, his friends in bonds,
Himself withered with debts ; and in that minute
Had I his usage and unkindness added,
'Twould have confounded every thought of good :
Where now, his riots fathering on his youth,
Which time and tame experience will shake off—
Guessing his kindness to me (as I smoothed him
With all the skill I had—though his deserts
Are in form uglier than an unshaped bear),
He's ready to prefer him to some office
And place at court ; a good and sure relief
To all his stooping fortunes. 'Twill be a means,
I hope, to make a new league between us, and
Redeem his virtues with his lands.

Serv. I should think so, mistress. If he should not now be kind to you, and love you, and so raise[1] you up, I should think the devil himself kept open house in him.

Wife. I doubt not but he will. Now pr'ythee leave
I think I hear him coming. [me :

Serv. I am gone. [*Exit.*

Wife. By this good means I shall preserve my
And free my husband out of usurers' hands. [lands,
Now there's no need of sale ; my uncle's kind :
I hope, if aught, this will content his mind.
Here comes my husband.

Enter Husband.

Hus. Now, are you come ? Where's the money? Let's see the money. Is the rubbish sold ? those wiseacres, your lands ! Why, when ? The money ?— where is it ? Pour it down ; down with it, down with it : I say pour't on the ground ; let's see it, let's see it !—

Wife. Good sir,
Keep but in patience, and I hope my words
Shall like you well. I bring you better comfort
Than the sale of my dowry.

Hus. Ha ! what's that ?

Wife. Pray do not fright me, sir, but vouchsafe me hearing. My uncle, glad of your kindness to me and mild usage (for so I made it to him), hath, in pity of your declining fortunes, provided a place for you at court, of worth and credit; which so much overjoyed me—

Hus. Out on thee, filth !
Over and overjoyed, when I'm in torment ?
[*Spurns her.*
Thou politic whore, subtiler than nine devils ! Was this thy journey to nunck ? to set down the history of me, of my state and fortunes ? Shall I, that dedicated myself to pleasure, be now confined in service ? to crouch and stand like an old man i'the hams, my hat off? I that could never abide to uncover my head i'the church ? Base slut ! this fruit bear thy complaints.

Wife. O, Heaven knows
That my complaints were praises and best words
Of you and your estate. Only, my friends
Knew of your mortgaged lands, and were possessed
Of every accident before I came.
If you suspect it but a plot in me,
To keep my dowry, or for mine own good,
Or my poor children's (though it suits a mother
To show a natural care in their reliefs),
Yet I'll forget myself to calm your blood :
Consume it, as your pleasure counsels you.
And all I wish even clemency affords ;
Give me but pleasant looks and modest words.

Hus. Money, whore, money, or I'll—
[*Draws a dagger*

Enter a Servant *hastily.*

What the devil ! How now ? thy hasty news ?

Serv. May it please you, sir ——

Hus. What ! may I not look upon my dagger ?— Speak, villain, or I will execute the point on thee: quick, short !

Serv. Why, sir, a gentleman from the university stays below to speak with you. [*Exit.*

Hus. From the university ? so ; university :—that long word runs through me. *Exit.*

Wife. Was ever wife so wretchedly beset ?
Had not this news stepped in between, the point
Had offered violence unto my breast.
That which some women call great misery
Would show but little here ; would scarce be seen
Among my miseries. I may compare,
For wretched fortunes, with all wives that are.
Nothing will please him, until all be nothing.
He calls it slavery to be preferred ;
A place of credit, a base servitude.
What shall become of me, and my poor children,
Two here, and one at nurse ? my pretty beggars ![2]
I see how ruin with a palsying[3] hand
Begins to shake the ancient seat to dust :
The heavy weight of sorrow draws my lids
Over my dankish[4] eyes : I scarce can see :
Thus grief will last ;—it wakes and sleeps with me.
[*Exit.*

SCENE IV.—*Another Apartment in the same.*

Enter Husband *and the* Master *of a College.*

Hus. Please you draw near, sir ; you're exceeding welcome.

Mast. That's my doubt ! I fear I come not to be welcome.

Hus. Yes, howsoever.

Mast. 'Tis not my fashion, sir, to dwell in long circumstance, but to be plain and effectual : therefore to the purpose. The cause of my setting forth was piteous and lamentable. That hopeful young gentleman, your brother, whose virtues we all love dearly, through your default and unnatural negligence, lies in bond executed for your debt—a prisoner ; all his studies amazed, his hope struck dead, and the pride of his youth muffled in these dark clouds of oppression.

Hus. Umph, umph, umph !

Mast. O, you have killed the towardest hope of all our university : wherefore, without repentance and

1 "*Cherish* you up" in previous editions.

2 So, in the same spirit, Macduff speaks of "my pretty chickens," &c.

3 "Palsy" in the old copies.

4 Other copies read "*darkish*" as well as "*dankish*." The latter is the more appropriate word, but reads unpleasantly in the line.

amends, expect ponderous and sudden judgments to fall grievously upon you. Your brother, a man who profited in his divine employments, and might have made ten thousand souls fit for heaven, is now, by your careless courses, cast into prison, which you must answer for; and assure your spirit it will come home at length.

Hus. O God! oh!

Mast. Wise men think ill of you; others speak ill of you; no man loves you; nay, even those whom honesty condemns, condemn you. And take this from the virtuous affection I bear your brother: never look for prosperous hour, good thoughts, quiet sleep, contented walks, nor anything that makes man perfect, till you redeem him. What is your answer? How will you bestow him? Upon desperate misery, or better hopes? — I suffer till I hear your answer.

Hus. Sir, you have much wrought with me; I feel you in my soul: you are your art's master. I never had sense till now; your syllables have cleft me. Both for your words and pains I thank you. I can not but acknowledge grievous wrongs done to my brother; mighty, mighty, mighty, mighty wrongs. — Within, there!

Enter a Servant.

Hus. Fill me a bowl of wine. [*Exit* Servant.] Alas! poor brother, bruised with an execution for my sake!

Mast. A bruise indeed makes many a mortal sore,
Till the grave cure them.

Re-enter Servant *with wine.*

Hus. Sir, I begin to you; you've chid your welcome.

Mast. I could have wished it better for your sake. I pledge you, sir: To the kind man in prison.

Hus. Let it be so. Now, sir, if you please to spend but a few minutes in a walk about my grounds below, my man here shall attend you. I doubt not but by that time to be furnished of a sufficient answer, and therein my brother fully satisfied.

Mast. Good sir, in that the angels would be pleased,
And the world's murmurs calmed; and I should say,
I set forth then upon a lucky day.

[*Exeunt* Master *and* Servant.

Hus. O thou confused man! Thy pleasant sins have undone thee; thy damnation has beggared thee. That Heaven should say we must not sin, and yet made women! give our senses way to find pleasure, which, being found, confounds us! Why should we know those things so much misuse us? O, would virtue had been forbidden! We should then have proved all virtuous; for 'tis our blood to love what we are forbidden. Had not drunkenness been forbidden, what man would have been fool to a beast, and zany to a swine — to show tricks in the mire? What is there in three dice,[1] to make a man draw thrice three thousand acres into the compass of a little round table, and with the gentleman's palsy in the hand shake out his posterity thieves or beggars? 'Tis done; I have done't, i'faith: terrible, horrible misery! — How well was I left! Very well, very well. My lands showed like a full moon about me; but now the moon's in the last quarter — waning, waning; and I am mad to think that moon was mine; mine, and my father's, and my forefathers'; generations, generations. — Down goes the house of us; down, down it sinks! Now is the name a beggar; begs in me. — That name which, hundreds of years, has made this shire famous, in me and my posterity runs out. In my seed five are made miserable besides myself: my riot is now my brother's gaoler, my wife's sighing, my three boys' penury, and mine own confusion.
Why sit my hairs upon my cursèd head?

[*Tears his hair.*

Will not this poison scatter them? O, my brother!
In execution among devils that
Stretch him and make him give;[2] and I in want,
Not able to relieve[3] nor to redeem him!
Divines and dying men may talk of hell,
But in my heart her several torments dwell:
Slavery and misery! Who, in this case,
Would not take money up upon his soul?
Pawn his salvation, live at interest?
I, that did ever in abundance dwell,
For me to want, exceeds the throes of hell.

Enter a little Boy *with a Top and Scourge.*

Son. What ails you, father? Are you not well? I can not scourge my top as long as you stand so. You take up all the room with your wide legs. Puh! you can not make me afraid with this; I fear no vizards, nor bugbears.

[*He takes up the* Child *by the skirts of his long coat with one hand, and draws his dagger with the other.*

Hus. Up, sir, for here thou hast no inheritance left.

Son. O, what will you do, father? I am your white boy.

Hus. Thou shalt be my red boy; take that.

[*Strikes him.*

Son. O, you hurt me, father.

Hus. My eldest beggar,
Thou shalt not live to ask a usurer bread;
To cry at a great man's gate; or follow,
"Good your honor," by a coach; no, nor your brother:
'Tis charity to brain you.

Son. How shall I learn, now my head's broke?

Hus. Bleed, bleed, [*Stabs him.*
Rather than beg. Be not thy name's disgrace:
Spurn thou thy fortune's first; if they be base,
Come view thy second brother's. Fates! My children's blood
Shall spin into your faces; you shall see,
How confidently we scorn beggary!

[*Exit with his* Son.

SCENE V.

A Maid *discovered with a* Child *in her arms; the* Mother *on a couch by her, asleep.*

Maid. Sleep, sweet babe; sorrow makes thy mother sleep:
It bodes small good when heaviness falls so deep.
Hush, pretty boy; thy hopes might have been better.
'Tis lost at dice, what ancient honor won:
Hard, when the father plays away the son!

[1] The game called *passage*, or *pass-dice*, was played with three dice. See note to "Sir John Oldcastle," page 104.

[2] Steevens detects a pun in this passage. Leather, he reminds us, when stretched, is said "to give"—that is, yield.
[3] "For to live" in other editions.

Nothing but misery serves[1] in this house;
Ruin and Desolation. Oh!

Enter Husband, *with his* Son *bleeding.*

Hus. Whore, give me that boy.
[*Strives with her for the* Child.
Maid. O, help, help! Out, alas! murther, murther!
Hus. Are you gossiping, you prating, sturdy quean?
I'll break your clamor with your neck. Down stairs;
Tumble, tumble, headlong. So:—
[*He throws her down and stabs the* Child.
The surest way to charm a woman's tongue,
Is—break her neck: a politician did it.[2]
Son. Mother, mother; I am killed, mother!
[Wife *awakes.*
Wife. Ha, who's that cried? O, me! my children
Both bloody, bloody! [both!
[*Catches up the youngest* Child.
Hus. Strumpet, let go the boy; let go the beggar.
Wife. O, my sweet husband!
Hus. Filth, harlot!
Wife. O, what will you do, dear husband?
Hus. Give me the bastard!
Wife. Your own sweet boy—
Hus. There are too many beggars.
Wife. Good my husband—
Hus. Dost thou prevent me still?
Wife. O, God!
Hus. Have at his heart.
[*Stabs at the* Child *in her arms.*
Wife. O, my dear boy!
Hus. Brat, thou shalt not live to shame thy house—
Wife. Oh, Heaven! [*She is hurt, and sinks down.*
Hus. And perish!—Now be gone: [one.
There's whores enough, and want would make thee

Enter a Servant.

Serv. O, sir, what deeds are these?
Hus. Base slave, my vassal!
Com'st thou between my fury to question me?
Serv. Were you the devil, I would hold you, sir.
Hus. Hold me? Presumption! I'll undo thee for it.
Serv. 'Sblood! you have undone us all, sir.
Hus. Tug at thy master?
Serv. Tug at a monster.
Hus. Have I no power? Shall my slave fetter me?
Serv. Nay, then the devil wrestles: I am thrown.
Hus. O, villain! now I'll tug thee, now I'll tear thee;
Set quick spurs to my vassal;[3] bruise him, trample him.
So: I think thou wilt not follow me in haste.
My horse stands ready saddled. Away, away;
Now to my brat at nurse, my sucking beggar:
Fates, I'll not leave you one to trample on! [*Exeunt.*

SCENE VI.—*Court before the House.*

Enter Husband; *to him the* Master *of the College.*

Mast. How is it with you, sir?
Methinks you look of a distracted color.
Hus. Who, I, sir? 'Tis but your fancy.

[1] Query: *survives?*
[2] This is supposed to allude to the imputed murder of his wife by the earl of Leicester.
[3] He uses his spurs in the struggle. The rowel in that day was no bad substitute for the dagger. Their points were more than an inch long, sharp, and with broad blades.

Please you walk in, sir, and I'll soon resolve you:
I want one small part to make up the sum,
And then my brother shall rest satisfied.
Mast. I shall be glad to see it: sir, I'll attend you.
[*Exeunt.*

SCENE VII.—*A Room in the House.*

The Wife, Servant, *and* Children *discovered.*

Serv. Oh, I'm scarce able to heave up myself,
He has so bruised me with his devilish weight,
And torn my flesh with his blood-hasty spur:
A man before of easy constitution,
Till now hell power supplied, to his soul's wrong:
O, how damnation can make weak men strong!

Enter the Master *of the College and two* Servants.

Serv. O, the most piteous deed, sir, since you came!
Mast. A deadly greeting! Hath he summed up these
To satisfy his brother? Here's another;
And by the bleeding infants, the dead mother.
Wife. Oh! oh!
Mast. Surgeons! surgeons! she recovers life:—
One of his men all faint and bloodied!
1 *Serv.* Follow; our murtherous master has took horse
To kill his child at nurse. O, follow quickly.
Mast. I am the readiest; it shall be my charge
To raise the town upon him.
1 *Serv.* Good sir, do follow him.
[*Exeunt* Master *and two* Servants
Wife. O, my children!
1 *Serv.* How is it with my most afflicted mistress?
Wife. Why do I now recover? Why half live,
To see my children bleed before mine eyes?
A sight able to kill a mother's breast, without
An executioner.—What, art thou mangled too?
1 *Serv.* I, thinking to prevent what his quick mischiefs
Had so soon acted, came and rushed upon him.
We struggled; but a fouler strength than his
O'erthrew me with his arms: then did he bruise me,
And rend my flesh, and rob'd me of my hair;
And like a man in execution mad,
Made me unfit to rise and follow him.
Wife. What is it has beguiled him of all grace,
And stole away humanity from his breast?
To slay his children, purpose to kill his wife,
And spoil his servants—

Enter a Servant.

Serv. Please you to leave this most accursed place:
A surgeon waits within.
Wife. Willing to leave it?
'Tis guilty of sweet blood, of innocent blood:
Murder has took this chamber with full hands,
And will ne'er out as long as the house stands.
[*Exeunt.*

SCENE VIII.—*A High Road.*

Enter Husband. *He falls.*

Hus. O, stumbling jade! The spavin overtake thee!
The fifty diseases stop thee![4]

[4] There is an old book by Gervase Monkham, entitled "The Fifty Diseases of a Horse." A similar speech occurs in *Taming of the Shrew.*

Oh, I am sorely bruised! Plague founder thee!
Thou runnest at ease and pleasure. Heart of chance!
To throw me now, within a flight o' the town,
In such plain even ground too! 'Sfoot! a man
May dice upon't, and throw away the meadows.
Filthy beast!
[*Cry within.*] Follow, follow, follow.
Hus. Ha! I hear the sounds of men, like hue and
Up, up, and struggle to thy horse; make on; [cry.
Despatch that little beggar, and all's done.
[*Cry within.*] Here, here; this way, this way.
Hus. At my back? Oh,
What fate have I! my limbs deny me go.
My will is baited; beggary claims a part.
O, could I here reach to the infant's heart!

Enter the Master *of the College, three* Gentlemen, *and* Attendants *with Halberds.*

All. Here, here; yonder, yonder!
Mast. Unnatural, flinty, more than barbarous!
The Scythians, even the marble-hearted Fates,
Could not have acted more remorseless deeds,
In their relentless natures, than these of thine.
Was this the answer I long waited on?
The satisfaction for thy prisoned brother?
Hus. Why, he can have no more of us than our
And some of them want but fleaing. [skins,
1 Gent. Great sins have made him impudent.
Mast. He has shed so much blood, that he can not blush.
2 Gent. Away with him, and bear him to the jus-
A gentleman of worship dwells at hand: [tice.
There shall his deeds be blazed.
Hus. Why, all the better.
My glory 'tis to have my action known;
I grieve for nothing, but I missed of one.
Mast. There's little of a father in that grief:
Bear him away. [*Exeunt.*

SCENE IX.—*A Room in the House of a* Magistrate.

Enter a Knight *and three* Gentlemen.

Knight. Endangered so his wife? murdered his children?
1 Gent. So the cry goes.
Knight. I am sorry I e'er knew him;
That ever he took life and natural being
From such an honored stock, and fair descent,
Till this black minute without stain or blemish.
1 Gent. Here come the men.

Enter Master *of the College, &c., with the* Prisoner.

Knight. The serpent of his house! [Oh!] I am sor-
For this time, that I am in place of justice. [ry,
Mast. Please you, sir——
Knight. Do not repeat it twice; I know too much:
Would it had ne'er been thought on! Sir, I bleed for you.
1 Gent. Your father's sorrows are alive in me.
What made you show such monstrous cruelty?
Hus. In a word, sir, I have consumed all, played away long-acre; and I thought it the charitablest deed I could do, to cozen beggary, and knock my house o' the head.
Knight. O, in a cooler blood you will repent it.
Hus. I repent now that one is left unkilled:
My brat at nurse. I would full fain have weaned him.
Knight. Well, I do not think, but in to-morrow's
The terror will sit closer to your soul, [judgment,
When the dread thought of death remembers you:
To further which, take this sad voice from me,
Never was act played more unnaturally.
Hus. I thank you, sir.
Knight. Go lead him to the gaol:
Where justice claims all, there must pity fail.
Hus. Come, come; away with me.
[*Exeunt* Husband, *&c.*
Mast. Sir, you deserve the worship of your place;
Would all did so! In you the law is grace.
Knight. It is my wish it should be so.—Ruinous[1]
The desolation of his house, the blot [man!
Upon his predecessors' honored name!
That man is nearest shame, that is past shame.
[*Exeunt*

SCENE X.—*Before* Calverly Hall.

Enter Husband *guarded*, Master *of the College*, Gentlemen, *and* Attendants.

Hus. I am right against my house—seat of my ancestors:
I hear my wife's alive, but much endangered.
Let me entreat to speak with her, before
The prison gripe me.

His Wife *is brought in.*

Gent. See, here she comes of herself.
Wife. O my sweet husband, my dear distressed
Now in the hands of unrelenting laws, [husband
My greatest sorrow, my extremest bleeding;
Now my soul bleeds.
Hus. How now? Kind to me? Did I not wound
Left thee for dead? [thee?
Wife. Tut, far, far greater wounds did my breast feel;
Unkindness strikes a deeper wound than steel.
You have been still unkind to me.
Hus. I'faith, and so I think I have.
I did my murders roughly out of hand,
Desperate and sudden; but thou hast devised
A fine way now to kill me: thou'st given mine eyes
Seven wounds apiece. Now glides the devil from me,
Departs at every joint; heaves up my nails.
O catch him, torments that were ne'er invented!
Bind him one thousand more,[2] you blessed angels,
In that pit bottomless! Let him not rise
To make men act unnatural tragedies;
To spread into a father, and in fury
Make him his children's executioner;
Murder his wife, his servants, and who not?—
For that man's dark, where heaven is quite forgot.
Wife. O my repentant husband!
Hus. O my dear soul, whom I too much have wronged!
For death I die, and for this have I longed.
Wife. Thou shouldst not, be assured, for these
If the law could forgive as soon as I. [faults die,
[*The two* Children *laid out.*
Hus. What sight is yonder?
Wife. O, our two bleeding boys,
Laid forth upon the threshold.

[1] I should prefer *ravenous* here. "Ruinous" is an epithet quite too feeble and inexpressive for such a case.
[2] Years, understood.

Hus. Here's weight enough to make a heartstring [crack!
O, were it lawful that your pretty souls
Might look from heaven into your father's eyes,
Then should you see the penitent glasses melt,
And both your murders shoot upon my cheeks!
But you are playing in the angels' laps,
And will not look on me, who, void of grace,
Killed you in beggary.
O that I might my wishes now attain,
I should then wish you living were again,
Though I did beg with you, which thing I feared:
O, 'twas the enemy my eyes so bleared!
O, would you could pray Heaven me forgive,
That will unto my end repentant live!
Wife. It makes me e'en forget all other sorrows,
And live apart with this.
Offi. Come, will you go?
Hus. I'll kiss the blood I spilt, and then I'll go:
My soul is bloodied, well may my lips be so!
Farewell, dear wife; now thou and I must part:
I, of thy wrongs repent me, with my heart.
Wife. O stay; thou shalt not go!
Hus. That's but in vain; you see it must be so.
Farewell, ye bloody ashes of my boys!
My punishments are their eternal joys.
Let every father look into my deeds,
And then their heirs may prosper, while mine bleeds.
[*Exeunt* Husband *and* Officers.
Wife. More wretched am I now in this distress,
Than former sorrows made me.
Mast. O kind wife,
Be comforted; one joy is yet unmurdered;
You have a boy at nurse: your joy's in him.
Wife. Dearer than all is my poor husband's life.
Heaven give my body strength, which yet is faint
With much expense of blood; and I will kneel,
Sue for his life, number up all my friends
To plead for pardon for my dear husband's life.
Mast. Was it in man to wound so kind a creature?
I'll ever praise a woman for thy sake.
I must return with grief; my answer's set;
I shall bring news weighs heavier than the debt.
Two brothers — one in bond lies overthrown —
This on a deadlier execution. [*Exeunt.*

THE END OF A YORKSHIRE TRAGEDY.

INTRODUCTION

TO

THE TRAGEDY OF LOCRINE.

The tragedy of "Locrine" was originally printed in quarto, under the following title: "The lamentable Tragedie of Locrine, the Eldest Sonne of King Brutus, discoursing the Warres of the Britaines and Hunnes, with their Discomfiture. The Britaines' Victorie, with their Accidents, and the Death of Albanact. No less pleasant and profitable. Newly set foorth, ouerseene and corrected by W. S. London, printed by Thomas Creede, 1595." The play was entered on the books of the Stationers' Company on the 20th of July, 1594. It was not included among the works of Shakspeare until seventy years after its first publication. There is no tradition which ascribes it to him. The publishers who classed it with his known writings, seem to have taken its authorship for granted; whether on the simple authority of the initials W. S., which accompanied its original publication, or on the strength of evidence which has not come down to us, can not now be ascertained. What value to attach to these initials is another difficult question; and, if Shakspeare's, the further question is, in what degree he participated in the production of a piece, of which we are told only that it was "*newly set foorth, ouerseene and corrected*" by him. Mr. Steevens says: "Supposing for a moment that W. S. here stood for our great poet's name (which is extremely improbable), these words prove that Shakspeare was not the *writer* of this performance. If it was only set forth, overseen, and corrected, it was not composed by him." This conclusion, however confident, Mr. Knight stops with a *non sequitur*. He shows an exact parallel to the title-page of "Locrine," in one of the generally-recognised plays of Shakspeare, viz.: "A pleasant, conceited Comedie, called Love's Labour Lost. As it was presented before her Highness the last Christmas. *Newly corrected and augmented* by W. Shakspeare." But, though we show that in plays unquestionably from the hands of the great master, he was modestly set forth as the corrector and augmentor only, it does not follow necessarily that *our* W. S. is William Shakspeare. About the time of the publication of this play of "Locrine," England was in possession of a certain William Stafford, who published political pamphlets bearing his initials only. Still, as Stafford's pamphlets were never imputed to Shakspeare, by any of the myriad admirers of the latter, so it is equally certain that neither the friends nor the foes of Stafford ever laid "Locrine" at his door. In 1596, however, one William Smith was living and writing, whose claims to its authorship might be urged more plausibly. He was the author of a collection of sonnets; and in 1600, a love-poem appeared in "England's Helicon," bearing the initials W. S. This also may have proceeded from the pen of William Smith. Another of the Smith family, about the same period, is known to have had a right to these initials, who is even known as a writer for the stage. This was Wentworth Smith, who, according to Mr. Knight, wrote many dramatic pieces "in conjunction with the best poets of that prolific period." We regret that Mr. Knight has not given us some specimens from the numerous dramas of this author, by which we could have formed some general idea with regard to his peculiar qualities. Our own collection of ancient British dramatic authors contains nothing which enables us to form a judgment in relation to his claims to "Locrine." Mr. Collier, in his "Annals of the Stage," tells us only that he was the author of "The Italian Tragedy" and "Hector of Germany," and was concerned in the production of the "Six Yeomen of the West," with William Haughton, John Day, and Richard Hathwaye; none of them quite worthy to be distinguished with the "best poets of that prolific period." Were any of the writings of Wentworth Smith extant, it would have been only proper, on the part of Mr. Knight, to have followed the suggestion of his name, in this connexion, with some specimens of his muse. It might then have been possible, by a comparison of his verses with those of "Locrine," to determine in what degree the internal evidence was likely to sustain his initials in the claim to the authorship, not of "Locrine" only, but of "Titus Andronicus," which not only equally suffers from like doubtful paternity, but the characteristics of which, to our notion, justify us in tracing it to the same sources with the former play. But of this, hereafter.

Here, then, amid a great variety of conflicting claims, a nearly equal doubt hanging over all, the field of conjecture lies sufficiently open. The critics have partially availed themselves of its privileges. Tieck, the German, describes "Locrine" as the earliest of Shakspeare's dramas. He suggests that the story has a political application — and was intended to shadow forth the nature and character of the commotions which troubled the peace of England, in consequence of the sympathy accorded to Mary Stuart, then in the bonds of Elizabeth. He supposes it to have been written prior to the execution of the former, and probably in order to the justification of that sharp judgment which led her to the block. But the English reader will smile at such an opinion. There is nothing of a modern complexion in "Locrine." The story is an old one. The author religiously follows the tradition — quite as slavishly, indeed, as it is possible for a dramatic author to follow; and, as for any effect which the sentiment of "Locrine" would have produced on the popular feeling or patriotism of the English, at the juncture alluded to, it will be only necessary to advert to the prevailing passion of the piece, which is revenge, and which is made throughout to occupy almost exclusively the attention of the spectator — to show how little were the politics of the time in the contemplation of the writer. Doubtless, a few lines, here and there, might have a present application, but these are evidently grafts on the original, rudely introduced, and probably by another hand than that of the author. Proof of this, indeed, occurs to us in a single instance, which probably led Tieck to his singularly foreign conjecture. The play, as we have seen, was entered on the books of the Stationers' Company on the 20th July, 1594. But the piece concludes with certain lines which fix the date in the thirty-eighth year of Queen Elizabeth's reign, which began on the 17th of November, 1595, nearly eighteen months after: —

"Lo here the end of lawless treachery,
Of usurpation, and ambitious pride!
And they that for their private amours dare
Turmoil our land, and set their broils abroach,
Let them be warnēd by these premises.
And as a woman was the only cause
That civil discord was then stirrēd up,
So let us pray for that renownēd maid
That eight-and-thirty years the sceptre swayed,
In quiet peace and sweet felicity:
And every wight that seeks her grace's smart,
Would that this sword were piercēd in his heart!"

This passage was evidently written after the entry at Stationers' Hall. It is probably the only passage in the play which has a direct political bearing on the events of the time. The allusion to Mary Stuart and her lovers is quite as obvious as that to Elizabeth. The speech is spoken by Atē, who acts as chorus throughout, and with this speech the play is concluded. But, if the reader will look to the piece itself, he will find the appropriate conclusion in the language of Guendeline, and that probably which alone was made by the author. Indeed, the conclusion thus made is singularly appropriate, and in point of style is equally excellent and Shaksperian. The language is noble, to the purpose, and the verse perfectly unexceptionable. Let the reader compare the structure of this last speech with any of the favorite passages of "Titus Andronicus;" compare it with the extravagance of most of the speeches of "Locrine" itself, to appreciate the evident improvement of the author under practice.

The lines which we have quoted are evidently an excrescence on the original production. They are not needed to the conclusion, which they absolutely cumber and impair. We have no doubt that they were written long after the play itself, and were intended for a present occasion. When Mr. Knight asserts that "the piece, if acted at all, was presented in the latter part of the year of which the first edition (that of 1595) bears the date," we are doubtful of the sources of his conclusion. If these verses only, it will suffice to take for granted that the play was *certainly* produced in the thirty-eighth year of Queen Elizabeth, possibly in the presence of the court; but how frequently before, is not concluded by the graft above quoted, which seems rudely fastened upon the tail of the piece. Its matter, certainly, is not woven in with the web, as would have been the case were the conjectures of Tieck raised upon any just foundation. But nothing can be more idle than his theory. We could scarcely conceive of a piece, presented to an English audience, so thoroughly passionate — after its own artificial style of passion — and so little given to passing politics, as this tragedy. "Locrine" was translated by Tieck into the German. He describes the piece, tolerably justly, as "bearing the marks of a young poet unacquainted with the stage, who endeavors to sustain himself constantly in a posture of elevation; who purposely (?) neglects the necessary rising and sinking of tone and effect; and who, with wonderful energy, endeavors, from beginning to end, to make his personages speak in the same highly-wrought and poetical language, while, at the same time, he shakes out all his school learning on every possible occasion." Commenting on this description, Mr. Knight remarks: "It must be evident to all our readers that these characteristics are the very reverse of Shakspeare." But this somewhat begs the question. The questions are, whether Shakspeare was not once a rude beginner — a boy — an apprentice in his art — whether his first steps were not like those of other boys, feeble and indiscreet — whether, differing from all other great writers of whom we have any precise knowledge, he at once sprang to maturity at a bound, like the armed Minerva, even from his birth, — and was the mature master-mind, at the opening, which we find him at the crowning scenes of his drama? If we are to be referred to his masterpieces, by which to determine all his performances, from the first feeble and rude beginnings of his career, whenever the crudities of these imputed dramas are under consideration, there is an end of inquiry and argument. The question is, whether these inartificial characteristics of "Locrine" — the absence of proper discrimination in tone — the neglect of a nice use of the light and shadow — a disregard to the more delicate effects arising from the softening tints — the ambitious and unnatural elevation of the dialogue, and the outshaking of all the school learning in possession of the writer, — whether these are not just as likely to have been the characteristics of the boy Shakspeare as of any other boy? — and when these are found with a real presence of poetry — a copious flow of language — a rich and generous fancy — and a frequent and curious felicity in phrase — all of which appear in "Locrine," — whether, then, the initials W. S., and the tacit assumption by the earliest editors of Shakspeare's writings, do not justify us in the ascription of this performance to his inexperienced muse? On this inquiry let us pass to other authorities. Schlegel says of "Locrine:" — "The proofs of the genuineness of this piece are not altogether unambiguous; — the grounds for doubt, on the other hand, are entitled to attention. However, this question is immediately connected with that respecting 'Titus Andronicus,' and must be, at the same time, resolved in the affirmative or negative."

Mr. Knight dissents entirely from this opinion; and, with all deference, we beg to dissent from him. He thinks the differences are as strikingly marked between "Locrine" and "Titus Andronicus," "as between 'Titus Andronicus' and 'Othello;'" a most monstrous heresy, in which, we suspect, Mr. Knight will find few readers of Shakspeare to concur. He objects to "Locrine" as a work of Shakspeare, chiefly on these grounds; namely: because the characters in "Locrine" speak rather out of books, than because of their passions; because of the large amount of classical and mythological imagery which Locrine employs; the pedantry of the author; his frequent repetition of phrases, in order to be rhetorical and forcible; and other like platitudes, which need no more particular designation. These objections are illustrated by numerous examples, and by such a studious exaggeration of the merits of "Titus Andronicus," and such an equally studied depreciation of the contrasted piece, that we are constrained to feel that the critic's ingenuity is rather too much at the expense of his ingenuousness, to suffer us to let the case go to judgment upon his showing only. While it will not be difficult to concur with Mr. Knight in much of his criticism, the points which are most essential to this question are the very ones which he seems to have considered in the spirit of a partisan. "Locrine," as a work of art, is a very crude performance. It must be considered the work, not of an artist, but an apprentice. The story is put together clumsily: the characters are not discriminated, and the attempts at the humorous are wretched in the last degree. As little may be said for the tastes and the proprieties of the piece which offend us as in "Titus Andronicus." Mr. Knight doubts if it is by a young person at all; but the very inequalities which exist in the production — the superiority of the versification — its frequent power and beauty, so singularly in contrast with the crude judgment of the writer, in all that relates to design and character, — seem to be conclusive that the author was a young beginner, fresh from his classical studies, who had scarcely yet begun to think for himself, and whose chief employment hitherto had been that naturally of all young poets — the acquisition of the arts of utterance — an acquisition which must inevitably precede the knowledge of character, and the philosophy which discriminates it happily, under the lead of experience. Such a writer will naturally elevate his school classics into undue place and inappropriate importance in connexion with labors, which, if not wholly, are in great measure foreign to his objects. We do not discover the vast dissimilarity which Mr. Knight perceives between "Locrine" and "Titus Andronicus." The latter is undoubtedly the better play. It is more decidedly a work of art. It is a great improvement, in this respect, upon "Locrine;" but, if the two plays be by the same hand, then was "Locrine" necessary, as a preparatory exercise to "Titus Andronicus." The latter has all the advantage in propriety and power. Its characterization is more perfect; its development of plan and purpose more unique and classical; and its variety of action, and its regard to cadence in the utterances, under various situations, of the persons of the drama, afford proofs of a large advance by the author of the one over the writer of the other production. But the faults of the two pieces are precisely of the same description: consisting, in excess, of bloody and brutal moods; an untamed and unmeasured ferocity; a tedious sameness of tone, unsparing resentments, and horrible purposes, which are left totally unrelieved by the redeeming interposition of softer fancies — of pity, or hope, or even love. In point of style and expression, the resemblance of faults between the two is even more decided, and the objections here, which Mr. Knight makes to "Locrine," will especially apply to the other piece. In both we have the same frequent repetition of phrase, either to intensify the sound by reiteration, or to patch out an imperfect line — the same free use of heathen mythology — and the same frequent employment of fragmentary lines of Latin, either incorporated with, or closing the paragraph. The structure of the verse of "Titus Andronicus" is singularly like that of "Locrine." They are both full and sounding, and ample always to overflow in the rhythm. The sense is usually clear and transparent, and the energy of the lines is quite remarkable, showing a strength and resource in the author, in one of the first essentials of his art, infinitely in advance of those acquisitions of knowledge and thought which can only result from constant attrition and frequent experience with the world of man. This goes to prove the immature years of the author. The inequalities which he exhibits are precisely such as mark the productions of all youthful poets of genius, showing a more perfect mastery over versification than thought — showing the utterance more malleable than the idea.

Our convictions are that "Locrine" and "Titus Andronicus" are from the same hand. No matter by whom, the former was the first written. With all its crudities, excesses, and absurdities, "Locrine" seems to us to be the legitimate sire of the other and the better play. We believe them both to be Shakspeare's, and that "Locrine" was probably his very first attempt in the tragic drama, when he may have been fifteen or sixteen years old. About the same time, he may have attempted the comic muse — may have written "The London Prodigal," "The Widow of Watling Street," and other of those puny performances, in which we see nothing but the feeble, first beginnings of one in his accidence. It is true that — mere versification alone excepted — "Locrine" exhibits few or none of those higher and finer traits of genius which prove or promise the master. It is the "'prentice han'" alone that it betrays. But the boy, even when a genius, always begins to write after a copy. He must and does usually write from books. His first years are simply years of training, in which he learns little more than the use of his tools. Rhyme and the facilities of speech are the chief objects of attainment at this period; are all that he aims at, and all that he acquires — that insensible growth of the thought alone excepted, which seldom startles by a too sudden exhibition. In his early practice at the arts of utterance, he simply repeats the sentiments and remoulds the forms set and prescribed by other hands, precisely as the schoolboy, in writing, copies after engraved copies. It is only when he becomes a sufficient master of versification, that he can possibly look into the stores of his own thought, and shape into proper language the more original ideà. It is only when his tongue becomes sufficiently freed, that he begins to speak from his own experience and heart. This is a common history. Who predicates, ordinarily, of the first exercises of the boy-poet, the heights of fame which his future wing will reach?

But "Locrine," though unworthy of the *master* Shakspeare — though decidedly inferior to "Titus Andronicus," which it most resembles — though grossly deformed by an under-current of vulgarity intended for humor, and which affords us no glimpses whatever of that ripe excellence to which we owe Sir John Falstaff and the appropriate circle which revolve around that great centre of wit and merriment — is yet not without certain merits of poetry which we should not overlook. It possesses some characteristics which remind us of Shakspeare, however faintly. We find these in the usually abrupt manner in which the persons of the drama enter upon the business of the scene; in the noble comparisons and figures which suggest themselves, as if without effort or premeditation, to the speaker; in the presence of an overflowing and exuberant imagination; in the occasional reflection which the contemplative mood acknowledges, even in the moment of action and performance; and in that genius which frequently snatches its grace beyond the reach of art, in the felicitous expression, the happy phrase, the bold figure, the delicate and unique fancy. Mr. Knight, in his hostility to this play, has been pleased to quote largely of those passages which betray the feeble hand and the crude and unenlightened taste. Many of his instances of repetition in phrase, which he assumes to have been deliberate results of judgment, are really only the makeshifts with which the inexperienced framer of blank verse patched out his halting heroics. Others are examples of bad taste and prurient metaphor. Some of these examples are chiefly reprehensible as they are detached by the critic from their appropriate connexion, and huddled, by him, into association with other similarly-conceived passages — the whole, together, forming a formidable array, which would scarcely prove so offensive, if not thus obtruded, in masses, upon the reader. As Mr. Knight has not scrupled to select the objectionable specimens, it will not be denied us the privilege of detaching a few more favorable samples from the same source, which, to us, indicate resources of fancy and power such as might well, under good training, ripen into excellence. We need not discriminate the passages we select, or specially designate in what their merit consists. We leave that to the reader. Some are given as specimens of a versification equally bold, sweet, and transparent — are samples of a dawning and vigorous fancy; others, again, commend themselves by the dignity and grace of the style and manner; and others, yet again, for that prompt entrance upon the action, with the energy of a thought already prepared for all its interests, which so remarkably distinguishes the more earnest portions of Shakspeare's writings. We proceed to our examples.

Brutus is about to die, exhausted by age. He speaks: —

——"These never-daunted arms,
That oft have quelled the courage of my foes,
Now yield to death, o'erlaid with crooked age,
Devoid of strength and of their proper force;
Even as the lusty cedar, worn with years,
That far abroad her dainty odor throws,
'Mongst all the daughters of proud Lebanon."

Estrild, the spouse of Humber, is ravished with the natural beauties of Albion: —

"The airy hills enclosed with shady groves,
The groves replenished with sweet-chirping birds,
The birds resounding heavenly melody —
Are equal to the groves of Thessaly;
Where Phœbus, with the learnēd ladies nine,
Delight themselves with music's harmony,

And, from the moisture of the mountain-tops
The silent springs dance down with murmuring streams,
And water all the ground with crystal waves.
The gentle blasts of Eurus' modest wind,
Moving the pattering leaves of Sylvan's woods,
Do equal it with Tempe's paradise;
And thus consorted all to one effect,
Do make me think these are the happy isles,
Most fortunate, if Humber may them win."

Humber, the invader, declares the sources of his hope in conquering the Trojans:—

——"Where resolution leads the way,
And courage follows with emboldened face,
Fortune can never use her tyranny!—
For valiantness is like unto a rock
That standeth on the waves of ocean,
Which, though the billows beat," &c.

Albanact is reported as approaching with a powerful army. Humber replies with promising—

——"Entertainment good enough,—
Yea, fit for those that are our enemies,
For we'll receive them at the lance's point," &c.

Hubba, the son of the invader, betrays a tone and spirit that remind us of Harry Hotspur, and the prince, his emulous rival. When told of Albanact's approach—

"*When as the morning shows his cheerful face,*
And Lucifer, mounted upon his steed,
Brings in the chariot of the golden sun,
I'll meet young Albanact in open field,
And crack my lance upon his burgonet."

Humber says:—

"Spoke like a warlike knight," &c.
"Therefore, to-morrow, ere fair Titan shine,
And bashful Eos, messenger of light,
Expels the liquid sleep from out men's eyes,
Thou shalt," &c.

The two preceding passages which we have italicized are not only beautiful in phrase, but seem to us to be full of the Shaksperian transparency and fancy.—A captain, about to impress a cobbler for the wars, finds him merrily singing at his board. The manner of the speech which he utters, pausing in the action to indulge in the reflection which the scene provokes, is also eminently that of Shakspeare:—

"The poorest state is farthest from annoy!—
How merrily he sitteth," &c.

Here follows just such a picture as Shakspeare frequently draws—in which, in the progress of the ordinary narrative, the speaker elevates into poetry his statements of the fact, by a graphic delineation of what is conspicuous in his group:—

"After we passed the groves of Caledon,
We did behold the straggling Scythians' camp,
Replete with men, stored with munition.
There might we see the valiant-minded knights
Fetching careers along the spacious plains;-
Humber and Hubba, armed in azure blue,
Mounted upon their coursers white as snow."

How well, simply, and becomingly, is the following order given!—

"Hubba, go take a cornet of our horse,
As many lancers, and light-armèd knights,
As may suffice for such an enterprise,
And place them in the grove of Caledon;
With these, when as the skirmish doth increase,
Retire thou from the shelter of the wood,
And set upon the weakened Trojans' backs;—
For policy, [when] joined with chivalry,
Can never be put back from victory."

These speeches are wholly free from stiltishness, which is the besetting infirmity of the author of "Locrine"—his wild, unpruned taste and excess of ardor usually spoiling his best passages. But such exaggerations ordinarily deform the writings of all young authors, particularly when the fancy is abundant. The *openings* of many of the speeches in "Locrine" frequently remind us of the *manner* of Shakspeare, and the *manner* is one of the most important matters in such a discussion. His hero enters upon the scene conscious fully of his situation, its exigencies, and what is due to his own character; and his speech usually begins generously and nobly. Thus Hubba, after a severe fight with Albanact, enters, exclaiming—

"How bravely this young Briton, Albanact,
Darteth abroad the thunderbolts of war," &c.

Thus, for a few lines, what is spoken is at once forcible, appropriate, and excellently given; but soon the speaker, in the very affluence of the poet, begins to multiply his images, to pile figure upon figure, and, without enlarging or advancing the idea, to cumber it with unnecessary phrases. We see, from the beginning of the speech, that the author knows what should be said in the place, but not *how* much, or in exactly what language. These are matters that experience alone can teach.—Albanact appears, fatally hurt. Here, again, is a felicitous beginning of his speech—at once opening upon the obvious point of the subject, and in appropriate language:—

"Injurious Fortune, hast thou crossed me thus?—
Thus, in the morning of my victories—
Thus, in the prime of my felicity,
To cut me off by such hard overthrow!
Hadst thou no time thy rancor to declare,
But in the spring of all my dignities?"

So far, the speech reads well. But what follows is mere raving, the result of abundant fancy in the author, as yet ungoverned by judgment and unrestrained by taste. It is in his very abundance that he wastes and impairs his possessions.—Corineius rebukes the idle sorrow that weeps for Albanact, without seeking to revenge him:—

"In vain you sorrow," &c.
"He loves not most that doth lament the most,
But he that seeks t'avenge the injury.
Think you to quell the enemy's warlike train
With childish sobs and womanish laments?
Unsheath your swords," &c.

Examples of the fancy, rising from and adorning the subject, are frequent, even in the crudest passages. Here, speaking of the resources of his province, Camber describes—

——"the fields of martial Cambria,
Close by the boisterous Iscan's silver streams,
Where lightfoot fairies skip from bank to bank,
Full," &c.

The speech of Humber at the opening of Scene 3 in Act IV., full of bombast as it is, reminds us, in one of its figures, of the famous passage in "Macbeth," where the bloody hands of the murderer promise to incarnardine the sea—

"Making the green one red."

A moment after, in a figure of vision, he sees the approaching conflict, and falsely predicts his own successes:—

"Methinks I see both armies in the field!—
The broken lances climb the crystal skies:
Some headless lie; some breathless on the ground,
And every place is strewed with carcasses!
Behold, the grass hath lost his pleasant green," &c.

The soliloquy of Hubba will not fail, in its felicity of comparison, its sweetness and force of language, and the peculiarity of some of its lines, which we have italicized, to remind the reader very sensibly of Shakspeare:—

"Let come what will, I mean to bear it out,
And either live with glorious victory,
Or die with fame renowned for chivalry!
He is not worthy of the honeycomb,
That shuns the hive because the bee hath stings!
That likes me best that is not got with ease,
Which thousand dangers do accompany:
For nothing can dismay our regal mind,
Which aims at nothing but a golden crown."

Beaten, a fugitive, and dying of famine, Humber says:

"Thou great commander of the starry sky,
That guid'st the life of every mortal wight,
From the enclosures of the fleeting clouds
Rain down some food."

There is a beauty in the following passage which, it is highly probable, did not escape the sight of Milton, who seems to have read this play with attention.—Locrine describes the secret spot where he has concealed Estrild:—

"Nigh Deucolitum, by the pleasant Lee,
Where brackish Thamis *slides with silver streams,*
Making a breach into the grassy downs,
A curious arch of costly marble wrought
Hath Locrine framèd underneath the ground;
The walls whereof, garnishèd with diamonds,
With opals, rubies, glistering emeralds,
And interlaced with sunbright carbuncles,
Lighten the room with artificial day:
And from the Lee, with water-flowing pipes
The moisture is derived into this arch,
Where I have placed fair Estrild secretly.
Thither eftsoons, accompanied by my page,
I visit covertly my heart's desire,
Without suspicion of the meanest eye,
For love aboundeth still with policy."

Of this passage Mr. Knight remarks—we need not say how unjustly—that it is the only example in the play approaching to something like natural and appropriate language. We could show many quite as appropriate and natural, and more noble. We proceed with our illustrations.—Humber, describing the terrible state in which he has lived as a fugitive, says forcibly:—

"Caves were my beds, and stones my pillow-biers,
Fear was my sleep, and horror was my dream."

Locrine, reproached with his lusts by Thrasymachus, is told—

"If princes stain their glorious dignity
With ugly spots of monstrous infamy,
They lose their former estimation,
And throw themselves into a hell of hate."

Guendeline's lament, though obscure and disfigured by instances of unformed and unlicensed taste, is not without its appropriate beauties:—

"Ye gentle winds, that, with your modest blasts,
Pass through the circuit of the heavenly vault,
Enter the clouds unto the throne of Jove,
And bear my prayer to his all-hearing ears!—
For Locrine hath forsaken Guendeline,
And learned to love proud Humber's concubine.
Ye happy sprites that, in the concave sky,
With pleasant joy, enjoy your sweetest love,
Shed forth those tears with me, which then you shed,
When first you wooed your ladies to your wills!—
Those tears are fittest for my woful case,
Since Locrine shuns my nothing-pleasant face."

The homeliness of the figure, in the hands of this author, as in those of Shakspeare, not unfrequently illustrates successfully the most elevated topic; thus:—

"Alas! my lord, the horse will run amain,
When as the spur doth gall him to the bone:
Jealousy, Locrine, hath a wicked sting."

Events in the natural world are made to shadow forth happily the crises in the affairs of man:—

"Behold, the circuit of the azure sky
Throws forth sad throbs, and grievously suspires,
Prejudicating Locrine's overthrow!"

Here follow several fragments remarkable for the freshness and felicity of phrase, warmth of fancy, and occasional stern force of the figure they exhibit. We may add, that, considered through the proper medium, they do not unfrequently or doubtfully denote that riper genius by which their crude virtues might have been rendered perfect. Detailing the evil omens that accumulate at the prospect of civil war, the ghost of Corineius tells us, among other things, of—

"The wat'ry ladies, and the lightfoot fawns,
And all the rabble of the woody nymphs,
Trembling, all hide themselves," &c.

Parting with Estrild, after his overthrow, and when about to commit suicide, Locrine speaks of her as—

——"Beauty's paragon,
Framed in the front of forlorn miseries."

Estrild, preparing to die also, says of the world:—

"What else are all things that this globe contains,
But a confusèd chaos of mishaps?
Wherein, as in a glass, we plainly see
That all our life is but a tragedy."

Thrasymachus, when he discovers the bodies of the two, exclaims—

"Nor doth thy husband, lovely Guendeline,
That wonted was to guide *our starless steps,*
Enjoy this light: see where he murdered lies!
And by him lies his lovely paramour,
Fair Estrild, gorèd with a dismal sword—
And, as it seems, both murdered by themselves,
Clasping each other in their feebled arms,
With loving zeal—as if, for [qu.: in?] company,
Their uncontented corses [ghosts?] were content
To pass foul Styx."

Without altering much of this matter, or adding much to its idea, the mature Shakspeare—the genius grown — would havè made it equally chaste, appropriate, and beautiful. — Sabren apostrophizes the —

——"Dryadés and lightfoot Satyri—
The gracious fairies, who, at eventide,
Their closets leave, with heavenly beauty stored,
And on their shoulders spread their golden locks," &c.

She says, again, failing to commit suicide ; —

"Her virgin hand too weak to penetrate
The bulwark of her breast"—

and, apostrophizing Death —

"Hard-hearted Death, that, when the wretched call,
Art farthest off, and seldom hear'st at all;
But, in the midst of Fortune's good success,
Uncallĕd comes and shears our life in twain!" —

we are reminded of Milton, who seems clearly to have imitated the passage, while improving it : —

"But the fair guerdon when we hope to find,
And think to burst out into sudden blaze,
Comes the blind Fury with the abhorred shears,
And slits the thin-spun life."

Let the reader look to the passage in the second scene of Act III., where Thrasymachus reports the defeat and death of Albanact, and observe how few and insignificant would be the alterations which are necessary to make this simple statement of facts a noble and poetical narrative of Shakspeare. Let him turn again to the opening speech of Humber, in the commencement of the second act, and note the lines of frequent beauty, and the figures at once noble and appropriate, which are found amid numerous crudities. How happily is courage counselled to perseverance by the comparison of the snail, who, feeble and crawling slowly, at length ascends the loftiest heights, scaling the walls of the stateliest castle! — and the proud boast of the Scythian emperor, that he —

"Leads Fortune tied [up] in a chain of gold,
Constraining her to yield unto his will,
And grace him with her regal diadem."

Even in the ludicrous portions of the piece, those which are mistakenly designed for the humorous, we discern glimpses of a conception, that, with a full development of the powers of expression on the part of the author, might have been reasonably expected to arrive at a birth equally legitimate and excellent. Thus, in the battle-scene where Albanact is beaten and slain, Strumbo, who is the buffoon of the piece, feigns death on the field, as Falstaff does in a like situation, in order to escape danger; and is lamented by his apprentice in a characteristic howl, which rouses the counterfeit as effectually as does the promise of Hal to have the fat knight disembowelled rouse Falstaff. In the latter instance the conception finds appropriate development, — the importance of the character concerned being duly raised, so as to interest us, even in his cowardice; — an advantage which Strumbo does not possess — to say nothing of that happy employment of language — playful, adroit, accomplished — in Falstaff, which could only have been acquired by long practice, and the experience of maturest years.

We give, in a cluster, several examples of that bold and somewhat abrupt, but truly dramatic manner of opening speech and scene, in which this play abounds, and which distinguishes the manner of Shakspeare :

"What! is the tiger started from his cave?"

Again : —

"What basilisk hath hatchĕd in this place?"

Again : —

"Was ever land so fruitless as this land?"

Again : —

"Thus, from the fury of Bellona's broils,
With sound of drum and trumpet's melody
The Britain king returns triumphantly."

The maturer writer would have said : —

"The British king triumphantly returns."

Again : —

"Now am I guarded with a host of men,
Whose haughty courage is invincible!"

Again : —

"Thus are we come, victorious conquerors,
Unto the flowing current's silver streams,
Which, in memorial of our victory,
Shall be," &c.

We finish our examples with the speech of Guendeline already referred to, and which is the proper conclusion of the drama. We have indicated this speech as an instance of transparent, dignified verse, highly appropriate to the party and the occasion, and as decidedly in Shakspeare's manner. At all events, it will not be difficult to find the strong parallelism which exists, in tone, manner, and general sentiment, between it and the closing speech in "Titus Andronicus." We place the two in opposition, that the reader may more readily judge for himself of the propriety of these comparisons between things acknowledged, as *wholes*, to be unequal : —

Guendeline. One mischief follows on another's neck!
Who would have thought so young a maid as she,
With such a courage would have sought her death?
And—for because this river was the place
Where little Sabren resolutely died—
Sabren, for ever, shall this same be called.
And, as for Locrine, our deceasĕd spouse,
Because he was the son of mighty Brute,
To whom we owe our country, lives, and goods,
He shall be buried in a stately tomb,
Close by his agĕd father Brutus' bones,
With such great pomp and great solemnity
As well beseems so brave a prince as he.
Let Estrild lie without the shallow [shadowy?] vault,
Without the honor due unto the dead,
Because she was the author of this war.
Retire, brave followers, unto Troynovant,
Where we will celebrate these exequies,
And place young Locrine in his father's tomb.

Even the topics in the speech from "Titus Andronicus" are singularly like those of the preceding. Here it follows : —

Lucius. Some loving friends convey the emperor hence,
And give him burial in his father's grave:
My father, and Lavinia, shall forthwith
Be closĕd in our household's monument.
As for that heinous tiger, Tamora,
No funeral rite, nor man in mournful weeds,
No mournful bell shall ring her burial;
But throw her forth to beasts and birds of prey:

Her life was beast-like, and devoid of pity;
And being so, shall have like want of pity.
See justice done to Aaron, that damned Moor,
By whom our heavy haps had their beginning:
Then, afterward, to order well the state;
That like events may ne'er it ruinate.

We conclude by repeating our concurrence with the German and our disagreement with the English critics. We hold this play of "Locrine" to be from the same hand with that of "Titus Andronicus," and we believe that hand to have been Shakspeare's.

Enough on this head. It now only remains to say something of the old tradition which forms the subject of "Locrine." This seems to have been a favorite one with the early poets. The story appears in the first pages of Geoffrey of Monmouth, whence it passes as an improbable legend into most of the subsequent historians. In Geoffrey of Monmouth it occupies some thirty pages. Milton, in his "History of England," condenses it sufficiently to enable us to use it here: —

"After this, Brutus, in a chosen place, builds Troja Nova, changed in time to Trinovantum, now London, and began to enact laws, Heli being then high-priest in Judea; and, having governed the whole isle twenty-four years, died, and was buried in his new Troy. His three sons, Locrine, Albanact, and Camber, divide the land by consent. Locrine has the middle part, Lœgria; Camber possessed Cambria, or Wales; Albanact, Albania, now Scotland. But he in the end, by Humber, king of the Huns, who with a fleet invaded that land, was slain in fight, and his people drove back into Lœgria. Locrine and his brother go out against Humber; who, now marching onward, was by them defeated, and in a river drowned, which to this day retains his name. Among the spoils of his camp and navy were found certain young maids, and Estrildis above the rest, passing fair, the daughter of a king in Germany; from whence Humber, as he went wasting the seacoast, had led her captive; whom Locrine, — though before contracted to the daughter of Corineus — resolves to marry. But being forced and threatened by Corineus, whose authority and power he feared, Guendolen the daughter he yields to marry, but in secret loves the other: and ofttimes retiring, as to some private sacrifice, through vaults and passages made under ground, and seven years thus enjoying her, had by her a daughter equally fair, whose name was Sabra. But when once his fear was off, by the death of Corineus, not content with secret enjoyment, divorcing Guendolen, he made Estrildis now his queen. Guendolen, all in rage, departs into Cornwall, where Madan, the son she had by Locrine, was hitherto brought up by Corineus, his grandfather; and gathering an army of her father's friends and subjects, gives battle to her husband by the river Sture; wherein Locrine, shot with an arrow, ends his life. But not so ends the fury of Guendolen; for Estrildis, and her daughter Sabra, she throws into a river: and, to leave a monument of her revenge, proclaims that the stream be thenceforth called after the damsel's name, which, by length of time, is now changed to Sabrina or Severn." — Milton uses the subject in his "Comus:" —

"There is a gentle nymph not far from hence,
That with moist curb sways the smooth Severn stream:
Sabrina is her name, a virgin pure;
Whilome she was the daughter of Locrine,
That had the sceptre from his father Brute.
She, guiltless damsel, flying the mad pursuit
Of her enragéd stepdame, Guendolen,
Commended her fair innocence to the flood,
That stayed her flight with his cross-flowing course."

It was again employed in the "Mirror of Magistrates," and by Spenser in his "Faerie Queen." Michael Drayton, in his "Polyolbion," also makes it the subject of his muse in a chant of fifty lines; and as he is a poet but little read — a sturdy native muse — who deserves more consideration than he finds, we are tempted to embrace his treatment of the story in this connexion: —

"Oh, ever-during heir
Of Sabrine, Locrine's child (who of her life bereft,
Her ever-living name to thee, fair river, left) —
Bruté's first-begotten son, whom Gwendolin did wed;
(But soon th'inconstant lord abandonéd her bed,
Through his unchaste desire for beauteous Elstred's love).
Now that which most of all her mighty heart did move,
Her father, Cornwall's duke, great Corineius dead,
Was, by the lustful king, unjustly banishéd.
When she, who, to that time, still with a smoothéd brow,
Had seemed to bear the breach of Locrine's former vow,
Perceiving still her wrongs insufferable were;
Grown big with the revenge which her full breast did bear,
And aided to the birth with every little breath —
(Alone she being left the spoil of love and death,
In labor of her grief, outrageously distract,
The utmost of her spleen on her false lord to act) —
She first implores their aid, to hate him whom she found;
Whose hearts unto the depth she had not left to sound.
To Cornwall then she sends (her country) for supplies;
Which, all at once, in arms, with Gwendolin arise.
Then with her warlike power her husband she pursued,
Whom his unlawful love too vainly did delude.
The fierce and jealous queen, then void of all remorse,
As great in power as spirit, while he neglects her force,
Him suddenly surprised, and from her ireful heart,
All pity clean exiled (whom nothing could convert),
The son of mighty Brute bereavéd of his life: —
Amongst the Britons here, the first intestine strife,
Since they were put a-land upon this promised shore.
Then crowning Madan king, whom she to Locrine bore,
And those which saved his soil to his obedience bought:
Not so with blood sufficed — immediately she sought
The mother and the child; whose beauty when she saw,
Had not her heart been flint, had had the power to draw
A spring of pitying tears; when, dropping liquid pearl
Before the cruel king, the lady and the girl
Upon their tender knees begged mercy! — Wo for thee,
Fair Elstred, that thou shouldst thy fairer Sabrine see,
As she should thee behold, the prey to her stern rage
Whom kingly Locrine's death sufficed not to assuage! —
Who from the bord'ring cliffs thee with thy mother cast
Into thy christened flood, the whilst the rocks aghast
Resounded with your shrieks; till in a deadly dream
Your corses were dissolved into that crystal stream,
Your curls to curléd waves, which plainly still appear,
The same in water now, that once in locks they were:
And as ye wont to clip each other's necks before,
Ye now, with liquid arms, embrace the wand'ring shore."

Spenser's narrative may be found in the tenth canto of his "Faerie Queen," including half a dozen stanzas from xiv. to xx. The various treatment of the subject by these several writers deserves the consideration of all those who would again employ the theme, which, by-the-way, is but little impaired by use, however frequent, for the purposes of the future dramatist.

THE TRAGEDY OF LOCRINE,

THE ELDEST SON OF KING BRUTUS.

PERSONS REPRESENTED.

TROJANS OR BRITONS.

BRUTUS, *King of* Britain.
LOCRINE, *his eldest son, and successor.*
CAMBER, ALBANACT, } *younger sons of* Brutus.
CORINEIUS, ASSARACUS, } *brothers of* Brutus.
THRASYMACHUS, *son of* Corineius.
MADAN, *son of* Locrine *and* Guendeline.
DEBON, *a veteran officer.*
STRUMBO, *a cobbler.*
TROMPART, *his apprentice.*
OLIVER, *an old man.*
WILLIAM, *his son.*
Ghosts of Albanact *and* Corineius.
Captain, Page, Soldiers, &c.

HUNS OR SCYTHIANS, OTHERWISE NORTHMEN.

HUMBER, *the Chief.*
HUBBA, *his son.*
SEGAR, THRASSIER, } *Captains.*
Soldiers, &c.

WOMEN.

GUENDELINE, *daughter of* Corineius, *and wife of* Locrine.
ESTRILD, *wife of* Humber, *and afterward mistress of* Locrine.
SABREN, *her daughter by* Locrine.
DOROTHY, MARGERY, } *wives of* Strumbo.
ATE, *as Chorus.*

ACT I.

SCENE I.—*A Forest. Thunder and Lightning.*

Enter ATE, *habited in sable, a burning torch in one hand, a bloody sword in the other. A lion then appears, pursuing a bear, which he destroys. Then follows an archer who slays the lion, and departs. After the dumb show disappears,* ATE *remains.*

In pœnam sectatur et umbra.[1]

Atë. A mighty lion, ruler of the woods,
Of wondrous strength and great proportion,
With hideous noise scaring the trembling trees,
With yelling clamors shaking all the earth,
Traversed the groves, and chased the wand'ring beasts.
Long did he range among the shady trees,
And drave the silly beasts before his face;
When, suddenly, from out a thorny bush,
A dreadful archer with his bow ybent,
Wounded the lion with a dismal shaft.—
So he him struck, that it drew forth the blood,
And filled his furious heart with fretting ire;
But all in vain he threat'neth teeth and paws,
And sparkleth fire from forth his flaming eyes,
For the sharp shaft gave him a mortal wound.
So valiant Brute, the terror of the world,
Whose only looks did scare his enemies,
The archer, Death, brought to his latest end.
Oh, what may long abide above this ground,
In state of bliss and healthful happiness! [*Exit.*

SCENE II.—*A Chamber in the Royal Palace.*

Enter BRUTUS, *carried in a chair;* LOCRINE, CAMBER, ALBANACT, CORINEIUS, GUENDELINE, ASSARACUS, DEBON, THRASYMACHUS.

Brut. Most loyal lords, and faithful followers,
That have with me, unworthy general,
Passëd the greedy gulf of the ocean,
Leaving the confines of fair Italy,—
Behold, your Brutus draweth nigh his end,
And I must leave you, though against my will.
My sinews shrink, my numbered[2] senses fail,

1 "*In pœnam sectatur et umbra.*"—"The shade or ghost pursues for punishment!" This line, though it occurs in the old copies immediately under the name of Atë, does not appear intended to form any portion of her soliloquy. A space occurs between it and the lines which follow, and leaves it standing as a sort of epigraph to the speech. The fragmentary character of the line leaves something doubtful in its sense. *Umbra,* which is ghost or shade, may be used to signify spectre or Fate; it may refer to Death, or to Atë herself; and it is possible that a vague reference may be intended to former crimes or offences of Brutus, who is thus pursued by the avenging deities. And yet the Trojan Brutus seems to have lived to be an old man.

2 The senses are numbered, it is true; but, in all probability, the author meant to say, "numbëd." The rhythm is satisfied with either word.

A chilling cold possesseth all my bones,
Black, ugly Death, with visage pale and wan,
Presents himself before my dazzled eyes,
And, with his dart, preparéd is to strike.
These arms, my lords, these never-daunted arms,
That oft have quelled the courage of my foes,
And eke dismayed my neighbor's arrogance,
Now yield to death, o'erlaid with crookéd age,
Devoid of strength and of their proper force;
Even as the lusty cedar worn with years,
That far abroad her dainty odor throws,
'Mongst all the daughters of proud Lebanon! —
This heart, my lords, this ne'er appalléd heart,
That was a terror to the bord'ring lands,
A doleful scourge unto my neighbor kings,
Now, by the weapons of impartial Death,
Is clove asunder and bereft of life;
As when the sacred oak, with thunderbolts,
Sent from the fiery circuit of the heavens,
Sliding along the air's celestial vaults,
Is rent and cloven to the very roots.
In vain, therefore, I struggle with this foe:
Then welcome death, since God will have it so.

Assar. Alas, my lord, we sorrow at your case,
And grieve to see your person vexéd thus: —
But whatsoe'er the fates determined have,
It lieth not in us to disannul;
And he that would annihilate his mind,
Soaring with Icarus too near the sun,
May catch a fall with young Bellerophon.
For when the fatal sisters have decreed
To separate us from this earthly mould,
No mortal force can countermand their minds.
Then, worthy lord, since there's no way but one,
Cease your laments, and leave your grievous moan.

Corin. Your highness knows how many victories,
How many trophies I erected have
Triumphantly in every place we came.
The Grecian monarch, warlike Pandrassus,
And all the crew of the Molossians; —
Goffarius, the strong-arméd king of Gaul; —
Have felt the force of our victorious arms,
And to their cost beheld our chivalry.
Where'er Ancora, handmaid of the sun,
Where'er the sun, bright guardian of the day,
Where'er the joyful day with cheerful light,
Where'er the light illuminates the world,
The Trojan's glory flies with golden wings; —
Wings that do soar beyond fell Envy's flight.
The fame of Brutus and his followers
Pierceth the skies, and with the skies, the throne
Of mighty Jove, commander of the world.
Then, worthy Brutus, leave these sad laments,
Comfort yourself with this your great renown,
And fear not Death, though he seem terrible.

Brutus. Nay, Corineius, you mistake my mind,
In construing wrong the cause of my complaints: —
I feared not t'yield myself to fatal Death;
God knows it was the least of all my thoughts:
A greater care torments my very bones,
And makes me tremble at the thought of it;
And, in your lordings doth the substance lie.

Thrasy. Most noble lord, if aught your loyal peers
Accomplish may, to ease your ling'ring grief,
I, in the name of all, protest to you,
That we will boldly enterprise the same,
Were it to enter to black Tartarus,
Where triple Cerberus with his venomous throat,
Scareth the ghosts with high resounding noise.
We'll either rend the bowels of the earth,
Searching the entrails of the brutish earth,
Or, with his Ixion's overdaring, soon,
Be bound in chains of ever-during steel.

Brut. Then hearken to your sovereign's latest [words,
In which I will, unto you all, unfold
Our royal mind and resolute intent.
When golden Hebe, daughter to great Jove,
Covered my manly cheeks with youthful down,
The unhappy slaughter of my luckless sire,
Drove me, and old Assarachus, mine eame,[1]
As exiles from the bounds of Italy.
So that perforce we were constrained to fly
To Grecia's monarch, noble Pandrassus.
There I, alone, did undertake your cause;
There I restored your antique liberty,
Though Grecia frowned, and all Molossia stormed —
Though brave Antigonus, with martial band,
In pitchéd field encountered me and mine —
Though Pandrassus and his contributaries,
With all the rout of their confederates,
Sought to deface our glorious memory,
And wipe the name of Trojan from the earth.
Him did I captivate with this mine arm,
And by compulsion forced him to agree
To certain articles which we did propound.
From Grecia, through the boisterous Hellespont,
We came into the fields of Lestrigon,
Whereat our brother Corineius was;
Which, when we passed the Cicilian gulf,
And so transfretting the Illician sea,
Arrivéd on the coast of Aquitain;
Where, with an army of his barbarous Gauls,
Goffarius and his brother Gathelus,
Encount'ring with our host, sustained the foil,
And, for your sakes, my Turnus there I lost:
Turnus, that slew six hundred men-at-arms,
All in an hour, with his sharp battle-axe.
From thence, upon the strands of Albion,
To Corus-haven happily we came,
And quelled the giants, come of Albion's race,
With Gogmagog, son to Samotheus,
The curséd captain of that damnéd crew,
And in that isle at length I placéd you.
Now, let me see if my laborious toils,
If all my care, if all my grievous wounds,
If all my diligence, were well employed.

Corin. When first I followed thee and thine, brave [king,
I hazarded my life and dearest blood
To purchase favor at your princely hands;
And, for the same, in dangerous attempts,
In sundry conflicts, and in divers broils,
I showed the courage of my manly mind.
For this I combated with Gathelus,
The brother to Goffarius of Gaul;
For this I fought with furious Gogmagog,
A savage captain of a savage crew;
And, for these deeds, brave Cornwall I received,
A grateful gift given by a gracious king:
And, for this gift, this life and dearest blood
Will Corineius spend for Brutus' good.

Deb. And what my friend, brave prince, hath vowed [to you,
The same will Debon do unto his end.

[1] Brother.

Brut. Then, loyal peers, since you are all agreed,
And resolute to follow Brutus' hests,[1]
Favor my sons — favor these orphans, lords,
And shield them from the dangers of their foes.
Locrine, the column of my family,
And only pillar of my weakened age —
Locrine, draw near — draw near unto thy sire,
And take thy latest blessing at his hands:
And, for thou art the eldest of my sons,
Be thou a captain to thy bretheren,
And imitate thy agèd father's steps,
Which will conduct thee to true honor's gate:
For, if thou follow sacred virtue's lore,
Thou shalt be crownèd with a laurel-branch,
And wear a wreath of sempiternal fame,
Sorted amongst the glorious, happy ones.

Loc. If Locrine do not follow your advice,
And bear himself in all things like a prince,
That seeks to amplify the great renown
Left unto him for an inheritance,
By those that were his ancestors,
Let me be flung into the ocean,
And swallowed in the bowels of the earth; —
Or, let the ruddy lightning of great Jove
Descend upon this my devoted[2] head.

Brut. [*taking* GUENDELINE *by the hand*]. But — for I see you all to be in doubt —
Who shall be matchèd with our royal son?
Locrine, receive this present at my hand:
A gift more rich than are the wealthy mines
Found in the bowels of America.[3]
Thou shalt be 'spoused to fair Guendeline:
Love her, and take her, for she is thine own,
If so thy uncle and herself do please.

Corin. And herein how your highness honors me,
It can not now be in my speech expressed;
For careful parents glory not so much
At their [own] honor and promotion,
As for to see the issue of their blood
Seated in honor and prosperity.

Guend. And far be it from my pure maiden thoughts
To contradict her agèd father's will;
Therefore, since he to whom I must obey,
Hath given me now unto your royal self,
I will not stand aloof from off the lure,
Like crafty dames that most of all deny
That which they most desire to possess.

Brut. [*to* LOCRINE, *who kneels*]. Then now, my son, thy part is on the stage,
For thou must bear the person of a king.
[*Crowns* LOCRINE.
Locrine, stand up, and wear the regal crown,
And think upon the state of majesty,
That thou with honor well may'st wear the crown;
And if thou tenderest these my latest words,
As thou requir'st my soul to be at rest,
As thou desirest thine own security,
Cherish and love thy new-betrothèd wife.

Loc. No longer let me well enjoy the crown
Than I do peerless Guendeline.

Brut. Camber!

Cam. My lord.

Brut. The glory of mine age — [the son]
And darling of thy mother Junoger —
Take thou the south for thy dominion.
From thee there shall proceed a royal race,
That shall maintain the honor of this land,
And[4] sway the regal sceptre with their hands.
[*Turning to* ALBANACT.
And Albanact, thy father's only[5] joy,
Youngest in years, but not the young'st in mind,
A perfect pattern of all chivalry,
Take thou the north for thy dominion; —
A country full of hills and ragged rocks,
Replenishèd with fierce, untamèd beasts,
As correspondent to thy martial thoughts.
Live long, my sons, with endless happiness,
And bear concordance firm among yourselves;
Obey the counsels of these fathers grave,
That you may better bear out violence!
But suddenly, through weakness of my age,
And the defect of youthful puissance,
My malady increaseth more and more,
And cruel death hasteneth his quickened pace,
To dispossess me of my earthly shape:
Mine eyes wax dim, o'ercast with clouds of age;
The pangs of death compass my crazèd bones; —
Then[6] to you all my blessings I bequeath,
And, with my blessings, this my fleeting soul.
My glass is run, and all my miseries
Do end with life. Death closeth up mine eyes,
My soul in haste flies to the Elysian fields. [*Dies.*

Loc. Accursèd stars, damned and accursèd stars,
T'abbreviate my noble father's life!
Hard-hearted gods, and [ye] too envious fates,
Thus to cut off my father's fatal thread!
Brutus, that was a glory to us all —
Brutus, that was a terror to his foes —
Alas! too soon, by Demogorgon's knife,
The martial Brutus is bereft of life.

Corin.[7] No sad complaints may move just Eacus —
No dreadful threats can fear Judge Rhadamanth.
Wert thou as strong as mighty Hercules,
That tamed the huge[st] monsters of the world —
Plead'st thou as sweet, on the sweet-sounding lute,
As did the spouse of fair Eurydice,
That did enchant the waters with his noise,
And made the stones, birds, beasts, to lead a dance,
Constrained the hilly trees to follow him —
Thou couldst not move the judge of Erebus,
Nor move compassion in grim Pluto's heart;
For fatal Mors expecteth all the world,
And every man must tread the way of death!
Brave Tantalus, the valiant Pelops' sire,
Guest to the gods, suffered untimely death;
And old Teithonus, husband to the Morn;
And eke, grim Minos, whom just Jupiter
Deigned to admit unto his sacrifice! —
The thundering trumpets of blood-thirsty Mars —

1 The old copy reads "*hosts:*" the word is unquestionably *hests*.

2 The old copy reads "devolted," which might have been revolted. *Devoted* is probably the word.

3 A correspondent hints that this must be a misprint for *Armenia*, or possibly *Armorica*. "Locrine," however, was written during Queen Elizabeth's reign, when the wealth of America, newly found, was the common talk. Our early dramatists never scrupled at an anachronism; and I have no doubt that, however improperly, *America* was the word intended.

4 "*That* sway" in the old copies.

5 Perhaps we should read *other* or *youngest* joy. We have no reason to suppose that there is any fault found with the other sons.

6 "*This* to you all," in former copies.

7 In all previous editions, this line, which evidently belongs to Corineius, is given to Locrine.

The fearful rage of fell Tisiphone —
The boist'rous waves of humid Ocean, —
Are instruments and tools of dismal Death.
Then, noble cousin, cease to mourn his chance,
Whose age and years were signs that he should die.
It resteth now that we inter his bones,
That was a terror to his enemies.
Take up his corse, and, princes, hold him dead,
Who, while he lived, upheld the Trojan state.
Sound drums and trumpets; march to Trinovant,
There to provide our chieftain's funeral.[1] [*Exeunt.*

SCENE III. — *The House of* STRUMBO, *the* Cobbler. *He appears above, in a Gown, with Ink and Paper in his hand.*

Strum. Either the four elements, the seven planets, and all the particular stars of the pole Antastic, are adversitive against me, or else I was begotten and born in the wane of the moon, when everything, as Lactantius, in his fourth *Book of Constultations*, doth say, goeth arsward. Ay, masters, ay; — you may laugh, but I must weep; you may joy, but I must sorrow: shedding salt tears from the watery fountains of my moist, dainty, fair eyes, along my comely and smooth cheeks, in as great plenty as the water runneth from the bucking-tubs, or red wine out of the hogsheads; for, trust me, gentlemen, and my very good friends, and so forth — the little god, nay, the desperate god, Cuprit, with one of his vengible birdbolts, hath shot me unto the heel; so, not only, but also, oh, fine phrase, I burn, I burn, and I burn a! — in love, in love, and in love a! — Ah, Strumbo, what hast thou seen? Not Dina with the ass, Tom? Yea, with these eyes thou hast seen her, and therefore pull them out; for they will work thy bale. Ah, Strumbo, hast thou heard the voice of the nightingale? — but a voice sweeter than hers? — yea, with these ears hast thou heard them, and therefore cut them off, for they have caused thy sorrow. Nay, Strumbo, kill thyself, drown thyself, hang thyself, starve thyself. Oh! but then I shall leave my sweetheart. Oh, my heart! Now, pate,[2] for thy master. I will 'dite an aliquant love-'pistle to her; and then she, hearing the grand verbosity of my scripture, will love me presently. [*Writes, and then reads.*] My pen is naught, gentlemen; lend me a knife. I think the more haste the worst speed. [*Writes again, and reads.*] *So it is, Mistress Dorothy, and the sole essence of my soul, that the little sparkles of affection kindled in me toward your sweet self, have now increased to a great flame, and will, ere it be long, consume my poor heart, except you, with the pleasant water of your secret fountain, quench the furious heat of the same. Alas! I am a gentleman of good fame and name; majestical; in apparel comely; in gait portly. Let not, therefore, your gentle heart be so hard as to despise a proper, tall young man of a handsome life, and, by despising him, not only but also to kill him. Thus, expecting time and tide, I bid you farewell. Your servant, Signor Strumbo.*

O, wit! O, pate! O, memory! O, hand! O, ink! O, paper! Well, now I will send it away. Trompart, Trompart! what a villain is this! Why, sirrah, come when your master calls you. Trompart!

Trom. [*entering*]. Anon, sir.

Strum. Thou knowest, my pretty boy, what a good master I have been to thee ever since I took thee into my service.

Trom. Ay, sir.

Strum. And how I have cherished thee always, as if thou hadst been the fruit of my loins, flesh of my flesh, and bone of my bone.

Trom. Ay, sir.

Strum. Then show thyself herein a trusty servant, and carry this letter to Mistress Dorothy, and tell her — [*Whispers in his ear and exit* TROMPART.

Strum. Nay, masters, you shall see a marriage by-and-by. But, here she comes. Now must I frame my amorous passions.

He descends and enter DOROTHY *and* TROMPORT.

Doro. Signor Strumbo, well met. I received your letter by your man here, who told me a pitiful story of your anguish, and so, understanding your passions were so great, I came hither speedily.

Strum. Oh, my sweet and Pigsney,[3] the fecundity of my ingeny[4] is not so great, that may declare unto you the sorrowful sobs, and broken sleeps that I [have] suffered for your sake; and therefore I desire you to receive me into your familiarity.

For your love doth lie,
As near and as nigh,
Unto my heart within,
As mine eye to my nose,
My leg unto my hose,
And my flesh unto my skin.

Dor. Truly, Master Strumbo, you speak too learnedly for me to understand the drift of your mind, and therefore tell your tale in plain terms, and leave off your dark riddles.

Strum. Alas, Mistress Dorothy, this is my luck, that when I most would, I can not be understood: so that my great learning is an inconvenience to me. But, to speak in plain terms, I love you, Mistress Dorothy, if you like to accept me into your familiarity.

Dor. If this be all, I am content.

Strum. Say'st thou so, sweet wench, let me lick thy toes. Farewell, mistress. [*To the audience.*] If any of you be in love, provide ye a cap-case[5] full of new coined words, and then shall you soon have the *succado de labres*,[6] and something else. [*Exeunt.*

SCENE IV.—*An Apartment in the Palace.*

Enter LOCRINE, GUENDELINE, CAMBER, ALBANACT, CORINEIUS, ASSARACHUS, DEBON, THRASYMACHUS.

Loc. Uncle and princes of brave Britany,
Since that our noble father is entombed,

[1] The traditional history of Brutus is abridged by Milton in his "History of England." He says: "After this, Brutus, in a chosen place, built Troja Nova, changed in time to Trinovantum, now London, and began to enact laws, Heli being then high-priest in Judea; and having governed the whole isle twenty-four years, died, and was buried in his new Troy. His three sons, Locrine, Albanact, and Camber, divided the land by consent. Locrine has the middle part, Lœgria; Camber possesses Cambria, or Wales; Albanact, Albania, now Scotland," &c.

[2] Scratching his head.

[3] Some ridiculous diminutive, signifying tenderness.

[4] It is scarcely necessary to seek a meaning for this perverse nonsense, but Strumbo would seem to say that his genius is not so fecund as to enable him to say how much he had suffered.

[5] The printers say, "a case of caps," "small caps," &c. A case of caps of new-coined words, might almost be taken from the printing-office.

[6] Sweet smack of the lips.

As best beseemed so brave a prince as he,
If so you please, this day, my love and I,
Within the temple of Concordia,
Will solemnize our royal marriage.
Thrasy. Right noble lord, your subjects every one,
Must needs obey your highness at command,
Especially in such a cause as this,
That much concerns your highness' great content.
Loc. Then frolic, lordings, to fair Concord's walls,
Where we will pass the day in knightly sports,
The night in dancing and in figured masks,
And offer to God, Risus, all our sports. [*Exeunt.*

ACT II.

SCENE I.

Enter ATE, *as before. Thunder and lightning, then a mask:* PERSEUS *and* ANDROMEDA, *hand in hand, and* CEPHEUS *with swords and targets. Then opposite,* PHINEUS, *all black in armor, with* Ethiopians *after him, driving in* PERSEUS, *and taking away* ANDROMEDA. *Then all depart but* ATE.

Regit omnia numen.[1]

Atê. When Perseus married fair Andromeda,
The only daughter of King Cepheus,
He thought he had established well his crown,
And that his kingdom should for aye endure.
But lo! proud Phineus, with a band of men,
Composed[2] of sun-burned Ethiopians,
By force of arms, the bride he took from him,
And turned their joy into a flood of tears!
So fares it with young Locrine and his love;—
He thinks this marriage tendeth to his weal,
But this foul day, this foul accursèd day,
Is the beginning of his miseries.
Behold, where Humber and his Scythians
Approacheth nigh with all his warlike train!—
It needs not, I, the sequel should declare,[3]
What tragic chances fell out in this war. [*Exit.*

SCENE II.—*The Seacoast of* Britain.

Enter HUMBER, HUBBA, ESTRILD, SEGAR, *and their* Soldiers.

Hum. At length the snail doth climb the highest tops,
Ascending up the stateliest castle walls;—
At length the water, with continual drops,
Doth penetrate the hardest marble stone;—
At length we are arrived in Albion,—
Nor could the barbarous Dacian's sovereign,
Nor yet the ruler of brave Belgia,
Stay us from cutting over to this isle!—
Whereas I hear, a troop of Phrygians,
Under the conduct of Posthumius' son,
Have pitchèd up lordly pavilions,
And hope to prosper in this lovely isle:
But I will frustrate all their foolish hopes,
And teach them that the Scythian emperor
Leads Fortune tied in a chain of gold,
Constraining her to yield unto his will,
And grace him with her regal diadem:
Which I will have, maugre their treble hosts,
And all the power their petty kings can make.
Hub. If she that rules fair Rhamnis' golden gate,
Grant us the honor of the victory,
As hitherto she always favored us,
Right noble father, we will rule the land,
Enthronizèd in seats of topaz stones,
That Locrine and his brethren all may know,
None must be king but Humber and his son.
Hum. Courage, my son;—fortune shall favor us,
And yield to us the coronet of bays,
That decketh none but noble conquerors!—
But what saith Estrild[4] to these regions?
How liketh she the temperature thereof?
Are they not pleasant in her gracious eyes?
Est. The plains, my lord, garnished with Flora's wealth,
And overspread with parti-colored flowers,
Do yield sweet contentation to my mind;—
The airy hills, enclosed with shady groves,—
The groves replenished with sweet chirping birds,—
The birds resounding heavenly melody,—
Are equal to the groves of Thessaly,
Where Phœbus, and those learned ladies, nine,
Delight themselves with music's harmony,
And, from the moisture of the mountain tops,
The silent springs dance down with murmuring streams,
And water all the ground with crystal waves!—
The gentle blasts of Eurus' modest wind,
Moving the fluttering[5] leaves of Sylvan's woods,
Do equal it with Tempe's paradise,
And thus consorted[6] all to one effect,
Do make me think these are the happy isles!—
Most fortunate if Humber may them win.
Hub. Madam, where resolution leads the way,
And courage follows with emboldened pace,
Fortune can never use her tyranny!—
For valiantness is like unto a rock
That standeth on the waves of ocean,
Which, though the billows beat on every side,
And Boreas fell, with his tempestuous storms,
Bloweth upon it with a hideous clamor,
Yet it remaineth still immoveable.
Hum. Kingly resolved, thou glory of thy sire!—
But, worthy Segar, what uncouth novelties[7]
Bring'st thou unto our royal majesty?
Seg. My lord, the youngest of all Brutus' sons,
Stout Albanact, with millions of men,
Approacheth nigh, and meaneth, ere the morn,
To try your force by dint of fatal sword.
Hum. Tut!—let him come with millions of hosts,
He shall find entertainment good enough,
Yea, fit for those that are our enemies:
For we'll receive them at our lances' points,
And massacre their bodies with our blades.
Yea, though they were in number infinite,
More than the mighty Babylonian queen,

1 "*Regit omnia numen.*"—"The Divinity [Fate] rules all things." We repeat the note here which occurs at the opening of the first act. The Latin epigraph may or may not belong to the speech of Atê. It would seem needless to be spoken in her case.
2 "*Contrived,*" in the original.
3 In the old copies this line runs thus:—
"I need not I, the sequel shall declare."

4 This name is printed in the old copies sometimes as we have here written, and sometimes *Elstrid.* We shall make it uniform throughout.
5 "*Pittering*" in the old copy. It might be "pattering," but "fluttering" seems most appropriate.
6 "*Comforted*" in the original. The correction is found in Rowe's edition.
7 Uncourtly news—which would better suit the rhythm.

Semiramis, the ruler of the west,
Brought 'gainst the emperor of the Scythians,
Yet would we not start back one foot from them:
That they might know we are invincible.

Hub. Now, by great Jove, the supreme king of [heaven,
And the immortal gods that live therein,
When, as the morning shows his cheerful face,
And Lucifer, mounted upon his steed,
Brings in the chariot of the golden sun,
I'll meet young Albanact in open field,
And crack my lance upon his burgonet,
To try the valor of his boyish strength! —
There will I show such rueful spectacles
And cause so great effusion of blood,
That all his boys shall wonder at my strength! —
As when the warlike queen of Amazon,
Penthesilea, arméd with her lance,
Girt with a corslet of bright-shining steel,
Cooped up the faint-heart Grecians in their camp.

Hum. Spoke like a warlike knight, my noble son;
Nay, like a prince that seeks his father's joy.
Therefore, to-morrow, ere fair Titan shine,
And bashful Eos messenger of light,
Expels the liquid sleep from out men's eyes,
Thou shalt conduct the right wing of the host; —
The left wing shall be under Segar's charge,
The rearward shall be under me, myself;
And lovely Estrild, fair and gracious,
If Fortune favor me in mine attempt,
Thou shalt be queen of lovely Albion.
Fortune *shall* favor me in mine attempt,
And *make* thee queen of lovely Albion.
Come, let us in, and muster up our train,
And furnish up our lusty soldiers,
That they may be a bulwark to our state,
And bring our wishéd joys to perfect end. [*Exeunt.*

SCENE III. — *The Cobler's Stall of* STRUMBO.

STRUMBO, DOROTHY, *and* TROMPART, *at work, and singing.*

Trom. We coblers lead a merry life:
Chorus. Dan, dan, dan, dan.
Strum. Void of all envy and strife:
Chorus. Dan, diddle dan.[1]
Dor. Our ease is great, our labor small;
Strum. And yet our gains be much, withal:
Dor. With this art so fine and fair, —
Trom. No occupation may compare:
Strum. For merry pastime and joyful glee, —
Dor. Most happy men we coblers be:
Trom. The can stands full of nappy ale,
Strum. In our shop still, withouten fail:
Dor. This is our meat, this is our food; —
Trom. This brings us to a merry mood:
Strum. This makes us work for company:
Dor. To pull the tankards cheerfully:
Trom. Drink to thy husband, Dorothy.
Dor. Why then, my Strumbo, here's to thee:
Strum. Drink thou the rest, Trompart, amain:
Dor. When that is gone, we'll fill't again:
Chorus. Dan diddle dan.

Enter Captain.

Capt. The poorest state is farthest from annoy!
How merrily he sitteth on his stool; —
But when he sees that needs he must be pressed,
He'll turn his note and sing another tune.
Ho, by your leave, master cobler.

Strum. You are welcome, gentleman. What will you? Any old shoes or buskins; or will you have your shoes clouted? I will do them as well as any cobler in Cathnes whatsoever.

Capt. [*showing him press-money*]. O, master cobler, you are far deceived in me; for, do you see this? I come not to buy any shoes, but to buy yourself. Come, sir, you must be a soldier in the king's cause.

Strum. Why, but hear you, sir! — Has your king any commission to take any man against his will? I promise you, I can scant[2] believe it; — or did he give you commission?

Capt. Oh, sir, you need not care for that. I need no commission. Hold here, I command you, in the name of our king Albanact, to appear to-morrow in the townhouse of Cathnes.

Strum. King Nactabell! — I cry God mercy! — what have we to do with him, or he with us? But you, sir, Master Capontail, draw your pasteboard, or else I promise you I'll give you a canvasado, with a bastinado over your shoulders, and teach you to come hither with your implements!

Capt. I pray thee, good fellow, be content. I do the king's command.

Strum. Put me out of your book, then.

Capt. I may not. [STRUMBO *snatching up a staff.*] No! wilt come, sir? Will your stomach serve you? By Gog's blewhood and halidom, I will have a bout with you. [*They fight.*

Enter THRASYMACHUS.

Thrasy. How now? what noise, what sudden clamor's this?
My captain and the cobbler hard at fight?
Sirs, what's your quarrel?

Capt. Nothing, sir, but that he will not take press-money.

Thrasy. Here, good fellow, take it at my command,
Unless you mean to be stretched.

Strum. Truly, master gentleman, I lack no money. If you please, I will resign it to one of these poor fellows.

Thrasy. No such matter:
Look, you be at the common-house to-morrow.
[*Exeunt* THRASYMACHUS *and the* Captain.

Strum. O wife, I have spun a fair thread. If I had been quiet, I had not been pressed, and therefore well may I lament. But come, sirrah, shut up, for we must to the wars. [*Exeunt.*

SCENE IV. — *The Camp of* ALBANACT.

Enter ALBANACT, DEBON, THRASYMACHUS, *and other* Lords.

Alb. Brave cavaliers, princes of Albany,
Whose trenchant blades, with our deceaséd sire,
Passing the frontiers of brave Grecia,
Were bathéd in our enemies' lukewarm blood,
Now is the time to manifest your will,
Your haughty minds and resolutions!
Now opportunity is offeréd

1 Each line is followed by the chorus, as the first two. We omit them, as the monotonous recurrence of "Dan, dan, diddle dan," sung or unsung, would only fatigue.

2 *Scant*—scarce.

To try your courage and your earnest zeal,
Which you always professed[1] to Albanact;
For, at this time, yea, at this present time,
Stout fugitives, come from the Scythian's bounds,
Have pestered every place with mutinies:
But trust me, lordings, I will never cease
To persecute the rascal runagates,
Till all the rivers, stainèd with their blood,
Shall fully show their fatal overthrow.

Deb. So shall your highness merit great renown,
And imitate your agèd father's steps.

Alb. But tell me, cousin, cam'st thou through the plains,
And saw'st thou there the faint-heart fugitives
Mustering their weather-beaten soldiers?
What order keep they in their marshalling?

Thrasy. After we passed the groves of Caledon,
We did behold the straggling Scythians' camp,
Replete with men, stored with munition.
There might we see the valiant-minded knights
Fetching careers[2] along the spacious plains;—
Humber and Hubba, armed in azure blue,
Mounted upon their coursers white as snow,
Went to behold the pleasant flow'ring fields;—
Hector and Troilus, Priam's lovely sons,
Chasing the Grecians over Simoeis,
Were not to be compared to these two knights.

Alb. Well hast thou painted out, in eloquence,
The portraiture of Humber and his son;—
As fortunate as was Polycrates:
Yet should they not escape our conquering swords,
Or boast of aught but of our clemency.

[*Cries without.*]—*Enter* STRUMBO *and* TROMPART.

Strum. and Trom. Wildfire and pitch, wildfire and pitch!

Thrasy. What, sirs!—what mean you by these clamors made—
These outcries raisèd in our stately court?

Strum. Wildfire and pitch, wildfire and pitch!

Thrasy. Villains! I say, tell us the cause hereof.

Strum. Wildfire and pitch, wildfire and pitch!

Thrasy. Tell me, you villains, why you make this noise,
Or, with my lance, I'll prick your bowels out.

All. Where are your houses, where's your dwelling-place?

Strum. Place? ha, ha, ha! laugh a month and a day at him. Place! I cry God mercy! why, do you think that such poor, honest men as we be, hold our habitacles in kings' palaces? Ha, ha, ha! But, because you seem to be an abominable chieftain, I will tell you our state[3]—

From the top to the toe,
From the head to the shoe;
From the beginning to the ending,
From the building to the burning.

This honest fellow and I had our mansion-cottage in the suburbs of this city, hard by the temple of Mercury; and [these], by the common soldiers of the ———,[4] the Scythians—what do you call them?—with all the suburbs, were burnt to the ground, and the ashes are left there for the country wives to wash bucks withal.

And that which grieves me most,
My loving wife, O cruel strife!
The wicked flames did roast.
And therefore, Captain Crust,
We will continually cry,
Except you seek a remedy
Our houses to re-edify,
Which now are burnt to dust!

Both cry. Wildfire and pitch, wildfire and pitch!

Alb. Well, we must remedy these outrages,
And throw revenge upon their hateful heads:
And you, good fellows, for your houses burnt,
We will remunerate you store of gold,
And build your houses by our palace-gate.

Strum. Gate? O, petty treason to my person! nowhere else but by your backside? Gate? oh how I am vexed in my choler! Gate? I cry God mercy, do you hear, master king? If you mean to gratify such poor men as we be, you must build our houses by the tavern.

Alb. It shall be done, sir.

Strum. Near the tavern! ay, by'r lady, sir, it was spoken like a good fellow. Do you hear, sir? when our house is builded, if you do chance to pass or repass that way, we will bestow a quart of the best wine upon you. [*Exit.*

Alb. It grieves me, lordings, that my subjects' goods
Should thus be spoilèd by the Scythians,
Who, as you see, with lightfoot foragers
Depopulate the places where they come.
But, cursèd Humber, thou shalt rue the day
That e'er thou cam'st unto Cathnesia! [*Exeunt.*

SCENE V.—*The Camp of* HUMBER.

Enter HUMBER, HUBBA, SEGAR, THRASSIER, *and* Soldiers.

Hum. Hubba, go take a cornet of our horse,
As many lancers, and light-armèd knights,
As may suffice for such an enterprise,
And place them in the grove of Caledon;
With these, when as the skirmish doth increase,
Retire thou from the shelter of the wood,
And set upon the weakened Trojans' backs;—
For policy, [when] joined with chivalry,
Can never be put back from victory. [*Exit* HUBBA.

Enter ALBANACT, *with his* Militia.

Alb. Thou base-born Hun, how durst thou be so bold
As thus[5] to menace warlike Albanact,
The great commander of these regions?
But thou shalt buy thy rashness with thy death,
And rue too late thy over-bold attempts;
For, with this sword, this instrument of death,
That hath been drenchèd in my foemen's blood,
I'll separate thy body from thy head,
And set that coward blood of thine abroach.

Strum. Nay, with this staff, great Strumbo's instrument,
I'll crack thy cock's-comb, paltry Scythian!

Hum. Nor reck I of thy threats, thou princox boy,
Nor do I fear thy foolish insolency;
And, but thou better use thy bragging blade

1 "*Protest*" in the folio.
2 "*Carriers*" in the old copy.
3 "*Your state*" in the folio.
4 I have here suppressed a vulgarity.
5 "*Once*" in the folio.

Than thou dost rule thy overflowing tongue,
Superbious Briton, thou shalt know too soon
The force of Humber and his Scythians. [*They fight.*
HUMBER and his troops are driven in.

Strum. O, horrible! O, terrible! [*Exeunt.*

SCENE VI.—*Another part of the Field of Battle.*

Alarums. Enter HUMBER *and his* Soldiers.

Hum. How bravely this young Briton, Albanact,
Darteth abroad the thunderbolts of war!
Beating down millions with his furious mood,
And in his glory triumphs over all,
Moving the massy squadrons off the ground!
Heap hills on hills, to scale the starry sky!—
As when Briareus, armed with hundred hands,
Flung forth a hundred mountains at great Jove;
As when the monstrous giant Monichus
Hurled Mount Olympus at great Mars' targe,
And shot huge cedars at Minerva's shield!
How doth he overlook, with haughty front,
My fleeting host, and lifts his lofty face
Against us all, that now do fear his force—
Like as we see the wrathful sea from far,
In a great mountain heap[1] with hideous noise,
With thousand billows, beats against the ships,
And toss them in the waves like tennis-balls!
[*Alarums.*
Ah me! I fear my Hubba is surprised!
[*Exit* HUMBER.

Alarums. Enter ALBANACT.

Alb Follow me, soldiers, follow Albanact:
Pursue the Scythians, flying through the field;
Let none of them escape with victory!
That they may know the Briton's force is more
Than is the power of all the trembling Huns.

Thrasy. Forward, brave soldiers, forward! keep the chase!
He that takes captive Humber, or his son,
Shall be rewarded with a crown of gold. [*Exeunt.*

SCENE VII.—*Another part of the Field.*

Alarums. Enter HUMBER, *pursued by* DEBON. HUBBA *enters behind, kills* DEBON, *and exit.* STRUMBO *falls, pretending to be slain. Enter* ALBANACT, *wounded.*

Alb. Injurious fortune, hast thou crossed me thus?
Thus, in the morning of my victories—
Thus, in the prime of my felicity,
To cut me off by such hard overthrow!
Hadst thou no time thy rancor to declare,
But in the spring of all my dignities?
Hadst thou no place to spit thy venom out,
But on the person of young Albanact?
I, that erewhile did scare mine enemies,
And drove them almost to a shameful flight;
I, that erewhile, full lion-like did fare
Amongst the dangers of the thick-thronged pikes—
Must now depart, most lamentably slain
By Humber's treacheries and Fortune's spites!
Cursed be her charms, damned be her cursèd charms,
That doth delude the wayward hearts of men—
Of men that trust unto her fickle wheel,
Which never leaveth turning upside down!

1 "*Heap't*" in former copies.

O gods! O heavens! allot me but the place
Where I may find her hateful mansion.
I'll pass the Alps to watery Meroe,
Where fiery Phœbus in his chariot,
The wheels whereof are decked with emeralds,
Casts such a heat, yea, such a scorching heat,
As spoileth Flora of her chequered grass!—
I'll overturn the mountain Caucasus,
Where fell Chimera, in her triple shape,
Rolleth hot flames from out her monstrous paunch,
Scaring the beasts with issue of her gorge!—
I'll pass the frozen zone, where icy flakes,
Stopping the passage of the fleeting ships,
Do lie, like mountains, in the congealed sea!—
Where, if I find that hateful house of hers,
I'll pull the fickle wheel from out her hands,
And tie herself in everlasting bands!
But all in vain I breathe these threatenings:
The day is lost; the Huns are conquerors;
Debon is slain; my men are done to death;
The currents swift swim violent with blood;
And last—O, that this last night so long last!—
Myself, with wounds past all recovery,
Must leave my crown for Humber to possess. [*Falls*

Strum. Lord have mercy upon us, masters! I think this is a holyday: every man lies sleeping in the fields; but, God knows, full sore against their wills.

Enter THRASYMACHUS.

Thrasy. Fly, noble Albanact, and save thyself!
The Scythians follow with great celerity,
And there's no way but flight, or speedy death;
Fly, noble Albanact, and save thyself. [*Alarums.*

Alb. Nay, let them fly that fear to die the death,
That tremble at the name of fatal Mors:
Ne'er shall proud Humber boast or brag himself
That he hath put young Albanact to flight;
And lest he should triumph at my decay,
This sword shall 'reave his master of his life,
That oft hath saved his master's doubtful life!
But oh! my brethren, if you care for me,
Revenge my death upon his traitorous head.
Et vos queis domus est nigrantis regia ditis,
Qui regitis rigido Stygios moderamine lucos;
Nox cæci regina poli, furialis Erinnys,
Diique deæque omnes Albanum tollite regem,
Tollite flumineis undis rigidaque palude;
Nunc me fata vocant, hoc condam pectore ferrum.[2]
[*Stabs himself.*[3]

2 There is certainly great dignity in thus dying with one's mouth full of Latin hexameters. These verses are probably original with the author, and if the play be Shakspeare's, will certainly justify the claim of Ben Jonson of a "little Latin" in his behalf. The reader may be curious to see King Albanact's speech in the vernacular. A learned friend, to whom the Latin verses of this play were all submitted, if possible for verification with those of known classical authors, suggests, that, as we do not hear of Stygian *groves* in our mythology, we should probably read, for "*lucos,*" in the second line, *lacos*:—but the banks of the Stygian lake may have had their woods, and I prefer that the word should stand as in the old folio. Our rendering is almost literal:—

"And you who sway in Pluto's royal house,
And govern with stern power the Stygian realms,
Night, queen of cloudy heavens—thou fearful fury,
And you, ye gods and goddesses, receive
The Alban sovereign to your gloomy lake
And ever-flowing streams!—The summoning fates
Decree, and through this bosom goes the sword."

3 Milton's history of the defeat of Albanact is as follows: "He [Albanact], in the end, by Humber, king of the Huns, who with a fleet invaded that land [Scotland—Albania], was slain in fight, and his people drove back into Lœgria."

Enter TROMPART, *who sees* STRUMBO.

Trom. Oh! what hath he done? his nose bleeds: but I smell a fox; look where my master lies. Master, master!

Strum. Let me alone, I tell thee, for I'm dead.
Trom. Yet one word, good master.
Strum. I will not speak, for I am dead, I tell thee.
Trom. And is my master dead?
O, sticks and stones, brickbats and bones,
And is my master dead?
O you cockatrices, and you bablatrices,
That in the woods dwell;
You briers and brambles, you cook-shops and shambles,
Come, howl and yell!
With howling and shrieking, with wailing and weeping,
Come you, lament;
O colliers of Croyden, and rustics of Royden,
And fishers of Kent;—
For Strumbo the cobbler, the fine, merry cobbler,
Of Cathnes town,
At this same stour, at this very hour,
Lies dead on the ground!
O, master! thieves, thieves, thieves!

Strum. Where be they? Cox me tunny, bobekin, let me be rising. Be gone; we shall be robbed by-and-by. [*They run off.*

SCENE VIII.—*The Camp of the* Huns.

Enter HUMBER, HUBBA, SEGAR, THRASSIER, ESTRILD, *and* Soldiers.

Hum. Thus, from the dreadful shocks of furious Mars'
Thund'ring alarums, and Rhamnusia's drum,
We are retired with joyful victory.
The slaughtered Trojans, weltering[1] in their blood,
Infect the air with their [dead] carcasses,
And are a prey for every ravenous bird.
Est. So perish they that are our enemies!
So perish they that love not Humber's weal!—
And, mighty Jove, commander of the world,
Protect my love from all false treacheries.
Hum. Thanks, lovely Estrild, solace to my soul!
But, valiant Hubba, for thy chivalry
Declared against the men of Albany,
Lo!—here a flowering garland wreathed of bay,
As a reward for this thy forward mind!
[*Crowns* HUBBA.
Hub. This unexpected honor, noble sire,
Will prick my courage unto braver deeds,
And cause me to attempt such hard exploits,
That all the world shall sound of Hubba's name.
Hum. And now, brave soldiers, for this good success,
Carouse whole cups of Amazonian wine,[2]
Sweeter than nectar or ambrosia;
And cast away the clouds of cursèd care
With goblets crowned with Semeleius' gifts!—
Now let us march to Abis' silver streams,
That clearly glide along the champaign fields,
And moist the grassy meads with humid drops.
Sound drums and trumpets—sound up cheerfully,
Sith we return with joy and victory. [*Exeunt.*

[1] I have substituted *weltering* for "*squeltering*," the word employed in the old copies, and in its day quite legitimate, but having the same meaning with the modern word.

[2] It is difficult to say what sort of beverage this could have been. From its name it should unite the virtues of both sexes, the strength of the one with the sweetness of the other: a good name for a drink.

ACT III.

SCENE I.

Enter ATE, *as before. A dumb Show. A Crocodile lies on a River's Bank; a little Snake stings it, and both fall into the Water.*

Atè. Scelera in authorem cadunt.[3]
High on a bank by Nilus' boisterous[4] streams,
Fearfully sat the Egyptian crocodile,
Dreadfully grinding, in her sharp long teeth,
The broken bowels of a silly fish:
His back was armed against the dint of spear,
With shields of brass that shone like burnished gold;
And, as he stretchèd forth his cruel paws,
A subtle adder, creeping closely near,
Thrusting his forkèd tongue into his claws,
Privily shed his poison through his bones,
Which made him swell, that there his bowels burst
That did so much in his own greatness trust.
So Humber, having conquered Albanact,
Doth yield his glory unto Locrine's sword.
Mark what ensues, and you may eas'ly see
That all our life is but a tragedy. [*Exit.*

SCENE II.—Troynovant. *An Apartment in the Royal Palace.*

Enter LOCRINE, GUENDELINE, CORINEIUS, ASSARACUS, THRASYMACHUS, *and* CAMBER.

Loc. And is this true? is Albanactus slain?
Hath cursèd Humber, with his straggling host—
With that his army made of mongrel curs—
Brought our redoubted brother to his end?
O, that I had the Thracian Orpheus' harp,
For to awake, out of the infernal shade,
Those ugly devils of black Erebus
That might torment the damnèd traitor's soul!
O, that I had Amphion's instrument,
To quicken, with his vital notes and tunes,
The flinty joints of every stony rock,
By which the Scythians might be punishèd!
For, by the lightning of Almighty Jove,
The Hun shall die had he ten thousand lives!
And, would to God he had ten thousand lives,
That I might, with the arm-strong Hercules,
Crop off so vile a hydra's hissing heads!
But, say, my cousin, for I long to hear,
How Albanact came by untimely death?
Thrasy. After the traitorous host of Scythians
Entered the field with martial equipage,
Young Albanact, impatient of delay,
Led forth his army 'gainst the straggling mates,
Whose multitude did daunt our soldiers' minds.
Yet nothing could dismay the froward prince;
Who,[5] with a courage most heroical,
Like to a lion 'mongst a flock of lambs,
Made havoc of the faint-heart fugitives,
Hewing a passage through them with his sword!

[3] "*Scelera in authorem cadunt.*"—The author, or doer, is responsible, or answerable, for the crime or deed. In imitable blank verse:—

"The criminal must answer for his crime!"

It will be observed that here the printer has made the vertigraph a part of the speech of Atè.

[4] The epithet here is better suited to the rhythm than the river.

[5] I substitute *who* for "but," which is the word in previous editions.

Yea, we had almost given them the repulse,
When suddenly, from out the silent wood,
Hubba, with twenty thousand soldiers,
Cowardly came upon our weakened backs,
And murdered all with fatal massacre;
Amongst the which, old Debon, martial knight,
With many wounds was brought unto the death;
And Albanact, oppressed with multitudes,
Whilst valiantly he felled his enemies,
Yielded his life and honor to the dust.
He being dead, the soldiers fled amain,
And I alone escapéd them by flight,
To bring you tidings of these accidents.

Loc. Not agéd Priam, king of stately Troy,
Grand emperor of barbarous Asia,
When he beheld his noble-minded sons
Slain trait'rously by all the myrmidons,
Lamented more than I for Albanact.

Guend. Not Hecuba, the queen of Ilium,
When she beheld the town of Pergamus,
Her palace, burnt with all-devouring flames,
Her fifty sons and daughters, fresh of hue,
Murdered by wicked Pyrrhus' bloody sword,
Shed such sad tears as I for Albanact.

Cam. The grief of Niobe, fair Athens' queen,
For her seven sons magnanimous in field,
For her seven daughters fairer than the fair'st,
Is not to be compared with my laments.

Cor. In vain you sorrow for the slaughtered prince,
In vain you sorrow for his overthrow;
He loves not most that doth lament the most,
But he that seeks t'avenge the injury.
Think you to quell the enemy's warlike train
With childish sobs and womanish laments?
Unsheath your swords, unsheath your conquering swords,
And seek revenge, the comfort for this sore!
In Cornwall, where I hold my regiment,
Even just ten thousand valiant men-at-arms,
Hath Corineius ready at command!—
All these, and more, if need shall more require,
Hath Corineius ready at command.

Cam. And, in the fields of martial Cambria,
Close by the boisterous Iscan's silver streams,
Where lightfoot fairies skip from bank to bank,
Full twenty thousand brave, courageous knights,
Well exercised in feats of chivalry,
In manly manner most invincible,
Young Camber hath, with gold and victual:
All these, and more, if need shall more require,
I offer up t'avenge my brother's death.

Loc. Thanks, loving uncle, and good brother too:
For this revenge—for this sweet word revenge—
Must ease and cease my wrongful injuries;
And, by the sword of bloody Mars, I swear,
Ne'er shall sweet quiet enter this my front,[1]
Till I be 'vengéd on his trait'rous head
That slew my noble brother Albanact.
Sound drums and trumpets; muster up the camp;—
For we will straight march to Albania. [*Exeunt.*

SCENE III.—*The Banks of the River, afterward the* Humber.

Enter HUMBER, ESTRILD, HUBBA, THRASSIER, *and* Soldiers.

Hum. Thus are we come, victorious conquerors,
Unto the flowing current's silver streams—
Which, in memorial of our victory,
Shall be agnominated by our name,
And talkéd of by our posterity!—
For sure, I hope, before the golden Sun
Posteth his horses to fair Thetis' plains,
To see the water turnéd into blood,
Changing his bluish hue to rueful red,
By reason of the fatal massacre
Which shall be made upon the virent plains.

The Ghost *of* ALBANACT *enters, and stretches his Arm over* HUMBER.

Ghost. See how the traitor doth presage his harm.
See how he glories at his own decay!—
See how he triumphs at his proper loss!—
O Fortune, vile, unstable, fickle, frail!

Hum. Methinks I see both armies in the field!
The broken lances climb the crystal skies:
Some headless lie; some breathless on the ground;
And every place is strewed with carcasses.—
Behold, the grass hath lost his pleasant green,
The sweetest sight that ever might be seen.

Ghost. Ay, traitorous Humber, thou shalt find it so;
Yea, to thy cost, thou shalt the same behold,
With anguish, sorrow, and with sad laments.
The grassy plains, that now do please thine eyes,
Shall, ere the night, be colored all with blood;
The shady groves that now enclose thy camp,
And yield sweet savor to thy damnéd corps,[2]
Shall, ere the night, be figured all with blood!—
The profound stream that passeth by thy tents,
And with his moisture serveth all thy camp,
Shall, ere the night, converted be to blood—
Yea, with the blood of these thy straggling boys:
For now revenge shall ease my lingering grief,
And now revenge shall glut my longing soul. [Ghost *disappears.*

Hub. Let come what will, I mean to bear it out,
And either live with glorious victory,
Or die with fame renowned for chivalry!
He is not worthy of the honeycomb,
That shuns the hive because the bees have stings!
That likes me best that is not got with ease,
Which thousand dangers do accompany;
For nothing can dismay our regal mind,
Which aims at nothing but a golden crown,
The only upshot of mine enterprise.
Were it enchanted in grim Pluto's court,
And kept for treasure 'mongst his hellish crew,
I'd either quell the triple Cerberus,
And all the army of his hateful hags,
Or roll the stone with wretched Sysiphus.

Hum. Right martial be thy thoughts, my noble son,
And all thy words savor of chivalry!—

Enter SEGAR, *in haste.*

But, warlike Segar, what strange accidents
Make you to leave the warding of the camp?

Seg. To arms, my lords, to honorable arms!—
Take helm and targe in hand;—the Britons come,
With greater multitude than erst the Greeks
Brought to the ports of Phrygian Tenedos.

Hum. But what sayeth Segar to these accidents?
What counsel gives he in extremities?

1 *Brain*—he touches his forehead.

2 "Corps"—in the sense of body; though it may be *corps*—or body of men. *Corse* would be the better substitute.

Seg. Why this, my lord: experience teacheth us
That resolution is sole help at need;
And this, my lord, our honor teacheth us—
That we be bold in every enterprise.
Then, since there's no way but to fight or die,
Be resolute, my lord, for victory.

Hum. And resolute, Segar, [do] I mean to be!—
Perhaps some blissful star will favor us,
And comfort bring to our perplexéd state.
Come, let us in and fortify our camp,
So to withstand their strong invasion. [*Exeunt.*

SCENE IV.—*Before the Hovel of a* Peasant.

Enter STRUMBO, TROMPART, OLIVER, *and his Son* WILLIAM.

Strum. Nay, neighbor Oliver, if you be so hot, come, prepare yourself; you shall find two as stout fellows of us as any in all the north.

Oli. No, by my dorth, neighbor Strumbo, Ich zee dat you are a man of small 'zideration, dat will zeek to injure your old vreends,—one of your vamiliar guests; and, derefore, zeeing your 'pinion is to deal withouten reazon, Ich and my zon William will take dat course dat shall be fardest vrom reazon.—How zay you—will you have my daughter or no?

Strum. A very hard question, neighbor; but I will solve it as I may. What reason have you to demand it of me?

Will. Marry, sir, what reason had you when my sister was in the barn to ——[1]

Strum. Mass! thou sayst true! Well, but would you have me marry her therefore? No, I scorn her, and you—and you. Ay, I scorn you all.

Oli. You will not have her then?

Strum. No, as I am a true gentleman.

Will. Then will we school you, ere you and we part hence. [*They fight.*

Enter MARGERY, *who snatches the staff out of her* Brother's *hand.*

Strum. Ay, you come in pudding-time, or else I had drest them.

Mar. You, Master Sauce-box, Lobcock, Coxcomb; you Slopsauce, Lickfingers,—will you not hear?

Strum. Who speak you to,—me?

Mar. Ay, sir, to you—John Lackhonesty, Little-Wit,—is it you that will have none of me?

Strum. No, by my troth, Mistress Nicebice!—how fine you can nick-name me! I think you were brought up in the university of Bridewell, you have your rhetoric so ready at your tongue's end;—as if you were never well warned when you were young.

Mar. Why, then, Goodman Codshead, if you will have none of me, farewell.

Strum. If you be so plain, Mistress Driggle-draggle, fare you well.

Mar. Nay, Master Strumbo, ere you go from hence we must have more words;—you will have none of me? [*She strikes him.*

Strum. Oh, my head, my head;—leave, leave, leave;—I will, I will, I will.

Mar. Upon that condition, I let thee alone.

Oli. How now, Master Strumbo; hath my daughter taught you a new lesson?

Strum. Ay, but hear you, Goodman Oliver, it will not be for my ease to have my head broken every day, therefore remedy this, and we shall agree.

Oli. Well, zon, well, for you are my zon now;—all shall be remedied. Daughter, be friends with him. [*They embrace.*

Strum. You are a sweet nut!—the devil crack you [*aside*]. Masters, I think it be my luck!—my first wife was a loving quiet wench, but this, I think would weary the devil. I would she might be burnt as my other wife was; if not, I must run to the halter for help. O, codpiece, thou hast undone thy master; this it is to be meddling with warm plackets. [*Exeunt.*

[1] I omit a simple grossness.

SCENE V.—*The Camp of* Locrine.

Enter LOCRINE, CAMBER, CORINEIUS, THRASYMACHUS, *and* ASSARACHUS.

Loc. Now am I guarded with a host of men,
Whose haughty courage is invincible!—
Now am I hemmed with troops of soldiers,
Such as might force Bellona to retire,
And make her tremble at their puissance!—
Now sit I like the mighty god of war,
When arméd with his coat of adamant,
Mounting his chariot drawn with mighty bulls,
He drove the Argives over Xanthus' streams.
Now, cursed Humber, doth thy end draw nigh;—
Down goes the glory of thy victories,
And all thy fame, and all thy high renown,
Shall in a moment yield to Locrine's sword!—
Thy bragging banners crossed with argent streams,
The ornaments of thy pavilions,
Shall all be captivated by this hand;—
And thou, thyself, at Albanactus' tomb,
Shalt offeréd be, in satisfaction
Of all the wrongs thou didst him when he lived.
But canst thou tell me, brave Thrasymachus,
How far we are distant [now] from Humber's camp?

Thrasy. My lord, within yon foul accurséd grove
That bears the tokens of our overthrow,
This Humber hath entrenched his damnéd camp.
March on, my lord, because I long to see
The treacherous Scythians weltering in their gore.

Loc. Sweet Fortune, favor Locrine with a smile,
That I may 'venge my noble brother's death,
And, in the midst of stately Troynovant,
I'll build a temple, to thy deity,
Of perfect marble, and of jacinth stones,
That it shall pass the high Pyramides,
Which, with their tops, surmount the firmament.

Cam. The arm-strong offspring of the 'doubted knight,
Stout Hercules, Alcmena's mighty son,
That tamed the monsters of the threefold world,
And rid the oppresséd from the tyrant's yoke,
Did never show such valiantness in fight,
As I will now for noble Albanact.

Corin. Full fourscore years hath Corineius lived,
Sometimes in war, sometimes in quiet peace,
And yet I feel myself to be as strong
As erst I was in summer of mine age,
Able to toss this great unwieldy club,
Which hath been painted with my foemen's brains;
And, with this club, I'll break the strong array
Of Humber, and his straggling soldiers,
Or lose my life amongst the thickest press,
And die with honor in my latest days.

Yet, ere I die, they all shall understand,
What force lies in stout Corineius' hand.

Thrasy. And if Thrasymachus detract the fight,
Either for weakness or for cowardice,
Let him not boast that Brutus was his eame,
Or that brave Corineius was his sire.

Loc. Then, courage, soldiers, for your safety first,
Next for your peace, last for your victory. [*Exeunt.*

SCENE VI. — *The Field of Battle.*

Alarums. Enter HUBBA *and* SEGAR *on one side, and* CORINEIUS *opposite.*

Corin. Art thou that Humber, prince of fugitives,
That, by thy treason, slew'st young Albanact?

Hub. I am his son that slew young Albanact,
And if thou take not heed, proud Phrygian,
I'll send thy soul unto the Stygian lake,
There to complain of Humber's injuries.

Corin. You triumph, sir, before the victory,
For, not so soon, is Corineius slain.
But, cursèd Scythians, you shall rue the day,
That ere you came into Albania. [*They fight.*
So perish they that envy Britain's wealth,
So let them die with endless infamy,
And he that seeks his sovereign's overthrow,
Would this my club might aggravate his wo.
[CORINEIUS *slays both* HUBBA *and* SEGAR, *and exit.*

SCENE VII. — *Another part of the Field.*

Enter HUMBER, *in flight.*

Hum. Where may I find some desert wilderness,
Where I may breathe out curses as I would,
And scare the earth with my condemning voice; —
Where every echo's repercussion
May help me to bewail mine overthrow,
And aid me in my sorrowful laments? —
Where may I find some hollow uncouth rock,
Where I may damn, condemn, and ban my fill,
The heavens, the hell, the earth, the air, the fire,
And utter curses to the concave sky.
Which may infect the airy regions,
And light upon the Briton Locrine's head? —
You ugly spirits that in Cocytus mourn,
And gnash your teeth with dolorous laments; —
You fearful dogs that in black Lethe howl,
And scare the ghosts with your wide open throats; —
You ugly ghosts that, flying from these dogs,
Do plunge yourselves in Puryphlegiton; —
Come, all of you, and, with your shrieking notes
Accompany the Briton's conquering host.
Come fierce Erinnys, horrible with snakes,
Come, ugly Furies, armèd with your whips; —
You, threefold judges of black Tartarus,
And all the army of your hellish fiends; —
With new-found torments rack proud Locrine's bones!
O gods and stars! — damned be the gods and stars,
That did not drown me in fair Thetis' plains! —
Curst be the sea, that, with outrageous waves,
With surging billows, did not rive my ships
Against the rocks of high Ceraunia,
Or swallowed me into her watery gulf! —
Would God, we had arrived upon the shore
Where Polyphemus and the Cyclops dwell; —
Or, where the bloody Anthropophagi,
With greedy jaws, devour the wand'ring wight.

Enter the Ghost *of* ALBANACT.

But why comes Albanactus' bloody ghost,
To bring corrosive[1] to our miseries?
Is't not enough to suffer shameful flight,
But we must be tormented now with ghosts —
With apparitions fearful to behold?

Ghost. Revenge, revenge for blood!

Hum. So, naught will satisfy you, wandering ghost,
But dire revenge; nothing but Humber's fall; —
Because he conquered you in Albany?
Now, by my soul, Humber would be condemned
To Tantalus' hunger, or Ixion's wheel,
Or to the vulture of Prometheus,
Rather than that this murder were undone!
When, as I die, I'll drag thy cursèd ghost
Through all the rivers of foul Erebus —
Through burning sulphur of the limbo-lake,
To allay the burning fury of that heat
That rageth in mine everlasting soul!
[*Exit* HUMBER.

Ghost. Vindicta! vindicta!
[*Exit.*

ACT IV.

SCENE I.

Enter ATE, *as before. A dumb Show follows, representing* OMPHALE, *Daughter to the* King *of* Lydia, *having a Club in her hand, and a Lion's Skin on her back;* HERCULES *following with a Distaff.* OMPHALE *turns, takes off her Pantofle,*[2] *strikes* HERCULES *on the head, then departs; he following submissively.* ATE *remains.*

Atè. Quem non Argolici mandata severa tyranni,
Non potuit Juno vincere, vicit amor.[3]
Stout Hercules the mirror of the world,
Son to Alcmena and great Jupiter,
After so many conquests won in field,
After so many monsters quelled by force —
Yielded his valiant heart to Omphale; —
A fearful woman, void of manly strength,
She took the club, and wore the lion's skin:
He took the wheel, and maidenly 'gan spin. —
So martial Locrine, cheered with victory,
Falleth in love with Humber's concubine,
And so forgetteth peerless Guendeline.
His uncle Corineius storms at this,
And forceth Locrine for his grace to sue;
Lo! here the sum:[4] the process doth ensue. [*Exit.*

SCENE II. — *The Camp of* LOCRINE.

Enter LOCRINE, CAMBER, CORINEIUS, ASSARACUS, THRASYMACHUS, *and* Soldiers.

Loc. Thus from the fury of Bellona's broils,
With sound of drum, and trumpet's melody,
The Briton king returns triumphantly! —
The Scythians, slain with great occision,

1 "A *corsive*" in the folio. 2 "Pantofle"—slipper.

3 "*Quem non Argolici mandata severa tyranni,*
Non potuit Juno vincere, vicit amor."
He whom the tyrant's mandate could not move,
Nor Juno's self subdue, submits to love.

4 "Sum," for *summary*; "process"—the details which are to follow.

Do equalize the grass in multitude,
And with their blood have stained the streaming brooks,
Offering their bodies and their dearest blood
As sacrifice to Albanactus' ghost.
Now, cursĕd Humber, hast thou paid thy due
For thy deceits and crafty treacheries,
For all thy guiles and damnĕd stratagems,
With loss of life, and everduring shame!
Where are thy horses, trapped with burnished gold?
Thy trampling coursers, ruled with foaming bits?
Where are thy soldiers, strong and numberless,
Thy valiant captains, and thy noble peers?
Even as the country clowns, with sharpest scythes,
Do mow the withered grass from off the earth—
Or, as the ploughman, with his piercing share,
Rendeth the bowels of the fertile fields,
And rippeth up the roots with razors keen—
So Locrine, with his mighty curtle-axe,
Hath croppĕd off the heads of all thy Huns!—
So Locrine's peers have daunted all thy peers,
And drove thine host unto confusion—
That thou may'st suffer penance for thy fault,
And die, for murdering valiant Albanact.

Corin. And thus, yea, thus, shall all the rest be served,
That seek to enter Albion 'gainst our will.
If the brave nation of the Troglodytes—
If all the coal-black Ethiopians—
If all the forces of the Amazons—
If all the hosts of the barbaric lands—
Should dare to enter this our little world,—
Soon should they rue their overbold attempts:
That, after us, our progeny may say,
There lie the beasts that sought t'usurp our land!

Loc. Ay, they are beasts that seek t'usurp our land,
And like to brutish beasts they shall be served;
For mighty Jove, the supreme King of heaven,
That guides the concourse of the meteors,
And rules the motion of the azure sky—
Fights always for the Briton's safety.
But stay: methinks I hear some shrieking noise,
That draweth near to our pavilion.

Enter Soldiers, *bringing in* ESTRILD.

Est. What prince soe'er, adorned with golden crown,
Doth sway the regal sceptre in his hand,
And thinks no chance can ever throw him down,
Or that his state shall everlasting stand,
Let him behold poor Estrild in this plight,
The perfect platform of a troubled wight.

Once was I guarded with mavortial bands,
Compassed with princes of the noblest blood;
Now am I fallen into my foemen's hands,
And, with my death, must pacify their mood.
Oh, life! the harbor of calamities,
Oh, death! the haven of all miseries!

I could compare my sorrows to thy wo,
Thou wretched queen of wretched Pergamus,
But that thou viewedst thy enemies' overthrow,
Nigh to the rock of high Caphareus;
Thou saw'st their death, and then departed'st thence:
I must abide the victor's insolence!

The gods, that pitied thy continual grief,
Transformed thy corse, and with thy corse, thy care:
Poor Estrild lives, despairing of relief,
For friends in trouble are but few and rare.

What said I—few?—ay, few, or none at all,
For cruel death made havoc of them all.

Thrice happy they, whose fortune was so good,
To end their lives, and with their lives their woes.
Thrice hapless I, whom Fortune so withstood,
That cruelly she gave me to my foes!
Oh, soldiers!—is there any misery
To be compared to Fortune's treachery?[1]

Loc. Camber, this same should be the Scythian queen.

Cam. So we may judge by her lamenting words.

Loc. So fair a dame mine eyes did never see!—
With floods of wo o'erwhelmed she seems to be.

Cam. Oh! Locrine, hath she not a cause for grief?[2]

Loc. [*aside*]. If she hath come to weep for Humber's death,
And shed salt tears for his [dread][3] overthrow,
Locrine may well bewail his proper grief,—
Locrine may move his own peculiar wo!
Humber,[4] being conquered, died a speedy death;
I, being the conqueror, live a lingering life,
And feel the force of Cupid's sudden stroke.
I gave him cause to die a speedy death:
He left me cause to wish a speedy death!
Oh! that sweet face, painted with Nature's dye,
Those roseal cheeks, mixed with a snowy white;
That decent neck, surpassing ivory;
Those comely breasts, which Venus well might spite—
Are like to snares by wily fowlers wrought,
Wherein my yielding heart is pris'ner caught.
The golden tresses of her dainty hair,
Which shine like rubies glittering in the sun,
Have so entrapped poor Locrine's lovesick heart,[5]
That from the same no way it can be won.
How true is that which oft I've heard declare,
One drachm of joy must have a pound of care!

Est. Hard is their fall, who, from a golden crown,
Are cast into a sea of wretchedness!

Loc. Hard is their thrall, who, [still] by Cupid's frown,
Are wrapped in waves of endless carefulness!

Est. Oh, kingdom, subject to all miseries![6]

Loc. Oh, love, extrem'st of all extremities!

[LOCRINE *sinks into a seat.*

[1] Tieck, the German critic, describes these verses as "the beautiful-rhymed stanzas in the fourth act, which so distinctly remind us of his [Shakspeare's] sonnets, and the 'Venus and Adonis,' that these alone would prove the genuineness of the drama." While very far from agreeing with Tieck, as regarding these stanzas as conclusive of the authenticity of the play as one of Shakspeare's, we are yet free to say that they do recall the "Venus and Adonis," though evidently composed by a less mature intellect. Still, we do not regard them by any means as indicative of that higher poetical power of which more certain proofs are to be found in this drama, in spite of all its crudities of plan and composition.

[2] The words of Camber in the old folio are, "Oh, Locrine, hath she not a cause for *to be sad?*" We plead guilty to the alteration, which is called for by good taste and the rhythm, rather than the necessity of the speech.

[3] The original runs thus: "And shed salt tears for *her* overthrow"—a line which lacks in measure, and in which it is evident that we must substitute *his* for "her."

[4] The old folio reads, "*He* being conquered," meaning Humber, but really referring to Locrine himself.

[5] The rhyme here fails us. The reader, if he prefer it, may read the line thus:—

"Have so entrapped poor Locrine's heart in snare."

[6] Estrild, in the old copies, is made to say—

"O kingdom, *object* to all miseries"—

which is clearly faulty. The kingdom she apostrophizes is her fortunes. To speak of them as a kingdom—"a sea of wretchedness"—as she does in an immediately preceding passage, "*subject* to all miseries," would seem to be appropriate enough.

1 *Sold.* My lord, in ransacking the Scythian tents,
I found this lady; and to manifest
The earnest zeal I bear unto your grace,
I here present her to your majesty.
2 *Sold.* He lies, my lord; I found the lady first,
And here present her to your majesty.
1 *Sold.* Presumptuous villain, wilt thou take my prize?
2 *Sold.* Nay, rather thou depriv'st me of my right.
3 *Sold.* Resign thy title, caitiff, unto me,
Or, with my sword, I'll pierce thy coward loins.
2 *Sold.* Soft words, good sir; 'tis not enough to speak:
A barking dog doth seldom strangers bite.
Loc. Irreverent villains, strive you in our sight?
Take them hence, gaoler, to the dungeon;
There let them lie and try their quarrel out.
But thou, fair princess, be no whit dismayed,
But rather joy that Locrine favors thee.
Est. How can he favor me that slew my spouse?
Loc. The chance of war, my love, took him from thee.
Est. But Locrine was the causer of his death.
Loc. He was an enemy to Locrine's state,
And slew my noble brother Albanact.
Est. But he was linked to me in marriage-bond,
And would you have me love his slaughterer?
Loc. Better to love,[1] than not to live at all.
Est. Better to die renowned for chastity,
Than live with shame and endless infamy.
What would the common sort report of me,
If I forget my love, and cleave to thee?
Loc. Kings need not fear the vulgar sentences.
Est. But ladies must regard their honest name.
Loc. Is it a shame to live in marriage-bonds?
Est. No, but to be a strumpet to a king.
Loc. If thou wilt yield to Locrine's burning love,
Thou shalt be queen of fair Albania.
Est. But Guendeline will undermine my state.
Loc. Upon mine honor, thou shalt have no harm.
Est. Then lo! brave Locrine, Estrild yields to thee;
And, by the gods whom thou dost invocate,
By the dread ghost of thy deceasèd sire,
By thy right hand, and by thy burning love,
Take pity on poor Estrild's wretched thrall!
Corin. Hath Locrine then forgot his Guendeline,
That thus he courts the Scythian's paramour?
What! are the words of Brute so soon forgot?
Are my deserts so quickly out of mind?
Have I been faithful to thy sire now dead?
Have I protected thee from Humber's hand,
And dost thou 'quite me with ingratitude?
Is this the guerdon for my grievous wounds?
Is this the honor for my labors past!
Now, by my sword, Locrine, I swear to thee,
This injury of thine shall be repaid!
Loc. Uncle, scorn you your royal sovereign,
As if we stood for ciphers in the court?
Upbraid you me with these your benefits?
Why, 'twas a subject's duty so to do.
What you have done for our deceasèd sire,
We know, and all know, you have your reward.
Corin. Avaunt, proud princox, brav'st thou me withal?
Assure thyself, though thou be emperor,
Thou ne'er shalt carry this unpunishèd.
Cam. Pardon my brother, noble Corineius;
Pardon this once, and it shall be amended.
Assar. Cousin, remember Brutus' latest words,
How he desirèd you to cherish them:
Let not this fault so much incense your mind,
Which is not yet passèd all remedy.
Corin. Then, Locrine, lo! I reconcile myself:
But, as thou lov'st thy life, so love thy wife;
And,[2] if thou violate these promises,
Blood and revenge shall light upon thy head!
Come, let us back to stately Troynovant,
Where all these matters shall be settlèd.
Loc. [*aside*]. Millions of devils wait upon thy soul;
Legions of spirits vex thy impious ghost;
Ten thousand torments rack thy cursèd bones!—
Let everything that hath the use of breath,
Be instruments and workers of thy death! [*Exeunt.*

SCENE III.—*A Forest.*

Enter Humber, *his Garments torn and bloody, his Hair dishevelled, and armed only with a Spear.*

Hum. What basilisk hath hatchèd in this place,
Where everything consumèd is to naught?
What fearful fury haunts these cursèd groves,
Where not a root is left for Humber's meat?
Hath fell Alecto, with envenomed blasts,
Breathèd forth poison on these tender plains?
Hath triple Cerberus, with contagious foam,
Sowed aconit among these withered herbs?
Hath dreadful Fames, with her charming-rods,
Brought barrenness on every fruitful tree?
What! not a root, nor fruit, nor beast, nor bird,
To nourish Humber in this wilderness?—
What would you more, you fiends of Erebus?
My very entrails burn for want of drink!
My bowels cry to Humber, *Give us meat!*—
But wretched Humber can bestow no meat;
These foul, accursèd groves afford no meat;
This fruitless soil, this ground, brings forth no meat;
The gods, hard-hearted gods, yield me no meat!
Then how can Humber give you any meat?
[*Retires back.*

Enter Strumbo, *a Pitchfork in his hand, and a Scotch-Cap on his head.*

Strum. How do you, masters? how do you? How have you 'scaped hanging this long time? I'faith, I have 'scaped many a scouring this year, but, I thank God, I have past them all with a good couragio, and my wife and I are in great love and charity now, I thank my manhood and my strength: for I will tell you, masters, upon a certain day at night I came home, to say the very truth, with my stomach full of wine, and ran up into the chamber, where my wife soberly sat rocking my little baby, leaning her back against the bed, singing lullaby. Now, when she saw me come with my nose foremost, thinking that I had been drunk, as I was indeed, [she] snatched up a fagot-stick in her hand, and came furiously marching toward me with a big face, as though she would have eaten me at a bit—thundering out these words unto me: *Thou drunken knave, where hast thou been so long? I shall teach thee how to benight me another*

[1] In the original, the line runs—
"Better to *live*, than not to live at all"—
which is meaningless. Locrine means to say, "Better to love, and love even your conqueror, than to forego life altogether," which might otherwise be her fate.

[2] "*But*" in the old folio.

time!—and so she began to play knaves trumps.—Now, although I trembled, fearing she would set her ten commandments[1] in my face, I ran within her, and taking her lustily by the middle, I carried her valiantly —— —— ——,[2] and so banished brawling for ever. And, to see the good will of the wench, she bought with her portion a yard of land, and by that I am now become one of the richest men in our parish. Well, masters, what's o'clock? It is now breakfast time; you shall see what meat I have here for my breakfast.[3] [*Sits down and displays food.*

Hum. [*coming forward*]. Was ever land so fruitless as this land?
Was ever grove so graceless as this grove?
Was ever soil so barren as this soil?
Oh, no! the land where hungry Fames dwelt
May no ways equalize this cursèd land;
No, even the climate of the torrid zone
Brings forth more fruit than this accursèd grove.
Ne'er came sweet Ceres, ne'er came Venus here;
Triptolemus, the god of husbandmen,
Ne'er sowed his seed in this foul wilderness.
The hunger-bitten dogs of Acheron,
Chased from the ninefold Puryphlegiton,
Have set their footsteps in this damnèd ground.
The iron-hearted furies, armed with snakes,
Scattered huge hydras over all the plains,
Which have consumed the grass, the herbs, the trees,
Which have drunk up the water-flowing springs.

[STRUMBO, *hearing the voice, starts up, puts his meat in his pocket, and seeks to hide.*

Thou great commander of the starry sky,
That guid'st the life of every mortal wight,
From the enclosures of the fleeting clouds
Rain down some food, or else I faint and die;
Pour down some drink, or else I faint and die!

[*Seeing* STRUMBO.

O Jupiter! hast thou sent Mercury,
In clownish shape, to minister some food?—
Some meat, some meat, some meat!

Strum. O, alas! sir, you are deceived. I am not Mercury; I am Strumbo.

Hum. Give me some meat, villain! give me some meat,
Or 'gainst this rock I'll dash thy cursèd brains,
And rend thy bowels with my bloody hands.
Give me some meat, villain; give me some meat!

Strum. By the faith of my body, good fellow, I had rather give a whole ox, than that thou shouldst serve me in that sort! Dash out my brains? O, horrible! terrible! I think I have a quarry of stones in my pocket. [*Aside.*

[*As he offers food, the* Ghost *of* ALBANACT *enters, strikes him on the hand, and* STRUMBO *runs out.* HUMBER *follows him.*

Ghost. Lo here the gift of fell ambition,
Of usurpation, and of treachery!
Lo here the harms that wait upon all those
That do intrude themselves in other lands,
Which are not under their dominion. [*Exit* Ghost.

SCENE IV.—*A Chamber in the Royal Palace.*

Enter LOCRINE *alone.*

Loc. Seven years hath agèd Corineius lived
To Locrine's grief and fair Estrilda's wo,
And seven years more he hopeth yet to live!—
Oh! supreme Jove, annihilate this thought!
Should he enjoy the air's fruition?
Should he enjoy the benefit of life?
Should he contemplate [still] the radiant sun,
That makes my life equal to dreadful death?
Venus, convey this monster from the earth,
That disobeyeth thus thy sacred 'hests.
Cupid, convey this monster to dark hell,
That disannuls thy mother's sugared laws.
Mars, with thy target all beset with flames,
With murdering blade, bereave him of his life,
That hindereth Locrine in his sweetest joys!—
And yet, for all his diligent aspect,
His wrathful eyes piercing like lynxes' eyes,
Well have I overmatched his subtlety.
Nigh Deucolitum, by the pleasant Lee,
Where brackish Thamis slides with silver streams,
Making a breach into the grassy downs,
A curious arch, of costly marble wrought,
Hath Locrine framèd underneath the ground;
The walls whereof, garnished with diamonds,
With opals, rubies, glistering emeralds,
And interlaced with sunbright carbuncles,
Lighten the room with artificial day;—
And, from the Lee, with water-flowing pipes,
The moisture is derived into this arch,
Where I have placed fair Estrild secretly:—
Thither, eftsoons, accomp'nied by my page,
I visit covertly my heart's desire,
Without suspicion of the meanest eye;
For love aboundeth still with policy;—
And thither still means Locrine to repair,
Till Atropos cut off mine uncle's life.[4] [*Exit.*

SCENE V.—*The entrance of a Cave, near which runs the River, afterward the* Humber.

Enter HUMBER, *solus.*

Hum. *O vita misero longa, fœlici brevis!*
Eheu malorum fames extremum malum.[5]
Long have I livèd in this desert cave,
With eating haws and miserable roots,
Devouring leaves and beastly excrements;
Caves were my beds, and stones my pillow-biers,
Fear was my sleep, and horror was my dream;
For still methought, at every boisterous blast,
Now Locrine comes—now, Humber, thou must die!
So that, for fear and hunger, Humber's mind
Can never rest, but always trembling stands.
Oh, what Danubius now may quench my thirst?
What Euphrates, what lightfoot Euripus,
May now allay the fury of that heat,
Which, raging in my entrails, eats me up?
Ye ghastly devils of the ninefold Styx,
Ye damnèd ghosts of joyless Acheron,
Ye mournful souls, vexed in Abyssus' vaults,
Ye coal-black devils of Avernus' pond—

1 Her ten fingers; the phrase is proverbial.
2 I have here suppressed an offensive grossness.
3 This history is addressed to the audience.

4 Milton thus describes this artificial grotto, and the secret intercourse of Estrild and Locrine: Locrine, "ofttimes retiring, as to some private sacrifice, through vaults and passages made under ground, and seven years thus enjoying her, had by her a daughter equally fair, whose name was Sabra."

5 It is difficult to say why these commonplace lines were not done originally into English. They are wholly independent of each other: "*O vita, misero longa, fœlici brevis!*"—O life! long to the wretched—to the happy, short! "*Eheu malorum fames extremum malum*"—Alas! of all evils, hunger is the worst.

Come, with your flesh-hooks rend my famished arms,
These arms that have sustained their master's life;
Come, with your razors rip my bowels up;
With your sharp fire-forks crack my starvéd bones!
Use me as ye will, so Humber may not live!—
Accurséd gods, that rule the starry poles,
Accurséd Jove, King of the accurséd gods—
Cast down your lightning on poor Humber's head,
That I may leave this death-like life of mine!—
What! hear you not, and shall not Humber die?
Nay, I will die, though all the gods say nay.
And, gentle Aby, take my troubled corpse—
Take it and keep it from all mortal eyes,
That none may say, when I have lost my breath,
The very floods conspired 'gainst Humber's death!
[*Flings himself into the river.*[1]

Enter the Ghost *of* ALBANACT.

Ghost. En cædem sequitur cædes, in cæde quiesco![2]
Humber is dead!—joy heavens, leap earth, dance [trees!
Now may'st thou reach thy apples, Tantalus,
And with 'em feed thy hunger-bitten limbs;
Now, Sysiphus, leave the tumbling of thy rock,
And rest thy restless bones upon the same;
Unbind Ixion, cruel Rhadamanth,
And lay proud Humber on the whirling wheel!
Back will I post to hell-mouth Tænarus,
And pass Cocytus, to the Elysian fields,
And tell my father Brutus of these news.
[*Exit* Ghost.

ACT V.

SCENE I.

Enter ATE, *as before. Dumb Show:* JASON *leading* CREON'S Daughter; MEDEA *following, hath a Garland in her hand, and, putting it on* CREON'S Daughter's *head, setteth it on fire; then killing* JASON *and her, departs.*

Até. Non tam Trinacriis exæstuat Ætna cavernis,
Læsæ furtivo quam cor mulieris amore.[3]
Medea, seeing Jason leave her love,
And choose the daughter of the Theban king,
Went to her devilish charms to work revenge;
And, raising up the triple Hecaté,
With all the rout of the condemnéd fiends,
Framéd a garland by her magic skill,
With which she wrought Jason and Creon's ill.
So Guendeline, seeing herself misused,
And Humber's paramour possess her place,
Flies to the dukedom of Cornubia,
And with her brother, stout Thrasymachus,
Gathering a power of Cornish soldiers,
Gives battle to her husband and his host,
Nigh to the river of great Mercia!—

1 Milton's history thus: "Locrine and his brother go out against Humber, who, now marching onward, was by them defeated, and in a river drowned, which to this day retains his name."

2 Lo! death to death succeeds—in death I rest.

3 "*Non tam Trinacriis exæstuat Ætna cavernis,*
Læsæ furtivo quam cor mulieris amore:"—
Not with such tumult, in Sicilia's caves,
Does Ætna rage, as doth the woman's heart,
When roused to madness by clandestine fires!

The chances of this dismal massacre,
That which ensueth shortly will unfold. [*Exit*

SCENE II.—*A Chamber in the Royal Palace.*

Enter LOCRINE, CAMBER, ASSARACUS, *and* THRASYMACHUS.

Assar. But tell me, cousin, died my brother so?
Now, who is left to hapless Albion,
That, as a pillar, might uphold our state—
That might strike terror to our daring foes?
Now, who is left to hapless Britany,
That might defend her from the barbarous hands
Of those that still desire her ruinous fall,
And seek to work her downfall and decay?

Cam. Ay, uncle, death's our common enemy;
And none but death can match our matchless power.
Witness the fall of Albioneius' crew;
Witness the fall of Humber and his Huns;
And this foul death hath now increased our wo,
By taking Corineius from this life,
And in his room leaving us worlds of care.

Thrasy. But none may more bewail his mournful [hearse
Than I, that am the issue of his loins!
Now, foul befall that curséd Humber's throat,
That was the causer of his lingering wound.

Loc. Tears can not raise him from the dead again.
But where's my lady-mistress, Guendeline?

Thrasy. In Cornwall, Locrine, is my sister now,
Providing for my father's funeral.

Loc. And let her there provide her mourning weeds,
And mourn for ever her own widowhood:
Ne'er shall she come within our palace-gate,
To countercheck brave Locrine in his love.
Go, boy, to Deucolitum, down the Lee,
Unto the arch where lovely Estrild lies:
Bring her and Sabren straight unto the court;
She shall be queen in Guendeliné's room.
Let others wail for Corineius' death:
I mean not so to macerate my mind
For him that barred me from my heart's desire.[4]

Thrasy. Hath Locrine then forsook his Guendeline?
Is Corineius' death so soon forgot?
If there be gods in heaven, as sure there be—
If there be fiends in hell, as needs there must—
They will revenge this thy notorious wrong,
And pour their plagues upon thy curséd head!

Loc. What, prat'st thou, peasant, to thy sovereign?
Or art thou strucken in some ecstasy?
Dost thou not tremble at our royal looks?
Dost thou not quake when mighty Locrine frowns?
Thou beardless boy, were't not that Locrine scorns
To vex his mind with such a heartless child,
With the sharp point of this my battle-axe
I'd send thy soul to Puryphlegiton.

Thrasy. Though I be young and of a tender age,
Yet will I cope with Locrine when he dares.
My noble father, with his conquering sword,
Slew the two giant kings of Aquitaine:
Thrasymachus is not degenerate,
That he should fear and tremble at the looks
Or taunting words of a venerean squire.

Loc. Menacest thou thy royal sovereign?
Uncivil, not beseeming such as thou.

4 "But when once his [Locrine's] fear was off, by the death of Corineius, not content with secret enjoyment, divorcing Guendolen, he made Estrilde now his queen."
MILTON.

Injurious traitor — for he is no less
That at defiance standeth with his king —
Leave these thy taunts, — leave these thy bragging words, —
Unless thou mean'st to leave thy wretched life.

Thrasy. If princes stain their glorious dignity
With ugly spots of monstrous infamy,
They lose their former estimation,
And throw themselves into a hell of hate.

Loc. Wilt thou abuse my gentle patience,
As though thou didst our high displeasure scorn?
Proud boy, — that thou may'st know thy prince is moved —
Yea, greatly moved, at this thy swelling pride, —
We banish thee for ever from our court.

Thrasy. Then, losel Locrine, look unto thyself:
Thrasymachus will revenge this injury. [*Exit.*

Loc. Farewell, proud boy, and learn to use thy tongue.

Assar. Alas! my lord, you should have called to mind
The latest words that Brutus spake to you:
How he desired you, by the obedience
That children ought to bear [unto] their sire,
To love and favor Lady Guendeline:
Consider this, that, if the injury
Do move her mind, as certainly it will,
War and dissension follow speedily.
What though her power be not so great as yours,
Have you not seen a mighty elephant
Slain by the biting of a silly mouse? —
Even so the chance of war inconstant is.

Loc. Peace, uncle, peace, and cease to talk hereof;
For he that seeks, by whispering this or that,
To trouble Locrine in his sweetest life,
Let him persuade himself to die the death.

Enter the Page, *with* Estrild *and* Sabren.

Est. O, say me, page, [and] tell me, where's the king?
Wherefore doth he send for me to the court?
Is it to die? — is it to end my life?
Say me, sweet boy: tell me, and do not feign.

Page. No, trust me, madam; if you will credit the little honesty that is yet left me, there is no such danger as you fear; — but prepare yourself: yonder's the king.

Est. Then, Estrild, lift thy dazzled spirits up,
And bless that blessed time, that day, that hour,
That warlike Locrine first did favor thee. —
Peace to the king of Britany — my love! —
Peace to all those that love and favor him!
[*She kneels.*

Loc. [*raising her*]. Doth Estrild fall, with such submission,
Before her servant, king of Albion?
Arise, fair lady, leave this lowly cheer;
Lift up those looks that cherish Locrine's heart,
That I may freely view that roseal face
Which so entangled hath my lovesick breast.
Now, to the court, where we will court it out,
And pass the night and day in Venus' sports.
Frolic, brave peers; be joyful with your king!
[*Exeunt.*

SCENE III. — *The Camp of* Guendeline.

Enter Guendeline, Thrasymachus, Madan, *and* Soldiers.

Guen. Ye gentle winds, that, with your modest blasts,
Pass through the circuit of the heavenly vault,
Enter the clouds unto the throne of Jove,
And bear my prayer to his all-hearing ears! —
For Locrine hath forsaken Guendeline,
And learned to love proud Humber's concubine.
Ye happy sprites that, in the concave sky,
With pleasant joy, enjoy your sweetest love,
Shed forth those tears with me, which then you shed,
When first you wooed your ladies to your wills! —
Those tears are fittest for my woful case,
Since Locrine shuns my nothing-pleasant face.
Blush heavens, blush sun, and hide thy shining beams,
Shadow thy radiant locks in gloomy clouds —
Deny thy cheerful light unto the world,
Where nothing reigns but falsehood and deceit!
What said I? — falsehood? — ay, that filthy crime:
For Locrine hath forsaken Guendeline.
Behold! the heavens do wail for Guendeline:
The shining sun doth blush for Guendeline:
The liquid air doth weep for Guendeline:
The very ground doth groan for Guendeline!
Ay, they are milder than is Britain's king,
For he rejecteth luckless Guendeline.

Thrasy. Sister! complaints are bootless in this cause! —
This open wrong must have an open plague;
This plague must be repaid with grievous war;
This war must finish [soon] with Locrine's death:
His death will soon extinguish our complaints.

Guen. O no, his death will more augment my woes!
He was my husband, brave Thrasymachus;
More dear to me than th'apple of mine eye;
Nor can I find in heart to work his scath.

Thrasy. Madam, if not your proper injuries,
Nor my exile, can move you to revenge —
Think on our father Corineius' words; —
His words to us stand always for a law.
Should Locrine live, that caused my father's death?
Should Locrine live, that now divorceth you?
The heavens, the earth, the air, the fire, reclaims:
And then why should we all deny the same?

Guen. Then, henceforth, farewell womanish complaints! —
All childish pity henceforth, then, farewell! —
But, cursèd Locrine, look unto thyself,
For Nemesis, the mistress of revenge,
Sits armed at all points on our dismal blades;
And cursèd Estrild, that inflamed his heart,
Shall, if I live, die a reproachful death!

Madan. Mother, though nature makes me to lament
My luckless father's froward lechery —
Yet — for he wrongs my lady-mother thus —
I, if I could, myself would work his death.

Thrasy. See, madam, see, the desire of revenge
Is in the children of a tender age. —
Forward, brave soldiers, into Mercia,
Where we shall brave the coward to his face.
[*Exeunt.*

SCENE IV. — *The Camp of* Locrine.

Enter Locrine, Estrild, Sabren, Assaracus, *and* Soldiers.

Loc. Tell me, Assaracus, are the Cornish chuffs
In such great number come to Mercia?
And have they pitched there their [clownish] host,
So close unto our royal mansion?

Assar. They are, my lord, and mean incontinent
To bid defiance to your majesty.
Loc. It makes me laugh, to think that Guendeline
Should have the heart to come in arms against me.
Est. Alas! my lord, the horse will run amain
When as the spur doth gall him to the bone!
Jealousy, Locrine, hath a wicked sting.
Loc. Say'st thou so, Estrild—beauty's paragon?
Well, we will try her choler to the proof,
And make her know, Locrine can brook no braves.
March on, Assaracus: thou must lead the way,
And bring us to their proud pavilion. [*Exeunt.*

SCENE V.—*The Field of Battle.*

Thunder and Lightning. Enter the Ghost *of* CORINEIUS.

Ghost. Behold! the circuit of the azure sky
Throws forth sad throbs,[1] and grievously suspires,
Prejudicating Locrine's overthrow:
The fire casteth forth sharp darts of flames;
The great foundation of the triple world
Trembleth and quaketh with a mighty noise,
Presaging bloody massacres at hand.
The wand'ring birds that flutter in the dark,
When hellish Night, in cloudy chariot seated,
Casteth her mists on shady Tellus' face,
With sable mantles covering all the earth—
Now fly abroad, amid the cheerful day,
Foretelling some unwonted misery.
The snarling curs of darkened Tartarus,
Sent from Avernus' ponds by Rhadamanth,
With howling ditties pester every wood.
The watery ladies,[2] and the lightfoot fawns,
And all the rabble of the woody nymphs,
Trembling, all hide themselves in shady groves,
And shroud themselves in hideous, hollow pits.
The boisterous Boreas thund'reth forth revenge:
The stony rocks cry out for sharp revenge:
The thorny bush pronounceth dire revenge!—
[*Alarums.*
Now, Corineius, stay and see revenge—
And feed thy soul with Locrine's overthrow!
Behold, they come; the trumpets call them forth;
The roaring drums summon the soldiers!
Lo where their army glistereth on the plains!
Throw forth thy lightnings, mighty Jupiter,
And pour thy plagues on cursèd Locrine's head!
[Ghost *disappears.*

Enter LOCRINE, ESTRILD, ASSARACUS, SABREN, *and* Soldiers, *on one side;* THRASYMACHUS, GUENDELINE, MADAN, *and their* Followers, *opposite.*

Loc. What! is the tiger started from his cave?
Is Guendeline come from Cornubia,
That thus she braveth Locrine to the teeth?—
And hast thou found thine armor, pretty boy,
Accompanied with these thy straggling mates?
Believe me, but this enterprise was bold,
And well deserveth commendation.
Guen. Ay, Locrine, trait'rous Locrine, we are come,
With full pretence to seek thine overthrow.
What have I done, that thou shouldst scorn me thus?
What have I said, that thou shouldst me reject?
Have I been disobedient to thy words?
Have I bewrayed thy arcane secrecy?
Have I dishonored thy marriage-bed
With filthy crimes or with lascivious lusts?—
Nay, it is thou that hast dishonored it:
Thy filthy mind, o'ercome with filthy lusts,
Yieldeth unto affection's filthy darts.
Unkind, thou wrong'st thy first and truest fair;[3]
Unkind, thou wrong'st thy best and dearest friend;
Unkind, thou scorn'st all skilful Brutus' laws,
Forgetting, father, uncle, and thyself.
Est. Believe me, Locrine, but the girl is wise,
And well would seem to make a vestal nun:
How finely frames she her oration!
Thrasy. Locrine, we came not here to fight with words—
Words, that can never win the victory;
But—for you are so merry in your frumps—
Unsheath your swords, and try it out by force,
That we may see who hath the better hand.
Loc. Think'st thou to dare me, bold Thrasymachus?
Think'st thou to fear me with thy taunting braves,
Or do we seem too weak to cope with thee?
Soon shall I show thee my fine-cutting blade,
And with my sword, the messenger of death,
Seal thee a quittance for thy bold attempts. [*Exeunt.*

SCENE VI.—*The entrance of a Cave.*

Alarums. Enter LOCRINE *and* ESTRILD, *in flight.*

Loc. O fair Estrilda, we have lost the field!
Thrasymachus hath won the victory,
And we are left to be a laughing-stock,
Scoffed at by those that are our enemies.
Ten thousand soldiers, armed with sword and shield,
Prevail against an hundred thousand men.
Thrasymachus, incensed with fuming ire,
Rageth amongst the faintheart soldiers,
Like to grim Mars, when, covered with his targe,
He fought with Diomedes in the field,
Close by the banks of silver Simois. [*Alarums.*
O, lovely Estrild, now the chase begins:
Ne'er shall we see the stately Troynovant,
Mounted with coursers garnished all with pearls;
Ne'er shall we view the fair Concordia,
Unless as captives we be thither brought.
Shall Locrine then be taken prisoner
By such a youngling as Thrasymachus?
Shall Guendeline [then] captivate my love?
Ne'er shall mine eyes behold that dismal hour;
Ne'er will I view that ruthful spectacle;
For, with my sword, this sharpest curtle-axe,
I'll cut in sunder my accursèd heart!
But O, ye judges of the ninefold Styx,
Which, with incessant torments, rack the ghosts
Within the bottomless Abyssus' pits;
Ye gods, commanders of the heavenly spheres,
Whose will and laws irrevocable stand—
Forgive, forgive this foul, accursèd sin!—
Forget, O gods, this foul, condemnèd fault!—
And now, my sword, that, in so many fights,
[*Kisses his sword.*
Hast saved the life of Brutus and his son,
End now his life that wisheth still for death,
Work now his death that hateth still his life!

1 A correspondent suggests that we should read *sobs* for "throbs." Either word will answer. Perhaps we might read, "throes *with* sad throbs." The last two words, which were "grievous suspirs," I have altered to *grievously suspires*—a correction absolutely called for by the verse.

2 A phrase which would scarcely satisfy *naiad* or *nereid*.

3 "*Fear*" in former editions.

Farewell, fair Estrild, beauty's paragon,
Framed in the front of forlorn miseries,
Ne'er shall mine eyes behold thy sunshine eyes,
But when we meet in the Elysian fields:
Thither I go before with hastened pace.
Farewell, vain world, and thy enticing snares!
Farewell, foul sin, and thy enticing pleasures!
And welcome, death, the end of mortal smart,
Welcome to Locrine's overburdened heart!
[*Stabs himself.*

Est. Break, heart, with sobs and grievous [sad] suspires!
Stream forth, ye tears, from out my wat'ry eyes!
Help me to mourn for warlike Locrine's death;
Pour down your tears, you watery regions,
For mighty Locrine is bereft of life!
O, fickle fortune! O, unstable world!
What else are all things, that this globe contains,
But a confusèd chaos of mishaps?
Wherein, as in a glass, we plainly see
That all our life is but a tragedy.
Since mighty kings are subject to mishap—
Since martial Locrine is bereft of life—
Shall Estrild live, then, after Locrine's death?
Shall love of life bar her from Locrine's sword?
O no!—this sword, that hath bereft his life,
Shall now deprive me of my fleeting soul:
Strengthen these hands, O mighty Jupiter!
That I may end my woful misery!
Locrine, I come! Locrine, I follow thee![1]
[*Kills herself.*

Alarums Enter SABREN.

Sab. What doleful sight, what ruthful spectacle,
Hath Fortune offered to my hapless heart?
My father slain with such a fatal sword!—
My mother murdered by a mortal wound!—
What Thracian dog, what barbarous myrmidon,
Would not relent at such a ruthful case?
What fierce Achilles, what hard, stony flint,
Would not bemoan this mournful tragedy?
Locrine, the map of magnanimity,
Lies slaughtered in his foul, accursèd cave;—
Estrild, the perfect pattern of renown—
Nature's sole wonder—in whose beauteous breasts
All heavenly grace and virtue were enshrined—
Both massacred, are dead within this cave;
And with them dies fair Pallas and sweet Love!
Here lies a sword, and Sabren hath a heart:
This blessed sword shall cut my cursèd heart,
And bring my soul unto my parents' ghosts—
That they that live, and view our tragedy,
May mourn our case with mournful plauditees.
[*Offers to kill herself.*
Ah me! my virgin's hands are too, too weak,
To penetrate the bulwark of my breast!
My fingers, used to tune the amorous lute,
Are not of force to hold this steely glaive;—
So am I left to wail my parents' death,
Not able for to work my proper death!—
Ah, Locrine, honored for thy nobleness!
Ah, Estrild, famous for thy constancy!
Ill may they fare that wrought your mortal ends!
[*Retires back.*

Enter GUENDELINE, THRASYMACHUS, MADAN, *and* Soldiers.

Guen. Search, soldiers, search!—find Locrine and his love!
Find the proud strumpet, Humber's concubine,
That I may change those her so pleasing looks,
Into a pale and ignominious aspect.
Find me the issue of their cursèd love—
Find me young Sabren, Locrine's only joy—
That I may glut my mind with lukewarm blood,
Swiftly distilling from the bastard's breast!
My father's ghost still haunts me for revenge,
Crying, *Revenge my over-hastened death!*
My brother's exile, and mine own divorce,
Banish remorse clean from my brazen heart—
All mercy from mine adamantine breast.

Thrasy. Nor doth thy husband, lovely Guendeline,
That wonted was to guide our starless steps,
Enjoy this light. See where he murdered lies,
By luckless lot and froward, frowning fate;—
And by him lies his lovely paramour,
Fair Estrild, gorèd with a dismal sword;—
And, as it seems, both murdered by themselves,
Clasping each other in their feebled arms,
With loving zeal—as if, for company,
Their uncontented corses were content
To pass foul Styx in Charon's ferry-boat.

Guen. And hath proud Estrild then prevented me?
Hath she escapèd Guendelina's wrath,
By violently cutting off her life?
Would God she had the monstrous Hydra's lives,
That every hour she might have died a death,
Worse than the swing of old Ixion's wheel—
And every hour revive to die again!
As Titius, bound to houseless Caucason,
Doth feed the substance of his own mishap,
And every day, for want of food, doth die,
And, every night, doth live again to die.
But stay: methinks I hear some fainting voice,
Mournfully weeping for their luckless death.
[SABREN *comes forward.*

Sab. Ye mountain-nymphs, that in these deserts reign,
Cease from your hasty chase of savage beasts;
Prepare to see a heart, oppressed with care;
Address your ears to hear a mournful style:
No human strength, no words,[2] can work my weal,
Care in my heart so tyrant-like doth deal.
Ye Dryades and lightfoot Satyri—
Ye gracious fairies, who, at eventide,
Your closets leave with heavenly beauty stored,
And on your shoulders spread your golden locks—
Ye savage bears in caves and darkened dens—
Come, wail with me the martial Locrine's death;
Come, mourn with me for beauteous Estrild's death!
Ah! loving parents, little do ye know
What sorrow Sabren suffers for your thrall!

Guen. But may this be, and is it possible?—

[1] Milton thus: "Guendolen, all in rage, departs into Cornwall, where Madan, the son she had by Locrine, was hitherto brought up by Corineius, his grandfather; and, gathering an army of her father's friends and subjects, gives battle to her husband, by the river Sture: wherein Locrine, shot with an arrow, ends his life."

[2] "*Work*" is the word in the folio. A correspondent suggests *worth.* I prefer *words,* as she has just before, in the previous line, appealed to the mountain-nymphs "to hear a mournful *style,*" which she instantly abandons, saying, "No *words* can work my weal."

Lives Sabren yet to expiate my wrath?
Fortune, I thank thee for this courtesy:
And let me never see one prosperous hour,
If Sabren die not a reproachful death.

Sab. Hard-hearted Death, that, when the wretched [call,
Art farthest off, and seldom hear'st at all,
But in the midst of Fortune's good success,
Uncallèd comes, and shears our life in twain!
When will that hour, that blessed hour, draw nigh,
When poor, distressèd Sabren may be gone? —
Sweet Atropos, cut off my fatal thread! —
What art thou, Death? — shall not poor Sabren die?

Guen. [*advancing*]. Yes, damsel, yes! Sabren shall surely die,
Though all the world should seek to save her life;
And not a common death shall Sabren die:
But, after strange and grievous punishments,
Shortly inflicted on thy bastard head,
Thou shalt be cast into the cursèd streams,
And feed the fishes with thy tender flesh.

Sab. And think'st thou, then, thou cruel homicide,
That these thy deeds shall be unpunishèd?
No, traitor, no! the gods will 'venge these wrongs;—
The fiends of hell will mark these injuries.
Ne'er shall these blood-sucking, [these] mastiff[1] curs,
Bring wretched Sabren to her latest home.
For I, myself, in spite of thee and thine,
Mean to abridge my former destinies;
And that which Locrine's sword could not perform,
This present stream shall present bring to pass.[2]
[*She flings herself into the river.*

Guen. One mischief follows on another's neck!
Who would have thought so young a maid as she,
With such a courage would have sought her death?
And — for because this river was the place
Where little Sabren resolutely died—
Sabren, for ever, shall this same[3] be called.
And as for Locrine, our deceasèd spouse,
Because he was the son of mighty Brute,
To whom we owe our country, lives, and goods,
He shall be buried in a stately tomb,
Close by his agèd father Brutus' bones,
With such great pomp and great solemnity
As well beseems so brave a prince as he.
Let Estrild lie[4] without the shallow vault,
Without the honor due unto the dead,
Because she was the author of this war.
Retire, brave followers, unto Troynovant,
Where we will celebrate these exequies,
And place young Locrine[5] in his father's tomb.
[*Exeunt.*

Enter ATE.

Atê. Lo here the end of lawless treachery,[6]
Of usurpation, and ambitious pride; —
And they, that for their private amours, dare
Turmoil our land, and set their broils abroach,
Let them be warnèd by these premises; —
And, as a woman was the only cause
That civil discord was then stirrèd up,
So let us pray for that renownèd maid,
That eight-and-thirty years the sceptre swayed
In quiet peace and sweet felicity;[7]
And every wight that seeks her grace's smart,
Would that this sword were piercèd in his heart!
[*Exit.*

1 "*Masty*" in the old editions.

2 Milton somewhat differs from this story. He says: "But not so ends the fury of Guendolen; for Estrildis and her daughter Sabra she throws into a river; and, to leave a monument of revenge, proclaims that the stream be thenceforth called after the damsel's name, which, by length of time, is changed now to Sabrine, or Severn." Milton refers to this incident in his "Comus." He deifies the damsel:—

"There is a gentle nymph not far from hence,
That with moist curb sways the smooth Severn stream:
Sabrina is her name, a virgin pure;
Whilome she was the daughter of Locrine,
That had the sceptre from his father Brute.
She, guiltless damsel, flying the mad pursuit
Of her enragèd stepdame, Guendolen,
Commended her fair innocence to the flood,
That stayed her flight with his cross-flowing course."

3 A correspondent suggests that for "this *same*," we should read "this *stream*"—an alteration which would be a decided improvement upon the tame and feeble language which is employed.

4 "Let Estrild *be*," is the language of the ancient folio.

5 "*Young* Locrine" would seem to be a strange epithet on the lips of his younger wife. Should it not be "*your* Locrine?"

6 Is it not just as likely that Atê meant to say *lechery?*

7 This passage fixes the date of one performance of "Locrine," the thirty-eighth year of the reign of Elizabeth. It is by no means conclusive of its original production or exhibition; only, of one performance, at this period, the copy used then being that from which the publication was subsequently made. The MS. might have been altered a hundred times, and, for aught we know, have been used for the reigns before and after. This is mentioned, as these three lines might be assumed as of positive authority in determining the question of authorship. The old dramatists and the managers altered their plays very frequently, to suit the reign and the occasion, availing themselves of every current event which might enable them to make a popular hit during the performance.

THE END OF THE TRAGEDY OF LOCRINE.

Popular Work! Twelfth Thousand Now Ready!

LEWIE, OR THE BENDED TWIG.

BY COUSIN CICELY,

Author of "Silver Lake Stories," etc., etc.

One Volume 12mo., - - - - - Price $1.00

ALDEN, BEARDSLEY & CO., AUBURN, N. Y., } *Publishers.*
WANZER, BEARDSLEY & CO., ROCHESTER, N. Y., }

"Mother! thy gentle hand hath mighty power,
For thou alone may'st train, and guide, and mould
Plants that shall blossom, with an odor sweet,
Or, like the cursed fig-tree, wither, and become
Vile cumberers of the ground."

Brief Extracts from Notices of the Press.

* * * A tale which deserves to rank with "The Wide, Wide World." It is written with graphic power, and full of interest.—*Hartford Repub.*

* * * Her writings are equal to the best. She is a second Fanny Fern—*Palmyra Democrat.*

* * * It is recommended by its excellent moral tone and its wholesome practical inculcations.—*N. Y. Tribune.*

* * * Full of grace and charm, its style and vivacity make it a most amusing work. For the intellectual and thinking, it has a deeper lesson, and while it thrills the heart, bids parents beware of that weakness which prepares in infancy the misery of man. "Lewie" is one of the most popular books now before the public, and needs no puffing, as it is selling by thousands.—*N. Y. Day Book.*

* * * The moral of the book is inestimable. The writer cannot fail to be good, as she so faithfully portrays the evils which owe their origin to the criminal neglect of proper parental discipline.—*Hunt's Merchants' Magazine.*

* * * The plot is full of dramatic interest, yet entirely free from extravagance; the incidents grow out of the main plot easily and naturally, while the sentiment is healthy and unaffected. Commend us to more writers like Cousin Cicely—books which we can see in the hands of our young people without uneasiness. Books which interest by picturing life as it is, instead of giving us galvanized society.—*National Democrat.*

* * * A touching and impressive story unaffected in style and effective in plot.—*N. Y. Evangelist.*

* * * The story of the Governess, contained in this volume, is one of rare interest.—*Highland Eagle.*

* * * The story is a charming one—the most affecting we ever read.—*Jersey Shore Republican.*

* * * "Cousin Cicely" is just the person to portray family scenes. * * * This story will be profitable reading.—*Daily Capital City Fact Columbus, Ohio.*

* * * The contents of the work are of the first order, and unexceptionable.—*Hartford Daily Times.*

* * * Let every youth peruse it, and we promise them they will find their hearts and lives improved by it.—*Advocate, Batavia.*

Truth is the basis of the work before us. In it the accomplished authoress has done an honor to her sex, and we doubt not secured blessings upon many households by the publication of this finished and elegant little volume. Her former labors have endeared her to *children.* The present one should secure for her the affection and gratitude of *parents.*—*Geneva Courier.*

* * * It is lively without triviality, and replete with interest from the first to the last.—*New York Day Book.*

* * * Believing this work adapted to lead mothers to *rightly train* the little shoots springing up around the parent tree, and to restrain their wandering inclinations, we commend it to their perusal.—*Student.*

Cousin Cicely is gifted with rare powers. It is of home incidents she writes, and in a manner highly attractive. * * * Traces with graphic force the loved and petted child. The volume is full of instruction to parents, and should have a place in every family library.—*Providence Daily Post.*

* * * Cousin Cicely is well known, and a work from her pen will meet with ready welcome.—*Providence Daily Times.*

* * * Her works are of decided merit, and should be possessed by all.—*Rochester Daily American.*

* * * She has got the hearts of parents and children through the Silver Lake Stories and Lewie.—*Rochester Daily Democrat.*

* * * The moral of the story is good, and the plot is so touching, that we cannot wonder at the book's success.—*N. Y. Commercial Adv.*

* * * Agnes, the sister of spoiled Lewie, is treated with unmotherly injustice; grows up a character of uncommon loveliness; and, though "only a Governess," marries splendidly.—*N. Y. Church Journal.*

* * * Downright interesting story. It is crowded with domestic pictures, true to nature. * * * The short and melancholy career of poor Lewie, shows the importance of properly managing children.—*Western Literary Messenger.*

* * * The description of an American home is true to the life. Many of the incidents are truly affecting. * * * Passages of remarkable beauty of expression and sentiment. We give the following as a specimen of the thought and style which characterizes the work: "It is strange how much a human heart may suffer and beat on and regain tranquility, and even cheerfulness at last. It is a most merciful provision of Providence, that our griefs do not always fall as heavily as they do at first, else how could the burden of this life of change and sorrow be borne. But the loved ones are not forgotten when the tear is dried, and the smile returns to the cheek; they are remembered, but with less of sadness and gloom in the remembrance; and at length, if we can think of them as happy, it is only a pleasure to recall them to mind."—*Patriot, Jackson Michigan.*

* * * Of remarkable and intense interest to the general reader and the scholar. * * * Its contents are worthy of examination.---*Palmyra Glee Book.*

* * * The facts which are given to prove the identity of Mr. Williams with the *Dauphin,* are of an exceedingly interesting character, and deserve a careful examination. The extraordinary resemblance which the Indian Missionary bears to the portraits of Louis XVI. and Louis XVIII. is not the least remarkable part of the matter. We commend this readable book to the attention of our friends, as one well worthy of notice.—*Fred. Douglass' Paper, Rochester.*

* * * Two of the most interesting periods in all the history of that nation. * * * Some of the more striking points in the history of those events.—*Rochester Daily Advertiser.*

* * * The sketches are written in pleasant style, and are authentic. * * * It can be read with pleasure and profit by all persons who would have a correct statement of two most important events.—*Rochester Daily American.*

* * * The fate of the Hugenots of France—and the mysterious history of the Dauphin or son of Louis XIV., constitute the points of attraction in this book—*The Wesleyan, Syracuse, N. Y.*

* * * These are portions of history of remarkable interest. * * * Every new book upon the subject is eagerly snatched up by the public, especially by a lively and graphic pen, like the one which drew these sketches. The work is replete with interest, and will repay a perusal. * * * The author's object has been to re-produce these great eras with vividness and freshness, rather than to express any novel views respecting them. He has certainly produced vivid pictures, and condensed a variety of historic information that ought to be in every reader's possession. The idea is a capital one, which ought to be more fully carried out. The reader may be assured of a very impressive and readable book.—*N. Y. Tribune.*

* * * The volume will be found a very attractive one to young readers and should have a place in all the libraries for young men.—*N. Y. Mirror.*

* * * This is a book of great interest and excellence. It contains two stories; but each one is full of stirring events; each developes an era in the history of France.—*Boston Traveller.*

This work is of great interest and of usefulness to the general reader, the student and statistician. It is a sketch of Biographies, thrilling incidents and recitals, replete with Historical Fact and valuable information, divested of the prolixity which necessarily appertains to standard Historic works. * * * We commend the book as a digest of History.—*The American Citizen.*

www.ingramcontent.com/pod-product-compliance
Lightning Source LLC
LaVergne TN
LVHW011227110826
845150LV00006B/1569

* 9 7 8 1 4 2 5 5 1 5 0 1 0 *